VICO AND NAPLES

VICO AND NAPLES

THE URBAN ORIGINS
OF MODERN
SOCIAL THEORY

BARBARA ANN NADDEO

CORNELL UNIVERSITY PRESS
Ithaca and London

First published 2011 by Cornell University Press

Printed in the United States of America

Library of Congress Cataloging-in-Publication Data

Naddeo, Barbara Ann.
Vico and Naples : the urban origins of modern social theory / Barbara Ann Naddeo.
    p. cm.
  Includes bibliographical references and index.
  ISBN 978-0-8014-4916-1 (cloth : alk. paper)
1. Vico, Giambattista, 1668–1744.   2. Social sciences—Philosophy—History.   3. Cities and towns—Philosophy—History.   4. Naples (Kingdom)—Historiography.   5. Rome—Historiography.   I. Title.
  B3583.N33 2011
  195—dc22   2010035481

Cornell University Press strives to use environmentally responsible suppliers and materials to the fullest extent possible in the publishing of its books. Such materials include vegetable-based, low-VOC inks and acid-free papers that are recycled, totally chlorine-free, or partly composed of nonwood fibers. For further information, visit our website at www.cornellpress.cornell.edu.

Cloth printing   10 9 8 7 6 5 4 3 2 1

To Helidon and Sicile

❧ CONTENTS

❧ ACKNOWLEDGMENTS

The origins of this book have as much to do with my own interests as they do with serendipity. Indeed, this book began with an invitation by Peter Reill to present a paper on Vico at a conference sponsored by the UCLA Center for Seventeenth- and Eighteenth-Century Studies and by the Fondazione Cini of Venice, Italy, which generously hosted the event in its grand setting on the Isola di San Giorgio Maggiore. At that conference, "Interpretazioni Vichiane" (22–23 November 2002), I had the opportunity to first meet a number of outstanding Vico scholars and to begin my own endeavors that have yielded this book. This project was then ideated and nurtured in conversation with other historians, both European and American, to whose great intellectual generosity I am profoundly indebted.

In Italy, the argument of this book was first broached and passionately debated with a number of exemplary scholars, and it is now my great pleasure to be able to thank Michèle Benaiteau, Brigitte Marin, Giovanni Muto, Anna Maria Rao, Manuela Sanna, and Piero Ventura for having listened and responded so constructively to my thoughts at the beginning of this project. On this side of the Atlantic, this book further benefited from the great interest and engagement of members of the faculty at Stanford University, where I was an Andrew W. Mellon fellow in the Humanities (2002–4). Among the many stimulating conversations I had at Stanford, I particularly would like to acknowledge those with Keith Baker, Paula Findlen, Jessica Riskin, and a visiting colleague, Sheryl Kroen, who helped me enormously with the conceptualization of this book and a number of other completed and ongoing projects. At the City College of New York, this project was then formalized in discussion with my former chair, Darren Staloff, for whose great encouragement I remain most grateful, and sustained by the indispensable support of my colleagues in the History Department.

The research for this book could not have been undertaken without the generous financial support of a number of institutions. The research funds and flexibility of the Andrew W. Mellon Fellowship of Scholars in the Humanities at Stanford made it possible for me to make a first foray into the libraries and archives of Naples with Vico specifically in mind. After I tested the waters and formulated this project, a Franklin Research Grant from the American Philosophical Society and grant monies from the Research Foundation of the City University of New York made possible new, crucial research in the libraries and archives of Vienna and of Naples in summer 2006. My receipt of a National Endowment for the Humanities Fellowship at the Newberry Library (2006–7) then provided what was the ideal setting for the completion of the nonarchival research for this book and my commencement of its writing. It would be impossible for me to overstate just how important and fruitful that year at the Newberry was for me. In the first place, the outstanding collection of early modern Italian literature at the library and its most helpful staff made the Newberry a most congenial and productive setting in which to work. What was more, at the Newberry I had the great fortune of enjoying the conversation and sociability of Elena Bonora, David Karmon, Carmen Nocentelli, Babs Miller, Diana Robin, Justin Steinberg, and Richard Wistreich, whose great interest in and encouragement of my work helped to sustain me both intellectually and morally. I would also like to note that I am thankful to the NEH Fellowship at the Newberry Library for making possible my intensive labor on this project without the sacrifice of my role as a parent at a time when my child, Sicile, was still but a toddler. The continued support of the Research Foundation of the City University of New York further made possible my return to Italian libraries and archives as the need arose while I was drafting and editing this book. Finally, I am indebted to the Columbia University Seminars for financial assistance with the production costs of this book.

Access to the collections of several institutions as well as the unfailing help and good humor of their staffs have also played crucial roles in facilitating the research for this book. At the Biblioteca Nazionale di Napoli, I owe profound thanks to Patricia Nocera and her staff in Circulation, who have worked tirelessly on my behalf for longer than I wish to admit. At the BNN, I am also thankful to the librarians of the Department of Rare Books and Manuscripts for their assistance with my consultation of the papers, letters, and rare books of Vico and others they conserve, and for their most patient advice on questions that arose regarding their holdings while I was writing this book. At the Archivio di Stato di Napoli, the research for this book long profited from access to the extraordinary patrimony of the Archive and the dutiful assistance of a number of its archivists, whose aid, instruction, and, no less, distraction all were greatly appreciated. The administrators of the Società Napoletana di Storia Patria granted me access to their library and permission for the reproduction of a number of their manuscripts, which were of invaluable importance to this project. Similarly, the director of the Archivio storico diocesano di Napoli permitted me to consult the holdings of that institution and kindly introduced me to both the strengths and weaknesses of its collections as regarded the topic of this book and others. The staff of the Haus- Hof- und Staatsarchiv and of the Österreichische Nationalbibliothek in Vienna helped me find my bearings within their rich collections of materials regarding the Habsburgs' Italian lands, which clarified the larger political context of Vico for me in ways that the extant secondary literature simply could not. In the Vatican, my work with the rich papers of the Congregation of the Index and the Congregation of the Holy Office conserved in the Archivio della Congregazione per la Dottrina della Fede was greatly aided by the generous advice of Daniele Ponziani and the most efficient work of the staff; and in the Archivio Segreto Vaticano (Secret Vatican Archives), Giovanni Castaldo kindly accommodated my schedule so that I could coordinate my work there with my research in the ACDF. Members of the research staff and personnel at the Istituto per la storia del pensiero filosofico e scientifico moderno in Naples—formerly known as the Centro di Studi Vichiani—repeatedly and most generously shared their expertise and resources regarding Vico with me, and it is with the greatest gratitude that I thank them here.

Last but not least, the outstanding collections, study spaces, flexible hours, and professional staff of the New York Public Library also proved to be the greatest of resources and the one to which I regularly turned when all else seemed to fail. I also would like to acknowledge that this book never could have been completed as is without the constant assistance of the staff of the Interlibrary Loan Office at the City College of New York, which most reliably procured a large amount of secondary literature for this project. For their help with some of the technical work related to the research for and production of this book I would also like to thank my former students Julia Bernier and Jesse Meredith.

Many colleagues have responded to sections of this book and provided valuable criticism and suggestions for its improvement. In particular, at Columbia University I thank the members of the Seminar on Eighteenth-Century European Culture and the members of the Seminar on Modern Italian Studies for hosting my presentation of sections of this work on a few occasions. At the Graduate Center of the City University of New York, this work also benefited greatly from its discussion in the Talk Series sponsored by the Eighteenth-Century Reading Room and in the writing workshop in the social sciences sponsored by the CUNY Faculty Fellowship Publication Program led by Steve Steinberg. For their close reading and detailed comments on a large part of the manuscript, I especially thank Anthony Grafton, Roberto Mazzola, Helena Rosenblatt, and Richard Saller. For their expert response to a number of the finer points of this book I would like to thank Elena Bonora, Girolamo Imbruglia, Marco Nicola Miletti, Anna Maria Rao, Giovanni Romeo, Lucia Gualdo Rosa, Manuela Sanna, and Piero Ventura. Needless to say, the remaining shortcomings are my responsibility alone.

John Ackerman at Cornell University Press has been the very best of editors, and I would like to thank him here for his great diligence and unfailing commitment to scholarship and humanity.

My father, Vincent Naddeo, has been an unyielding source of strength and support for me and my family as we have confronted the challenges of seemingly interminable intellectual labor with a child and in a big city, and I thank him for his great faith in our abilities and countless more. While I have been immersed in intellectual labor family members and some dear friends have helped to surround my daughter with love. I especially thank Genevieve Connor, Myla Goldberg, Lorraine McEvilley, and the members of the Windsor Terrace–Kensington Babysitting Cooperative for their vision and sense of extended family, and both my parents and in-laws, who have been the best of good sports and done their share of child rearing with the greatest of love. Finally, and most important, I note that this journey has been shared with my spouse, Helidon Gjergji, who most lovingly has encouraged and distracted me to the best of his abilities. Consequently, this book is dedicated to him, to our daughter, and to our love.

Introduction
Vico and Naples

I. Vico, the Metropolitan Question, and the Emergence of Social Theory

In this book I specifically examine the oeuvre of Giambattista Vico (1668–1744), the famed professor of Rhetoric at the University of Naples, whose magnum opus, the *Scienza nuova* (3rd ed., 1744), has been hailed by so many contemporary scholars as the precursor of modern social theory and its disciplinary affiliations.[1] Since the 1960s, Vico has often been cited by historians of the social scientific disciplines as a most precocious forerunner, and, as such, a legendary sort of founding figure whose genius transcended his own circumstances. Consequently, as concerns Vico's own social science, sight of the forest has been lost through the trees, as the historical contribution and circumstances of his thought have been neglected.

Paradoxically, the aspects of Vico's social theory that have been least studied are its most obvious, namely, that Vico made an iconic metropolis the privileged object of his investigation and that he individuated in the *iter*—or procedural acquisition—of civic citizenship a law of development pertaining to humans across the globe. Specifically, Vico identified in the origins of Rome the template for the formation of society from a state of nature. Similarly, he found in the history of Roman factionalism and the plebeian contest for rights a universal typology of societal development, or what constituted the history of civilization in his early texts. Thus, my book takes as its own thematic focus the centrality of the metropolis and the metropolitan question to Vico's social thought. It also offers a historical account of why Vico specifically identified the metropolis as the site for the contest of rights, and why he believed that contest to be utterly transformative of human nature.

Methodologically, in this book I seek to wed texts to their contexts in ways that have often eluded historians. It is my working assumption that some of the most innovative, if not inflammatory, claims of the past regularly escape contemporary readers simply because we do not share the original frames of reference presumed by their authors. Consequently, in this book I set out to do two things. First, I identify not only the commonalities but also the differences of Vico's texts from the traditions in which he was working, by exhibiting both the debts and departures of his ideas from them. As Vico was a neoclassicist whose idiom was that of the ancient Romans, I examine the novel content with which Vico invested both the history and theory of the Roman polity, novelties that shifted the very terms in which political belonging was cast and shocked Vico's contemporaries. In other words, it is my contention that Vico's contribution to social thought was encoded in his unique interpretation of the Roman polity, and that we can begin to appreciate that same contribution only if we situate the uniqueness of his interpretation in the historical perspectives of antiquity and of early modern Naples. I thus seek to decipher what Vico's interpretation of Roman history meant to him, without losing sight of the pitfalls, or unintended consequences, of his working within overdetermined frames of reference. Simply put, in this book I pinpoint and contextualize the specificities of Vico's interpretation of history to make manifest his politics, however subtle they may have been.

Second, in this book I participate in the debate about the relationship between the transformations of society and the emergence of social theory in early modern Europe. I provide an example of why one eighteenth-century figure found it appropriate to describe the polity of the capital city in terms of a society, and why he further hypothesized that the laws of behavior animating that same polity were exhibited by groups whose identity and coherence were rooted in what were extrapolitical realities. In particular, I argue that Vico's social theory was a product of his observations regarding the social transformations of his own metropolitan habitus, and I show why that was the case, as the transformations of society and of theory do not necessarily correspond. Put somewhat differently, this book evidences that Vico's theoretical convictions about the nature of the Roman polity and significance of Roman citizenship were first formulated within an assessment of his own urban environment: that of the capital city of Naples. It makes plain that the very occasion for Vico's first foray into social theory was one that dramatically tested the municipality of Naples and gave contemporaries reason to reevaluate the criteria for and meaning of citizenship in the capital. In sum, it finds in the highly politicized judgment Vico passed on both the municipality and its rivals that novel content with which he would invest the *iter* of civic citizenship for ancient Romans and, analogously, for humanity.

While the historiography has acknowledged the literal prescience of the *Scienza nuova* (1744), little has been done to contextualize its innovation either in the oeuvre or experience of Vico himself. Indeed, the foremost twentieth-century advocates of Vico assiduously maintained that his work was not only vanguard but also untimely and apolitical.[2] Moreover, these claims faithfully reproduced Vico's own disingenuous pronouncements about his alienation from his intellectual milieu, pronouncements that he had carefully crafted to account for his failure to win promotion to the coveted Morning Chair of Civil Law.[3] Although meant to be a corrective, the historiographical response then erred on the side of recasting Vico as overly typical of his age, that is, as a prodigious and recondite polymath, whose works represented the summation and apotheosis of late Renaissance and baroque epistemologies.[4] In dialectical fashion, subsequent literature has thus attempted to restore the work of Vico to its immediate context, but has differed on whether that context was "European" or "Neapolitan," and in both cases has presented Vico's topics as somewhat belated rejoinders to the once-burning and manifold questions of the Republic of Letters, especially as they concerned religious belief.[5] Intrigued by not only the contemporaneity but also the politics of Vico's oeuvre, I have taken the clues for my own work from scholars who have suggested the importance of the jurisprudential tradition for the hallmarks of Vichian social theory, which I herewith examine from its first formulation in Vico's early historical and rhetorical texts through its permutations in his legal works and the first edition of the *Scienza nuova*.[6]

As I show in the chapters that follow, Vico derived both the categories and norms of his social theory from the jurisprudential tradition of Roman law. Furthermore, Vico's theory manifestly historicized the juridical categories and norms of Roman law to provide a novel account of the formation of the urban polity and, more important, the nature of its foundational contract. What is more, this same debt of Vico's social theory to Roman jurisprudence explains both some of its peculiarities as well as some of its more comparable, European-wide features, such as its characteristic materialism. As will become clear, the benchmark status of property for political belonging evidently was as much a debt to the recent legacy of a Hobbes or a Locke as it was to the shared legacy of Roman jurisprudence, which already in its classical age had introduced the category of "things," or property, as an essential attribute of persons and the constitutive bond among individuals in society.[7] Beyond his debts to the legacy of canonical theorists and jurists, this present book also establishes Vico's affinity for contemporary politics and political factions, and argues that we can understand both the jurisprudential beginnings and *iter* of his social theory precisely in this same context.[8]

Consequently, in this book I begin by examining the political occasion for Vico's first reflections about the nature of urban society and social relations. And I show that Vico therewith employed old concepts to the novel ends of diagnosing and accounting for the atypical behavior of new metropolitan groups, whose innate desires and goals he would grant the quality of finality, or teleology, in his subsequent work.

The first chapter presents the occasion for Vico's foray into social theory, that is, his composition of a history of the failed Neapolitan revolt of 1701, known as the *Coniuratio principum Neapolitanorum*. Although commissioned by the political brokers of the Spanish regime, Vico's history evidently failed to please the representatives of the status quo, as it challenged their neat incrimination of the urban underclasses with its attention to the unusual ways in which extrapolitical processes had both destabilized and reshaped the behavior of the traditional orders of the Kingdom in general and those of the capital city of Naples in particular. By examining Vico's account of revolt in light of the normative explanations of the period, this chapter underscores just what an astute critic of contemporary politics and society Vico was and the extent to which his keen sense of the obsolescence of civic citizenship and the municipality of Naples informed his alternative account of this episode of revolt against the Spanish.

The second chapter then examines Vico's advocacy of global citizenship, or cosmopolitanism, as it was expressed in the inaugural addresses he delivered to the student body of the University of Naples between 1699 and 1708. In particular, this chapter traces Vico's abandonment of an emotive notion of cosmopolitanism for a commercial one, and explains his idealization of commercial sociability with reference to the conclusions he had drawn about the protagonists and nature of the metropolitan community in his history of the revolt of 1701. It thus shows how Vico arrived at the idea that all human relations are transactional in nature, and therefore forms of commerce, and that both the mutual obligations and actionable rights of humans most appropriately can be conceived in terms of international commercial law. Finally, it contextualizes these seemingly moral philosophical claims about the obligations and rights of humans within the contemporary legal battles of the Kingdom, especially as they concerned the jurisprudential tradition of its arbiter of Roman law, that is, the supreme court of the Kingdom, the Sacro Regio Consiglio.

Chapter 3 considers both the legal aspirations and jurisprudential works of Vico, and reconstructs his first full-blown account of Roman law and society in light of the jurisprudential tastes of his target audience, the leading members of the Neapolitan judiciary. It begins with an ample reconstruction of Vico's life and work between the publication of his last inaugural address, the *De ratione* (1709), and the drafting of his legal treatise known as the *Diritto universale,* which comprised the volumes *De uno* (1720), *De constantia* (1721), and *Notae* (1722). In particular, the second section identifies Vico's motivations for undertaking a legal treatise, and it reconstructs the publication history and reception of both *De uno* and *De constantia,* which not only were subjected to scrupulous censorship but also occasioned some scandal.

The third section of this chapter considers the history of law and society immanent to the legal treatise. In particular, the third section reconstructs Vico's unique history of Rome, which, it shows, made novel claims about the origins and laws of development characteristic of cities and, by analogy, world polities. Furthermore, this section evinces that Vico's unique history of Rome couched the theme of natural, or human, rights in the political idiom available to him, namely that of citizenship, and that he therewith lodged the sharpest critique with not only the classical notion of citizenship as a set of political liberties but also the social inequities constraining the practical meaning of that same political category. In his legal works, Vico provocatively rewrote the history of Roman citizenship as a history of the plebeians' gradual acquisition of natural property rights. Against the traditional historical grain, Vico argued that the political watershed of the Roman Republic was marked by the Lex Poetelia Papiria (326 BCE), which forbade the enslavement of plebeians for debt. Similarly, he conceptualized the successive victories of the plebeians as their progressive acquisition of full possession of their own persons and, subsequently, lands and things, departing from the revered historical record of Livy to engage in contemporary debates about the rights indiscriminately due to humans and the path to civilization. This third section thus underscores Vico's idealization of the late Roman Republic as a *societas,* or commercial partnership, that engaged its members in the practice of commerce. It also makes plain that this idealization was intended as a counterpoint to the condition of not only the earlier Republic but also the modern capital, which, as this chapter also establishes, was implicated in Vico's reconstruction of the origins and nature of Roman political civilization.

Finally, the third section of this chapter assesses the influence of Vico's target audience, that is, the leading members of the Neapolitan judiciary, on his arguments concerning the nature and ends of Roman jurisprudence. In his legal treatise, Vico arguably rewrote the history of Roman jurisprudence to support the innovations of the contemporary Neapolitan judiciary, whose judicial program had sought to further social reform. Therein, he insisted that the end of jurisprudence was justice, which he significantly equated with "equity," a precept of the *ius gentium,* or "law of nations," that was often invoked in contemporary courts to overrule traditional privileges in favor of the public welfare. This section thus makes plain the intimate connections between Vico's endorsement of an equity-oriented form of Roman jurisprudence and his politicking among the high-ranking judiciary of Naples. At the same time, it also explains why the judiciary failed to take an interest in Vico's legal treatise, which not only endorsed the natural jurisprudence of the courts but also its codification.

The last chapter of this book, chapter 4, gives content to Vico's famous claim in his *Autobiografia* that he became a philosopher only because he failed to become a professor of law. In the first place, it shows that Vico's politicking among the judiciary was untimely—and hence a miserable failure—by narrating Vico's unsuccessful bid for the highly remunerative Morning Chair of Civil Law at the University of Naples, a position whose award traditionally was contingent on the favor of not only the professoriate but also the heads of the Kingdom's tribunals. It further recounts the great personal difficulty with which Vico drafted and sought to publish the first edition of the *Scienza nuova,* for which he failed to secure the financial support of the learned Cardinal Corsini. Finally, the book ends where most books on Vico begin, that is, with the first edition of the *Scienza nuova,* in which Vico generalized the hypotheses of his legal works to make applicable to world society those insights about the nature of citizenship and rights of humans that he heretofore more narrowly had exemplified with his history of the Roman metropolis.

Though an intellectual biography of Vico, this book does more than reconstruct the career of one of the eighteenth century's most intriguing thinkers. In it I seek to answer a number of the big questions surrounding the relationship between the actual transformation of society and the advent of social theory at the end of the Old Regime. Above all else, this book evidences something that all students of early modern Europe intuitively know but that the historiography heretofore has failed to reconstruct in all its due complexity, namely, the relationship between the advent of the metropolis and the emergence of a cosmopolitan theory of society that

posited commerce as the constituent relation and right among humans. Cosmopolitanism was one of the most common and powerful critiques leveled
at the Old Regime by its critics. At the same time, it was predicated on a
sense of anachronism that itself must be explained and politically aligned. As
I argue here, the metropolitan question made meaningful, if not necessary, the
coinage of an extrapolitical notion of cosmopolitan society by making plain
the utter disconnect between the rhetoric and realities of the civic polity, or
city. Thus, this book concretely weds a history of semantics to one of metropolitan politics, restoring to both the invention and critique of "society" its
fullest political dimension.[9]

What is more, with its contextualization of cosmopolitanism, this book
also helps to identify and account for the genesis of a modern rights theory that places its primary emphasis on contractualism, individuating the
metropolitan roots of one of modernity's most central political concepts.
Curiously, the centrality of contractualism to modern rights theory has been
importantly qualified by the historiography on political thought, which,
unintentionally perhaps, has shifted the gaze of the literature from the nature
of the original political contract to questions regarding the possibility and
conditions of individual liberty within political civilization. One vein of this
historiography in particular has reconsidered early modern contractual theory in terms of its upshot for the model of freedoms enjoyed within political civilization, as if the debates about political rights themselves had been
subordinate to concerns about political liberty per se. Consequently, this vein
has focused on the reconstruction of the political concept of "liberty" and its
manifold associations, and has hypothesized the existence of three historical
types of such, two "positive" and one "negative," which together purportedly
represented the range of opinions characteristic of the early modern period.
According to this view, the first type of "liberty" was "positive" and premised
on a "participatory" notion of political freedom, while the others were "negative" and espoused either a "liberal," that is, Hobbesian, or a "neo-Roman"
notion of the same, which in the latter case amounted to a definition of
liberty as freedom from forms of political dependency and the concomitant
representation of the citizen in the decisions of the political community.[10]
Despite the dichotomous nature of the vantage points it has considered, the
emphasis of this vein can be said to have limited its purview to texts in which
the polity and politics were presumed to function independently of what
we would call social constraints. Indeed, the very enthusiasm this vein has
expressed for the "neo-Roman" definition of "liberty" as a political condition opposite to the one of "slavery" has both overstated the metaphorical
meaning with which republican theorists invested this status of persons and,

consequently, obscured the ongoing historical relevance of its more funda-mental juridical meaning, that is, the right to the possession of oneself and of one's labor. In other words, this vein has focused its study of political thought to suggest that questions of equity—whether legal, moral, or economic—did not factor into that set of conditions proposed as necessary for the "liberty," or freedom, of the individual within political civilization. In other words, with its particular choice of traditions, it has downplayed, if not neglected, the centrality of extrapolitical rights to some notions of freedom in the early modern period—such as the importance that the rights tradition specifically gave to the potentiality and self-realization of humankind, as well as to the manifold extrapolitical contingencies that could impede the same.[11]

Another vein of the historiography has complemented the first by spe-cifically considering the history of rights theory over the longer *durée* and has argued that the genealogy of a modern notion of individual rights, or subjective liberties, developed internal to the ancient and medieval tradition of natural law.[12] Perhaps the most suggestive and important insight of this vein of historiography has been the emphasis it has placed on the ongo-ing importance of Roman law for circumscribing the rights and obliga-tions of individuals. In particular, its study of the ever-changing semantics of the Latin word *ius,* law or right, since antiquity has brought to the fore the centrality of allied Roman legal concepts—such as, *potestas,* or power, and of *dominium,* or possession—to the definition of the essential condi-tion and irreducible rights of the individual. If implicitly, then, this vein has reminded us of the unequivocal significance of Roman jurisprudence for the development of a modern rights theory; and it has cast light upon the assumptions of that same rights theory as they regarded the rule of law, or the political order as it were. At the same time, the history of rights theory—initially at least—shied from contextualizing the literature it unearthed and from reconstructing the occasions for either the transmission or incommu-nicability of that literature's ideas to political worlds of thought and action. What is more, this vein has upheld a distinction between types of rights that was not itself historical: that is, the one between "objective," or claim-based, and "subjective," or agency-based, rights. As I show in this book, however, Vico's innovation of a subjective notion of rights went hand-in-hand with his revising and advocating an objective notion of the same. Drawing and expanding on the findings of this literature, the historiography of political thought of the early Enlightenment too has emphasized the importance of the idiom and concepts of Roman law for the emergence and diffusion of a modern notion of freedom—that is, what it was more restrictively called an "economic" notion of freedom, by which it meant the right and ability of the individual to engage in commerce.[13]

In many ways, this book has profited from the insights, conclusions, and even shortcomings of all this scholarship. I have tried to write a book that would live up to the methodological program of the first vein of historiography on political thought;[14] and with this methodology, I have sought to account for that pertinence of Roman law to the modern notion of individual rights so strongly suggested by the latter two veins. In the first place, I have sought to reconstruct the meanings of Vico's utterances and texts by restoring them to their contexts. Second, I have sought to show that the "economic" definition of freedom pertained to Vico's world of concerns in his early works and that the pertinence of that definition is best accounted for by Vico's debts to contemporary Roman jurisprudence. As this book makes plain, Vico's contribution to the redefinition of political freedom and individual rights had its roots in the institutional problems confronting the judiciary of his own day. Similarly, I argue that Vico should be understood as participating in a set of reflections and theoretical solutions that were common to those of the judiciary and its successors during the European Enlightenment. Put somewhat differently and plainly, this book evinces that both Roman law and the practice of jurisprudence by the courts was an important source for innovations in thought about the polity and the rights due to its constituency.

Finally, this book revisits an old, unresolved theme within the historiography of early modern Europe: that of the relationship between jurisprudence and social science.[15] As the book suggests, the blossoming of the social sciences in the Kingdom of Naples had something to do both with the agenda of jurisprudence and with the failure of the same to accommodate and effectively administer the natural claims made on the polity by social groups, both displaced and entrenched, in search of justice. Through its reconstruction of Vico's own intellectual career, furthermore, this book makes manifest that the uncoupling of social theory from jurisprudence leveled a heady critique at the shortcomings of jurisprudence as a palliative for the challenges of the capital city—especially as those shortcomings concerned the rights of new metropolitan groups. And it provides an example of the professional trajectory that so often culminated in the vocation of social science: that of critics who viewed themselves as the heirs and successors of the judiciary in the twilight of its efforts at reform.

II. Questions of Citizenship and Society in Metropolitan Naples

Circa 1730, the city of Naples was famously described as a gigantic head set upon a frail, thin body, a grotesque corporeal metaphor for the relationship between the capital and provinces of the Kingdom that would be invoked repeatedly over the course of the eighteenth century.[16] More incisively than the political brief in which it was employed, this metaphor conveyed how contemporary authorities perceived the origins and consequences of the demographic growth of Naples, which throughout the early modern period steadily grew at a dramatic rate to become the third-largest metropolitan area in Europe by 1730.[17] Picturing Naples as the colossal head of an attenuated Kingdom, this metaphor suggested that the urbanization of Naples was the product of migration from the provinces to the capital of such relatively great size that it sapped the former while enlarging the latter to the point of utter monstrosity, or what we would call preternaturality.

If this metaphor overstated the effects of urbanization for the provinces of the Kingdom, it faithfully represented the source and consequences of population growth for Naples itself, which like all other major European capitals was dependent on immigration for its demographic increase and infamously outgrew the limits of its own municipal structures.[18] However apt eighteenth-century Neapolitans considered this metaphor for their particular circumstances, this image of the capital city had both European-wide currency and longevity, becoming by midcentury what was an almost hackneyed way for contemporaries to convey the sorts of challenges posed by the unprecedented growth of Europe's capitals, or what contemporary historians have dubbed the metropolitan question.[19] Throughout the long eighteenth century, indeed, gross immigration to capital cities was epochal, and the sheer demographic size of capitals such as London, Paris, and Naples increasingly dwarfed the towns of their respective kingdoms, be they near or far from the metropolitan center.

For instance, we know that London drew as many as twelve thousand immigrants a year by the outset of the eighteenth century and that it absorbed about half the natural increase of provincial England in its entirety.[20] As a result, "by 1700 it almost certainly contained a tenth of the total population of England and before 1800 it was always at least ten times larger than the next English town."[21] While these trends made and sustained London as the single largest capital in all of Europe throughout the eighteenth century, the comparable figures for Naples are even more stunning. Although it ranked behind London and Paris in terms of its aggregate population, Naples was truly immense in relation to the other towns of its Kingdom, and doubtless its hypertrophic growth was sustained by waves of immigration from the provinces that stabilized, if not depressed, the population of the same. In light of its immensity, historians of the Kingdom have been careful to note that the demographic growth of Naples was equally an indication of a more general trend investing the entire Kingdom over the course of the eighteenth century.[22] Nonetheless, relative to other towns of the Kingdom the capital grew at what was a disproportionate rate. As is well known, between 1657 and 1707 the population of Naples increased by a spectacular 47 percent, and it doubled in the course of the century, while that of the major towns in its most immediate hinterland, for instance, increased but modestly or stagnated.[23] As a consequence, by 1700 approximately 10 percent of the Kingdom resided in Naples proper and a stunning 33 percent of the same additionally inhabited the territory within 50 kilometers of its city limits, making the metropolitan area of the capital a literal metonym for the Kingdom of Naples.[24] By 1800, indeed, the capital could boast close to half a million inhabitants, and it figured as twenty times larger than the second-largest peninsular city of the Kingdom, that is, Bari.[25] With the continuous growth of its population, the capital famously morphed far beyond the confines of its "City," or municipality, rendering the demographic map of Naples increasingly incommensurable with the political territory of its municipality. In the eighteenth century, especially, most of the demographic growth of the metropolitan area of Naples took place in its outlying circles of suburban residential developments (*borghi*), agricultural communities, and villages (*casali*) belonging to the City of Naples, but only tenuously controlled by it.[26] The image of Naples as a gigantic head set upon a frail, thin body, in sum, conveyed the nature and immediate problems of an urban community swollen by immigration and sprawling beyond the grasp of its own municipal jurisdiction.

Beyond the very real challenges this image conveyed, for contemporaries it further bore the problem of political categorization. For it equally represented a political typology that posited the capital in contradistinction to the prevailing models of urban community, namely, those of the Greek *polis* and of the Roman *civitas*. Representing the capital as the site of implosion of a larger constellation of political territories, this image constructed an urban type whose hallmarks were its openness, extraordinary demographic size, and, most conspicuously, the overwhelming foreignness of its constituency.

Conceptually, this urban type thus presented a novelty that posed the problem of political oxymoron: that of a city whose political identity was vested neither in its citizenry nor in its capacity to integrate others into the civic self. Since the time of Aristotle, the *polis* had been synonymous with its exclusive citizenry, or *politai*, that corporation of free adult men whose duty was to rule and to be ruled, and with that citizenry's enjoyment of the "good life," a telos that Aristotle thought was predicated on the purported self-sufficiency, or near autarky, of the civic community.[27] Analogously, the boundaries of the Roman *civitas*, too, had been coextensive with its citizenry.

Indeed, at the time of the Republic, Cicero used that Latin word to signify both the condition of citizenship and the body of the citizen community subject to a common law.[28] As the rhetoric of ancient history had suggested to its heirs, furthermore, the imperial Roman *civitas* had been an expansionary polity that proved eminently capable of incorporating the peoples of its new territories into the civic self with its successive grants of Roman citizenship to Latins, Italians, and provincials, respectively.[29] To the extent that it lent itself to metaphor, the image of an infinite set of concentric circles perhaps best would have captured the nature of the Roman *civitas*,[30] which, after the imperial edict of the Antonine constitution in 212 CE, could claim to have encompassed the Empire in its entirety and to have earned the epithet of the *urbs orbs*, or *cosmopolis* as it were.[31] In light of the centrality of citizenship to the ancient typologies of the city, then, the preternaturality attributed to the modern capital is hardly surprising. It was in stark contrast to both the boundedness of the *polis* and the integrative capacity of the imperial *civitas* that the typology of the capital figured as a behemoth and plurality of political subjects. Consequently, the typology of the capital presented the uncanny and novel problem of how to understand the nature of an urban polity whose actual constituency conspicuously exceeded that of its nominal citizenry.

In the seventeenth and eighteenth centuries, this problem was most patently addressed by the coinage and usage of new language to denote the capital itself. The modern usage of the word "metropolis," for instance, was a by-product of this era of hypertrophic growth; and it appeared unusually early in Naples, where, to my knowledge, it was first employed by Capaccio in his famous guide to the city, *Il forastiero* (1632), to capture not only the splendor but also the grandeur of Naples,[32] a connotation that it would maintain in the eighteenth century as well.[33] If a less dramatic representation of change than the oft-used head metaphor, this semantic innovation too articulated a shift in the political ontology of the capital city of Naples; posited in contradistinction to the "city," the "metropolis" semantically conveyed the anachronism of the capital as a discrete civic polity, whose internal dynamics and fortune could be accounted for by the laws of classical politics. For in the city of classical politics, there had been no place for the analysis of the claims and behavior of outsiders, who simply were viewed as alien to the political, cultural, and even moral orders of the civic community.[34] What is more, once dislodged from the field of political analysis, study of the city necessitated not only a new taxonomy but also a new teleology that could subsume the diverse members of its constituency. It begged the redefinition of citizenship for a world where the characteristic modalities of the civic community were not only strained but also in the process of being superseded.

Perhaps the best-known response to these questions and others like them in the eighteenth century was to invent the "nation"—as had Jean Bodin and, to very different ends, as would Jean-Jacques Rousseau[35]—that is, to extend the extant political categories of "citizenry" and "civic community" to embrace the larger, eclectic whole. As this book will show, another response was to discern in the implosive city the privileged site for the investigation of "society"—or what was a metapolitical sphere of human association and interaction—and to provide a new narrative of the *iter* and ends of civic citizenship that squared with those new realities and policies governing the metropolitan community.

In early modern Italy, the *iter* of civic citizenship had defined the political obligations and rights of the extant members of the city as well as provided the practical means for the integration of outsiders into the ranks of the civic community.[36] Typically, immigrants to cities could apply for citizenship once they had fulfilled the residency, tax, and property requirements stipulated by municipal statutes. Customarily, the award of citizenship then conferred on the individual the title of "true and original citizen of the city," or "antique, true and natural citizen of the city," so that his citizenship did not differ in kind from that of citizens-by-birthright, with whom he then (theoretically) shared the same burdens and rights of membership in the civic community.[37] Beyond the customary duties and privileges, the acquisition of citizenship bore for the same individual the fiction of naturalization. As studies of the *consilia,* or opinions, of prominent Renaissance jurists have shown, the conferral of citizenship was viewed not only as a juridical contract between the city and its new member but also as a formal acknowledgment of the new member's acquired political essence, or second political nature, be that new essence or nature understood as the product of juridical art itself or prolonged civic habit.[38] In other words, with its bestowal of a new juridical persona upon its recipient, the award of citizenship was a process that both dramatized and formalized the acquisition of a new political culture, making for a legal equivalent of the process of civilization *avant la lettre.*

As in the city-states of northern Italy, in the Kingdom of Naples the award of citizenship was primarily the prerogative of local municipalities, and it distinguished its recipient as the free and privileged member of a distinct civic community. In the capital of the Kingdom, however, the real perquisites and political duties of municipal citizenship were the most advantageous and honorific, making citizenship in the City of Naples a coveted good for much of the early modern period. Unlike the citizens of other communities, the citizen of Naples enjoyed numerous fiscal exemptions and jurisdictional privileges throughout the Kingdom of Naples.[39] In the first place, the Neapolitan citizen was exempt from cadastral taxation in Naples, or what was called the "focatico," and from numerous duties imposed on goods at the customs houses of the capital and Kingdom. In the legal realm, the Neapolitan also enjoyed the so-called *privilegio del foro,* the right for his case to be judged in Naples and thus by Neapolitan law, regardless of the provenance of the other party, as well as a set of legal protections that most famously included freedom from torture in the informational phase of a trial and from the confiscation of one's property. Finally, the citizen of Naples also possessed the right and duty to participate in the government of the municipality, which in addition to the governance of the polity also had the political privilege of officiating on behalf of the entire Kingdom in both the political dialogues and rituals conducted with the Spanish Empire.[40] Thus, the patent of citizenship in the City of Naples secured for its bearer a superior status that was literally honored throughout the Kingdom: it had cachet, both literally and symbolically.

As in the city-states of northern Italy, in the City of Naples the acquisition of citizenship was a well-codified process regulated by the practices and norms of juridical culture that both dramatized and formalized belonging to the civic corps. Significantly, integration into the citizenry and municipal governance of Naples could occur at one of two social levels: that of the civic patriciate or that of the *Popolo,* or People. In the case of the former, the acquisition of citizenship was the product of the admission of an individual to one of the five patrician *piazze,* or local parliaments of Naples, the accession to which had less to do with the civic qualifications than with the political and personal allegiances of the successful candidate.[41] As the civic patriciate was an exclusive body, most aspirants thus petitioned for citizenship at the rank of the Popolo, which beginning around 1500 increasingly required that one submit the requisite documentation to the Kingdom's preeminent fiscal organ, the Regia Camera della Sommaria, which evaluated it and ultimately conferred the patent and perquisites of municipal citizenship on the successful candidate. Beyond birthright, the primary qualification for citizenship was demonstrable possession of immovable property in Naples, that is, a home, which was the benchmark for residency.[42] In addition to this relatively steep property requirement, the qualifications for citizenship in Naples included the testimony of a number of key members of the civic community on behalf of the candidate, for whose good civic standing and Catholic orthodoxy they vouched, making the process of application an opportunity not only for an evaluation of the urban polity but also for a strengthening of ties among its own members, in spite of the centralization and juridical standardization of the process itself. In other words, the process demanded, as Piero Ventura has put it, "constant contractualism" with the state,[43] which served to adjudicate the status and rights of its new constituents and strengthen the fabric of the urban community. At the same time, the process of citizenship also renewed the municipality, whose corporation it symbolically reaffirmed and literally sustained with its admittance of new members to the Piazza del Popolo, the popular component of the municipal government of Naples, which effectively policed the polity and often served as a political partner of the viceroy on the ground. In sum, the institution of citizenship in early modern Naples was vital to both to the political fiction and function of the City, whose corporation was vested in its citizenry.

In light of the status and importance of citizenship in early modern Naples, its waning as an institution well before its formal abrogation by the nation-state is striking and warrants both explanation and investigation. Although not quantified, historiographical studies have suggested that the request for Neapolitan citizenship declined relative to the actual population growth of the capital in the second half of the seventeenth century, a political trend that partially could be explained by demographics, that is, by the ever-larger presence in the capital of immigrants excluded from the prospect of citizenship because of its exigent qualifications.

Beyond this demographic explanation, recent studies have offered two further reasons to account for this trend, one fiscal and one professional/cultural.[44] For those who did qualify, in the second half of the seventeenth century it seems that the patent of citizenship was no longer an efficacious means to attain more than the symbolic ends of civic distinction. In the first place, the patent yielded fewer tax exemptions after 1647, when the reforms of the viceroy, the Count of Oñate, eliminated most of the customs duties imposed on goods entering the capital in the wake of popular revolt in Naples. Furthermore, the significance of fiscal reform for the institutional bankruptcy of citizenship was compounded by the geographical limits of its political privileges. After the plague of 1656–57, just as earlier, much of the demographic growth of the city of Naples was accommodated by its district—that is, by its immediate suburbs and villages—where qualified residents could apply for Neapolitan citizenship bearing the qualification *de casalibus,* or of the district, which entitled them to the same privileges as those of a citizen *de ortu,* or of Naples, save participation in the Piazza del Popolo.[45] Consequently, the "constant contractualism" of residents of the district of Naples had been first and foremost about the fiscal prerogatives due its propertied class. Without the lure of those prerogatives, it is easy to imagine why the institution became less attractive to many of its prospective candidates. Just as citizenship no longer carried the same fiscal benefits after 1650, neither did it provide its titleholder with a competitive edge in qualification for the profession of government administration. Beyond its loss of fiscal might, the patent of citizenship also seems to have lost ground to other qualifications for office, such as a university degree, or *dottorato,* as the reflections of a contemporaneous jurist employed in the capital, Francesco D'Andrea, suggest.[46] In his celebrated personal memoir, the *Avvertimenti ai nipoti,* D'Andrea exclaimed that the essential qualification for office in Naples was "merit," rather than "birth, money, or even the honor of citizenship (*cittadinanza*)," which he therewith discounted as a nice but meaningless embellishment of the credentials requisite for a career in administration.[47]

Although it had lost its attractiveness, the category of citizenship seems to have persisted, if only to beg reinvention. Indeed, a better-known example of that reinvention is the way that D'Andrea and other members of the judiciary in Naples literally reappropriated and redefined the more antique Italian word for citizenship, that is *civiltà,* to refer to their own order of educated legal professionals, a usage that apparently was so widely diffused by the eighteenth century that it was reiterated in the sociological profiles of the city offered by numerous tourist guides.[48] With the waning of citizenship as an institution, then, the *iter* of civic citizenship gradually was lost as a procedure but gained as a model for thinking about the nature of distinctions among the constituents of a polity, whose demographic boundaries exceeded those of the municipality. In other words, it became a template for a theory of naturalization, whose subjects were those of the burgeoning metropolis.

Viewed retrospectively, it is easy to underestimate the sea change brought on by the obsolescence of civic citizenship in the early modern metropolis. Beyond the political challenges it must have posed to the municipality's governance on the ground and partnership with the court, the waning of citizenship additionally undermined the municipality as the telos of political incorporation, as well as the normative grid by which to assess and account for the relative status, rights, and obligations of the metropolitan community's members. Its waning thus made necessary, if not urgent, an alternative account of the union and ends of human beings, as well as the liberties and claims of the individual within the metropolitan community. In other words, it made meaningful the posing of those questions that otherwise were thought to apply to a fictional state of nature, namely, the occasion for the formation of what we would call "society" and the nature, obligations, and rights that its human relationships entailed. As this book shows, this sea change provided the context for the emergence of social theory in the city of Naples, which both adapted and transformed the criteria of early modern citizenship to hypothesize anew political belonging for the modern world.

If social theory hypothesized anew civic belonging, then it also challenged those models of social organization and comportment that heretofore had been the gold standard of behavior for the most ambitious members of the civic community of Naples. For the idea of *Napoli gentile*—that is, the idea of Naples as the seat of an illustrious nobility and a theater for that nobility's exhibition of its courtesy and power—had been among the most antique, oft-quoted, and tenacious tropes particular to the capital.[49] What is more, this trope was not without an undeniable foundation in reality. As is well known, Naples had long boasted its own indigenous caste of nobility, that is, the civic patriciate, which proudly drew its members from the ranks of the most illustrious families of the Kingdom.[50] In fact, the families with the largest feudal holdings in the Kingdom all enjoyed the privilege of membership in the patrician *piazze* of Naples,[51] and typically divided their time between their feudal estates and urban residences in the capital.[52]

Consequently, Naples truly was not only the capital of the Kingdom but also the capital of the Kingdom's feudal magnates; for contemporaries, it housed not only the representatives and institutions of royal governance but also those of, what the eighteenth-century itself called, the feudal system.[53] Among the many types of capital cities characteristic of early modern Europe, then, Naples is perhaps most comparable to Madrid, which has been referred to as a city "in the feudal order."[54] Beyond the ranks of the civic patriciate, other illustrious representatives of the Kingdom's nobility, or "barons," populated the capital in the early modern period. They had been invited by Viceroy Pedro de Toledo to maintain a residence in Naples, and the consequences for the capital's urban fabric are well known. Waves of immigration by the Kingdom's barons grossly enlarged the city and transformed it into a spectacle of palatial residences and, no less, a semiotic field of noble blazonry.[55] This imprint left no less a mark on the religious fabric, institutions, and customs of the capital, which benefited from the countless bequests of chapels, charities, reliquaries, and their associated festivities.[56] In the political field, furthermore, this same invitation unleashed among the barons a fierce competition for citizenship in the patrician *piazze* of Naples—which, as noted, held the keys to the political prerogative of civic governance for the nobility—and a keen vying for precedence and visibility in the rituals of the capital.[57] At the same time, the high concentration of nobles reproduced within the urban landscape social forms of organization and customs that had been typical of the barons' feudal estates. In the first place, it created a disproportionate number of jobs for domestic servants of various stations.[58] While the provenance of these servants has yet to be studied empirically, it is indubitable that many belonged to either the provincial households or communities of the barons themselves. As Tommasso Astarita has suggested in his study of the Caracciolo family, the resettlement—or seasonal residence—of the baronage in the capital provided opportunities for their vassals.[59] Consequently, it is easy imagine that Naples provided not only a spectacle of aristocratic station but also an ostentatious display of the aristocratic household and its customary forms of patronage. As Galanti commented in his reflections about the customs of Naples at the end of the eighteenth century: "Large is the number of domestics.... No one who has any pretense to station would know how to do without them. The custom of going about town in the morning without them has been introduced, but toward evening their company is reputed to be indispensable to the gentleman."[60] And it was precisely at the center of this great concourse of nobility and within its landscape pregnant with signs of genealogy and power that the young Vico was born, received his education, and nursed his ambitions for the remainder of life.

CHAPTER 1

The Origins of Vico's Social Theory

*Vichian Reflections on the Neapolitan Revolt of 1701
and the Politics of the Metropolis*

I. Introduction: Vico's Politics and the Political Origins of His Social Theory

In 1697 the civic political career of Giambattista Vico was stillborn. In that year, Vico competed for a position in the municipal government of Naples for which he qualified as a citizen of the capital, a title and identity that he proudly touted at the time. Indeed, that same year Vico prominently had signed his elegy on behalf of the deceased Catherine of Aragon as "Giambattista Vico, Citizen of Naples," lending the luster of his civic qualifications to his yet modest literary credentials.[1] Given his lineage, Vico's claim to citizenship in the City of Naples must have been a point of pride, as his own father, Antonio di Vico, was a recent immigrant to the capital from the village of Maddaloni—a farming community and fief of the powerful Carafa family in the province of Naples—where Vico's grandfather, Aniello, had labored as a peasant. Consequently, for Giambattista citizenship in the capital of Naples—which bore not only a coveted set of political privileges and fiscal immunities but also cultural cachet throughout the Kingdom—marked a rupture with the humble status of his rural ancestors as well as a new departure for the genealogy of his own family.[2] What was more, for Giambattista citizenship in the capital of Naples made juridically possible his pursuit of professional opportunities in the administration of the state, from which vassals

20   **CHAPTER 1**

customarily were excluded.[3] Regardless of his civic qualification, the position of Secretary of the City, a post that often was awarded to members of the Popolo of Naples who had some literary distinction, was given to another, namely Giovanni Brancone. This rejection by the municipality seems to have demoralized Vico, who retrospectively would mention it only in the context of the ostensible reluctance with which he then applied for another position, the lectureship in Rhetoric at the University of Naples.[4] Notwithstanding the tendentiousness of his *Autobiografia,* with his failure to obtain the post of Secretary of the City, Vico did set his sights on the University of Naples and successfully compete for a lectureship there, abandoning the more traditional avenue of municipal patronage for that of the state as a way to prosper in the capital.

For most of his long life, Vico was employed at the University of Naples as the professor of Rhetoric (1699–1741),[5] a position whose primary responsibility was the instruction of first-year students in the classical art of oratory, proficiency in which was required for formal admission to the university's course in legal studies and for candidacy for the doctorate of law.[6] Relative to most other positions within the university faculty, the one in Rhetoric was of lesser rank and salary.[7] Nonetheless, its award to Vico at the age of thirty not only acknowledged the growing reputation but also the political connections and allegiances of the young literatus. As the University of Naples was a public entity administered by the state, the award of the position in Rhetoric was a form of political patronage, which in the case of Vico recognized and rewarded his outstanding literary contributions to illustrious ceremonies of state wherein he honored the Spanish rulers of the Kingdom with an eloquence equal only to that of his unabashed obsequiousness.

In addition to his activities as a private tutor, prior to his university appointment Vico had accepted a number of commissions for ceremonies and publications celebrating members of the viceroyal court, for which he produced elegant hyperbolic works that evidently earned him both the respect and obligation of their sponsors and cohort. As Vico proudly noted in his *Autobiografia* (1725), in 1696 he had composed an oration praising the governance of Francesco Benavides, Count of Saint Stephan, the viceroy of Naples (1688–96) beloved by the Neapolitans, on the occasion of his departure.[8] Of incomparable eloquence, it was given pride of first place in the elegant commemorative volume edited by Nicola Caravita,[9] the learned Neapolitan jurist and loyal partisan of the Spanish administration, who Vico later claimed had facilitated his candidacy for the position in Rhetoric in 1697.[10] Whether or not Vico owed his university position to Caravita, we do know that the former contributed work to events and publications coordinated by the latter of high political profile throughout 1697, such as, Latin verse for a reading at the viceroyal palace in celebration of the name day of Charles II, the king of Spain, as well as a Latin oration and poem for the commemoration of the deceased Catherine of Aragon, the mother of the new viceroy, Luis de la Cerda, Duke of Medinaceli (1696–1701).[11] Needless to say, occurring just prior to his competition for the position in Rhetoric, these events provided Vico with ample occasion to demonstrate both his oratorical skill and, more important, his political allegiance to the Spanish before the leading members of the Kingdom's ruling class.

Once instated in the Chair of Rhetoric (1699) at the university, Vico nonetheless worked to maintain his public profile. Not only did he continue to frequent the circle about Caravita, who hosted an academy attended by distinguished local and Spanish men of learning, but he also secured membership in the most politicized of intellectual forums in Naples, namely, the newly established viceroyal academy, known as the Accademia Medinaceli. Presided over by no one less than the Duke of Medinaceli himself, on his admission to the Accademia Vico pronounced a lecture on the ancient Roman custom of feasting, a notably sociological reading of the Roman *cena* (supper) that was probably most compelling for its entertainment value.[12] In short, at the outset of his career Vico strategically worked to win and cultivate the favor of the ruling caste of the Kingdom, be it by the art of baroque adulation or by the antiquarian indulgence of Roman bonhommerie.

Initially, on both the counts of eloquence and politics Vico's demonstration must have been quite convincing, as in 1702 he was commissioned by the viceroy of Naples, Marquis of Villena and Duke of Escalona (1702–7), to memorialize what were among the most delicate political episodes of the last decade of Spanish rule, first, the visit to the Kingdom of Philip V (17 April–2 June 1702), the Bourbon heir to Charles II, whose succession to the Spanish throne was then in the process of contestation by the means of international warfare,[13] and, second, the history of the failed coup d'état (23–24 September 1701) directed against the regime of the Duke of Medinaceli just one year after the announcement of the same Bourbon succession in 1700.[14] For the former, the royal visit to Naples, Vico reportedly penned on the shortest of notice a Latin panegyric to Philip V, the *Panegyricus Philippo V,* which he allegedly published at his own cost and distributed to the new king, whom he presented with a manuscript copy of the oration, and among his court, upon whose members he showered numerous printed ones.[15] If the details concerning the publication and distribution of the *Panegyricus* are in fact correct, then there is good reason to believe that both the efforts and expenses incurred by Vico were not in vain. For some thirty-two years later (1734), when he sought to curry the favor of the rein-stated Bourbon dynasty, he would choose to give some prominence to the *Panegyricus* in a curriculum vitae calculated to build a case for his merit of royal patronage, or what was a sinecure.[16] Listed and elaborated on before his more famous philosophical works, Vico clearly considered the *Panegyricus* to be a key selling point of his career to the new Bourbon king, Charles (designated but not invested as VII), who himself was the son of Philip V. In light of the outcome of Vico's request, his appointment as Royal Histo-riographer of the Kingdom, the *Panegyricus* presumably passed as evidence of services faithfully rendered to and well received by King Philip V during his contested reign over the Kingdom (1701–7). Indeed, in hindsight, Vico's praise of Philip V in 1702, that is just five years before he surrendered the Kingdom to imperial forces during the War of the Spanish Succession, easily lent itself as proof of unwavering loyalty to the Bourbon dynasty through both good times and bad.

However, as the omissions of the same vita suggest, Vico's track record was blemished, and the prominence granted the *Panegyricus* surely was also calculated to mitigate the poor publicity, if not outright disrepute, brought Vico by his subsequent commissioned work, namely, the history of the failed coup d'état directed against the regime of the Spanish viceroy, Medinaceli, in 1701. For the same vita, Vico cautiously omitted mention of the history, now conventionally entitled the *Coniuratio principum Neapolitanorum* (dated to circa 1703–4), although it presumably had been commissioned by Vice-roy Villena and composed by Vico to apologize for the Bourbon succession to the Spanish throne and to discredit the purported ends of the Neapoli-tan insurrectionaries.[17] The *Coniuratio* was never published, however, as it was censored by the viceroy's handpicked examiners, the trusted Antonio Giudice, the Prince of Cellammare, and Restaino Cantelmo, the Duke of Popoli, who reportedly declared that both it and the history of another author were "too offensive to the majesty of the sovereign and to the honor of several noble families."[18] While the exact objections of the censors to the publication of the history remain obscure, for those high-ranking servants of the Spanish crown, the *Coniuratio* clearly failed to persuasively defend the political status quo of the Kingdom and to respect the honor of its nobility. The viceroyal examiners also may have balked at Vico's representation of the political pretenses of the coup's protagonists, pretenses that he implicitly was obliged to either denounce as illegitimate or politely neglect as ridiculous. In any case, for the likes of Giudice and Cantelmo, Vico had failed to deliver a history that could adequately serve the propagandistic ends of the Spanish on the ideological front of the War of the Spanish Succession.

For Vico, in turn, the censure of his history evidently was a source of immediate frustration and of lasting embarrassment. In the first place, he surely would not have accepted the commission of a history of such great political delicacy had he not been sure that he could succeed splendidly at the task and therewith benefit from it. Despite the plausible validity of the objections to the *Coniuratio,* furthermore, given his track record in 1703–4, he must have experienced the censorship of his history as a betrayal of his steadfast loyalty to Spanish rule of the Kingdom in its hour of supreme trial. During his drafting of the *Coniuratio,* Vico had continued to demonstrate unwavering public support for a Bourbon succession to the Spanish throne. Most notably, in his correspondence he adamantly defended the leading tract on the juridical propriety of the Bourbon succession penned by the prominent jurist Serafino Biscardi, who was then regent of the Kingdom's preeminent ministry, the Consiglio Collaterale, or Council of State, and perhaps the single most staunch ally of the Spanish in the Kingdom.[19] For the Neapolitan coterie of philo-Spanish administrators, then, it was doubtless where Vico's political allegiances lay. Nonetheless, it was with mixed results that Vico publicly positioned himself as a staunch supporter of the Spanish Empire in the twilight of its Italian rule. Consequently, Vico not only omitted mention of the *Coniuratio* in his vita from 1734 but also covered over its tracks in his magisterial celebration of his intellectual career, the *Autobiografia,* which placed his philosophical works front and center.

If the *Coniuratio* marked a change in his political fortune, it also occasioned Vico's identification of those social issues with which he would grapple for the rest of his career. For rather than simply providing him with an opportunity to laud the Spanish Empire, the commission of the *Coniuratio* gave Vico occasion to analyze the instability of the Kingdom within it, the causes for which he identified in not only the larger European but also the local Neapolitan context. The narrative reconstruction of the failed coup d'état was predicated on the keen sense that political loyalties were delimited, if not determined, by what were larger processes investing the lives of individuals with otherwise discrete identities. Indeed, Vico's interpretation evinced a disconnect between the nominal identity and behavior of numerous participants in the coup; similarly, it also exposed the lines of division among preexisting groups. In short, it made conspicuous the limitations of those traditional categories employed to characterize and meaningfully order the constituents of the polity, while identifying new criteria to account for political behavior.

For Vico, in no place were these contradictions more accentuated than in the city of Naples, the actual theater of the revolt and, thus, the stage upon which the various social actors of the Kingdom converged to advance and/ or protect their ambitions. In the *Coniuratio,* more than a point of convergence, the capital was also a point of accentuation, however. Therein, Vico presented the urban polity as a field that reconfigured social alliances in what were unpredictable ways for contemporaries; it made of the so-called conspiracy a social war that both recalled and confounded the lessons of more ancient examples, as it exposed the vulnerability of allegiances born of both order and civic *patria.* In other words, it squarely destabilized the early modern categories of order and citizen as especially concerned the codes of political behavior normally connoted by them. What is more, as I argue in this book, this historical exercise not only sharpened but also broadened the practical horizons of citizenship in Vico's mind. In particular, it would lead him to revisit and selectively appropriate that ancient political philosophy most concerned with the boundaries of political membership, namely, Stoic cosmopolitanism. Thus, with the change in his political fortune Vico would elaborate a theory of citizenship for a globalizing world, while remaining keenly aware of the expectations of his audience, the contemporary circumstances of the Kingdom, and the diplomatic norms of his age.

II. *Historia magistra vitae:* The *Coniuratio principum Neapolitanorum* and Its Models

As a history, the *Coniuratio* recounted the story of the failed coup organized against the representative of the Spanish monarchy in Naples, Viceroy Luis Francisco de la Cerda, Duke of Medinaceli. The coup against the Spanish viceroy of Naples was organized in the ostensible favor of Habsburg Archduke Charles, the second son of Holy Roman Emperor Leopold I, whom the leading international powers had nominated to succeed the heirless Charles II in Spain, the Spanish Netherlands, and colonies, and whose own political ambition included rule of the Spanish possessions in Italy. The coup was plotted over the course of 1701, a year that marked the most vulnerable of transitions for the Spanish monarchy. Then, the appointed successor to the heirless Habsburg, the Bourbon Philip V, acceded to the Spanish throne and sought against many odds to establish his power over the monarchy and to maintain its many possessions intact. Most notably, the same consortium of European powers that had nominated Archduke Charles for succession to the Spanish throne joined forces to wage a war against Philip and his French ally in the War of the Spanish Succession (1701–14/20), which not only taxed the dwindling resources of the Spanish monarchy but also Philip's tenuous control over it. Furthermore, belligerent opposition from without the monarchy provided the ideal condition for the expression of staunch opposition from within by the grandees and baronage of the Spanish crown lands, who struggled to protect, if not reassert, local privileges in the face of the uniform regulations of a centralizing administration. Throughout the monarchy, opposition to the Bourbon succession also came in the form of revolt, as it did in the jewel of the monarchy's Italian possessions, the Kingdom of Naples, the reasons for which Vico captured with rhetoric inspired by the ancients and an analysis firmly rooted in the moderns.

Like most political histories penned by Italians since the Renaissance, the *Coniuratio* made manifest the contingency of Italy in general and the Kingdom of Naples in particular on the state of international affairs.[20] As the structure and content of its narrative evinced, the domestic fate of the Kingdom remained tied to the outcomes of pan-European warfare and the fortunes of its victors. The opening frame of Vico's account of the coup offered a punctilious discussion of the stratagems of individual European powers on the death of Charles II, rehearsing in detail for his reader the war of rhetoric and men brought to enforce rival claims to the Spanish throne and to win influence within the European orbit of its monarchy. What is more, it attributed the very origins and impetus of the Neapolitan revolt to the machinations of the European powers. Specifically, it identified in the diplomatic intrigue negotiated behind closed doors and in the warfare pursued on the ground by Leopold I the conception and sustenance of that scheme that would shake but not effectively end Spanish control of the Kingdom in 1701. Indeed, Vico credited the ideation of the coup to Leopold himself, who reportedly sent Neapolitan nobles of the sword in the imperial service as unofficial envoys to Rome, where they dutifully assessed the potential for Austrian support among the Kingdom's resident barons. Moving from the European theater of warfare to the Neapolitan stage of the revolt, then, the narrative trajectory of the *Coniuratio* found the conditions for local sedition in the schemes of the international powers. Vico patently viewed the ruthless vying of the European powers for influence in the Spanish world as a destabilizing force in the Kingdom, as it prompted the Kingdom's various orders and citizens to weigh the ostensible advantages of Austrian rule by a Habsburg against those of continued Spanish rule under a Bourbon.

As a genre, Vico's *Coniuratio* evidently was most indebted to that famous history of political revolt penned by the Roman author Gaius Sallustius Crispus, namely, the *Bellum Catilinae,* most commonly known as *The Conspiracy of Catiline,* which had recounted the plot hatched by the patrician Catiline to stage an armed insurrection against the Roman state toward the end of the Republic. Vico's debt was far from unique. For his model, Vico had chosen

a Roman history that long had ranked as a favorite of the reading public of
early modern Europe. As the work of Patricia Osmond has amply documented, throughout the Renaissance, manuscript copies and print editions
of Sallust were widely available to the literate public and voraciously read by
them. "From the advent of printing to the early seventeenth century," indeed,
"he headed the bestseller list of Roman historians," according to Osmond.[21]
If widely read and discussed, his work also was imitated by the most illustrious of Renaissance literati, from the patrician historian Bernardo Rucellai
in the fifteenth century to the Renaissance playwright Ben Jonson in the
early seventeenth.[22] That Vico chose Sallust's history as a model for his own
thus has been noted as if the choice were overdetermined by the canonical
status of Sallust, the cachet of Sallustian history, and Vico's own predilection
for the classics. As an explanation of Vico's choice, however, those observations veil the especial appropriateness of the *Bellum Catilinae* for his interpretation of the coup. As Patricia Osmond has argued, the reasons for the
undying popularity of Sallust most probably lay in the great adaptability of
his histories to the changing climate of political opinion, as there evidently
was something in them for almost every one of the political thinkers from
the fifteenth-century champions of civic Humanism to seventeenth-century
advocates of monarchy.[23] In the case of Camillo Porzio, for instance, the
author of a famous Sallustian history of the Renaissance Kingdom of Naples,
the history of the baronial revolt of 1485 entitled *La congiura de' baroni del
Regno di Napoli, contra il Re Ferdinando Primo* (1565), Sallust's hallmark account
of the degeneration of the Roman constitution provided what was a model
for not only the moral censure of the Kingdom's rebels but also the staunch
endorsement of monarchical rule.[24] As Porzio had done, so did Vico serve
himself of Sallustian tradition to censure the character of the Kingdom's
conspirators. Yet, at the same time, Vico employed Sallust in a key that was
distinct from the one of his Renaissance predecessors; and he did so to political ends that were different from those of Porzio. For Vico not only drew
on some exempla of Sallustian history to encode and validate his own positions, respectful of the Ciceronian aphorism held by Renaissance literati that
history was the great teacher of life,[25] but also tested the validity of others,
underscoring the irreconcilable differences between his modern world and
the ancient one. And it is the reason why Vico tested the validity of Sallust,
breaking ranks with his Renaissance predecessors, that is the ultimate argument of this chapter. With his Janus-faced citation of Sallust, Vico succeeded
well at both underscoring the resemblances and stating the differences of
his particular analysis of urban revolt from that of the canonical Roman.
Put somewhat differently, therewith Vico played on the expectations of his

learned audience to interrogate the value of the foremost model of urban factionalism for contemporary Naples and to bolster his own account of the instability of the capital's constitution.

Like Sallust, Vico emplotted his riveting tale of revolt as a conspiracy. Indeed, the very titles Vico presumably gave the two versions of his manuscript work both bore the Latin word for such, that is, "coniuratio." The only significant difference between the two titles lay in the qualification of the conspiracy, which the first described as "Partenopean," or Neapolitan ("De Parthenopea coniuratione"), and the second more specifically attributed to an unnamed cast of "Neapolitan princes" ("Coniuratio principum Neapolitanorum")—a revision that better inflected the emphasis of the work on the arguable social composition of the conspiratorial faction.

With Sallust, Vico shared the methodological conviction that good history instructed and that instruction was well served by that sort of character analysis that added to the storehouse of virtuous and vicious examples available to the literary public. A tale of conspiracy, Vico's narrative gave prominence to the protagonists of the coup, whose portraits he painted with a vividness and flourish for detail that matched, if not surpassed, Sallust's own. Like the portraits of the protagonists of Catiline's war, those of the *Coniuratio* first and foremost identified the desire for sedition in the nature of its instigators; they offered intense depictions of the character of their subjects, whose predisposition to political intrigue the portraits represented as a manifestation of the sheer and utter villainy of their personae. As Vico depicted them, in other words, the conspirators were personifications of vice. Recalling Sallust's harrowing psychological portrait of Catiline, Vico eloquently incriminated the ostensible mastermind of the Neapolitan plot, Giuseppe Capece, the son of the Marchioness of Rofrano, as an emblem of depravity with the following figure of his character: "an enigmatic young man of few means and insatiable desires... who was quick of hand, slow of tongue, keen of mind, tenacious in his proposals, audacious in their realization, and most faithful in the keeping of secrets."[26] Vico further shared his moral invective with the accomplices of Capece, whom he introduced to his readers as lawless men of unbridled ambition who readily stooped to any means to promote their personal gain. Taking roll of Capece's band, Vico listed with censure: Bartolomeo Ceva Grimaldi, the Duke of Telese, a maniacal assassin; Francesco Spinelli, the Duke of Castelluccia, a man of extravagant "leisure" who pondered nothing less than the "commonwealth"; Giambattista Di Capua, the Prince of Riccia, a figure of regal countenance whose "perfidy" was betrayed by "the perversity of his eyes"; and, most infamously, Gaetano Gambacorta, the Prince of Macchia, the reputation of whose lineage and personal service to the Spanish already had been tainted by his violent lapses of infidelity to the monarchy and by his poor judgment, which reportedly had been impaired by his penury.[27] As Vico's portraits impressed upon the imagination of his contemporary reader, the conspirators shared a proclivity for treachery, which suited them well for the perpetration of Capece's plot, in spite of the illustriousness of their lineage and the presumed gentility of their cohort.

Yet, the commonness of depravity alone could not explain the political concert of iniquity in the *Coniuratio*. With Sallust, Vico further shared the methodological conviction that good history accounted for the formation of political faction; and from Sallust he took the lesson that political faction was born of a commonality of interest, however base. Consequently, Vico's account of conspiracy strategically elaborated Sallust's own to argue that the collective action of the Neapolitan conspirators had been predicated on the coincidence of their material circumstances and goals. Despite his literary penchant for character analysis, Vico complemented his moral portraiture of the conspirators with an assessment of their personal fortunes, wherein he specifically located the conditions that made a cohesive faction out of men from distinct, if not rival, noble clans. In the prefatory remarks to his sketch of Capece's band, Vico squarely noted that for his accomplices Capece had sought out noblemen who were not only "faithful to himself" but also "avid for change" on account of their personal ruin. As had the accomplices of Catiline, those of Capece consequently evaluated the prospect of a regime change in terms of its potential for their personal profit. Indeed, they purportedly rallied around Capece's plot for a price. Couching his analysis of the conspirators' actions in the ostensible objectivity of popular saying, Vico reported: "They say it was for profound avidity that the conspirators shamefully sold the peace of the fatherland to the Germans."[28] And, as Vico further revealed, the price of the *patria* was a handsome one indeed, namely, the expropriation of a number of the Kingdom's most coveted feudal lands and offices for bestowal upon the noble insurrectionaries. If a display of his classical learning and talent for character analysis, then Vico's history of the Neapolitan coup evidently was also an analysis of the conspiratorial faction that underscored the primacy and cohesiveness of its members' material interests, and that particularly made manifest the systemic threat posed by noble forces out of step with a changing mode of capital accumulation.

Vico evidently availed himself of the *Bellum Catilinae* to persuasively package his own convictions about the nature of political alliance, and the challenges it posed for the contemporary Kingdom. As seen, by invoking Sallust, Vico's analysis of the conspirators restated with the authority of antiquity that the commonalities of what we would call class mattered more than either morality or social allegiance in the formation of political faction. Indeed, Vico's own inventory of the conspirators and subsequent analysis of the revolt pointed up how the interests of class trumped the differences of rank and order. For the conspirators were composed of impoverished representatives from the most sundry ranks of the Kingdom's nobility and the capital's commoners. As the political roles of these groups famously had been at odds in Vico's age, their collaboration would have struck contemporaries as unusual, if not outright disturbing, and thus worthy of explanation.[29] To this end, Vico's analysis of the Neapolitan conspirators first unveiled the limitations of social identity for explaining political behavior; it questioned the political relevance of those social categories employed to distinguish and order the constituency of the capital and its Kingdom, destabilizing the notion that social etiquettes also connoted political coalitions with time-honored roles in the capital's community. As will be seen, this insight was especially borne out by Vico's study of the popular forces to collaborate with the conspirators. In sum, the *Coniuratio* corroborated an ancient model of conspiracy while revising contemporary expectations of rank and order, especially as they pertained to the politics and political constitution of the capital's civic community.

III. The *Coniuratio* on the Politics of the Capital and Behavior of Its Commoners

As in the *Bellum Catilinae,* at the heart of the tale of conspiracy told by the *Coniuratio* was an examination of the politics of the capital. Indeed, at the center of Vico's gripping narrative was a report from the ground on the contemporary politics of the common citizenry of Naples, as evidenced by their deliberated reaction to the aristocratic insurrection against the regime of Medinaceli. Therewith, the *Coniuratio* identified and sought to account for the particularity of the urban alliance formed to perpetrate the plot of the conspirators, both hitching and distinguishing its analysis of political partisanship from that of the *Bellum Catilinae.* For Sallust, the ultimate task of his history had been to explain why the treacherous ambition of a patrician could find such ample support among the common citizens of Rome that it posed a real threat to the political status quo. For him, the answer to this question chiefly had lain in the factionalism of Roman politics and society, that is, in the growing disparity between the patricians and plebeians of the Roman commonwealth that had rendered the disenfranchised many hostile toward the privileged few. Significantly, this same answer helped to engender the model of Roman politics as a conflict of orders that located the desire for change and the potential challenge to the status quo in the urban plebs, or what moderns would call the masses. And it was this model of metropolitan politics as a conflict of orders that the *Bellum Catilinae* also helped to bequeath to posterity.

The reasons for the lasting success of Sallust's account of the plebeian faction can be found in his reliance on both historical fact and literary fiction. On the one hand, his account of plebeian partisanship recalled the political casualties of Sulla's infamous end to the Social War, which ironically had curtailed the rights of the Republic's plebs and redistributed much of their property holdings, exacerbating the preexisting divisions between the Roman patricians and plebeians. On the other hand, it availed itself of powerful literary *topoi* about the urban plebs that gave his account of factionalism the credence of a commonplace truth. As for so many Roman literati, for Sallust the urban plebs were akin to a parasitic and undifferentiated mob, which coalesced in the pursuit of sustenance and *otium,* or bread and circuses. Indeed, in the *Bellum Catilinae* Rome itself was comparable to a cesspool of the disenfranchised, prodigal, and reprobate, all of whom the *urbs* purportedly rendered characteristically idle and, as such, volatile. As Sallust famously remarked: "The young men who had maintained a wretched existence by manual labor in the country, tempted by public and private doles had come to prefer idleness in the city to their hateful toil; these like all the others battened on the public ills."[30] Not surprisingly, it was this prospectless urban mob fattened at the public expense from which the Roman conspirators easily lured their recruits with the promise of spoils, according to Sallust.[31] And it was on the marginalized plebeian assembly (*contio*), roused by the premeditated slander of the foremost representative of the senate, the famous consul Marcus Tullius Cicero, that the conspirators additionally counted in their call to arms.[32] It was the manipulation of the desperate many by the ambitious few, then, that produced the unholy alliance between the conspirators of Catiline and the urban plebs.

For an early modern like Vico the *Bellum Catilinae* was thus didactic. Specifically, it warned against the intrigue of the greedy and the volatility of the plebeian masses, which were so easily enlisted in the most pernicious of causes. More generally, it offered an important lesson about the extraordinary precariousness of things in the metropolis, whose political constitution was perennially threatened by the volatility of the plebeian mob. Yet, its powerful fiction of a plebeian mob also offered a powerful model against which to gauge and assess the dynamics of contemporary urban politics in early modern Europe, as Vico would do in his analysis of the forces of revolt in Naples.

Analogously to the *Bellum Catilinae,* in the *Coniuratio* both the viability
and denouement of insurrection were predicated on the support provided
by the urban populace. Consequently, eminent among Vico's concerns was
a vivid portrayal of the nature and behavior of the common citizenry of
Naples, which contemporaries generally called the "Popolo." To denote the
commoners of Naples, Vico employed the semantics of the *Bellum Catilinae,*
however. Like Sallust, Vico used the Latin term "plebs" to refer to the large
swath of commoners of the urban community, and his qualification of them
further recalled the caricature of the Roman plebs as a volatile mob.[33] Yet the
unfolding of the revolt demonstrated that semantic continuity alone proved
to be a misleading indicator of the actual political behavior of the Neapolitan
populace. Indeed, the response of the Neapolitan plebs to the conspirators
belied the volatility attributed to them by means of semantic association with
the Roman mob. It rather suggested that the Roman model of the urban plebs
did not faithfully represent the common people of Naples, whose constituency and political choices Vico compellingly narrated.

Like the choices of the Roman plebs in the *Bellum Catilinae,* those of
the Neapolitan plebs in the *Coniuratio* were utterly pivotal for the course
of revolt. Indeed, the original plan of the conspirators had been to have the
viceroy murdered at the hands of his servants and to take the main bulwark,
the Castel Nuovo, with the help of a contingent of turncoat guards. Once
foiled, however, the support of the urban populace was absolutely decisive
for both launching and later breaking the momentum of the insurrection
against the Spanish. Consequently, some of the most suspense-filled scenes
of the *Coniuratio* were devoted to the depiction of how despised representatives of the conspiracy strived to cajole members of the "plebs" into joining
their ranks. Approaching its climax, Vico's narrative turned to the ground to
follow the conspirators in their pursuit of popular support across those zones
of the city inhabited, as he specified, by members of the "basest plebs." And
there, at those neighborhood monuments of plebeian life—at the Pietra del
Pesce, the Conceria, and the Mercato—Gambacorta, the Prince of Macchia,
exercised his oratorical skills to persuade the plebs to take up arms. While
Vico noted that some were persuaded, under the guise of Herodotean objectivity, he also reported how others balked at Gambacorta's invitation and
promises. Indeed, in response to Gambacorta's virile rally to arms members
of the plebs ostensibly exercised not only precautionary restraint but also
political judgment, giving good reason for their refusal to enlist. Based on an
assessment of the stakes of insurrection, some politely declined their support
with the dictum "You seek to seize a better fortune; we live happily with
ours," citing the discrepancy of interests between the nobles and commoners

as their reason for keeping the peace.[34] The response of others was more contentious, however, invoking the political factionalism of the capital as reason for their refusal. For those representatives of the plebs, recent history had taught the populace to distrust the nobility, making an alliance with them inconceivable. Specifically, the nobility's betrayal of the popular cause during the landmark revolt of Masaniello (1647–8) had irreparably divided the commoners from them.[35] As one pleb remonstrated with some grandiloquence, when it would have been "fair" to support popular revolt against the excesses of the Spanish, the nobility rather chose to hinder it, in patent opposition to what was just.[36]

Yet members of the plebs did not fail to enlist in the cause of the conspirators, infusing the insurrection with both strength and momentum. In particular Vico noted that men from the very margins of the civic commoners, or what he called the "vile plebs,"[37] rallied to the cause of the conspirators with a furor equal to the lowliness of their station, breaking ranks with their more distinguished brethren. Swelling their ranks, furthermore, were criminals and outsiders such as those prisoners liberated by the conspirators (from the detention of the guilds, civil courts, and churches of Naples) as well as the peasant vendors at the Mercato who hailed from the vicinity of the capital. If Vico's report from the ground marshaled evidence for division between the noble and common orders, then it also suggested that a fracture effectively existed within the "plebs," or Popolo, itself. Qualifying the soldiers in the ranks of the conspirators as the vilest of men, Vico's account of popular support for the insurrection served as evidence for how social distinctions within the Popolo were further articulated as political differences in this episode of crisis. By both hitching his account to and distinguishing it from that of Sallust, then, Vico argued by example that the Roman notion of factionalism could not do justice to the complexity of the social fabric and, in similar fashion, civic politics of Naples.

First, the divisive reaction of the plebs to Gambacorta made plain that the body politic of Naples was divided not only among but also within its constituent orders. Moreover, it also implied that the Roman notion of the plebs as an impressionable collective entity did not pertain to the Neapolitan order of commoners. If members of the plebeian forces had rallied to the cause of the conspirators, then their behavior had to be explained in terms other than those of mob psychology. Finally, and most important, Vico's documentation of plebeian behavior built a case for the bankruptcy of the politics of the common citizenry of Naples—that is, for the demise of the Popolo as a united political front and consensual partner of the Spanish. It attested that the political will of the Neapolitan Popolo had been broken by both its political experience as well as its own internal social divisions. In other words, for Vico the historical record of the Neapolitan conspiracy had evidenced the political submission of the Popolo and had raised the issue of the relationship between the social stratification and political judgment of its members, whose condition and behavior he subsequently would correlate in the *Coniuratio.*

Vico's explanation of the behavioral fault line among the popular forces of Naples hinged on a single central distinction, namely, that of property. For Vico, those plebeians who joined the revolt were strictly limited to the "the most vile of men, good-for-nothings" who "squandered their resources on games, wine, and women."[38] As he further observed, they were men who possessed nothing more than "their lives and hope."[39] By contrast, propertied commoners, however modest, shunned the conspiracy and safeguarded both themselves and their things. Like the "modest citizens" (*modesti cives*) and "nobles of private wealth" (*privatae fortunae nobiles*), who in times of revolt typically brought their families to safety and secured their possessions, so too did the "artisans and shopkeepers" (*artifices ac mercatores*) of Naples secure their wares and retire to their homes, refusing the aid requested of them by the conspirators.[40] In other words, for Vico there were "plebs" and there were "base plebs," whom he regularly distinguished throughout his text by the linguistic means of qualification.[41] Thus, Vico's reconstruction of the rival alliances forged by representatives of the common people made plain that the political divide within the Popolo was drawn by the threshold of ownership. Similarly, Vico's analysis of the motley constituency of the rival factions suggested that their bases consisted in the shared outcomes of their members' risk assessment. As his analysis of the conspiratorial faction implied, the curious alliance of grand nobility and base plebeians was indeed natural, if one only considered the common results of their calculations: that they literally had nothing to lose and everything to gain from revolt. As concerned political partisanship, then, the commonality of individual prospects trumped that of order in the *Coniuratio,* offering a sociological explanation of political behavior where the logic of order and rank had lost its force.

That property should count as a determining factor of political behavior was not new with Vico, however. Indeed, since the times of the Romans, the possession and cultivation of landed property had been considered a virtue that nurtured one's loyalties to the customary laws and order of the civic polity. The very prejudices Sallust expressed against the urban immigrants from the countryside betrayed as much. So did the astonishment with which the citizenry of Naples ostensibly reacted to the news that the landed nobility of the Kingdom had conspired against the "civic polity" (*civitas*).[42] What was particular to Vico's observations about the political loyalties and obligations born of property was the kind that especially pertained. While the Romans had associated the cultivation of political loyalties and obligations with the possession of immoveable property, that is, land, Vico associated the same with the possession of movables, that is, things, such as the goods and wares of the artisan and merchant classes. Consequently, Vico's assessment of the citizens faithful to the polity was not only more inclusive than the Roman, whose fiction of the urban plebs simply had lumped the artisans and shop-keepers together with the destitute rest, but also fundamentally different. Importantly, it shifted the bar for civic loyalty from the profits of the land to those of industry and, more shockingly, commerce. In other words, it floated the claim that the regard for political order derived from the processes of exchange and capital accumulation.

For contemporaries, this point was most forcefully made by Vico's identi-fication of the capital's entrepreneurs as the pillars of civic order in times of revolt. As Vico specifically noted, beyond his inner circle, the viceroy placed his greatest trust in the "modest citizens" (*modesti cives*), an elusive subset of the Popolo that Vico took pains to distinguish linguistically,[43] and that contemporaries would have understood as characterized by not only their moral restraint but also moveable assets, given Vico's usage of the term.[44] In other words, Vico represented the history of the revolt as if the restoration of the peace had been facilitated by the discretion and loyalty of distinctly propertied men. Indeed, in his rendition of the restoration of law and order, Vico specifically cast these "modest citizens" in roles traditionally reserved for identifiable officers of the Popolo. According to Vico, at the very height of the revolt it was these "modest citizens" of means that the viceroy reportedly employed as scouts amid the destitute plebs to assess the extent and strength of their insurrection, replacing the captains of the *ottine* (civic districts) and their guards.[45] And it was they who apparently flanked the final cavalcade marking the return of law and order to the capital, replacing the rank and file of the Piazza del Popolo in that show of an enforced peace.[46] In other words, according to Vico, it was representatives of commerce and industry who personified the moral quality of *modestia*—that is, a most dignified form of discretionary restraint—and who, above the fray, remained most faithful to the civic polity. Consequently, one of the political lessons of the *Coniuratio* was that the economy of exchange civilized; therein, exchange rendered its subjects averse to lawlessness and inclined them toward the maintenance of a public authority committed to the rule of law and vested with the use of force. Regardless of one's rank, it edified its subjects politically by making real for them the benefits of political union and order. In addition, the *Coniuratio* also warned that the title of "citizen" was a far less reliable indicator of civic loyalty than a person's assets, whose accumulation was so dependent on political stability and the rule of law. As Vico's account of factionalism intimated, allegiance to the polity was better fostered by the practices of exchange than by those of citizenship alone, whose very significance was belied by the political contradictions of the revolt.

If Vico's analysis of the Neapolitan conspiracy dismissed Roman ideas about the civic orders as an anachronism, then it also questioned the actuality of the early modern notion of citizenship. In the first place, Vico employed the term "citizen" in an unconventional way; in the *Coniuratio*, it functioned as a sort of catchall for non-noble residents of the capital, be they registered members of the municipal citizenry, or not. For instance, Vico indistinctly identified both the plebeian forces of revolt and their most stalwart opponents, the entrepreneurs, as "citizens." In reality, we know that among both these groups there were great numbers of "foreigners," or "forestieri," the term that was used for residents of the capital hailing from other parts of the Kingdom and Italian peninsula, a fact that contemporaries especially noted in reference to the origins of the commoners of the city, or the nominal plebs.[47] Thus, Vico's blanket usage of the term citizen destabilized the traditional meaning of that political category. His usage forced a conflation between the mere residents and actual citizens of Naples, groups that customarily had been viewed as distinct and unequal. In similar fashion, it invested what had been a political term with sociological meaning, robbing it of the connotation of juridical exclusivity. What was more, this conflation inflected, if not acknowledged, that the effective community of the capital was significantly larger than the citizen body of its municipality, or *Città* as contemporaries called it, and the intrapersonal network of its government. If not in name, then in content it posited the conundrum of the metropolis: the challenge of an urban space that could physically integrate the persons but not honor the natural rights of its resident subjects.

In the *Coniuratio*, this conundrum was most dramatically evidenced by the symbolic actions of the nominal plebs at what was the climax of the revolt. In the heat of the insurrection and at the dead center of Vico's narrative the conspirators occupied the seat of the municipality, the church and complex of San Lorenzo, where their popular forces reportedly undertook the destruction of the acts of the civic corporation, endangering the coveted privileges and prerogatives of Naples conserved in its codices and volumes. By contemporary observers, this gesture of political violence generally was interpreted as evidence of the irrationality of the plebs, as the rhetoric of Vico and others indeed suggested. With the attempted destruction of those privileges from which they presumably benefited, the plebs were "intent upon their own destruction," as Vico put it.[48] This rhetoric notwithstanding, Vico's account of the course and demise of the violence implied that the occupation of San Lorenzo was a powerful symbol of popular revolt against exclusion from those same coveted privileges and prerogatives the anonymous commoners attempted to destroy. In other words, it suggested that the "plebs" partaking of the assault on the icons of the civic corporation were so in name only and that among the sources of malcontent was the exclusivity of Neapolitan citizenship and, similarly, of the capital's privileges and prerogatives. That the assault on the municipality was the unintended consequence of enlisting outsiders in the fray was made plausible by Vico's inclusion of peasants among Gambacorta's forces, and it was sustained by Vico's account of the quick reversal of the assault commanded by one of the leading conspirators. As Vico recounted it, the violence against the municipality was as swiftly reversed as it was apprehended by the patrician conspirator and preeminent citizen Tiberio Carafa, whose family exercised the greatest influence within the municipal corporation. Once the political violence had been subdued, furthermore, the conspirators peacefully regrouped the "plebs" before San Lorenzo, the seat of the municipality, for what Vico pictured to be a mock, and thus illegitimate, civic assembly, symbolism that would not have been lost on contemporaries. There, the leader of the insurrection, Gambacorta, proclaimed to acclamation the election of the Habsburg Archduke Charles in the name of the motley assembly of nobles and commoners. And he boldly declared that motley assembly the "most faithful People of Naples," appropriating the customary title of the citizen body of the municipality and its claim to sovereignty for whom they manifestly were not due.[49] Thus, the symbolism of the political violence and its permutation implicated among the leading causes for popular furor the nonrepresentativeness of the municipality and, in particular, the Piazza del Popolo, the civic parliament of the People that partnered with the civic patriciate to govern the City. It dramatically staged the claim that there was a lack of correspondence between the civic governance and social realities of the capital, and that this noncorrespondence had proved a powder keg. More specifically, it recognized that the capital, as a postcitizen polity, both hosted and frustrated the ambitions of newcomers, whose sense of entitlement and justice the municipality was ill-equipped to accommodate. If not with its words, then with its images of the revolt, the *Coniuratio* made plain just how empty was the municipality's claim to represent, and govern on behalf of, the body politic of the Kingdom.[50] And, most important, it made an utter sham of the conspirators' claims to avenge the *Città* and its political rights against the Spanish administration.

The civic society that followed on the restoration of law and order was illustrated by the denouement of the *Coniuratio*. Curiously, its account of the conspiracy extended beyond the temporal framework of the insurrection proper to describe the political consensus forged with the peace. The concerted show of force and munificence staged by the viceroy and municipality not only quelled the actual insurrection but also allegedly elicited political consensus, which was manifested in the popular applause and supplications that greeted both the military cavalcades enforcing the restoration of order.[51] Be that as it may, with the restoration of order the danger posed to the civic peace by the whimsicality of self-interest did not abate, as the last grand event of the *Coniuratio* made plain. As if warning his readers about the fragility of the contemporary peace, Vico additionally recounted the spectacular failure of the banks, tragically occasioned by what was merely false rumor. As Vico told this tragic episode, for the sake of revenge, an employee of the Banco della Pietà spread the false accusation that a personal enemy conspired to have the banks and houses of the rich sacked by the common people of Naples, unleashing panic among the nobility and wealthy citizens of the city. While the common people kept the peace, the wave of ungrounded fear that engulfed the depositors of the banks swiftly brought ruin to the largest financial institutions of Naples and, with them, the commerce of the Kingdom and numerous persons of private wealth.[52] What the insurrection of the discontented popular forces had left unharmed the baseless fear of their opponents devastated, in other words. As Vico noted with disapproval, the nobles of means fled to the fortified regions of Naples, abandoned themselves to fear, and demanded their deposits from the banks, when it would have benefited them more to defend the stability and well-being of the city.[53] If the tale of the conspiracy had denounced the self-interested calculations of the opponents of the regime, then this episode did as much with regard to its supporters, who ironically followed suit within the bounds of the law. The great irony of this episode made plain that there were limitations to the civilizing forces of capital accumulation when it was not subjected to the laws of justice. It illustrated that a state of nature could also exist within the parameters of civic society, if therein the prerogatives of the strong were let to prevail over the common interest. As Vico argued by example, if commerce civilized, then it strictly did so within limits, as self-interest provided a poor substitute for justice. This example dramatized the political quandary posed by the regulation of society by self-interest as opposed to the common good. It railed against the notion that the individual pursuit of what Vico would call utility could provide a sound foundation for the peaceful and prosperous regulation of society, a theme that Vico treated at length in his foremost theoretical works. Taken together with the political lessons offered by the conspiracy, those taught by the example of the bank failures gave a sense of urgency to those big questions concerning the rights, proscriptions, and ends of political society, questions to which Vico would dedicate the remainder of his career.

IV. The *Coniuratio,* the Competing Accounts, and the Archival Sources for the Revolt of 1701

That the Spanish disapproved of the *Coniuratio* was not without its evident reasons. In the first place, the lack of finality Vico gave the *Coniuratio* left the suppression of the coup hanging, undermining the supposed victory of the Spanish with lingering doubts about the stability and longevity of the peace achieved. Second, Vico spared few details regarding the Draconian measures with which the viceroy and his ministers executed the suppression of the revolt after the celebratory parade of force and munificence staged by the cavalcades, showing that the return of law and order to Naples was also paved with bloodthirsty vengeance and, consequently, the cultivation of enemies. Needless to say, inclusion of these details and others like them undeniably blunted the commemorative value of the *Coniuratio,* easily currying more disappointment than favor among the Spanish cohort. As his official task had been to commemorate the Spanish victory, it is clear that Vico overstepped the bounds of his commission. What is more, the questions that Vico's account posed regarding the actuality of the civic citizenry and municipality could not have pleased the Spanish either. Regardless of Vico's own position on them, those questions cut to the bone of unresolved tensions concerning the partnership between the capital and the Spanish viceroy, which the latter apparently would have preferred to see politicly reaffirmed.

Not surprisingly, the history that won official approbation, the *Conjuratio inita et extincta Neapoli anno MDCCI* by Carlo Maiello, rather simplistically diagnosed the revolt as the work of a few renegade barons whose perfidy was abetted by members of a moblike Popolo; and, by the same token, it reconstructed the response of Naples's political elites as evidence of their harmony and the good health of the political status quo.[54] In particular, the official history identified the momentary strength of the insurrection in the skill with which the notorious Gaetano Gambacorta, the Prince of Macchia, had agitated the naturally tumultuous "plebs."[55] And its denouement celebrated the fidelity of the Kingdom's nobility to the Spanish administration, by both recounting at some length and enumerating in an appendix the concourse of "patricians" to the forces lead by the able Restaino Cantelmo, the Duke of

Popoli, the mere sight of whose wondrous configuration allegedly quelled the fury of the "plebs," despite the strength of their own numbers.[56] In other words, the viceroyal censors preferred an account of the insurrection that employed without revision Sallust's notion of the Roman mob and affirmed without reservation the relationship between the Neapolitan patriciate and the viceroyal administration as one of heroic collaboration. In fact, they endorsed a history that squarely contradicted—and without the revision of the key political concepts and social categories of the Neapolitan polity— the official historical record as it is conserved in the Archivio di Stato in Naples.

It is hard to know what motivated Vico to write an account of the conspiracy that so exposed both the strengths and excesses of the former viceroy and his ministers in what were times of the utmost political instability and thus danger for presumed turncoats, be they soldiers in the military or intellectual corps, in the war on the imperial offensive against the Franco-Spanish alliance. Vico presumably believed that his record of loyalty to the Spanish had earned him a latitude of intellectual freedom that extended to an affair as delicate as that of a failed coup d'état. If the genre of the text itself may be taken as a reliable source of his working assumptions, it is clear that Vico viewed this commission as an opportunity to pen a text that would bring him literary glory, if not immortality, inasmuch as the intellectual liberties he took bore conspicuous resemblance to those of the most exemplary historians of ancient Rome. Modeling his method and ends on those of the greatest Roman authors, Vico shared the sense that the writing of history was a political vocation bearing the responsibility of moral instruction by example. Indeed, like the emperors and their cohorts in the histories by the Roman Tacitus, no one in the *Coniuratio* was above the criticism of character analysis, not even Vico's benefactors. Like the early modern proponents of Tacitism, Vico evidently was concerned about the political burden of the past for the present and the future.[57] By ending the *Coniuratio* on such a powerful note of irresolution, the implication was that its account of the recent past offered a diagnosis of the fragile present as well as a caveat for the unforeseeable future. The irresolution of the *Coniuratio* implied, in other words, that the very viability of the peace was at issue.

While a number of Vico's inclusions effectively disqualified the *Coniuratio* as a piece of state propaganda, many of its omissions equally served to aggrandize the decisions and actions of the viceroy and his ministers. If the *Coniuratio* admonished as regarded the future, then it also embellished what concerned the past so that the viceroy and his administration appeared to have been masters of a situation over which in reality their control was tenuous at best. As the institutional documents of the revolt conserved in the Archivio di Stato di Napoli evidence, the *Coniuratio* whitewashed the record of the interregnum and revolt, so that the insularity and vulnerability of the viceroyal administration throughout this period of crisis was withheld from the public. In other words, it eloquently papered over the extent to which this crisis tested the strained relationship of the viceroyal administration with the municipality. Rather than outright contradict the strain posed by the crisis, as had Maiello, Vico largely sought to smooth over it by censoring evidence of the uneasy collaboration of the viceroyal administration with the *piazze* documented in the minutes of the Consiglio Collaterale.

In further emulation of his predecessors, both ancient and modern, Vico evidently took the consultation of sources seriously.[58] As the comparison of Vico's history with the extant archival documentation of the events of 1700–01 indeed suggests, Vico must have sought and acquired access to the written testimonies of high-ranking officials of the Kingdom. Like the record of the emergency meetings of the Collaterale from 20 November 1700 conserved in the Archivio di Stato di Napoli, Vico's own account of what transpired between the viceroy and his advisory council on the death of Charles II identified the same as their main topics of discussion: the public announcement of the death of the king; the enlistment of the support of the Eletto of the Popolo; the precariousness of the banks; the reinforcement of the castles of Naples; the adequate provisioning of foodstuffs; and the commission of the Arte della Seta, or silk guild.[59] However, Vico's account of those topics both elided some of the very pressing concerns of the Collaterale while interjecting some of his observations as their own. On the one hand, as regarded the perceived threat to the public order, Vico understated the extent to which the viceroy and the Collaterale discerned in the patrician *piazze* a potential challenge to the viceroy's continued rule of the Kingdom. In the actual meetings, much discussion was devoted to how best inform the patrician *piazze* of the death of Charles II so as to avert any inopportune rivalry on their part and to co-opt their support for the political status quo.[60] Without yet knowing what formal provisions had been stipulated for the interregnum, the underlying concern of this heated discussion was that the *piazze* might take advantage of the situation's lack of clarity to question the legitimacy of the viceroy and to promote themselves as the legitimate claimants to the governance of the Kingdom. As the Eletto of the Popolo was indeed quick to warn the viceroy, since the incipience of the illness of Charles II there had been talk among the civic patriciate of the possibility of an interregnum.[61]

In reality, the allegiance of the civic patriciate to Spanish rule was doubted and its political challenge feared by the Collaterale. By the same token, the enlistment of the support of the Popolo of Naples was a question whose political delicacy the *Coniuratio* did not fully convey as well. Not only did the Collaterale call to their meeting the Eletto of the Popolo, a traditional ally of the viceroy within the municipality, but it also deliberated how to maintain the loyalty of the people on the ground. To that end, the viceroy ordered the Eletto to make the captains of the *ottine* privy to the death of Charles II in solicitation of their conduct as "good vassals of His Majesty,"[62] while others urged the viceroy to additionally enlist the solidarity of the governors of the Arte della Seta, various notaries, as well as prominent citizens with authority among the Popolo, such as Don Tomasso Mazzacara.[63] The suggestion of these exceptional measures notwithstanding, the Eletto agreed to the more usual one of seeking the support of his captains of the *ottine,* the captains of the municipal subdivisions and their companies, over whom he apparently maintained influence.[64]

As regarded the threat to public order in the *Coniuratio,* Vico rather interjected a reason for it that was all his own, namely, an analysis of the orders of Naples that correlated political constancy with possession of property. However commonplace it might have been to explain popular revolt in terms of material motivation, this same equation discounted the political resources of the powerful and elided social boundaries in counterintuitive ways for contemporaries. While in reality the civic patriciate was regarded as a formidable competitor to the political right to rule, in Vico's reckoning they were indistinguishable from the nobility at large, which in turn was apprehended as a source of political instability because inconstant in its avidity for material gain. As Vico generalized, there were among the Neapolitan nobles "few who possessed things and many who desired them";[65] and, in particular, the patrician *eletti* were for the most part engaged in unprofitable affairs and, consequently, were also the least appropriate candidates for the administration of the "republic," Vico added.[66] In other words, Vico's recomposition of the Neapolitan nobility along socioeconomic lines ran against both the grain of tradition and the reality of the dominant political blocks of the capital, however besieged it was by the economic forces of modernity.

Compared to the official record and other histories penned about the revolt, Vico's profile of the Popolo was unparalleled, as it suggested that the political role of the Popolo as a civic corps—that is, as a popular assembly and civic militia—had been supplanted by its de facto role as a social entity—that is, as an amalgam of diverse non-noble groups, whose better part constituted a tribunal of conscience for the municipality and Kingdom.

Indeed, the *Coniuratio* had achieved as much by offering an analysis of the revolt that not only recognized the social subdivisions within the Popolo per se but also politicized them in new ways; specifically, it underscored both the judiciousness of the common folk and the heroism of the middle strata like no other history. In the first place, Vico's stratification of the plebs and their political behavior was unique to his interpretation of the course of the insurrection. In the other surviving histories, the plebs were often spoken about in the singular and conflated with the "Popolo,"[67] or derisively the "Popolaccio,"[68] generalizing their behavior so that it implicated the larger swath of non-noble residents of Naples as rebels. Where the popular insurrection was rather attributed to the merely "vile" sectors of the population, the size of their ranks was described as if it were immense and the numerical remainder of the "Popolo" insignificant. Indeed, this was especially true of the account by Maiello, which described the party of Gambacorta at the climax of the revolt as consisting of the "entire city," or what was a "quasi infinite multitude of the Popolo."[69]

The one notable exception to these rules was the journal of the astute resident observer of Naples, the French-born Antonio Bulifon, whose account of the insurrection emphasized not only the specificity of the rebels' class but also the base materiality of their ends, as had Vico's.[70] In important contrast to Vico's representation of plebeian restraint and judgment, however, in Bulifon's account the judiciousness with which the plebs refused the conspirators support was sorely undercut by the context of their speech act—namely, their disillusion and grumbling over the conspirators' order to cease and desist from sacking—which robbed the plebeian refusal of the edifying connotation of political wisdom.[71]

Similarly, the centrality that Vico granted the so-called modest citizens of means is simply lacking in other narratives. While the members of the "Popolo" loyal to the regime were often identified as "citizens" in other accounts, the ostensible qualification for their loyalty was exclusively moral rather than material, as the appellation of "most honest citizens" (*onestissimi cittadini*) in Maiello's history implied,[72] and the term "good citizens" (*buoni cittadini*) in the minutes of the Collaterale describing the revolt confirmed.[73] What is more, Vico's substitution of representatives of the Piazza del Popolo by "modest citizens" of means in those pivotal acts of support for the regime obscured the very real role that traditional municipal forces had played in the maintenance and restoration of order. In reality, the viceroy seemed far more dependent on the strategic support of the *ottine* than the *Coniuratio* suggested. As described earlier, following the death of Charles II in 1700 the viceroyal administration relied on the municipal regiment to help maintain civic order. As the record of the Collaterale further suggests, much the same held true during the actual revolt of 1701. For example, among the "good citizens" to offer their assistance to the viceroyal administration during the insurrection of 1701 numbered the Dottor Aniello Mascolo, who reportedly offered not only his personal aid but that of his entire Ottina di Porto, one of the territorial subdivisions of the Piazza di Porto controlled by the Popolo and responsible for mounting a contingent of the municipal regiment in times of conflict.[74]

However contentiously, then, Vico clearly individuated in the "modest citizens" of means a powerful constituency that superseded the structures and forces of the Popolo as the partner of the viceroyal administration within the capital and kingdom. In them, he identified a bulwark of support for the Spanish—and, by association, their program of modernization—that contrasted with the sociopolitical divisiveness he ascribed to the larger popular estate. What was more, the very centrality Vico granted the "modest citizens" in the suppression of the revolt further downplayed, if not eclipsed, the spectacular presence of patrician members of the municipality in the cavalcade led by Cantelmo marking the restoration of law and order by the Spanish.[75] Therewith, Vico's narrative hinted at the obsolescence of the municipality as an institution of—and, indeed, competitor for—governance, although one also could have argued that its resilience was remarkable, especially in times of duress.

V. The *Coniuratio* and the Patrician Struggle for the Supremacy of the Municipality

When one further considers the international context in which it was penned, the politics of modernization advocated by the *Coniuratio* come into even sharper focus. After the failure of the coup, its surviving protagonists waged a war of words in defense of the privileged status and role of the municipality within the Kingdom and, more generally, the orbit of the Spanish Empire. Read in this context, the questions the *Coniuratio* posed regarding the representativeness of the municipality and its role in the restoration of law and order to the capital were fighting words indeed. For they contested the legitimacy of the very political claims made on behalf of the municipality by failed patrician conspirators. From their exile at the emperor's court in Vienna, the eminent Neapolitan patricians Francesco Spinelli, the Duke of Castelluccia, and Bartolomeo Ceva Grimaldi, the Duke of Telese, waged a war of propaganda on behalf of the civic body politic of Naples that invoked republican language to maintain both the naturalness of its political rights and the appropriateness of its political program for the contemporary world.

Not long after the suppression of the coup, Spinelli and Ceva Grimaldi both published and had circulated in Naples short treatises that disputed the legitimacy of Philip's rule over the Kingdom and that declared the ends of their armed opposition to his rule, ends with which they swore to return victorious to the Kingdom. From the imperial citadel on 22 October 1701, Spinelli penned his "Manifesto," which according to one historian was not only circulated in but also affixed to the street corners of Naples, keeping alive the ambitions of the opposition despite their terrible defeat.[76] Spinelli's "Manifesto" must have been read and discussed in the capital that fall, as it solicited an even more lengthy response, the "Risposta al manifesto di Francesco Spinelli," by an anonymous author who rallied to the defense of the political status quo with a supreme sense of irony and indignation. Despite the peace, in other words, the contention over the succession of Philip and rule of Medinaceli evidently had remained keen, and its supporters most defensive. From Vienna in December 1701, Ceva Grimaldi then came to the defense of Spinelli in his "Lettera," which most elegantly elaborated on both the political injustices of the Spanish that Spinelli had denounced as well as the political agenda for reform that he had proposed, communicating to their Neapolitan compatriots that the exiles had a consonant political vision from which little could dissuade them. Indeed, the passage of time only seems to have inspired Spinelli to sharpen his rancor into a political theoretical diatribe, the "Risposta alla Risposta data al manifesto di Don Francesco Spinelli," that contended no less than that Medinaceli had violated the constitution of the Kingdom with his disregard for civic tradition and unabashed favoritism of the magisterial class.[77]

The political bone of contention for both Spinelli and Ceva Grimaldi was first and foremost the contractual relationship between the Spanish monarchy and the Kingdom, which they believed Medinaceli had abrogated with his procedural defiance of civic tradition following the death of Charles II. According to that relationship, Spinelli and Ceva Grimaldi exclaimed, the accession of a new dynast to the Kingdom's throne had to be marked by the investiture of the Pope, the presumed feudal lord of the Kingdom, and, more important, by the acclamation of the people of the Kingdom. According to tradition, Spinelli and Ceva Grimaldi further lamented, to receive that acclamation the *piazze* of Naples ought to have been summoned and their oath of fidelity to the new dynast secured. Before this, it was simply illegitimate to declare Philip V the rightful successor of Charles II and, as a consequence thereof, the Duke of Medinaceli his representative in the Kingdom.

In sum, as Spinelli declared, purportedly with tears in his eyes, his opponent had violated the privileges of the City of Naples and deprived its *piazze* of that shadow of jurisdiction left them by the scourge of the Spanish; in other words, he explained, "Medinaceli would like to revoke the municipality's right [to rule], which itself derives from the common consensus, and transfer it to his few passionate friends, to whom it does not belong."[78] At issue, in other words, were not only the political privileges of the municipality of the capital per se but also the sovereignty of the Kingdom. For Medinaceli's disregard of civic tradition meant more than a neglect of political formalities for contemporaries; rather, it symbolized calculated defiance of the metonymic status of the municipality as the representative of the people and as the interlocutor of the Kingdom with the Spanish. As Spinelli's tearful objections expressed, the authority of popular consensus, and thus the very sovereignty of the Kingdom itself, derived from the representatives of the municipality's patrician and popular *piazze*. By making an utter sham of the civic rituals that forged and demonstrated their consensus, Medinaceli thus had failed to procure for the new order the mandate of the *piazze* and that of the people of the Kingdom.[79] With furor, Spinelli remarked that the solemn rituals of the municipality "are indeed a valid demonstration of the will of the people."[80] Consequently, more than an iron-fisted tactic by which to keep the peace, for members of the civic patriciate Medinaceli's audacious proclamation of Philip's succession to the thrones of the Spanish monarchy and its lands not only disrespected the traditions of Naples but also sought to force a change in the political equation between the Empire and the municipality of the capital that would irreversibly compromise the Kingdom. In other words, the proclamation had neglected to solicit the voluntarism quintessential to a contractual relationship, both subordinating the municipality of the capital to the Spanish monarchy and tentatively exploring the possibility of rule without the hallowed principle of the consent of the people.

The rhetoric the Neapolitan exiles brought to bear on their argument for the appropriateness of their leadership, moreover, was nothing short of a brilliant defense, as it effectively appropriated the sacrosanct political language of old to compete with the political forces of the new. While the exiles protested the violation of the political rights of the municipality of Naples, they also sought to preempt the criticism that they were defending the "private interests" (*interessi particolari*) of the nobility by invoking republican language to characterize their ends and by enumerating the same in the form of a coherent program of political reform. In the first place, the exiles repeatedly declared that their actions had been motivated by a sense of "justice" and a concern for the "public good." As Spinelli pronounced: "I hereby make manifest to all that our operation was sparked by the praiseworthy motivations of the advantage and liberty of the *patria*" and, as he added farther along, "for the recognition of justice and the public good."[81] If the failed insurrectionaries had acted out of a sense of justice and concern for the public good, then they had also done so in their capacity as true "citizens," added Ceva

Grimaldi, who characterized his cohort's efforts on behalf of the common good as the obligation of "every good citizen," thereby reserving that appellation for the patrician insurgents.[82]

Second, the exiles outlined an elaborate program of political reform for the Kingdom that anticipated on many counts precisely that which their local competitors for political influence later would demand of the successors to the Spanish.[83] Most prominently, they demanded "their own king," who would reside in Naples and, as the argument went, restore it to the ranks of a flourishing capital city. More important, they also demanded a number of provisions to foster the "prosperity" of the Kingdom, such as the encouragement of its commerce and the reservation of its offices for "nationals" (*nazionali*).[84] Speaking grandiloquently about the potential outcome of this program for the Kingdom, Ceva Grimaldi declared that it would "liberate the Kingdom from its no less ignominious than miserable condition as a province," representing his cohort as the liberators of the Kingdom from its state of servitude as a province of the Spanish Empire.[85] What is more, it promised to restore harmony to the orders of the capital and Kingdom of Naples. In contrast to the rule of the Spanish, it held out the hope of bridging those divisions both between and within the "nobility" and "people" that the Spanish had so deftly cultivated in their quest to divide and conquer the Kingdom.[86]

In both the political verbiage and content of their tracts, the surviving protagonists of the failed coup thus positioned themselves as the Kingdom's most loyal and capable citizens and, ergo, as the natural heirs to Charles II. Therewith, they also challenged the growing political powers of the local cadre of professionals who collaborated with the Spanish—namely, those "few passionate friends of the Duke of Medinaceli"—who hailed from the Kingdom's homegrown class of magistrates and doctors of law, which had clouded the prestige and mitigated the influence of the representatives of the civic body politic. Put somewhat differently, the civic patriciate in revolt used republican language of old and ideas of new to argue that both their lineage and perspective qualified them for political office in a way that mere certification could not.

The exiles' political flames seem to have been first fanned and then temporarily extinguished by the actual sojourn of Philip V in Naples (17 April–2 June 1702), during which the French Bourbon worked hard to win the trust of the capital and to secure the performance of those civic rituals customary for the formal approbation of a new dynast by the Kingdom. Philip's efforts did not succeed without the vehement protest that they were "contrary to the privileges and constitutions of the Kingdom," however.[87] If not heeded by the *eletti* of the municipality, the objections of this protest evidently were not alien to their concerns, which were perhaps most honestly expressed by the unusual and poorly excused postponement of their oath of fidelity to the new monarch after he himself had already sworn on the missal of the Secretary of the City in the Cathedral of Naples to uphold the "capitoli e privilegi" of the City and Kingdom. Although eventually carried out, the approbation of Philip's succession evidently was ambivalent indeed.

In light of the war of words waged by the exiles, Vico's sociological analysis of the revolt and, similarly, the beginnings of his social theory evidently were highly political. In that context, indeed, Vico's sociological account of political factionalism mounted a powerful polemic against the supremacy of the capital's municipality advocated by the patrician protagonists of the coup. In the first place, the unusual centrality that Vico's narration of the revolt granted to the attack of San Lorenzo, the seat of the municipality—an episode that was largely neglected by Maiello in his history, for instance—made painfully manifest the utter bankruptcy of the conspirators' claim that the municipality of Naples represented the people of the Kingdom and their interests. In other words, it challenged the notions of the sovereignty of the capital and the naturalness of its rights so ruthlessly championed by the patrician conspirators. Furthermore, Vico's depiction of the capital's orders as beset by class-based fissures made plain that the social preconditions for a civic politics of corporate consensus were wanting, exposing the political principles of the insurrectionaries as nostalgic at best. At the same time, Vico's argument for the anachronism of the municipality did not endorse without censure and political reservation the leadership of Medinaceli. If Vico challenged the advocates of a civic past, then he also criticized the prospect of an unchecked technocratic regime, whose rule of law was applied without the oversight, or countervailing political weight, of the citizen body it was supposed to privilege. In other words, in the *Coniuratio* Vico embraced the advent of the modern state with reservation, raising many of the hard political questions that his subsequent works would painstakingly address, such as how to attain the republican ends of the common good in a political community that was ruled not by its citizenry but by professional jurisprudents.

VI. Conclusion

Although it was not the text that secured his literary fame, the *Coniuratio* did launch Vico's career as a social theorist. As much as it was a history of the conspiracy the *Coniuratio* was also an argument about the nature and boundaries of political rights within a post-civic society. Significantly, that argument shifted the object of rights discourse from one pertaining to civic orders to one pertaining to civic classes. Of equal importance, it also relied on a number of assumptions about the polity of the capital that were themselves both novel and polemical. In the first place, this argument relied on the prescient insight that the body politic of the capital both effectively and justly exceeded that of its municipality. As has been explained, the unconventional use that Vico made of the term "citizen" invested it with a sociological meaning that suggested the exclusive juridical criteria for civic membership was an anachronism. In addition, his account of the symbolic destruction of the municipality during the raid of San Lorenzo showed that natural justice demanded superseding the limitation of the municipal privileges and rights to the juridically qualified few. Taken together, these two assumptions militated for a more fluid conception of the polity and political belonging, conceptions that Vico would work to enumerate with ever greater specificity over the course of his long career.

Second, Vico's argument also relied on his contention that the market economy civilized. As already noted, Vico's examples of political loyalty made plain that the economy of exchange not only enriched but politicized its protagonists by rendering their livelihood dependent on the rule of law and the judicious use of force exercised by a public authority. Vested with the defense of the persons and property of private individuals, the public authority readily was embraced as the natural advocate of the rights of private individuals in the *Coniuratio*. Contrariwise, for Vico, those excluded from the market economy also remained largely alien to the benefits and protections of public authority and, consequently, antagonistic to it. As seen, the groups left behind by the market economy included not only the army of the destitute but also representatives of the Kingdom's nobility, both patrician and baronial, whom the *Coniuratio* first and foremost showed were ever ready to exercise violence to defend and promote their particularistic rights against infringement by the regime. Thus, the real force of the argument of the *Coniuratio* lay in its conceptual substitution of the divisions of order by the clash of rights. What the blood and guts of its narrative made real was the political incompatibility of rights born of status with rights born of class, or what were rights born of war with rights born of commerce. It dramatized the antagonism between persons whose powers were rooted in the use of force and those whose powers were exercised in the exchange of things; and its lessons pointed to the obsolescence of the former to the advantage of the latter. In sum, what Vico individuated in the rivalry and outcome of the revolt was the temporal succession of juridically defined historical personae, or the reassertion and demise of the claimants of privilege vis-à-vis those of contract. For the successful claimants he further would postulate an achievement of full personality that located the rights of the historical subject in the acquisition of economic liberties.

This succession of juridical personae provided the backbone of that theoretical work that subsequently earned Vico literary immortality. In light of this, it bears mentioning two things before moving on to Vico's better-known texts: the *Orationes,* the *Diritto universale,* and first edition of the *Scienza nuova* (1725). In the first place, the content of the *Coniuratio* substantiates the scholarly assertion so often made about the *Scienza nuova* that Vico's social theory must have had some basis in reality. At the same time, it cannot be overstated just how argumentative Vico's view of this reality was in the *Coniuratio.* Vico's analysis of the revolt in the *Coniuratio* unequivocally interpreted political behavior and alliance to elide what were meaningful distinctions for contemporaries and to privilege the actors of the revolt as emblems of a larger dynamics of change. In other words, Vico's social theory had a basis in an interpretation of reality occasioned by the revolt of 1701. Second, as argumentative as Vico's analysis was, it is also true that the specificities of this revolt lent themselves to an interpretation that surpassed the models of both the ancients and moderns. In particular, the evident points of contrast between the revolt of 1701 and that of 1647 made compelling an interpretation of rebellion that went beyond the idea of a popular mandate for change as the force of the historical process. Indeed, the very currency of the popular retort regarding the baronial betrayal of the popular cause during the revolt of Masaniello illustrated as much. That Vico offered an interpretation that also marshaled the evidence for an evolutionary theory of society was the product of his own originality, however.

The *Coniuratio* would long remain a thorn in Vico's side. Not only had it displeased the Spanish, but once the imperial forces wrested the Kingdom from them, the Austrian power too noted its displeasure with the professor of Rhetoric, of whom it humiliatingly demanded funerary epithets for those barons fallen in the name of the emperor in 1701. As he had with the Spanish, so did Vico oblige with the Austrians, penning the most eloquent of commemorative verses for inscription upon the tombs of Giuseppe Capece and Carlo Di Sangro.[88] As part of his courtship of the new power, furthermore, Vico delivered a particularly brilliant oration on the value of education for the inauguration of the academic year in October 1708, a festive occasion that was apparently dedicated to the emperor.[89] That oration itself capped the series that Vico had been delivering since assuming the position in Rhetoric, a series in which he explicitly had broached the topic of global citizenship and whose philosophical permutations further inflected his analysis of metropolitan society in the *Coniuratio.*

❦ Chapter 2

Vico's Cosmopolitanism

*Global Citizenship and Natural Law in
Vico's Pedagogical Thought*

I. Introduction: Cosmopolitanism,
Ancient and Neoclassical

The earliest evidence of the significance of the *Coniuratio* for Vico's social theory can be found in the *Orationes,* the inaugural addresses Vico delivered before the student body and faculty of the University of Naples on 18 October between 1699 and 1708. Despite their pedagogical task to exhort the student body to study, taken as a whole the *Orationes* equally represented a foray into social theory that elaborated a new vision of cosmopolitanism.

In the European tradition, the theory of cosmopolitanism had been most fully articulated by the ancients, for whom it first and foremost had signified the apprehension of the commonality of humanity and the adventitiousness of one's local affiliations and identities.[1] The cosmopolitan viewed himself, or herself, as a "citizen of the world," as Diogenes the Cynic most famously put it.[2] They understood, as Plutarch remarked of Zeno, the early Hellenic Stoic, that one "should regard all humans as our fellow citizens and local residents, and there should be one way of life and order, like that of a herd grazing together and nurtured by a common law."[3] In its earliest Hellenic formulation cosmopolitanism thus rejected, if not outright discredited, local group and civic affiliations and exhorted its students to make humanity their first moral allegiance. To that end, in the place of the actual *polis* it further hypothesized the existence of a cosmic city that embraced both "gods and humans" alike and was itself ruled by a common "natural," or rational, law.[4] In view of its pointed critique of civic institutions and chauvinisms, it is perhaps not surprising that the idea of the cosmic city was first formulated by self-reputed outsiders, namely, Greek speakers who by virtue of their peripheral origins were both literally alien to the metropolitan center of the Hellenistic empire, Athens, and, it seems, conscious of the anachronism of that same center's preferred political status. Be that as it may, the idea of the cosmic city and its global citizenry was later revived and elaborated on with new emphases by the Roman Stoics, the survival of whose works transmitted the ancient ideals of cosmopolitanism to the conceptual palette of early modern Europeans and Enlightenment Europe.

For early moderns, the Stoic philosophers and teachers of the greatest influence were those of the imperial era of Roman history, namely, Seneca, the famed epistler, essayist, and tutor of Nero; Epictetus, the Greek slave manumitted in Rome who founded his own school of Stoic philosophy in Nicopolis; and Marcus Aurelius, the contemplative second-century emperor of Rome and author of the journal/notebooks known as the *Meditations*. Although an Academic skeptic, the great republican statesman and orator Marcus Tullius Cicero too bequeathed to posterity a highly regarded repository of Stoic beliefs and tenets through his eclectic philosophical works, and it is to those works that a number of Reformation and Enlightenment thinkers especially owed much of the foundation for their own moral and, no less, political philosophies, broadly conceived. As Gerhard Oestreich, Martin van Gelderen, Richard Tuck, Thomas Schlereth, Martha Nussbaum, and others have shown, Roman Stoic doctrine provided a set of moral concepts and teachings that not only appealed to the classically trained early modern philosophers from Lipsius to Kant but also proved most usable to them, particularly in their political writings that addressed the comportment appropriate to the individual and to his larger communities in times of uncertainty and conflict.[5] As this chapter shows, Vico's own interest in Stoicism similarly stemmed both from his profound knowledge of classical Latin literature and from the daunting ethico-political challenges posed by his immediate historical circumstances. In 1700, indeed, primary among the concerns of Vico's contemporaries was the political fate of the Kingdom on the imminent death of Charles II, the ambiguities of whose testament had rendered uncertain both the political future and peace of Naples.[6] By the same token, in the face of the political unknown and the reality of municipal impotence, the resilience and autonomy of the capital's quasi-autonomous political organs became increasingly important as a source of authority and a lifeline of order and normalcy for contemporaries. In light of this context, for Vico, what Stoicism provided was a model of allegiances that could reconcile the vested nature of the professional interests and ambitions of his audience, the university-trained cadre of jurists seeking employment and power within the capital's administrative organizations, with the instability of their political identity and, therefore, the nominal ends of their service.

As the literature has shown, Stoicism also informed the sociability and artistic genres of scholars and artists alike throughout the seventeenth century.[7] However pervasive and protean the culture of neo-Stoicism may have been in the seventeenth century, Vico took less of an interest in how the Stoic model of virtuous comportment applied to the protagonists of culture than it did to the actors of the political community of world nations. While Vico also lauded the cultivation of Stoic virtues by members of the Republic of Letters, then, his own employment of Stoic motifs contributed more to the creation of what Gerhard Oestreich has called the new "political man," whose great constancy and unrivaled wisdom purportedly suited him well for a life of public service.[8] In particular, Oestreich has shown how Justus Lipsius, the greatly influential Flemish humanist and moral philosopher (1547–1606), found in Roman Stoicism a model of praxis-oriented edification that befitted the constituents of changing constitutional forms. Specifically, according to Oestreich, Roman Stoicism offered Lipsius a model of moral instruction and allegiances that not only offered spiritual consolation and ethical guidance to the subject weary of temporal vicissitudes but also lent a transcendent identity and purpose to the same within the cadre of the absolutist state, the ethics of whose pursuits were complicated by the conflicts of, first, religious and, later, international warfare. Like Lipsius—and in contrast to the cultural proponents of seventeenth-century of neo-Stoic sociability—at the outset of the eighteenth century Vico helped to craft a persona for the civil servant, whose personal excellence reputedly lay in the training of his mind, the disciplining of his passions, and, consequently, the constancy of his political judgment. By weaving together Stoic instructions regarding not only the moral edification but also commitments of the wise man, Vico helped to develop the model of a political actor whose credentials were earned by dint of sheer study, whose judgment pertained to the administration of the state, and whose first allegiance was to humanity.

However, Vico's notion of cosmopolitanism was anything but static. Rather, it took on a variety of forms in the *Orationes* and his later works. This chapter specifically traces the changing nature and commitments of Roman Stoic cosmopolitanism in the *Orationes*. In particular, it shows that over the course of the *Orationes* Vico supplemented a primarily moral notion of cosmopolitanism with a commercial one that put a primacy on the economic agency of individuals and the culture of exchange among them. And it makes sense of this shift in Vico's focus by recalling the conclusions he had drawn about the bonds of community in the *Coniuratio,* and by laying bare the compatibility of commercial cosmopolitanism with a consequential position within the contemporary debate about the nature and aims of jurisprudence in the Kingdom. This chapter thus accounts for why Vico came to first espouse the notion of a community wherein all relations are transactional in nature and the rights and obligations of its members are conceived in terms of commercial law, or that sort of community the eighteenth century called "society." In this sense, it also identifies the origins of Vico's interest in the history of society, which in his legal works he both elaborated and complicated with distinctly programmatic ideas about justice. If Vico's engagement of cosmopolitanism was initially motivated by his pedagogical duties, as will be seen in chapter 3 it was later driven by his vocation to make evident the criterion proper to a universal system of justice. Vico only broached the question of universal justice, however, after considering the moral commitments of the individual to the self, one's immediate fellows and humanity as they had been formulated by the Roman Stoics, moral commitments which he faithfully restated but whose political lessons he proposed anew in the *Orationes.*

II. *Urbis Orbis:* Roman Stoicism and the Narrative of the *Orationes*

The thread of the narrative immanent to the *Orationes* exhibited a construed, if not belabored, coherence, as its focus steadily moved from the micro- to macrocosmic realms of the political world over the course of its exposition. As the manuscript tradition of the *Orationes* suggests,[9] Vico repeatedly revised the orations for publication (after 18 October 1706 and through 1709), both polishing his style and sharpening the conceptual content of his addresses to create out of the individual pieces a more cohesive text.[10] In light of his efforts to revise the manuscript of the orations for publication, it seems that Vico was wed to the argument of the work in its entirety and thought that it represented him well, despite his curious retrospective belittlement of the *Orationes* in the *Autobiografia.*[11] The revised text of the *Orationes* remained in manuscript form, perhaps for want of the patronage that he had sought from the young Neapolitan patrician Marcello Filomarino in December 1708. Nonetheless, in March or April 1709 Vico extended and published at his own cost the Seventh Oration (1708), *De nostri temporis studiorum ratione* (translated as *On the Study Method of Our Time*), which in so many ways gave programmatic content to the prior ones and set his sights on engaging the tradition of Roman jurisprudence.[12]

Although the individual themes of the addresses varied, the revised narrative of the six *Orationes* bore the unmistakable imprint of the Roman variation on Stoic cosmopolitanism. Cumulatively, it gave content to the cosmopolitan ideal of the individual's simultaneous membership in multiple communities, a hallmark of Roman Stoicism that Vico could have derived from his reading of Cicero, Seneca, or Marcus Aurelius.[13] In antiquity, this ideal had exhorted the individual to recognize his fellowship with and, by implication, responsibility to the rest of humankind, while also acknowledging and accepting the conventional bounds within which the cosmopolitan both acquired and lived his sense of world fellowship. As Seneca had perhaps most famously formulated this ideal in his moral essay *De otio,* or *On Leisure:*

> Let us grasp the idea that there are two commonwealths—the one, a vast and truly common state, which embraces alike gods and men, in which we look neither to this corner of earth nor to that, but measure the bounds of our citizenship by the path of the sun; the other, the one to which we have been assigned by the accident of birth.[14]

Despite the great popularity of Seneca throughout the early modern period, in the eighteenth century the Stoic image most often invoked to convey the individual's affiliation with both the local and global communities was that of a series of concentric circles emanating forth from the self to the outer limits of the cosmos.[15] As first formulated by Cicero and later elaborated by Hierocles, this image pictured the individual as surrounded by a series of ever larger circles of association—beginning with the self and expanding outward to incorporate one's family, tribesmen, fellow citizens, compatriots, and, finally, humanity—and it instructed, if not exhorted, people to grasp and thereby widen their spheres of identification and obligation.[16] In Vico's own work, this image provided the thematic structure of the *Orationes,* which progressively examined those same spheres of association, beginning with the microcosmic realm of the human mind and concluding with that of the world order. In other words, the *Orationes* literally gave social content to this ancient image of world fellowship, while offering a model of cosmopolitan consciousness and ethical behavior distinct from the Stoic and, as such, especially meaningful for Vico's contemporaries.

Although the narrative of the *Orationes* faithfully reproduced the architecture of that ancient image of world fellowship, its overarching argument did not do the same for the ethos of Roman cosmopolitanism. On a number of points, the *Orationes* masked in the semantic guise of ancient ethics principles of conduct that were markedly modern. Consequently, its practical lessons regarding the norms and ends of cosmopolitanism differed in important ways from those of Roman Stoicism. In light of these differences, it is essential to recall the importance that the ancient Stoics had placed on the translation of philosophical doctrines into analogous practices.

Indeed, as a practice, the Roman variation on Stoic cosmopolitanism evidently was the political corollary of the ethical principle of *oikeiosis*, which can be translated as "affinity."[17] The principle of oikeiosis itself had taught that all humans were sociable by nature and, as such, perfectly capable of widening their sphere of identification and benevolence as they progressively cultivated personal wisdom, or what was also called virtue. Consequently, for the Roman Stoic, cosmopolitanism had entailed both a moral education and a corresponding practical reorientation—it had presumed and advocated the individual's progression from a conventional set of ethical understandings and social bonds to one that was truly cosmic in its values and, analogously, social practices.[18] While the *Orationes* faithfully reproduced the idea of progression inherent to the philosophical tenet of oikeiosis, the practical lessons it taught less obviously followed from the personal wisdom of the Stoic sage than that of the moderns. As will be seen, the ethos of Vico's cosmopolitanism differed from that of the Roman Stoics on at least two important counts. In the first place, as a set of guiding ethical principles for the cosmopolitan it elaborated a notion of natural law that was distinct from the ancient one following from oikeiosis. Indeed, the *Orationes* expounded an idea of natural law that betrayed the very anthropology and ethics of oikeiosis while maintaining the semantic guise of continuity with that foundational tenet of Stoicism. Rather than solely derive the precepts of universal law from the feelings associated oikeiosis, more specifically, Vico proposed that the laws of nature also stemmed from the circumstances governing the formation of the first societies and their common conventions. Second, if Vico's image of cosmopolitanism evidently reflected that expansive notion of the Stoics, he complicated the Stoic notion of the outer sphere of world fellowship with reflections about warfare and international administration. Rather than pose warfare as a moral bind, however, Vico investigated the customs regulating war and its arguable functions. Significantly, Vico crafted both these distinctions after the fateful events of 1701, developing his perspective on the practical corollaries of global citizenship after his intellectual reflections on the contemporancity of the civic corporation under the duress of revolt and the specter of warfare.

III. *Orationes I–II:* Cultivation and the Self

In the first two orations, delivered in 1699 and 1700, respectively, Vico specifically addressed the nature of the innermost circle of association, that of the human mind, and the sort of education necessary for the individual's practical reorientation as a cosmopolitan. Therein, Vico most faithfully appropriated and, indeed, advocated Stoic beliefs and doctrines like nowhere else in the *Orationes,* discussing the nature of the mental landscape and the education of behavior with a set of metaphors and prescriptions true to both the psychology and the pedagogical aims of the Roman Stoics, especially as they had been represented by Cicero in the *Tusculan Disputations.* Reminiscent of its Stoic models, education, or "philosophy," was understood as more than the course of university accreditation—that is, it was understood as a course of personal cultivation, or what the ancient Greeks more generally called *padeia.*[19] As it specifically had for the ancient Stoics, so for Vico did education involve the curing of the spirit, or the excising from the mind the affliction of false judgments, so that it could attain a higher form of cognizance and ultimately apprehend truth.

Education was further important as the handmaiden to a practical ethics; Vico adopted the intellectualist position that the right form of knowing would produce the right sort of actions, and it was on the latter that he would set his store. Consequently, like the Stoics, in these orations Vico viewed the process of cultivation as the key to world citizenship and linked his discussion of personal edification to that of its more glorious political ends. At the same time, he elaborated on the political responsibility of the reeducated in a way that contrasted with his Stoic models, conflating what were the means with the ends of Roman cosmopolitanism.

In nuce, the first oration staged and responded to a simple, final question about the limits of human knowledge, to which it offered what was a decidedly Stoic response. In short, it asked: "If...man is endowed by nature with so many and great means to achieve wisdom, why is it that he is impeded and held back from the most excellent studies of the liberal arts and sciences?"[20] As staged by Vico, the bewilderment that question expressed regarding the limits of human knowledge followed from his claim that humans in general, and the members of his audience in particular, were eminently rational creatures. Over the course of his oration, indeed, Vico had prepared the terrain for this gnawing final question by developing a working model of human nature that enumerated the select beliefs of a number of currents of rationalism since the time of the ancient Greeks. The model drew its strength not from its originality but from a barrage of rationalistic tenets that added up to a eulogy of humans as the privileged possessors of reason and, as such, godlike creatures capable of the cultivation of wisdom and the apprehension of truth. At the very outset of the oration, Vico exhorted his audience to "Know thyself," citing the well-known ancient aphorism that most famously had been employed by Socrates to urge his students to recognize and connect with their rational soul, which, in the Platonic tradition, was believed to be that part of the soul capable of apprehending the true essence of things.[21] As employed by Vico, this same exhortation further served as proof of the quintessence of the human mind and, similarly, its godlike powers. Citing the canonical *Tusculan Disputations,* Vico restated with the authority of Cicero the latter's interpretation of the aphorism to assert that the locus of personal identity lay in the mind and that the mind itself was nothing less than "the image of Almighty God," glossing Cicero in turn with a conviction about human nature that recalled the one of Renaissance Neoplatonism.[22]

To his bombardment of rationalism, Vico also marshaled the belief of the Renaissance Neoplatonists in the capacious freedom of humans as beings in possession of not only reason but also free will. As if sounding the tocsin to study, Vico emphatically proclaimed with both the conviction of a Humanist and the persuasiveness of a great orator: "O listeners the mind is to you your own god.... [And your] becoming wise depends solely on the will!"[23] For his finale, Vico then mixed the metaphors of Neoplatonism with those of Cartesianism, further pleading with his listeners to search for the truths embedded in their minds, adding the promises of innatism to his already ample store of rationalistic rallying cries. Needless to say, this speaking in rationalistic tongues before the advent of Pangloss was firstly meant to serve Vico's rhetorical ends of emboldening the youth before him to study, by dramatizing those powers predisposing humankind to the acquisition of knowledge.

Yet, Vico's very own model of human nature seemed at best a swan song to rationalism. For as Vico's own response to his final gnawing question regarding the de facto limitations of human knowledge forewarned, the emotions and passions were the most insidious of foes. Invoking both the psychological model and pedagogical aims of the Stoics, Vico explained the spirit quickly would acquire knowledge were it not prevented by the passions.[24] And to this theme of the vexed relationship between the passions and the intellect Vico dedicated the second of his addresses contained in the *Orationes.* As if preparing his listener/reader for his next theme, Vico concluded the first oration by advising that his public approach their studies with the even-temperedness of the Stoic, or what was called *apatheia,* to the end of studying for the sake of wisdom alone rather than the shortsighted benefits of mere professional accreditation.[25] In light of the oration's final note, then, it is clear that even at this early stage in Vico's career his professed faith in human reason was qualified by a keen concern about the passions, and that his sense of humanity's great nobility was less an affirmation than a prognosis of development. While the problem of a pedagogue in its origins, the question of the subject and outcome of *padeia* would occupy Vico for the rest of his life, as would that of the means by which an imperfectly rational man could apprehend and implement political truths.

In the second oration, Vico purposefully invoked the tenets of Stoic psychology to woo with the most hortatory of tones the student body to diligent study. Therein, Vico both admonished his students of the consequences of slacking and held out before them the grand prospects of true knowledge, namely, the consummate privilege of world citizenship. To that end, he employed the ancient Stoic tropes of the sage and of the fool, and waxed most eloquently on the privileges of wisdom awarded the former and the punishments of ignorance due to the latter. Like the Stoics he so admired, Vico conceived of cosmopolitanism not only as an individual awareness of fellowship with humanity but also as a hard-earned cognition born of the individual's cultivation of enlightenment.[26] It was at once the fruit and reward of a mature intellect that effectively had transcended the limitations of the self, by superseding the false impressions of the senses regularly besetting the mind. Thus, cosmopolitanism solely was the achievement and condition of the wise, or the sage, who had learned to properly evaluate and process sense impressions to achieve what the Stoics called *apatheia,* or the joyful equanimity of spirit before both that which one could and that which one could not control. As Vico described the condition of the sage: "Through knowledge the wise separates the spirit from the concerns of the body, thus allowing him to devote himself to the better and godlike part."[27] In contrast to the blissful condition of the sage, Vico also conjured for his audience the ignominy and misery of the fool. Further drawing on the moral psychology of the Stoics and overlaying it with Christian contempt for the body, Vico presented the fool as a prisoner of his emotions and bodily passions, that is, as a hostage of his own assent to the barrage of false impressions of the senses and the lustful desires of the body. For Vico, this assent rendered the fool akin to a madman, depriving him of the very rationality that distinguished him as a member of humanity. Consequently, the fool was deprived of his humanity and barred from the privilege of world citizenship by his debased nature. As Vico maintained, the ignorance of the fool besieged the mind and debased the political spirit: "The weapon of the fool is his own unrestrained passion. The power that overcomes him is his remorse. The homeland of which he is deprived is the whole world. The wealth that he loses is human happiness."[28] By contrast, then, the ascent to world citizenship was paved by the acquisition of wisdom characteristic of the sage; it was marked by the achievement of freedom from the heinous tyranny of the impressions and crowned by the beatitude of infallible reasoning. More important, it also earned for its apostle the apprehension of and adherence to the very principles of humanity, that is, the laws of nature, or what were those inherently reasonable truths and standards of justice. As Vico summed it up: "What can one with more grandeur and honor say than 'I am a citizen of Rome' if not he who can declare 'I am a citizen of the universe,' which only the wise may do.... Who if not the wise can prove himself fit to be a citizen of this great city? It is he who knows and serves the law of nature and the universe."[29] Cosmopolitanism was, in short, a state of heightened awareness that both predisposed its agent to the sort of behavior, or actions, appropriate to a member of the world community and obligated him to the natural laws of justice.

The very loftiness of Vico's rhetorical tour de force naturally begs the question of what his pronouncements about the enlightenment of the passions and the reward of global citizenship possibly meant to contemporaries. To whom were the orations specifically addressed? And, similarly, what sort of practical role in society did Vico imagine for the so-called sage? Was that role a point of contention for contemporaries, and if so, why? What were those natural laws of justice to which Vico referred? And what sort of politics was implicit to their advocacy, if any? The first three of these questions are best answered by both selectively returning to the texts of the first two orations for Vico's own admissions as well as contextualizing Vico's lofty pronouncements within the history of the contemporary institutions and debates to which they were addressed. The latter ones similarly will be answered in the subsequent treatment of the later orations.

IV. The "Sage" in Context: The Profile and Expectations of Vico's Audience

Behind the impersonal grandeur of Stoic cosmopolitanism lay a concrete program for the governance of the Kingdom, which would have been perfectly evident to Vico's contemporaries. In the first place, Vico himself was unambiguous about the practical purposes of a university education, properly undertaken, and the role that his audience was expected to play in the community. Indeed, speaking in the presumed voice of the ministers of the Kingdom, Vico unabashedly invited the student body to study in preparation for service to the state, or *res publica*. As he promised his student public,

the reward of the wisdom acquired at university was a career in the administration of the state along with the many honors and prerogatives due its
importance: "This group of magistrates of great offices, which they exercise
with incredible prudence and wisdom, and which is the reward of their diligent studies, invite you to these same studies, so that, according to your own
merit, you too can become part of the administration of the state."[30] Doubt-
lessly, then, Vico's exhortations were addressed to the university's students of
law, which was the primary course of study offered by the university and
the one that prepared students for a career in the Kingdom's administrative
offices, which at the time largely consisted of tribunals.[31] In fact, the University of Naples was a royal institution that expressly had been founded by
Frederick II for the instruction of law and the formation of an administrative
corps for the Kingdom.[32] It was, in other words, "a school of the state," whose
governance, appointments, and curriculum were all shaped by the practical
political concerns of the monarch, which in the sixteenth and seventeenth
centuries were executed by his representative in the Kingdom, the Spanish
viceroy.[33] In like manner, throughout the early modern period the Faculty
of Law and its course of study dominated the curriculum of the university,
which remained renowned for its instruction in jurisprudence.[34] For these
reasons and others like them, the referents of Vico's adulation would have
been perfectly self-evident to contemporaries, and, furthermore, his praise of
them would have positioned Vico as a cultural spokesman for the social and
political ambitions of the doctors of law.[35]

With his citation of Stoic cosmopolitanism in the orations, Vico clearly
began to craft an ideology for the university-trained jurist, or what was a
cultural argument meant to serve him in his pursuit of social recognition and
political supremacy. The reasons for the utility of such an ideology were as
manifold as the forces of competition with the professional jurist himself.
In the first place, as regarded his social status, the doctor of law stood much
to gain from an ideology that effectively promoted social recognition for
his title of accreditation over those due him by birthright. For the study and
practice of jurisprudence was the career choice typical of non-nobles from
the provinces of the Kingdom.[36] As the vast majority of the courts were
located in the capital of the Kingdom, most professional jurists remained in
Naples, where their identity was marked by the undistinguished couplet of
the title of doctor and legal status as a *forestiero*, or foreigner of provincial origin, refracting the uneasy duality of the capital itself as both a metropolitan
center of administration and an autonomous municipality with its own distinct citizenry. As the inaugural orations primarily were addressed to foreign
doctors, it is easy to imagine the great appeal of Stoic cosmopolitanism for

Vico's public and the wide resonance of its premise that one's education, or acquired nature, was both distinctive per se and more significant than one's traditional group affiliations, such as order and municipal citizenship. Indeed, as the reconstruction of contemporary debates shows, Vico strategically looked to cosmopolitan models to endorse the contentions of university-trained jurists, whose very grounds for social and political advancement precisely hinged on discrediting the significance of order and citizenship within their field of operation.

If Stoic cosmopolitanism spoke to and greatly appealed to Vico's audience, it was not by merit of its premises alone, but also by virtue of the burning topicality of the same, as the most widely read nonjuridical works by doctors of law from the end of the seventeenth century perfectly make plain. Vico's cosmopolitanism effectively lent credibility to the bold argument by contemporaries for both the personal distinction and professional merit of university training. In the first place, it corroborated with time-honored Stoic pedagogical theory the polemical claim to nobility formulated by doctors of law for their formation and profession in books and manuscript works of wide circulation. It provided a respected frame of cultural reference for the assertion that a title of learning, such as doctorate of law, was intrinsically superior to those highly coveted, adventitious ones of contemporary society, such as citizen, and, most jealously, noble or civic patrician. As such, it was partisan to the efforts of illustrious jurists to stake a persuasive claim for the transformative powers of the law curriculum and the dignity of the legal profession. By the same token, the insistence that Vico's cosmopolitanism placed on the value of university training in preparation for service to the state also partook of a debate concerning the credentials for public office, once again aligning Vico with that cadre of jurists dismissive of corporate badges and steadfast in their pursuit of public glory. In other words, it proffered university training as an indispensable qualification for both those who were excluded from and those who enjoyed the traditional group affiliations of civic society.

Vico's grandiloquent presentation of university training as a process of edification culminating in incomparable personal dignity and political wisdom represented a philosophical paraphrase and endorsement of a no less articulate appeal on the part of contemporary jurists for recognition of the study and practice of jurisprudence as an exalting enterprise. Since the middle of the seventeenth century, a number of jurists had compiled studies of the Kingdom's tribunals featuring pointed reflections about the edifying nature of the doctorate of law.[37] In the landmark *De origine omnium tribunalium nunc in castro Capuano fidelissimae Civitatis Neapolis existentium* (1659–66), for instance, Niccolò Toppi had prefaced his work with a definition of nobility distinguishing that which derived from wealth, arms, and learning to the great advantage of the latter, strongly conveying his conviction that knowledge was the superior source of personal distinction and the true mark of aristocracy.[38] Even more famously, the preeminent jurist of the Kingdom at the time, the Campanian Francesco D'Andrea, specifically had addressed the transformative powers of jurisprudence in his widely circulated memoir penned just a few years prior to Vico's orations, the *Avvertimenti ai nipoti* (1695).[39] A plaidoyer for the inherent dignity of the legal profession, the very point of D'Andrea's memoir had been that the *iter* of jurisprudence fundamentally transformed and distinguished its subjects qua humans. As he most succinctly put it: "In Naples the practice of law is that which ennobles vile persons, raises the mediocre and even renders illustrious those belonging to the grand nobility."[40] What was more, for D'Andrea the identity of the legal profession trumped that of one's traditional group affiliations, vitiating all the adventitious badges of corporate society associated with birthright. Especially in Naples, D'Andrea boasted, the merit of the jurist reportedly transcended not only order by birth and rank by wealth but even the patent of citizenship: "There is no other city in the world where [one's] value is rewarded more and where a man can achieve such high offices, immense riches, supreme dignities and even govern the republic without having any other quality besides his own merit, not even the honor of citizenship."[41] In other words, the intrinsic value and exhibited merits of a career in jurisprudence were a more perfect form of distinction and political belonging for D'Andrea. Its more perfect distinction also rendered unnecessary, if not downright foolish, the entrenched social practice of overlaying the title of doctor with the material trappings of the civic patriciate and the feudal baronage. As D'Andrea repeatedly warned throughout his memoir, the coveted acquisition of feudal titles was inimical to the welfare of the jurist, as by the force of custom it not only retired him from the edifying practice of law but also obliged him to the ruinous prodigality of the nobility.[42] The large number of extant manuscript copies of the *Avvertimenti,* which evidently was recopied, annotated, and circulated throughout the first decade of the eighteenth century, strongly suggests that D'Andrea's argument was timely, provocative, and immensely influential. Indeed, Vico evidently shared and echoed D'Andrea's famous convictions regarding the intrinsic value of jurisprudence and the supreme dignity of the jurist. With the rhetoric of Stoicism, however, he additionally lent the asserted supremacy of the legal profession over traditional group affiliations that profound sense of social justice indelibly associated with cosmopolitanism.

That Vico's cosmopolitanism provided an endorsement of what was a well-known social agenda by highly regarded jurists did not make it any less polemical, however. As my own study of period manuscript literature suggests, around 1700 the bid to rank the significance of education and merit over that of order was bold indeed, regardless of its swift dissemination and future success. While contemporaries of Vico first crafted the trope of the jurist ennobled by merit alone, it was only the publicists of the later eighteenth century who made of that trope a commonplace.[43] Thus, it is important to recall that at the time of the orations it was not customary for students of jurisprudence to envision the credentials of the doctoral title, the lucre of law, and the prospect of public honors as either dignified per se or, for that matter, the sole payoffs of their course of study. Rather, around 1700 it remained fashionable for university-trained jurists to pen and to consume genealogies that held out the promise of a course of social mobility culminating in the acquisition of a noble title. Indeed, the very content and popularity of the anthologies penned by the jurist and noted publicist, "Doctor" Domenico Confuorto, manifest as much.[44] So do the commissions by leading jurists of family histories, which for a price were falsified to add the luster of antiquity and of titled nobility to the material patrimony of a career in jurisprudence.[45] Indeed, a number of those protagonists of the forum studied by publicists of the later eighteenth century, as those publicists themselves both admitted and criticized, tirelessly endeavored to procure feudal distinctions and rewrite their genealogies accordingly.[46] In short, those protagonists neither would have refound themselves in the trope of the jurist ennobled by merit alone nor would they have applauded it for its sanguinity. For example, even the staunchest exponents of the state around 1700 seem not to have escaped the "mania" of feudal title, as one critic put it. Indeed, the two mavericks of jurisdictionalism at the outset of the eighteenth century, Serafino Biscardi (1643–1711) and Alessandro Riccardi (1660–1726), both were consumed by the pretense of nobility, which led the first to seek admission to the civic patriciate of multiple provincial towns and the second to ensconce his own claims to feudal title in a family chapel erected in the Neapolitan Church of the Spirito Santo.[47] Thus, it was in this context that Vico weighed his words about the great dignity and finality of learning, and that his praise of world citizenship had meaning for his audience.

Needless to say, to speak about the transcendental distinction of world citizenship in a society where the cachet of civic and feudal title strongly persisted, indubitably, was to challenge the status quo. It represented an erudite, coded way of rejecting the traditional social ambitions of the judiciary, which had set its sights on the acquisition of not only the titles but also the lifestyle of the civic and feudal nobility. And it offered an alternative code of behavior and distinctions that set apart the university-trained corps of jurists, touting them as an exemplary and exclusive cadre.

If Vico knew and addressed the social aspirations of his public, then it seems that he was also fully cognizant of their political ambitions. For his Stoic pedagogy further took sides in the contemporary debate about the qualification for public office waged between noble and non-noble members of the judiciary. The debate itself concerned the criteria by which to determine the equitable award of office and had much bearing on the allocation of the highest magistracies of the Kingdom's tribunals. Around 1700, beyond the Consiglio Collaterale, or Council of State, the leading organs of the Kingdom were tribunals, or courts of law with distinct jurisdictions. Within those same tribunals numbered a hierarchy of positions, whose premier judicial posts, the magistracies, disproportionately had been awarded to members of the capital's patriciate for much of the seventeenth century, unhinging the link between merit and office at the upper echelons of state.[48] With his idealization of university training, then, Vico effectively advocated the credentials of the non-noble doctor of law over those of his patrician counterpart in the contest for the magistracies, as the patrician members of the judiciary customarily had received their legal education from private tutors, although university attendance theoretically was required of all candidates for the doctorate of law.[49]

What is more, to make university training the bar for political wisdom additionally suggested that the nonpatrician members of the judiciary were those best suited for the new and more comprehensive roles of the magistracies in the Kingdom. Beyond their judicial responsibilities, the magistrates increasingly were called on to fulfill political roles as counselors and administrators of state under the reign of Charles II (1665–1700);[50] and, as such, they increasingly served to govern the Kingdom in what was an ad hoc but preeminently practical way, effectively constituting something akin to a senatorial class.[51] Consequently, between the leading representatives of the tribunals and municipality of Naples there ensued a tug-of-war over the appropriate jurisdictions of each and, more acrimoniously, over the claim to sovereignty on the part of both, which in times of political transition became a very real struggle over the right to temporarily rule the Kingdom, as was indeed the case on the death of Charles II in September 1700.[52] Thus, at the time of the orations it was painfully evident to contemporaries that the contest for the leading magistracies entailed a contest for the de facto governance of the Kingdom both in times of peace and, especially, in those of war. Indeed, Vico himself explicitly extolled the role of the magistrates in the governance of the Kingdom, as if they fulfilled that of a senatorial class in the governance of a "republic," as he put it, imputing to them the autonomous powers and prestige of that Roman body.[53]

In light of this, then, the first orations represented a manifesto for the university-trained jurist's natural right to rule. Their Stoic cosmopolitanism advocated the ascendancy of a new political man, whose credentials lay not in his corporate affiliations but in the knowledge and, no less, behavior distinctive of his university formation. The *apatheia,* or constancy, instilled in that man by the university, furthermore, arguably equipped him well to serve the Kingdom in both times of stability and those of constitutional change. Considering the destabilizing prospect of regime change in the offing, this manifesto could not have been timelier. As we saw in chapter 1, the anticipated and imminent death of Charles II already had unleashed the political pretenses of the capital's municipality and the military machinations of the nobility, both of which would be brought to justice by the ablest of magistrates.

V. *Orationes III–V:* The Self, "Society," and a Modern Conception of Natural Law

In good Stoic fashion, with the progression of the *Orationes* so did Vico proceed to investigate those broader circles of association encompassing the intercourse and responsibilities of the aspiring jurist. Moving from the rationality of the mind to that of the group, with the third oration Vico began to formulate hypotheses about the origins and purposes of human associations that more specifically engaged the tradition of natural law. Whereas the first two orations had established the moral basis for the jurist's right to rule, the subsequent ones identified those norms that the jurist's rulings were expected to uphold, staking a first set of claims regarding the normative ends of natural law jurisprudence. While the semantics of the subsequent orations largely remained the same, the actual content of those Stoic concepts did change considerably. In the orations composed and delivered after 1701 Vico betrayed his literal faithfulness to the ancient Stoic ideals of cosmopolitanism and natural law to accommodate those observations about contemporary society he had formulated and dramatized in his exposition of the Neapolitan revolt. Indeed, Vico's revision of the Stoic ideals of cosmopolitanism and natural law marked the commencement of the Neapolitan's career as a modern social theorist and his advocacy of the legislation of reform by juridical ruling.[54]

Whereas Vico had written about world fellowship as a product of education in the early orations, in the subsequent ones, which were written and delivered after fall 1701, he presented it as the outcome of a process of societal formation that had been occasioned by human instinct and perpetuated by the limitations on its powers imposed by free will. Herewith, like so many of his predecessors, Vico assumed that humans were by nature social animals and that they developed their humanity in the context of association,[55] or what Vico called "society," whose general nature and particular forms he made the subject of his investigation. Over the course of the subsequent three orations, Vico first established the natural sociability of humans and the fundamental purposes of their "society" and then specifically examined three forms thereof: what he called "scholarly society"; the "patria," or nation; and, finally, "human society."

From a strictly narrative perspective, Vico's treatment of human affiliations followed perfectly from his treatment of the self in the first orations, as it gave content to those ever-wider spheres of association in which the cosmopolitan presumably held membership. Yet this continuity of narrative form did little to ensure that of narrative content. For the laws of fellowship Vico identified with humans in "society" contrasted markedly with those he had envisioned animating the self in his prior addresses. Previously, Vico had postulated that humans were by nature potentially rational beings who developed their humanity independently of one another through the cultivation of the mind and the disciplining of the body. Furthermore, he had believed that rational humans were animated by a sense of benevolence that directed their affinity for and interactions with their like. However, in the third oration, Vico curiously replaced this intellectualist notion of cosmopolitanism with a materialist one that took its model of human nature and association from the idiom of Roman commerce. Modeling the principles of human association on those of the Roman commercial venture, in the third oration Vico proposed that humans were quintessentially interdependent beings whose fellowship consisted in the reciprocal obligations and common transactions arising from their contract. What Vico postulated in the third oration, in other words, was what the historiography on the eighteenth century sometimes has called economic, or commercial, cosmopolitanism, a notion that envisioned human associations as "societies," or transactional communities, and human fellowship as a form of contractual exchange.[56] If the premises of Vico's cosmopolitanism were not unique, considering that the Neapolitan was, however precocious, just one of a number of eighteenth-century theorists to venture a materialist revision of Stoic cosmopolitanism, the programmatic aspects of his cosmopolitanism do stand apart, as they specifically endorsed a school of natural law of eminently practical application.[57] For Vico identified those natural laws of fellowship directing human association with those customary norms regulating the Roman commercial venture, supplementing his explanatory account of human association with the identification of a body of law and school of jurisprudence for its governance. Beyond the moral injunctions and proscriptions his contemporaries equated with natural law, then, Vico associated a juridical corpus and method of rendering justice that lent rhetorical support to the argument for the precedence of natural law jurisprudence in the courts, bringing the cycle of the *Orationes* to a most emphatic political close.

In the first two orations Vico specifically had identified natural law with those dictates of conscience quintessential to the cosmopolitan, who was characterized by the possession of reason and by an affinity for fellow humanity. Invoking the authority of Cicero in support of his own argument, Vico summarily had restated the Ciceronian definition of natural law proffered in the *Laws*, where the Roman most cogently had formulated the Stoic view that "law" was "right reason in commanding and forbidding," or the principled injunction and proscription of things by the fully developed faculty of human reason.[58] Importantly, this Ciceronian idea of natural law was predicated on three key assumptions, from which Vico would depart in his third inaugural address. In the first place, it was based on the notion of moral realism, wherein "moral properties inhere in their objects."[59] Consequently, it assumed a natural correspondence between the laws commanded by reason and their moral authority for humans. Second, this Ciceronian idea rested on the more ancient Stoic tenet that the imperatives of natural law and justice took precedence over those codified within agreements among humans, or what we would call conventional or customary justice. It implicitly had contradicted the notions that contractual agreements could provide natural justice and that self-interest, or utility, could direct the relations among humans to the end of virtue,[60] notions that had been expounded by both the ancient Epicureans and modern proponents of natural law such as Hobbes, whose influence was palpable in contemporary Naples.[61] Finally, and most important, in spite of the view of conventional justice it implied, this Ciceronian idea implicitly had identified natural with Roman law, which it upheld as a perfectly rational code of universal relevance and application.[62] As specific to Roman history this latter position may seem, in Vico's own time it was advocated by the foremost theoretician of law, Gian Vincenzo Gravina, who in his widely read magnum opus, the *Originum iuris civilis libri tres,* argued for the interpretation of Roman civil law as an inherently reasonable code of universal validity. In the orations predating the revolt of 1701, then, Vico had shared the Ciceronian assumptions regarding the intrinsic morality and, indeed, justice of human reason and the naturalness of Roman civil law.

In his very first address composed after the revolt of 1701, however, Vico abandoned the anthropological premises underlying the moral realism of the prior ones, making necessary a new definition of natural law. In the third inaugural address, which presumably was delivered in 1702, Vico floated a model of human nature that expressly denied humans the ability to follow the injunctions and proscriptions of their reason. Contrarily to the earlier addresses, and echoing a standard Christian position, in the third oration Vico viewed that capacious freedom of the human he once had so lauded as the greatest of liabilities. Betraying his former allegiances to rationalism, Vico criticized what Descartes had thought to be humanity's consummate point of pride as precisely its sorest weakness, namely, its distinction from the animals. In contradistinction to the beasts, Vico despaired, humans possessed not only reason but also a free will, which bedeviled them by decoupling their actions from the injunctions of their rational instincts. In comparison to the rest of creation, in other words, humans were singular, as their behavior was uniquely inconsistent with instinct and, as such, potentially self-destructive. By contrasting the indeterminate behavior of humans to the constancy of animals, Vico decried the vulnerability of humankind caused by the possession of a free will: "Indeed, the freedom of choice of the human spirit is the reason for all evil." For it permitted both glorious as well as foolhardy behavior. "He has built above him a great wall of stone, but it will crush him," he added.[63]

As concerned the laws of human association and fellowship, the upshot of this sobering caricature of the human condition was a model of community that both acknowledged and reconciled the naturalness of association with the diversity of behavior among associated humans. To accomplish such, Vico's model of community provided empirical evidence for a nominal understanding of the concept of oikeiosis, or natural sociability. On the basis of empirical observation, in the third oration Vico cited oikeiosis as the efficient cause of human association, while he deliberately repudiated its auxiliary significance for the actual comportment of humans in community, contradicting the Stoic belief in the predisposition of humanity to empathy and acts of benevolence toward their fellows.[64] As Vico described it in the third oration, then, the human condition in community was marked by an oxymoron, that is, by a subjection to the directive of oikeiosis and by a divorce from its principles of justice. And it was this oxymoron that Vico would seek to remedy with his notion of "society" and his proposals for its governance in the third address. For it was in the imperative for society that Vico would locate that of natural law. As he so notoriously had done and repeatedly would do over the course of his long career, Vico parted company with the premises of the classics he so revered to engage in debate with the moderns in the most coded and recondite of ways.

Within his own oeuvre the claims that Vico put forth regarding the nature and regulations of "society" breathed new life and overlaid with distinct meaning his ideas of world citizenship and natural law. With his adoption of "society" as the model for human community, Vico manifestly abandoned his restriction of world fellowship to the sentience of enlightened humans and his equation of natural law with the dictates of conscience immanent to the same. Indeed, it marked Vico's assumption that the basis for human fellowship in community lay in the externalities of nature and that the norms of natural justice for the community resided in the injunctions of human convention. In other words, however tentative, it marked Vico's recognition of and grappling with the idea that, more than a feeling, cosmopolitanism was the product of external circumstances and conventional agreements among the members of a world polity.

In the third oration, Vico cleverly broached the topic of "society" and its regulatory norms in what was otherwise a belletristic address ostensibly devoted to discussion of the illustrious Republic of Letters. Formally speaking, the primary objective of the third oration was to chasten the audience of student-scholars to pursue their studies with the greatest of justice, that is, with due regard to the conventions of the Republic of Letters.[65] However, the conventions that Vico put forth rather distinctly relied on his definition of the Republic of Letters as a "society,"[66] which he used as a platform from which to state what he associated with that term and what practical significance it bore for the governance of human communities. By "society," Vico meant the association and customary obligations of the members of a partnership, or *societas,* as it had been defined in classical Roman law. As a "society," then, the Republic was governed by the conventions of the Roman commercial venture, whose members, by legal definition, Vico reminded, purposefully pooled their resources for the sake of a common enterprise. "For all associations of men this is the intended law: that each member bring with him to share in common either his goods or his talents," he exclaimed, explicitly citing the contractual terms of the societas as if they were those of the scholarly community and, by implication here, all other human associations as well.[67] The primary obligation of membership in the Republic, Vico thus explained, was the duty to contribute to the community of learning to the best of one's ability. What was more, the standards of professional behavior for members of the Republic were set by those same norms that customarily had governed the obligations of the partnership's contract, the principles of "good faith" and "equity."

Lest there be any doubt as to their appropriateness for the Republic of Letters, Vico most vividly conveyed the great relevance of those principles for academic behavior with his innumerable examples of squabbles among petty scholars who had unfairly appropriated the work of some and judged others in bad faith.[68] After speaking of the improper use and deceitful judgments of intellectual property perpetrated by the incurably envious, Vico roused his audience of student-scholars to recognize those customary obligations of the societas as their own: "O eternal God! If in commercial societies the members are equitable and well disposed toward one another, will the members of scholarly societies act unfairly with one another?"[69] Clearly, Vico hoped not, employing his slight of rhetorical hand to universalize the pertinence of the concept of the societas and the customary duties of its contract. With much admonition and little ado, Vico's usage of the term "society" superimposed the nature of the Roman partnership upon associations; it forced a systemic equivalence between commercial and cultural societies that made both the purpose and regulatory norms of commerce synonymous with those of human associations at large. What is more, with his usage of "society," Vico acknowledged a human field of investigation whose object was clearly demarcated from that of politics: with it, he partook in the creation of modern social theory, by finding in a contemporary and, more important, extrapolitical form of the urban community evidence for universal patterns of association and for natural laws by which to govern humans qua humans.

If the purpose and norms of commerce pertained to small human associations in the third oration, then they were also proper to the relations among humans in the broader context of the world. Indeed, Vico also used the term "society" to denote humanity by qualifying it with the adjective human (humana societas).[70] Here, he employed the term "human society" as if it were a natural extension of the smaller association that he had heretofore discussed, and extended his analogy between the nature of the two to the guiding principles of both. Significantly, this particular usage of "society" represented a neologism in its day. As the work of Johan Heilbron, Daniel Gordon, and Keith Michael Baker has shown, at the outset of the eighteenth century the term "society" was not yet used to represent the collectivity of humanity but had a more restricted meaning: it typically referred to either contractual ventures or associations of friends engaged in cultural activities, such as conversation.[71]

Consequently, the advent of modern social theory has been dated to circa 1750, when the term "society" began to acquire a more comprehensive connotation, that is, one inclusive of all social units, or the "social world as a whole."[72] Thus, Vico's employment of "society" was both novel and precocious, as it created a hybrid out of the distinct contemporary meanings of the term, and as, with qualification, that hybrid took on the more comprehensive connotation of a collective humanity. Although this particular usage appeared only once in the third oration, it is nonetheless of unequivocal importance, as it introduced the notion of an all-inclusive collectivity of humanity, and it posited those same norms operative among "associates" of various kinds as relevant to the exchanges among the members of that inclusive whole. Indeed, in the third oration this term specifically appeared in Vico's example of a crime against "human society," namely, that of misleading a stranger who has lost his way, with which he embraced, if not engendered, a vision of human fellowship that lent the imperative of good faith to the Stoic obligations of world citizenship.[73] More than the origins and purposes of association, then, what Vico recognized in the legal fiction of the commercial *societas* were principles, or regulations, for a human *societas* that transcended the conflict of laws among political communities. In other words, therein he identified the duties, or reciprocal obligations, owed by humans to one another regardless of the personal legal distinctions among them, elevating the norms of commercial law to the stature of a cosmopolitan natural law.

With his recognition of the reciprocal obligations borne by the members of "human society," furthermore, what Vico acknowledged, in content if not name, is what we would call human rights, that is, a set of inviolable things possessed by and owed to us by universal accord, embedding into his materialistic revision of Stoic cosmopolitanism an embryonic theory of right to which he would give ample elaboration in his later legal works. Thus, already in the earliest stage of his career, Vico found in the commercial *societas* a model of human community that transcended the arbitrary distinctions of polities and located in commercial law a set of natural principles, or regulations, that superseded the particularisms of extant civil laws. The third oration thus marked Vico's entrée into speculating about the pertinence of natural law, most broadly understood, to the commonalities of human experience and behavior. Indeed, Vico's interest in natural law would not stagnate but flourish over the course of his career. For it was precisely the development of natural law and its relationship to the political culture of peoples that Vico would revisit and interpret anew in his later legal writings, wherein it would provide both the categories and backbone of his particular history of civilization.

However bold it was, Vico's identification of commercial as cosmopolitan natural law had important ancient and modern precedents, which can be found in the history of the juridical concept of the ius gentium, or law of nations. In addition, those same precedents explain the centrality of "good faith," or *bona fides,* to Vico's model of "society" in both its local and global incarnations. While the ius gentium was not a distinct body of law per se in the postclassical period, it was one of the three types of Roman law, and in the time of the Roman Empire it had connoted those norms and rules with which the Romans governed foreigners. In ancient Rome, the civil law, the *ius civile* or *ius Quiritium,* was made to apply only to Roman citizens, a practice that necessitated the creation of a body of extralegal procedures and rules for the adjudication of disputes among foreigners at Rome as well as between Romans and foreigners. These procedures and rules themselves were largely the creation of the Roman praetors, those magistrates bearing the powers, or *imperium,* of jurisdiction in civil affairs and whose rulings were famous for their interpretative spirit and practical innovation of the law.

Despite the murkiness of its beginnings, the origin of the ius gentium is generally traced to the institution in Rome about 242 BCE of the magistracy of the *praetor peregrinus,* who was "vested with jurisdictional powers in civil matters between foreigners and between foreigners and Roman citizens."[74] In stark contrast to the strict formalism of civil law, for the peregrine praetor's court a flexible formulary procedure was developed, which permitted the praetor to take into consideration the specific circumstances of a case and to accommodate the law to the new socioeconomic conditions of Rome's burgeoning commerce with foreigners. As Peter Stein has underscored, the formulary procedure thus became both the institution and vehicle for the introduction into Roman law of those norms and rules that would be most closely associated with the ius gentium.[75] At the beginning of his term, the praetor published what remedies he was prepared to grant, and it was specifically through the published edicts of the *praetor peregrinus* that over the years there emerged a "general system of rules governing the relations between free men as such, without reference to their nationality."[76]

One of the major innovations of this supranational system was its recognition of the "consensual contract," that is, the common commercial contract typically used for the institution of the commercial societas. Significantly, this sort of contract was bilateral and the product of consensus alone. Consequently, the content of the obligations that it imposed was determined by the moral concept of "good faith."[77] For instance, in the case of an action particular to the praetorian formula available to the litigants was the clause *ex bona fide,* which literally made "good faith" an actionable objection and "allowed the *iudex* (citizen judge) to take into account equitable pleas." With the passage of time, as Peter Stein has explained, "what good faith required became more and more onerous, as public opinion, expressed through the decisions of successive *iudices,* expected higher and higher standards of conduct from contracting parties."[78] Thus, the understanding that the members of "society" were held to the duties and obligations assumed in "good faith" ultimately derived from the development of praetorian law as it concerned the governance of commerce among aliens. That this same supranational system born of the praetorian edicts also should be identified as natural law, that is, as a set of inherently rational norms and rules common to all peoples, or human societas, was the further development of Roman jurisprudence in the first and second centuries CE, which importantly would inform the modern school of natural law jurisprudence.

By the time of Gaius, the second-century CE Roman jurist and author of a textbook entitled the *Institutes,* one school of legal thought strictly identified the ius gentium with a natural law of humanity.[79] As a historian of Roman law has explained, this theory "drape(d) a scientific cloak around the fact that a number of principles developed by the *praetor peregrinus* had proved useful also in the jurisdiction of the *praetor urbanus;* the recognition of the *fides* as a basis for actionable obligations is an example."[80] It was precisely this dressing of the ius gentium in the garb of natural law, then, that Vico invoked when he upheld the commercial societas and its principle of good faith as the model for human association. What is more, it was precisely this history of the ius gentium that Vico would interpret with the greatest of argumentative force in his legal tracts concerning universal law.

While we cannot know the exact extent to which Vico had mastered all the details of this legal tradition by this point in his career, it nonetheless is clear that he was well versed in the precepts of the ius gentium and familiar with its connotation as natural law from his reading of philosophical works by ancients and moderns alike. Setting a precedent, on which Vico evidently drew, in his final work, *De officiis,* Cicero famously had upheld the reciprocal obligations of the ius gentium as the foundation of natural justice and the universal duties of humans in community.[81] Indeed, Cicero had insisted that these universal duties were first and foremost composed of the obligations of good faith and equity, which he illustrated with numerous examples, including praetorian rulings where principles of general conduct were at issue.[82] If Vico derived his ideas regarding the ius gentium from Cicero, these ideas evidently were meaningful to him as a posture within modern natural law theory, however. For Vico not only shared Cicero's late convictions regarding the universality of the ius gentium. He also shared and departed from Cicero's broader theory of natural law as formulated in *De officiis* on precisely the same counts as did his older contemporary Samuel Pufendorf (1632–94), the famed German professor of law and statesman whose natural law treatises so influenced Enlightenment philosophers from Locke to Rousseau. Put somewhat differently, the working assumptions of the third oration resembled

Pufendorf's own citation of the ius gentium and departures from Roman Stoic natural law. Vico's antirationalistic anthropology, his moral nonrealism, his usage of the term "society," and, no less, the moral priority he gave the obligations of "good faith" and "equity" all recalled the hallmark premises of Pufendorf's monumental *De iure naturae et gentium libri octo* (1672), which famously had posited the Roman societas as the model of human association and the imperatives of *socialitas* as the prescriptions of its natural law.[83] In other words, for his contemporaries Vico's neoclassical idiom would have established his authority not only on the classics but also on the modern authors of natural law and effectively demonstrated his allegiance to both the ideas and politics of Pufendorf's social theory.

If a posture within the tradition of natural law, both ancient and modern, then the affinity that Vico demonstrated for Pufendorf is most important for what it tells us about the occasion for and the politics of social theory in Naples. The reasons for Vico's adoption of the natural law idiom of Pufendorf, I believe, are fourfold. In the first place, with the lessons of the third oration Vico explicitly engaged the tradition of natural law at what was the most public of university events, making a showy display of both his knowledge of and allegiances within that tradition on what was literally the eve of university reform.[84] At this watershed in its history, the university notably lacked instruction in natural and international law, although those subjects apparently were topical in contemporary Naples. According to contemporary accounts, natural law was widely discussed and hotly contested at the time; as Nicola Capasso, then a young and ambitious jurist, had put it in a lecture before the Accademia Medinaceli, "ius naturale" was "talked about by everyone" but "understood by few."[85] Consequently, Vico's display of natural law theory may have involved some calculation regarding the exigencies and opportunities posed by the ambitious program for university reform planned by the regent "protector" of the university, Andrea Guerriero, and by its modernizing rector, Cappellano Maggiore Don Diego Vincenzo de Vidania, for the upcoming academic year.

Second, by publicly engaging the tradition of natural law Vico not only demonstrated his credentials in that field of learning but also took sides in what was an acrimonious debate about the ostensible nature and ends of the polity in 1702. For public support of the natural law theory of Pufendorf equally represented a rebuff, however coded, of that modern position favored by the prior viceroy, who just had been recalled to Spain after his draconian repression of the Neapolitan revolt of 1701. Among those closest to the court of Medinaceli, it seems that the preferred vein of natural law had been that of Hobbes, whose theory (tacitly) had been cited to bolster the authority of the Spanish monarchy in the Kingdom and to justify the "reason of state" doctrine, or policy that favored the strength of the regime over that of its competitors at all costs.[86] In what was recent memory, in front of the Accademia Medinaceli Capasso had also repackaged the hallmark ideas of Hobbes on natural law and sovereignty for their application in the Kingdom, securing the continued favor of the viceroy, who expressed his great approbation of Capasso's demonstration of fidelity with the nomination of the latter to the Acting Chair of the prestigious professorship in Canon Law.[87] In what was even more recent and harrowing memory, furthermore, the "reason of state" doctrine had legitimated the viceroy's military trial, torture, and execution of the rebels of 1701, whose dead bodies were publicly desecrated in defiance of all customary standards of decency and, more significantly here, international norms governing the conduct of war, which from Cicero to Grotius famously had been associated with precepts of the ius gentium: that is, good faith, equity, and, by extension, clemency.[88] To identify the nature and governance of the community with that of the Roman societas, then, was to contradict the absolutist doctrines and "reason of state" policy associated with and legitimated by the natural law of Hobbes.

Third, Vico's usage of the Roman societas as a model of community also lent legitimacy to his own observations about who counted in the polity and why, as we know them from his history of the Neapolitan revolt of 1701. In the *Coniuratio,* Vico had identified in the *cives modesti,* or in what we would call the bourgeoisie, the pillars and stalwart defenders of the capital of the Kingdom, positing a correlation between the enterprise of capital accumulation and attachment to the political community that defied the traditional civic benchmarks for political belonging and allegiance. Thus, Vico's adoption of the term "society" invoked a model of community that could recognize and account for the agency of non-noble urban actors excluded from the traditional structure of the civic polity. In other words, it made comprehensible both the political value and behavior of industrious metropolitan actors lacking civic credentials, and it weakened the purchase of those time-worn civic measures of belonging and of duty. At the same time, the idea of "society" also rendered intelligible the multiple allegiances and non-normative behavior of capital city dwellers bearing traditional corporate identities, who had betrayed corporate order in favor of contractual relations, however debasing.

Fourth, given the immediate context of his address, Vico's adoption of the societas dramatically communicated a direct challenge to the corporate model of community offered by the *universitas,* which in early modern Naples denoted both the royal university as well as the local communities of the

Kingdom.[89] Most remarkably, perhaps, this address literally summoned the privileged members of a *universitas,* or royal corporation, dedicated to the study of civil and canonical law, to govern themselves as if they were the individual partners of a societas, and thus by the juridical norms of Roman commercial law, or what was the ius gentium. Consequently, it displayed utter disregard for both the legal persona of its audience, who together constituted a corporation possessing a number of prerogatives and privileges granted by the king, as well as for the primary ends of their study, namely, mastery of the corpus of Roman civil law. With disarming naturalness, then, it made a case for the moral priority of individual merits over those of the corporation and for the precedence of Roman commercial law over civil law.

Finally, Vico's advocacy of the ius gentium furthered the Neapolitan's efforts to promote both the prestige and powers of the judiciary within the Kingdom. For the ius gentium was associated with natural law jurisprudence, and, however ancient, its precepts maintained practical relevance for contemporary jurists. Indeed, the principles of "good faith" and "equity" Vico cited were also legal precepts employed by contemporary jurists to override the inequities occasioned by the conflict of laws within the Kingdom, especially as they concerned commercial disputes. Consequently, they were also tools that permitted the judiciary to wield discretionary power and to establish, to the great chagrin of imperial powers, a certain degree of autonomy within the administration of the state.

Thus, for Vico and his contemporaries, the idiom of Pufendorf's natural law was an intellectual weapon in the arsenal of change; it proffered fighting words of relevance to contemporary debates about the bar for membership in the community, the constitutive relationship among the community's members, and, most contentiously perhaps, those notions of sovereignty and legality that ought to inform its practical governance. While Vico had addressed his audience in the voice of an umpire of the scholarly community, the language of natural law he spoke leveled the most radical of critiques at the "reason of state" doctrine and at the system of Roman laws brought to bear on the adjudication of disputes. However deft his slight of rhetorical hand, it indubitably begged a reconceptualization of the polity on the terms of contractual enterprise and endorsed a school of natural jurisprudence that weighed in the favor of its commerce. In other words, Vico embraced the semantics of "society" because it represented both a conceptual and jurisprudential tool for reform. In Naples, social theory emerged as a direct challenge to the despotism of the Spanish monarchy and the ossified corporative structures of the Kingdom, and it endorsed a program for the juridical ruling and implementation of change.

The practical value of the *societas* for world administration was specifically examined by Vico in the fifth oration, which he apparently delivered
in 1706.[90] By then, some four years had intervened since the delivery of the
third oration, an interval that included a three-year hiatus in his recitation.
In the fourth oration (1705), Vico had addressed the reasons for this hiatus,
which he attributed to that initiative in university reform promulgated in
the winter of 1703 that had busied the faculty with self-assessment for some
two years.[91] Indeed, during that period, Vico was reviewed for the position
in Rhetoric, to which he was not only reappointed, but which apparently
was converted from a four-year lectureship to a "perpetual" chair.[92] While
university reform may have taken precedence over certain rituals, it also was
the case that the same hiatus coincided with the censure of the *Coniuratio*
(1703–4), and as such may have been a public manifestation, or avowal, by
Vico of the respectful caution due to the regime in response to its displeasure
with that work, despite the anti-Spanish sentiments of the university rector
Vidania. Indeed, when Vico did resume his delivery of convocation addresses
it was with a most patriotic of diatribes that adamantly reminded the students
of their duties to the republic, of the supreme usefulness of the honorable,
and of the finality of the common good, while lauding not only the *patria*
but also the Spanish monarchy and its empire.[93]

With the fifth oration, however, Vico turned his gaze from the politics of
the *patria* to that of the world of nations, whose means of justice he located in
the art of war. In light of that, it is noteworthy that the fifth oration also followed a significant change in the military fortune of the Bourbon claimants
to the Kingdom. With the battle of Blenheim in summer 1704, the French
armies had begun to suffer a series of reversals that eventually would cost
Philip V the Kingdom of Naples. Not surprisingly, this period in the Kingdom's history generally has been considered one of transition, during which
many of the leading Neapolitan administrators hedged their political bets;
and in this climate of anticipated change there may have been more readiness
to close an eye to what might have been considered the indiscretion of the
Coniuratio with regard to the Spanish. In any case, in the fifth oration, Vico
considered the value of the humanities for the art of war, which was at the
very least topical, if not provocative, for the members of his audience.

Whereas Vico had examined the model and principles of "society" in the
third oration, in the fifth he identified those of its global counterpart, or what
he called "human society." Generalizing from the principles of the former
for the latter, he specifically considered the obligations and laws governing
the political units of the world community, or its nations, as it were. All this
Vico packaged within the context of arguing about the relative importance

of the literary and military arts for the livelihood of any nation, a theme
that had been treated by a number of Renaissance scholars including Francis
Bacon, whose advocacy of their concurrence Vico essentially adopted.[94]

However, to the Renaissance debate Vico brought moral questions that
had lain beyond its scope. And in doing so, he gave content not only to the
moral obligations but also to the natural rights of agents within the world
order. In short, Vico argued that the literary arts were a handmaiden to the
military ones for the reason that international wars were analogous to a
judgment of civil law.[95] To demonstrate this analogy between civil law and
international wars, he first cited the celebrated Roman Stoic assertion that all
humans had two citizenships, one determined by the location of their birth
and another by the expanse of the cosmos, acknowledging both the duality
of the cosmopolitan's allegiances and the plurality of political orders constitutive of human society.[96] To substantiate his analogy, he then compared the
nature of the laws, intercourse, and means of redress available to the members
of the respective orders of human society, concluding that a just war had
the same function of redress among nations as the civil law had among the
individuals of a civic polity.[97]

Within the context of his address, the immediate purpose of Vico's particular analogy between civic and world society was to persuade his audience
of the moral responsibilities attendant to military command and of the great
utility of a philosophical education for the proper exercise of its offices. With
the most hortatory of tones, Vico enumerated the reasons for those philosophical virtues with which the military commander ought to be imbued:

> with justice, so that the reasons for war be just; with moderation, so that
> he would practice forgiveness as well as wrath; with restraint, so that
> he may extract from the defeated no more than what would threaten;
> with clemency, so that he would keep the captives alive rather than an-
> nihilate them. These are the virtues of the spirit that wisdom confers
> on the supreme commander.[98]

However, Vico's analogy was crafted with far more than an eye to persuasion
about the value of a philosophical education in time of war. In the fifth oration, he forayed into what we would call international law, as he made claims
about the actionable obligations and appropriate means of redress available
to nations across the globe. Universalizing the societas, Vico made both the
model and principles of the commercial "society" apply to the world of nations as a whole, so that the norms of the "consensual contract" to which
individuals were held similarly pertained to world political communities. In
addition, Vico concerned himself with the *iura,* or rights, of the transgressed

party in this oration. Although he preferred the terms "fas nationum" and "ius humanum" to "ius gentium" here,[99] it is nonetheless unequivocal that Vico engaged in the ongoing debate about the rights and redress granted by the ius gentium to its subjects. While Vico said less about the actionable obligations of nations than he had about those of associations, he said more about the ethical means of redress among the contracting nations of human society than he had about those available to partners. Clearly, war figured as that ethical means for Vico, provided, of course, that it had "just" cause and exercised "just" tactics.

Consideration of the justice of war in tandem with the natural rights of nations was not new to the tradition of the ius gentium, however. Among the ancients, Cicero had treated the causes and norms of just war in his same treatise on moral duties,[100] and among the moderns Francisco De Vitoria and Hugo Grotius famously had elaborated on the same in the context of developing a (modern) theory of the ius gentium as it concerned the rights of exploration.[101] To this tradition, however, Vico brought a keen interest in equity that would inform his own investigation of and elaboration on the ethical means of force well into the future.

VI. *Oratio VI* and *De ratione:* Pedagogy and Politics for the Austrian Regime

With the Austrian defeat of the Franco-Spanish alliance at Turin (1706) and the subsequent march on and occupation of the Kingdom by the imperial forces of General Daun (summer 1707), the Kingdom of Naples passed from the orbit of the Spanish into that of the Austrian Habsburg Empire, which would rule the Kingdom until 1734. Consequently, the final orations, delivered in 1707 and 1708, respectively, were pronounced before an audience that would have included representatives of the Hapsburg Empire enlisted for the governance of Austria's new Italian province. Indeed, the last oration was dedicated to the emperor and delivered in the presence of the viceroy of the Kingdom, the (anti-French) Cardinal Grimani, members of his retinue, and many royal ministers at what must have been the most solemn of convocations.[102] In the wake of this ceremony, Vico lengthened that oration and published it at his own cost as a small volume with the printer Felice Mosca, with whom he henceforth enjoyed a lifelong working relationship.[103] The published oration bore the title *De nostri temporis studiorum ratione,* known as *De ratione,* and brought him fame as a literatus and spokesperson for the judicious pursuit of modern learning among both scholars on the Italian peninsula and in northern Europe.[104] Beyond the fame they brought Vico, these final orations also brought his reflections on cultivation, cosmopolitanism, and natural law to a neat close by identifying the significance of learning for the association of humanity and that of jurisprudence for the effective governance of the same.

While the first orations had enumerated the personal outcomes of cultivation, these final two elaborated a pedagogical theory that purposefully proposed wherein that process of cultivation might consist. In other words, it made an issue of both the content and, more important, method of instruction imparted to contemporary youths. To that end, Vico specifically compared the sciences and scientific methods of ancient and modern times, and offered a series of criticisms and recommendations geared to the needs and ends of his contemporary world. As Vico formulated his theme in *De ratione*: "Which study method is finer and better, ours or the ancients'?"[105] As we shall see, the answer to that question for Vico lay in an assessment of the sciences that ultimately evaluated them in terms of their appropriateness for their subject and usefulness to society, bringing the criteria of Renaissance humanism to bear on his evaluation of modern learning.

Before engaging pedagogical theory and practice, Vico first addressed the importance of his final topic, which he attributed to the fallen state of humankind and its consequent need of edification. In contrast to the secular anthropology of his prior orations, these two specifically located the exigency for cultivation in the human condition produced by original sin, identifying in the biblical Fall of Man both the source of the problem that his recommendations were intended to remedy and, no less, the very reason for the empirical study of humans.[106] Although marked by differences in emphasis, taken together, Vico's last orations offered a critique of and program for modern education that was intentionally tailored to the ends of postlapsarian humans conjoined by their needs in society.[107] Consequently, they provided an evaluation of contemporary scientific method and a proposal for curriculum reform that was designed above all else to form out of fallen humanity virtuous men capable of wise rule and the sustenance of fellowship, or "human society," as he put it. On the eve of the Enlightenment in the Kingdom, this position was, needless to say, cautiously respectful of theological dogma,[108] if not, by the same token, purposively critical of the anthropological models underlying pedagogical reform in the Protestant lands.[109] Yet that same respect for dogma that Vico displayed did not exclude a vision for the formation of the individual that took its definition of virtue from the ancients and moderns rather than the pietistic literature of the Church.[110] Indeed, it cannot be overstated the extent to which Vico purposefully employed theological dogma to modern ends here: within the arch of his

own argument, he invoked dogma to foreground and lend legitimacy to a science of human nature and a corresponding theory of pedagogy that assumed
the efficacy of human free will and, in like manner, of human agency. Similarly, his bow to theological orthodoxy conspicuously did not carry over into
his curricular proposal, which included theology but also subordinated it in
importance to jurisprudence. What is more, jurisprudence itself represented
the culmination of the process of learning as well as a "moral theology" per
se, by which Vico meant a secular-oriented Christian ethics that administered
the polity with righteousness.[111] In other words, in Vico's curricular model
jurisprudence assumed the role of the so-called queen of the sciences, subordinating theology, however orthodox, to the ends of civil science.

The novelty of Vico's curriculum lay in its pedagogical premise that the
course of study ought to conform to the intrinsic nature of the human
mind rather than the extrinsic relationship among the extant disciplines of
knowledge.[112] This premise controverted the pedagogical models of both
tradition and modernity available to contemporaries in the Catholic lands.
At that time in the Kingdom and, more generally, in the Habsburg territories,
the *Ratio studiorum* of the Jesuit order remained the dominant curriculum
and mode of instruction, whose rigid program and techniques not only enforced intellectual mastery of grammar, philosophy, and theology but also
encouraged a strict emulation of authority.[113] Alternatively, the contending
pedagogical model in the Catholic lands was that of the Jansenists, whose
influential *Logique de Port-Royal* had instantiated the application of Cartesian
method to the disciplines of the humanities.[114] Despite the great repute and
broad dissemination of these models, by 1700 both had begun to fall into disfavor: the Jesuits, for their relentless dogmatism, both theological and methodological, and the Port-Royal, for their unorthodox cultivation of grace
and the universality of their application of Cartesian method to the sciences.
Thus, Vico contributed in a novel way to what was a preexisting critique of
Catholic pedagogy by insisting that an effective course of study was one that
befitted the nature of the mind itself.

For his model of the human mind, Vico seems to have drawn on the precepts of Aristotelian psychology, which had asserted that the mind possessed
a set of distinct powers, or cognitive faculties, that shaped its perceptions
into knowledge. To this Aristotelian doctrine, Vico significantly added the
dimension of temporality, however, conjecturing that the distinct faculties of
the mind held sway in what were distinct periods of the individual's life.[115]
For Vico, the most profitable curriculum, hence, modeled its course of study
on the course of the mind, instructing the student in the kinds of sciences
that were appropriate to his particular stage of mental development. In other

words, the ideal curriculum was predicated on an empirical understanding of the human mind, which envisioned it as subject to a sort of developmentalism that predisposed the human mental world to a slow but gradual progression from a state of simplicity to one of reason.

The originality and force of Vico's pedagogical theory of developmentalism derived both from the nature of its critique of the scientific revolution and from the precociousness with which it embraced a new form of empiricism. While Vico believed that the scientific revolution had enriched the field of human knowledge, Vico also blamed its very methods and practices for having dangerously limited the contemporary's experience of his world, if not deadened his faculties and distracted him from those sources of knowledge about human existence—such as, poetry, history, and the *ars topica*[116]— that could best impart to him the skills needed for the exercise of prudence. Most notably, Vico scathingly criticized "modern philosophical critique,"[117] or what was Cartesian method, citing its universal application of geometry as harmful to the "common sense" (*sensus communis*), which he viewed as the ultimate foundation of all knowledge.[118] For similar reasons, he censored the preeminence of the exact sciences and, in particular, physics, denouncing its findings as mere probabilisms masking as truths.[119] In sum, Vico noted, the greatest defect of modern learning was the priority given to the natural sciences over ethics, generally understood, and, more grievously, the science of politics, whose neglect hindered the ability of the Kingdom's youth to participate in the life of the community.[120] If Vico lambasted the culture of the scientific revolution, then he also formulated a notion of developmentalism that shifted the very terms of its debate about the relationship of humans to knowledge of the natural world.

Although Vico began *De ratione* with a reverent citation of the *De dignitate et de augmentis scientiarum* by Francis Bacon (1561–1626), he summarily dismissed Bacon's famous agenda for the advancement of knowledge, which had advocated an exhaustive "survey of learning" both humanistic and natural and a "building up of philosophy . . . by the Inductive,"[121] as vainglorious and sullied by futile proposals that were vexing to the nature of things and comparable to the prospect of paving the sea with stones.[122] Indeed, Vico's own empiricism was directed at the internal mind. Like his older contemporary Locke, Vico envisioned the mind as a mediator of experience and education as a moral affair, which, Vico added, ought to prioritize the knowledge of the humanities. As his notion of developmentalism made plain, Vico deplored the exact scientific foci and methods of contemporary education because he believed they conflated the means of knowledge with its ends, which, he exclaimed, were inseparable from the wisdom of experience.

Not surprisingly, in Vico's curriculum, jurisprudence represented both the highest form of learning and ultimate discipline in the course of study. Consequently, the single longest section of *De ratione* was dedicated to the study and practice of law. The ultimate point of this section was to pass judgment on the contemporary legal practices of the Kingdom, which Vico both scorned and lauded in turn. However, his discussion of present practices was foregrounded by a brief history of past ones that recounted the emergence of the corpus and institutions of Roman law. Needless to say, as was typical of Vico, this history of the Roman past was argumentative: in it, he couched an interpretation of the ends of law that spoke to both the origins and appropriate function of the ius gentium, past and present, presenting a first set of ideas on the topic that would figure so centrally in his later legal works.

Simply put, the lesson that Vico drew from the history of Rome was that the emergence of the ius gentium, or what he called praetorian law, had marked the demise of both civil law and Roman jurisprudence. As he presented it, the golden age of Roman law had transpired during the Republic, when the Law of the Twelve Tables was the civil law and the rendering of justice strictly conformed to its letter. For Vico, the rigorous enforcement of the law had borne great advantages for the Republic: "That body politic is most fortunate, indeed, where the rigorous observance of the law binds citizens together like the worship of an unknown god."[123] With the advent of the Principate and the developments of the Empire, however, the nature of jurisprudence slowly was transformed, according to Vico, from a formalistic "science of the written law" (*scientia iusti*) to an art, or technique, "by equity" (*aequitate*), which subordinated the literal provisions of the law to an interpretation of their "spirit" (*mens*).[124] For Vico, this was because of the new role and authority granted the praetors and praetorian law by the emperors, who ostensibly allowed those magistrates to mitigate the severity of the law in order to win the political favor of the masses.[125] Regardless of the historical value of this short account, the point of Vico's narrative was a political one: that the science of jurisprudence had evolved from being an instrument of justice to being a tool of constitutional change and, in so doing, had reneged on its function to serve the common good. Contrary to the history of the institution as we know it, Vico dated the codification of praetorian law to the Empire in order to associate it with the decline of republican political culture. What is more, praetorian law not only marked the decline of jurisprudence but also contributed to an assault on the public welfare according to Vico, because it effected the separation of private law from public law. Moreover, in the name of equity, praetorian law permitted the introduction of rulings favorable to private interest, or what he called "natural equity" (*aequitas naturalis*).[126] In sum, praetorian law had played a prominent role in the decline and fall of the *urbs orbis*.[127]

The importance of this history evidently lay in its heuristic value for the present. In the first place, the rigorous jurisprudence of the Republic plainly offered an instructive contrast to that of contemporary Naples, which Vico denounced as an "art of the equitable" (*ars aequi*). Second, the very short-comings of the ancient art of the Empire served to underscore those of its modern equivalent in Vico's own day. Yet, there were important differences between the equity-oriented jurisprudence of the Empire and that of con-temporary Naples, which, Vico lamented, had wreaked even more damage on the system of law than had its ancient predecessor. While contemporary jurists had betrayed the science of formal justice for the art of the equitable as had the praetors of the Empire, in contradistinction to the latter they did not employ fictions to produce equitable outcomes in conformance with the laws but rather interpreted the laws according to their "spirit" (*ex mente*) so as to accommodate the law to the facts, shamelessly producing a multitude of rulings and precedents that resembled "privileges" (*privilegia*).[128] Further-more, the interpretation of the law according to its spirit put at greatest risk precisely that which the science of law was intended to effect and protect, namely, what Vico called the *aequitas civilis*—that is, a type of equity that made the "common good" its primary beneficiary.[129] With his criticism of contemporary jurisprudence, in other words, Vico both reasserted the cen-trality of the public welfare to the task of the law and, therewith, affirmed the role of the courts in the good governance of the polity. As he exclaimed: "What is justice? It is the constant care for the common good. In what does the science of law consist? In the knowledge of the best government. What is law? It is an art of watching over the public interest."[130] Much like his ancient and Renaissance predecessors, then, Vico viewed jurisprudence as a *scientia civilis,* or civil science, whose primary end was to create and maintain the political community and advance the common good of its citizenry.[131] And it was precisely a jurisprudential program for this political directive that Vico would endorse with the best of his oratorical skill at the close of his discussion of law.

Despite his acerbic criticism of contemporary jurisprudence, the repub-lican overtones of Vico's legal idiom had what were concrete contemporary references, which he revealed like a deus ex machina at the end of his sec-tion on law. For there was a good example of the practice of jurisprudence in the Kingdom according to Vico, namely, the Court of the Sacro Regio Consiglio in Naples. In the early modern period, the Sacro Consiglio had functioned as the supreme court of the Kingdom. Specifically, it had been reformed by the Aragonese to render justice on behalf of the king; consequently, it adjudicated disputes in the name of the sovereign, and its sentences were equivalent to the will of the prince and, when "promulgated" twice, royal decrees.[132] Indeed, the published *Decisiones* of the Sacro Consiglio constituted another normative source for the law, both in the Kingdom and abroad.[133] More than exemplary, a number of things about this court made it truly exceptional, however, and its exceptions to the rules were what Vico found valuable in it.

In the first place, the procedure of the Sacro Consiglio was not limited to the rules of Roman civil law, but those stipulated at the discretion of the Court.[134] Furthermore, its investigation was guided by the general principle of ascertaining the truth solely on the basis of an analysis of the facts, or, as the motto of the Court ran, *de plano, sola facti veritate inspecta,* a hardheaded sort of empiricism that gave priority to sentences that provided what were "just" rather than "juridical" solutions.[135] More important, the hallmark of the Court's jurisprudence was its prerogative to decide *praeter,* or even *contra, legem*—that is, beyond or against the letter of the law—which in the decisional literature of the Court was upheld as an instrument for its adjudication by the "common sense."[136] Finally, the adjudication by the "common sense" itself was associated with the rendering of justice in accordance with the principle of equity, which since the sixteenth century had virtually been the vocation of the Court.[137] For Vico and his contemporaries, then, the Court was exemplary for its enforcement of the principles of the ius gentium, or what were understood to be those intrinsically rational norms derived from mercantile practices and common to diverse peoples; the Court was viewed, in sum, as a living institutional source of natural law.

The jurisprudential program that Vico identified for the governance of the political community and advancement of its common good, in other words, was that of the Sacro Regio Consiglio. Indeed, it was precisely the Court's principled prerogative to rule beyond, or even against, the letter of the law that Vico offered to his public both as a model of jurisprudence and as a potential fulcrum of change and prosperity for the Kingdom. In general, and with the most hortatory language, Vico advised the university and its monarch of the great benefits to be reaped for the Kingdom from the interpretation of Roman law "according to civil doctrine."[138] And, in particular, Vico extolled the decisions of the Sacro Consiglio taken "against [the letter of] Roman law" or, as he explicitly cited the formula of the Court, *"ex certis causis,"* which, he further affirmed, had given precedence to civil equity over private interests.[139]

What was more, and in conclusion, Vico recommended that this juridical prerogative be extended to all the royal courts of the Kingdom, a reform, he emphatically repeated, that would prove immensely beneficial to the welfare of the polity.[140] In other words, with his retreat from the history of jurisprudence into the practices of his present day Vico dramatically endorsed the technical provision of the judiciary for a commonsensical interpretation of the law, wherewith, he strongly suggested, the judiciary should favor and promote the welfare of the public over that of private individuals. Furthermore, by singling out the institution of the Sacro Consiglio for praise, it is fair to say that Vico advocated what was more than technical reform and augured what was more than mere prosperity for the Naples of his day. For however idealized Vico's presentation of the Sacro Consiglio may have been, implicit to his idealization of that particular court was perforce an endorsement of the outcomes that would result from its (more) regular employment of its acclaimed prerogatives. As the Sacro Consiglio functioned as a court of last instance for not only civil disputes among the Kingdom's nobility but also the appeals of their vassals,[141] to adjudicate *ex causis* in these matters importantly meant to decide above, it not against, the letter of the *jus regni*—that is, that bundle of Roman, feudal, customary, royal, and statutory laws applicable to the Kingdom—which, needless to say, privileged the Kingdom's baronage and, no less, the capital's civic patriciate. In other words, this prerogative provided the Court with an instrument for discretionary ruling, which, Vico evidently hoped, would be used in favor of the greater welfare of the Kingdom's subjects, regardless of their status and legal personae.

Whether or not the historical praxis of the Court itself warranted such commendation, it was reasonable for Vico to expect that his aspirations for the Sacro Consiglio were shared by its members and, more generally, by contemporary jurists allied with the Kingdom's new rulers, the Austrian Habsburgs.[142] In the first place, the Sacro Consiglio did have a history of investigation into baronial abuses, however circumstantial.[143] Second, and more significantly, the very change in the personnel of the Sacro Consiglio effected by the Austrians in 1707 had boded well for a state-centered approach to jurisprudence, as among the new appointees to the Court numbered Gaetano Argento, the rising star of Neapolitan jurisprudence and jurisdictionalism, who was then the leading lawyer in the city of Naples.[144] Third, that the newly reconstituted Sacro Consiglio seemed poised to assume a more state-centered approach to jurisprudence by the time of *De ratione* is additionally suggested by the *consulte* (memoranda and opinions) of the Court from that year, which document both the political directives the Sacro Consiglio had received from Vienna as well as the assignment of its new members to, and their opinions of, cases between barons and the sovereign as well as between barons and civic communities, whose legal rights had been curtailed, if not transgressed, by baronial claims.[145] Finally, the *sentenze* (sentences) of the Court from this period document that the reformed Sacro Consiglio did exercise its prerogative to rule *ex causis,* although only further study could settle whether or not the use of this prerogative yielded equitable solutions that arguably promoted the public welfare in the eyes of contemporaries.[146] Be that as it may, in light of the old competency and new constituency of the Court, Vico's call to decide cases *ex causis* was indubitably an exhortation to the new members of the Sacro Consiglio to use all the means at their disposal to administer change that favored the welfare of the public over that of the privileged elite of the Kingdom.

However rhetorical, in light of the historical nexus of the Court, in sum, Vico's call was a plea to the judiciary to bring the criteria of the common sense and of the common good to bear upon the (selection and) judgment of cases concerning baronial practices. Put somewhat differently, it implicitly advocated a judicial campaign against those privileges, oftentimes bound by feudal custom, hampering the prosperity of the Kingdom, and it squarely placed both its full political trust and oratorical weight behind a supreme sort of *imperium* for the judiciary. Indeed, Vico literally recommended that the praxis of the Sacro Consiglio be made customary for the Kingdom, arguing for the effective transformation of the judiciary into a vehicle of discretionary reform.[147] Finally, Vico's recommendation also represented a practical procedural remedy for the adjudication of disputes among individuals bearing distinct juridical personae, as was most emphatically the case for the inhabitants of the metropolis of the Kingdom of Naples, where the multiplicity of provincial legal identities was compounded by the legal privileges due the citizens of the capital. In other words, it represented a concrete proposal for the implementation of the rule of law, that is, a system wherein justice was rendered to all in accordance with principle rather than according to the adventitious identity of provenance and order.

That Vico would single out the Sacro Regio Consiglio as exemplary of natural law jurisprudence was both obvious and curious, however. For many of the leading battles waged in the name of natural law, or the ius gentium, on behalf of the state had been fought in the Regia Camera della Sommaria, which was the premier fiscal organ of the Kingdom. Although a *consigliere* of the Sacro Consiglio, for example, it was in his capacity as *avvocato fiscale* of the Sommaria that Francesco D'Andrea most famously invoked the principles of the ius gentium to counter what he deemed to be baronial abuses damaging to the welfare of the state.[148] Indeed, it was in the Sommaria that D'Andrea had offered his famous opinion on baronial tolls, which he viewed as contrary to both the ius gentium and the *salus reipublicae,* that is, the welfare of the state.[149] Beyond its prerogatives, then, what probably made the Sacro Regio Consiglio such an appropriate and potent institution of reform in the eyes of Vico was the royal authority with which it invested its judiciary and its symbolism as the constitution of the Kingdom. For the very identity of the Sacro Regio Consiglio rested upon the fiction of the "arms and body of the sovereign," which itself invested its judges with what was absolute, and indeed sacred, imperium. Furthermore, the status of its decisions as decrees further associated the Court with a political constitution that could respond to and promulgate change. In light of these salient features, it will not be surprising that Vico's later reconstructions of the history of Roman law would so pivot on the institution of magisterial imperium and the efficacy of magisterial rule as a positive force of change within the Roman polity. For *De ratione* was indeed a call to entrust greater discretionary, and thus political, power to the judiciary, as the arbiters and executioners of the sovereign's will.

VII. Conclusion

For all of its neoclassicism, then, the idiom of cosmopolitanism Vico employed in his later orations had as its points of reference the political battles fought in the Kingdom during the twilight of its Spanish rule. To speak about the welfare of "human society," as Vico did in *De ratione,* was to address the rights of political beings qua humans—rather than qua provenance and corporate order—and to contradict the systemic practice of permitting the powerful to purchase a justice favorable to their private interests. In similar fashion, for Vico to endorse "natural law" was to support both the jurisprudential instruments and efforts of a judiciary predisposed to forms of justice that honored the public welfare over traditional corporate privileges. And, finally, to speak about knowledge itself as the product of an empirically grounded "common sense" was to honor the principles of the jurisprudence of the Kingdom's highest court and, like that same jurisprudence, to value experience over method and equity over the formalities of political civilization. Put somewhat differently, the idiom of cosmopolitanism was the vehicle with which Vico reintroduced the political virtues and scientific values of republicanism to a world where princes ruled and citizens were not exemplary but just one type of consummately privileged political being. In other words, "human society" and "natural law" were the neoclassical code words with which Vico advocated the supercession of the polity, whose constituents bore incompatible, if not mutually unintelligible, legal personae and, consequently, rights.

Once it was published, Vico lost little time in circulating and promoting *De ratione,* which garnered him repute both in Naples and abroad. In his *Autobiografia,* Vico speaks of how it won for him both the praise and friendship of Domenico D'Aulisio, the most learned professor of Civil Law at the University of Naples, who on completing his reading of the work apparently honored Vico with an invitation to sit beside him during a public evaluation of candidates for a university position.[150] However, the cappellano maggiore and rector of the university, Vincenzo Vidania, rather, took respectful exception to *De ratione* by providing ample evidence to the contrary of Vico's claim that Roman jurisprudence had been the purview of the patriciate throughout the time of the Republic. This scholarly reproof seems not to have affected Vico's relationship with Vidania, to whom he respectfully replied in turn both personally and, later, publicly in his legal works.[151]

Vico must have arranged for copies of his book to be transported and distributed among literati in France, as *De ratione* was reviewed by the *Journal des sçavans* in 1709 and the prestigious *Mémoires de Trévoux* in 1712.[152] More important for Vico's reputation in Italy, *De ratione* was acclaimed by the Neapolitan prelate Biagio Garofalo in the first volume of what would become the preeminent contemporary literary journal in Italy, the *Giornale de' letterati d'Italia,* which had been founded in Venice by the luminary librettist Apostolo Zeno, the antiquarian Scipione Maffei, and the learned medical doctor Antonio Vallisneri.[153] Over the course of its existence, the same journal also would announce to its public and review many of Vico's subsequent works, helping to build for Vico what was a national reputation as a scholar, despite his lament of isolation in the *Autobiografia.* In fact, it would host the lively debate concerning Vico's first metaphysical work, the *De antiquissima Italorum sapientia ex linguae Latinae originibus eruenda* (1710),[154] between the reviewer, apparently the Cartesian Bernardo Trevisano, and Vico himself.[155] If his litigiousness earned him some notoriety with the *Giornale,* his Venetian interlocutors nonetheless publicized Vico's next major work, the *De rebus gestis Antonii Caraphaei libri quatuor,* which had launched Vico on his study and critical edition of *De iure belli ac pacis,* the magnum opus of Hugo Grotius, the progenitor of modern international law.[156] And it was to the work of both Pufendorf and now Grotius that Vico shortly would respond in kind with his own three-volume work on universal law.

CHAPTER 3

Vico's Social Theory

The Conundrum of the Roman Metropolis and the Struggle of Humanity for Natural Rights

I. Introduction: From Rhetoric to Law

With hindsight, Vico would reflect that the argument of *De ratione* (1709) represented a first draft of those ideas he would develop only a decade later in his legal works, the three-volume treatise commonly known as the *Diritto universale* (1720–22), which constituted a most protean disquisition on the origins and development of society and law.[1] In the interim, beyond the polemic concerning *De antiquissima,* Vico's intellectual life was less spectacularly marked by his duties as a pedagogue and by his acceptance and execution of literary assignments that won him more remuneration than glory. Therein, Vico undertook the first formal draft of his course in Rhetoric for the university, the *Institutiones oratoriae* (1710–11),[2] and excelled in his role as a teacher, his grand persona not only filling the lecture hall but also inviting the imitation of his most devoted students.[3] During this period, Vico also undertook numerous commissions, such as composing poetry for festive occasions,[4] funerary eulogies, and inscriptions,[5] as well as his famous biography of preeminent Neapolitan patrician and warrior Antonio Carafa, *De rebus gestis Antonii Caraphaei* (published in March of 1716), for which he received the handsome fee of one thousand ducats from its patron, his pupil Adriano Carafa.[6]

The latter work reportedly engaged Vico for some two years circa 1713–15, during which time he worked through the mass of documentary material contained in the private archive of Field Marshal Carafa, which was inherited by his nephew Adriano, while he was "wracked by the cruelest hypochondriac cramps in the left arm."[7] In addition to the pangs of his hypochondria, Vico apparently prepared *De rebus gestis* amid the felicitous "turmoil and distraction of the household and often in conversation with friends."[8] Indeed, Vico's endeavors from this period famously were punctuated by happy domestic events, such as, the birth in 1715 of his son Gennaro, whom Vico would choose as his successor to the Chair of Rhetoric, and the marriage in 1717 of his much loved and first-born daughter, Luisa, whose wedding Vico paid for with the proceeds from the Carafa commission and whom he already had favored with an education that made her a centerpiece of salon life in contemporary Naples.[9] The final product of his pained endeavors was a splendid publication in a one-volume quarto, replete with engravings, whose material specs Vico proudly would vaunt in the *Autobiografia*.[10] As he had with *De ratione,* so too with *De rebus gestis* did Vico further travail to distribute copies of his work, some of which were sold and others offered as gifts to those powerful culture brokers whose favor and patronage Vico continued to pursue. As research has uncovered, Vico sent a dedicated and annotated copy of *De rebus gestis* to Apostolo Zeno, the Venetian librettist and editor of the *Giornale de' letterati d'Italia,* who therein politely announced its publication.[11] And, as my own archival work has ascertained, *De rebus gestis* also circulated in Vienna, where among other libraries it could be found and read in the extensive collection of European literature amassed by Alessandro Riccardi, the illustrious Neapolitan jurist and leading figure of the Italian community in the Austrian capital, who there served the Council of Spain (from 1714) and, no less, as prefect of the Royal Library (from 1723).[12]

A portrait of the career of Carafa, the *De rebus gestis* flatteringly chronicled the duty of the Neapolitan count in the forces of the Austrian Habsburgs, whom he served with distinction in the occupation, recovery, and reintegration of Hungary from the Ottoman Empire. As Vico recounted, Carafa had enlisted in the army of Leopold I in 1665 and served first in Alsace and then in Royal Hungary, which he defended both from the incursions of Hungarian partisans—who conducted guerilla raids against the Austrian occupying forces—and from the advances of the Turks lead by the inimitable and ruthless Kara Mustafa, whom he additionally helped to repel from the Hungarian lands in that series of reconquests waged by the Austrians and their allies against the Ottomans beginning in 1683.

Although it was an account of the military deeds of Carafa, the *De rebus gestis* also assessed those same deeds according to the norms of the law of nations as they had been formulated by Hugo Grotius in *De iure belli ac pacis,* or *The Rights of War and Peace.* Indeed, the *De rebus gestis* literally dramatized the law of nations in the minds and actions of the historical personae it immortalized, further making the biography an excursus on the application of natural law to international conflicts. For Grotius, the law of nations was analogous to the rights of individuals, who, he imagined, self-evidently shared the same set of claims on one another regardless of their political citizenship. In *De iure belli,* Grotius famously had hypothesized that the natural sociability of humankind had entitled its members to natural rights, which he defined as moral faculties that granted individuals powers over themselves and their consensual agreements, and enjoined them to respect those of their fellows.[13] As its title implies, the vast majority of the *De iure belli* was more specifically devoted to the moral faculties and injunctions of the international parties to warfare, however. The overriding concern of Grotius, indeed, had been to show that there was a body of natural law that pertained to the conflicts of distinct nations, or what he called a *ius gentium et naturae* (a law of nations and of nature). Although the written laws of any individual nation could not be made to obligate distinct warring parties, Grotius claimed that there were binding ones (*iura*) that "Nature dictates, or the Consent of Nations (*consensus gentium*) has instituted"; as he put it: "There is some Right common to all Nations (*inter populos ius commune*), which takes Place both in the Preparations and in the Course of War."[14] Again, this claim rested on Grotius's keen sense of the analogy between the rights of nations and those of individuals. Likening the state to the moral individual in nature, Grotius had argued that the political entity too possessed natural powers and too was limited by moral injunctions, which in their complexity he called the law of nations, or ius gentium, thereby giving novel diplomatic content to that category of ancient Roman law.[15] The conceptual "building blocks" of the law of nations were the right of self-defense and the injunction, or law, of inoffensiveness, to whose precepts Grotius gave the most ample detail in his three-volume treatise.[16] Following from the right of self-defense were the many "just" causes of war and the natural rights of nations, which Grotius enumerated and discussed in books 1 and 2; and in giving meaning to the law of inoffensiveness, Grotius both specified and qualified those same rights with an exposition of the obligations and limitations on those party to warfare in book 3. For example, among the rights of the warring nations identified by Grotius numbered the right to kill enemies and to take prisoners, the right of plunder, the right of embassage, the right of postliminy, and the right of burial; and among the limitations imposed on the same, according to Grotius, were those following from the moral injunctions of moderation and probity, especially as those injunctions concerned the obligations contracted among the warring parties.

Making the law of nations the standard for righteous conduct in *De rebus gestis,* Vico thus paid especial tribute to Carafa by extolling him not only as a most capable warrior but also as a personification and arbiter of the precepts of international law. Instilling the fictional conscience of his protagonist with the dictates of *De iure belli,* Vico artfully couched the stratagems and ratiocinations of the Neapolitan patrician, whether manifestly just or utterly iniquitous, in the rhetoric of international rights and obligations.[17] With ingenious craft, Vico literally made Carafa a spokesperson for the natural injunctions of moderation and probity and had him uphold the rights of his adversaries and the obligations of diplomacy, however guilefully. By the same token, Vico both honored and vilified the opponents of the Habsburgs with regard to their respect for international law. Most notably, Vico presented the contention over the conditions of a peace between Habsburgs and Ottomans as stemming from their irreconcilable differences regarding the legitimacy of the law of nations. At the climax of the peace negotiations between the two empires, Vico heroized Carafa as a defender of the universal law of nations while excoriating the Ottoman ambassador as a realist and spokesperson for the parochial laws of his own people. In a theatrical dialogue that recalled Thucydides' canonical personification of might versus right,[18] the Ottoman representative was made to declare that an honorable peace could only be settled by force, as the religious customs of his people forbade the voluntary surrender of any territory to Christian opponents, while Carafa was permitted the high-minded reply that the dispute at hand was not between "the citizens of a single state" but two empires that "recognize a single law equal for all peoples."[19] According to Carafa, in other words, the laws of the Muslim God did not pertain to the governance of humanity. True to the principles of the law of nations, Carafa denounced the pretense that a customary belief and practice of the Ottomans should be intelligible and binding for all peoples. And under the guise of the habitual Christian criticism of the Ottomans, Vico upheld the more daring premise that the reason of all states was subordinate to a singular body of norms dictated by what Grotius had called the consensus of nations.

Thus, the composition of the *De rebus gestis* had marked more than the fulfillment of a handsome commission for Vico. For the composition of the Carafa biography evidently had occasioned Vico's most thorough mastery and assimilation of the principles of *De iure belli.* What is more, the literal personification of those principles in the mind and deeds of the biography's most illustrious protagonist indubitably established Vico as a partisan of the law of nations. As Carafa's righteous rejoinder to the Ottoman ambassador made manifest, Vico too held that there were norms common to all peoples and that those same norms constituted a body of unwritten laws to which all nations were obligated and subject.

With that same rejoinder, furthermore, Vico also followed Grotius into the more perilous waters surrounding the relationship between the norms of religion and those of nations. For Vico's dialogue about the possibility of a peace among religiously distinct camps implicitly broached the topic of the demarcation of natural law from theology and, no less, human from divine agency, a topic that Grotius himself notoriously had treated in the Prolegomena to the *De iure belli*. Indeed, Carafa's criticism of Ottoman parochialism recalled Grotius's infamous assertion that the obligations of the law of nations were independent of the very existence of God and that divine volition and religious norms were, by implication, exiguous to the standards of conduct for the behavior of humans and, no less, moral entities.[20] In other words, Vico's dialogue upheld the lesson, if not the letter, of Grotius's most notorious assertion of the moral independence of human societies from the governance of God and the dictates of religion. Clearly, then, in the interim between *De ratione* (1709) and the *Diritto universale* (1720–22), Vico not only mastered but also appropriated the tenets and credo of *De iure belli*, which would remain central to his own inquiries for the remainder of his long career.

Whereas Vico had incorporated the tenets of *De iure belli* into *De rebus gestis* with some subtlety, retrospectively, he would both flaunt his knowledge of Grotius and express his reservations about the same. In the *Autobiografia,* Vico specifically would claim that he had in this same period also undertaken the notes for an edition of *De iure belli* based on that of Gronovius, but had been compelled by his conscience to abandon them after completing only half the task. While it is hard to assess the veracity of this claim, as there is no evidence for Vico's work on an edition of *De iure belli* beyond a preface,[21] it is probably fair to say that this claim first and foremost was calculated to justify Vico's strong sense of the injustice of his contemporary lot.[22] First, this remark boasted that Vico had long had demonstrable expertise on the law of nations, expertise that, Vico plausibly believed, should have certified him in the eyes of his contemporaries for a more honorable form of public service than the one he held.[23] Second, the reason that Vico provided for his abandonment of an edition of *De iure belli* was no less defensive, as it conversely bolstered his credentials as an orthodox Catholic at a time when he evidently believed that those credentials were under siege. At that time, the public condemnation of Grotius primarily honored what was Catholic dogma. However widely circulated and read *De iure belli* may have been in Naples and, more generally, in the Catholic world,[24] in the 1720s Grotius still figured prominently on the Index of Prohibited Books, which specifically had proscribed not only his religious works but also his magnum opus on the law of nations with a decree in 1627 that was periodically renewed through 1900.[25] Thus, it is indubitable that a Neapolitan edition of *De iure belli*—and especially the notes on that passage in the Prolegomena where the Dutchman notoriously had hypothesized that the laws of nature would hold even in the absence of God—would have elicited a most careful reading and prohibition by the Congregation of the Index, if not the ire and investigation of the Holy Office of the Inquisition itself.[26] Thus, it is not surprising that Vico gave the convictions of his faith as the reason for his change of heart in the *Autobiografia* (1725);[27] as he claimed therein: "He abandoned the task, reflecting that it was not fitting for a man of Catholic faith to adorn with notes the work of a heretical author."[28] Rather, it is curious—and as such, telling of the intellectual commitments and editorial practices of contemporary Neapolitans—that Vico would have boasted in the first place of his work on what, perforce, would have been a clandestine edition of Grotius.[29] However inscrutable his actual commitments, then, it is most probable that Vico's retrospective remarks about his convictions were a piece with his contemporary efforts to earn the reputation of being a Catholic author, who in contradistinction to his contemporaries was committed to addressing the questions of his day within the limits of Church dogma. And to that end, Vico evidently misrepresented a number of the episodes in his own intellectual biography so as to make a case for the staunch orthodoxy of his beliefs.

As regards this incidence, for instance, in the *Autobiografia* Vico congratulated himself on his pious abandonment of *De iure belli* only after first misconstruing the ecclesiastical reception of the Carafa biography, which, he suggested, had earned him the acclaim of high-ranking figures within the papal court: Gianvincenzo Gravina (1664–1718), the renowned Arcadian poet and professor of Canonical Law at the Pontifical Academy; and Pope Clement XI (papacy: 1700–21) himself.[30] As the evidence for their alleged commendation was slim and both Clement XI and Gravina were long deceased by the time Vico publicized it in the *Autobiografia,* his claims to their support evidently was meant to constitute what was incontrovertible proof of his good standing with the Church.[31] Whatever his precise motivations for publicizing his expertise on *De iure belli* may have been, then, with hindsight Vico evidently thought that his association with Grotius had buttressed his credentials as a philosopher and could have tarnished them as a

Catholic, and that this latter fact was now a liability that he wished to avoid at all costs.

Although Vico famously cited Grotius as one of his four model authors in the *Autobiografia,* with the progress of his career he appropriated less and criticized more of Grotius's claims regarding the nature and application of the law of nations. Indeed, Grotius's idea of the law of nations provided both the normative point of reference and the central bone of contention of the *Diritto universale* (1720–22), in which Vico argued in the most nuanced of ways for the historicity of that concept. In his legal treatise and subsequent works, Vico hypothesized that the law of nations exclusively had pertained to a pre-political or civic state of war. What is more, Vico proposed that the importance of the law of nations lay in its legacy for the originary polity, or what he would call the city; in particular, Vico conjectured that the limitations of that law had shaped both the political nature of the city and the course of its history. Consequently, in the *Diritto universale* he took as his specific object of inquiry the legacy of the law of nations for the institutions of the city, that is, for the foundational contract of the city, the rights of its consenting members, and, most important, the logic of its subsequent internal disputes.

In the *Diritto universale,* the single most important political lessons Vico took from *De iure belli* were those that concerned the rights of individuals in the state of war. In particular, Vico took a keen interest in the wartime limitations placed on the natural rights of humans per the law of nations. Like so many of his predecessors and contemporaries, in his own work on the origins of law and society, Vico conjectured that cities universally had been formed to countervail the threat to human self-preservation posed by the recurrence of violence within a state of nature. However, the significance that Vico attributed to the city itself sharply distinguished his views from those of his interlocutors. Regardless of the differences among their political visions, in their respective narratives Hobbes, Locke, and Pufendorf similarly had assumed that a state of war had occasioned both the impetus for the union of nonagnatic individuals as well as that equality of duress requisite for their brokerage of a political contract by unconditional consensus.[32] In addition, they had claimed that the political contract itself had provided for the personal liberty and self-determination of its parties. In other words, these authors had viewed the political contract as an end in itself that had overcome the most fundamental injustices of warfare. Distinctively, Vico neither viewed the state of war as a temporary state of equality nor did he consider the foundational contract of the city as a supersession of its own conditions of production. Rather, as this chapter shows, the core problem of Vico's legal treatise was his conjecture that the original civic contract had failed to overcome the wartime limitations on natural rights and had failed to provide equally for the liberty and self-determination of its members. What the *Diritto universale* thematized, in other words, was the paradoxical nature of the right to the city, whose significance it therewith assessed for the history of civic society and its institutions.

According to Grotius, in wartime the natural right to personal liberty was strictly contingent on circumstance, and it could be voluntarily alienated or forcefully suspended per the law of nations. As Grotius explained, although "there is no Man by Nature Slave to another . . . it is not repugnant to natural Justice, that Men should become Slaves by a human Fact, that is, by Vertue of some Agreement, or in Consequence of some Crime" or in wartime "by the Law of Nations," which, Grotius clarified, ascribed to all prisoners of a "solemn" war the status of slaves.[33] Despite their natural rights qua humans, then, in wartime humans justly could be stripped of their freedom, either by the consensual surrender of their personal liberty in exchange for their lives or by the subjugating defeat of a just war.

Although Vico premised his own study of law and society on the contingency of freedom, he reached rather different conclusions regarding the significance of human servitude than had Grotius. Whereas Grotius had sought to identify the injunctions governing the extant institution of slavery, Vico probed the legacy of that institution in its incipience for the foundations of political civilization: specifically, he conjectured that the loss of human freedom in a pre-political state of war had been of the utmost importance for the status of individuals in the originary city. In contradistinction to his predecessors and contemporaries, Vico supposed that the foundational contract of the city had formally reproduced those accidental qualities acquired by humans in wartime. While the civic contract had provided equally for the personal security of its members, according to Vico it more significantly had preserved that loss of personal liberty, or human freedom, occasioned by the pre-civil state of war, conventionally instituting what was a political form of slavery. Thus, for Vico, it was simply impossible, if not delusional, to speak of the liberty of the city, as had so many writers about the civic polity since the early Renaissance.[34] In this sense, Vico's social theory distinctively anticipated that of Rousseau,[35] although both the historical account and political remedies of civic inequality that Vico proposed sharply differed from those of his successor. Indeed, as will become apparent, Vico authoritatively made his point about the inequities of the city by revisiting, and revising, the iconic history of Rome, in which he ostensibly found empirical evidence for that political form of slavery established by the foundational contract of the city.

Contrary to the hallowed traditions of political thought, then, Vico argued by Roman example that the originary city had been predicated on a political conundrum: that of a consensual contract among natural equals, which instituted among them an absolute inequality of rights in perpetuity. To the extent that the civic contract was held to the norms of the Roman law of contracts, this political conundrum further presented what was a legal paradox, as the obligations of the consensual contract per the Roman ius gentium imposed on its parties reciprocal rights and duties, whose content was determined above all else by the principle of equity.[36] And it was this legal paradox at the root of political civilization that Vico both explained and explored with his interpretation of the history of Rome and of Roman jurisprudence. If it were impossible to speak of the freedom of the city for Vico, then it was similarly inappropriate to speak of the political justice of consensus, whose role in the formation of the civic union evidently was subordinate to those necessities born of circumstance and made binding by instinct. For, in practice, consensus alone could not ensure the negotiation of an equitable political contract; it could not supplant the circumstantial differences in nature and, no less, power acquired by the contracting parties, whose asymmetrical positions rendered impossible the equal safeguarding of their rights. As a product of contract, the justice of the originary city thus was limited to those minimum provisions requisite for the consent of its parties, which, Vico reminded his reader, was not to be conflated with a more perfect "natural" justice. In other words, Vico assumed the provocative position that the civic community had been shaped not by the equality but by the casualties of war and that the community's contract had formalized the loss of personal freedom suffered by its wartime victims, the restitution of whose natural rights consequently became the *telos* of civic history. In the *Diritto universale,* the history of Rome thus bore evidence not only for the injustice of the civic contract but also for the struggle by the disenfranchised for human rights, a struggle whose progressive unfolding distinctly bore out the principles of equity per the Roman commercial ius gentium.

Yet, Vico's history of Rome did more than revisit the origins, contractual nature, and conflicts of that iconic city. In the *Diritto universale,* the history of Rome exemplified the history of civic justice from the inception of the polity to its maturation and demise. Beyond its particular emphasis, what was unique about this history of Rome was its instruction regarding the nature of political justice and the process by which that justice effectively was attained. With this history, Vico specifically hypothesized that justice was the outcome of an ongoing process of sociolegal reform, which was institutionalized by a succession of jurisprudential schools, whose respective tenets were appropriate to the exigencies of historical circumstance. And with that same history, Vico distinguished himself both as a historian of jurisprudence as well as an advocate of jurisprudential principles that were appropriate to the governance of his own contemporary polity.

As strictly concerned the tradition of legal thought, this neat conjecture significantly unraveled and distinguished that cluster of jurisprudential concepts that had been vying for association with the idea of a universal natural law since antiquity.[37] Traditionally, the term "natural law" (*ius naturale*) properly had been used to denote an ideal law, whose origin lay in natural reason and whose function was that of a higher universal standard. Contrariwise, the term "law of nations" (*ius gentium*) had been employed to convey a set of conventional practices presumably observed by all nations; but, with the passage of time it too was overlaid by the notion of "rationality," which likened, if not equated, it with the *ius naturale*. With his particular history of the schools and forms of civic justice, then, Vico both neatly distinguished the meaning of these terms and historicized them, by assigning the origins and pertinence of each to its own specific epoch of Roman history.

In the first place, Vico effectively differentiated the Stoic notion of natural law from the multiple meanings of the law of nations, among which he then further distinguished. As will be discussed, Vico made a pronounced distinction between the Grotian ius gentium, or law of nations, which he relegated to the conventions of pre-political states, and the Roman ius gentium, or commercial law, to which he gave the discrete content of the equity rulings of the ancient praetors and which he appointed as a model for the governance of the contemporary civic community. As the prior chapters suggested, Vico arguably had been preparing his entire career to lay out the intellectual distinctions among the various schools of natural law, making this product of patient study an unmistakably didactic contribution to the investigation of legal theory and society. At the same time, the distinctions Vico made were of a more practical significance than their recondite content suggests. In particular, Vico's history of the schools and forms of civic justice made a case for the actuality of the Roman ius gentium and, more important, its role as a corrective of positive law: it imagined a history of political civilization in which the rule of reason and equity figured not as an originary law that exclusively pertained to humans in a state of nature, as it had in Hobbes and Locke, but rather as set of jurisprudential principles that pertained to the social problems of humans in the city. As I specifically shall demonstrate, Vico's study of Rome importantly plotted a history of political civilization that was progressive and whose way stations were marked by the better provision for equity among the members of its civic community.

If Vico rewrote Roman history as a fulfillment of the jurisprudential principles of equity, he also imagined that equity would restore to the disenfranchised what he called "liberty," to which he thereby gave distinctive meaning as well. In contradistinction to his immediate predecessors and contemporaries, Vico's idea of liberty implied more than the Renaissance notion of "freedom from tyranny"[38] and the seventeenth-century vision of the personal freedom of humans in the state of nature.[39] Rather, it denoted full legal personality. By full legal personality, Vico primarily understood the positive freedom of the possession of oneself, one's labor, and one's property; for him, it meant a right that conveyed both moral and material ownership of oneself and one's activities. And it was this liberty of possession in the fullest sense of the word that history and its system of justice ideally were meant to achieve and to protect. While this notion of liberty recalled Locke's famous reasoning concerning the right to property,[40] Vico evidently had derived his from the Roman law of persons, in which full legal personality classically entailed the rights and duties of the paterfamilias: citizenship, the power of life and death over himself and his children, as well as the full rights of property.[41] By so giving to the modern idea of liberty the practical meaning of Roman legal personality, then, Vico effectively embedded into his history what was a novel account of citizenship. Vico importantly rewrote the history of Rome so that it wed the traditional *iter* of Roman citizenship to that of possession: he literally retold the history of the acquisition of citizenship as a history of the achievement of the positive rights of possession of oneself and of one's unencumbered property. Needless to say, with such a notion of citizenship Vico implicitly broached the ethical question of what constituted full participation in the civic community, to which he gave a decidedly economic gloss. Indeed, Vico's template of the activities and regulations of the community in the *Diritto universale* specifically recalled the Romanisms of Pufendorf, whose idea of *socialitas* Vico first had embraced in those *Orationes* composed after the revolt of 1701.

In sum, in this chapter I argue that Vico utterly transformed the definition of the city and the concept of civic citizenship by making the restitution of the natural rights of self-possession and of property the most fundamental purpose and hallmark of full participation in the civic community. What is more, I further show that with his history of Rome Vico proffered what was a model of citizenship for the metropolis and a school of jurisprudence for its governance. Therewith, he proposed a procedural model for the achievement of full agency in an urban community, the primary basis for whose bonds were contractual. And for that urban community quintessentially comprising diverse legal persons and challenged by the conflict of laws, he naturalized the adjudication of disputes by the principles of the ius gentium, upholding the universal promises of natural law as the distinctive rights of its members. In short, with his history of Rome Vico argued by example for the essentiality of natural law to the body politic and to the practical justice of the metropolis, whose metacivic community principally had been integrated by the artifice of contract and whose differences and commonalities reasonably were adjudicated by the norms of the community of nations, or human society, as it were.

While a number of Vico's contemporaries appreciated his original contribution to social theory, the most immediate and clamorous opinions voiced about the *Diritto universale* seem to have drawn attention to the religious themes of that text. As will be seen, the contemporary debate about the legal treatise was weighted to addressing the questions of faith that the treatise broached rather than its political content. As a consequence, Vico was forced to defend his religious views, creating a paper trail of documents that would greatly influence the questions brought to bear on the analysis of the *Diritto universale* by both contemporaries and the subsequent historiography. Indeed, in the *Autobiografia* Vico somewhat apologetically would speak about the *Diritto universale* as if it were evidence for the convictions of his faith and, in essence, a metaphysical tract that did little more than confirm the primacy of God as the source of all knowledge.

Influenced by the confident assertions of Vico's self-fashioning, in its turn the historiography has also emphasized the metaphysical aspects of the *Diritto universale,* which one contemporary critic has hailed as evidence of Vico's Catholic theodicy.[42] In this view, Vico's inquiries into law and society were an objection to the skepticism of modern political philosophers who had postulated that humans had been abandoned by God and thus were ruled by their mere instincts; and, in refutation of their skepticism, Vico presumably proposed that God had provided both the source and force of that motion, or *conatus,* animating the course of societal development, whose ends necessarily were just.[43] While this interpretation of the *Diritto universale* as a response to modern political philosophy is by no means unfounded, its physics rests on the assumption that for Vico the consequences of original sin and the Fall of humankind had necessitated the "continuous divine participation in the human realm."[44]

Yet, had this been Vico's position, then it would not have affirmed Catholic theology but rather would have contradicted Catholic theodicy since

Augustine, which had primarily laid the moral responsibility for the actions of fallen humanity with the free will. Indeed, to the extent that Vico's vision of human history was consonant with Catholic theology, it was because Tridentine theology expressly had reaffirmed the Catholic commitment to the role of free will and, consequently, of human agency in its own salvation, and not the contrary.[45] With regard to the particulars of Vico's legal treatise, furthermore, this interpretation has overstated the role of Providence in the course of human events and, no less, has obscured the function that Vico assigned to jurisprudence in the remedy of an imperfect civic world. Like Vico's self-representation, in other words, this interpretation has concealed some of the most salient contributions of the *Diritto universale* to social thought—its novel history of the city and citizen rights, its study of the judiciary, and its analysis of jurisprudence—on which this chapter shall focus. Nonetheless, by the time of the *Autobiografia* (1725), Vico did indeed have his own personal motivations for underscoring the orthodoxy and obscuring the politics of his legal writings, and it is to those circumstances that so shaped both the career of Vico and the legendary way that he retrospectively portrayed it for posterity that I shall now turn.

   In this chapter I first reconstruct the occasion, publication, and reception of the *Diritto universale*. As the reception of the *Diritto universale* was centered on the view of monotheism offered in that text, I then primarily treat the same in my reconstruction of the criticism of Vico's legal treatise by his foremost contemporary critics. The decision to primarily treat Vico's religious ideas as they were received itself rests on the fundamental conviction that in the *Diritto universale* these ideas were ancillary to Vico's social scientific project: in other words, it is my belief that they were meant to provide what was first and foremost a framework for the empirical study of humans, as opposed to a trenchant endorsement of either Catholic orthodoxy or Enlightenment beliefs per se. That the unquestionable truths of religion were meant to provide a framework for the study of humans is made apparent by the significance Vico attributed to the act of original sin and the Fall of humankind in the *Diritto universale*. Rather than necessitate the "continuous divine participation in the human realm," in Vico's narrative the Fall rendered humans autonomous subjects who, for their self-preservation, were forced to rely on their personal agency, or their exercise of what Vico called free will. In the *Diritto universale,* the Fall thus had marked the commencement of a temporal history of humanity that was animated by its striving for the restitution of a prelapsarian-like condition, wherein humans would enjoy a beatitude born not of divine grace but of the supreme justice of equity.

In light of this commencement and telos of human history, this chapter thus takes as its central subject Vico's social theory as it was articulated in his account of the foundation and development of Rome. In particular, it reconstructs his claims about the origin and nature of the metropolitan community as well as the rights to which its members were entitled and the forms of justice to which they were subject. Finally, this chapter concludes and segues to the next with a contextualization of Vico's boldest claims in the political context of contemporary Naples.

II. The Making of a Legend: The Publication and Reception of the *Diritto universale*

Both the circumstances and content of the *Diritto universale* strongly suggest that Vico ideated and wrote his three-volume legal treatise to qualify himself for the prestigious Morning Chair of Civil Law, whose incumbent had been forced into retirement in 1717 and then passed away in December of 1722, leaving the Chair officially vacant.[46] Given the prestige and handsome salary attached to this Chair, which was a "perpetual" appointment and paid its holder some six hundred ducats yearly, its opening represented what was a golden opportunity for Vico. The public announcement of the competition for the Morning Chair of Civil Law would not be made until after the death of its proprietor in January of 1723, but the multiple-year promise of a competition and the political nature of its selection evidently shaped both Vico's intellectual projects and his cultural politics in the interim. Indeed, when the announcement of the competition finally was made in the middle of January 1723 Vico promptly displayed not only his great eagerness for the position but also his readiness for its competition, by being the very first contender to formally present his credentials to the university for candidacy, which he did on the 24th of January 1723, that is, within a fortnight of the issue of its advertisement.[47] As Vico had well understood, however, his credentials were only as good as the political support that they would garner, as the selection of the finalist would be made not only by members of the university professoriate but also by the regents of the Consiglio Collaterale and the heads of the Kingdom's tribunals, all of whom had a single vote, making the appointment truly a highly political one.

Vico began canvassing for the Chair in 1719, when he delivered an inaugural address at the university that specifically presented in nuce the argument of his legal treatise before its most eminent audience.[48] Immediately following this public display, it seems that he lost no time in deferentially soliciting the response and support of the leading jurists among his public, whom he strategically would cite in the *Diritto universale* as having praised his address and emboldened him to develop it into the present work. As Vico memorialized this event in his Prologue to the first volume of his legal treatise, the *De universi iuris uno principio et fine uno* (1720), his address had been honored by the attendance of not only a number of "most learned men" but also by the presence of the single most illustrious Neapolitan jurist of the day, the regent Gaetano Argento, and by his nephew, Francesco Ventura, who under the patronage of his uncle figured as the next star of the Neapolitan judiciary. As if that were not enough evidence of their favor, Vico further boasted that on the completion of his delivery Argento publicly had lauded him for having spoken as an "orator, philosopher and jurist," and that in the more intimate sphere of the home Ventura had encouraged him to refine and expand his ideas into what became *De uno*.[49] Although Vico's account of the reception of his address most certainly erred on the side of self-promotion, it also colored and contextualized the past in such a way as to respectfully invite the patronage of Argento and Ventura. For Vico not only flattered Argento profusely but also honored Ventura by dedicating *De uno* and its companion volume to him, thus ingratiating himself with both jurists and, by the force of custom, obliging Ventura to future benefaction.

If, by his various demonstrations of deference and respect, Vico had sought to win the personal favor of Argento and Ventura, in the *Diritto universale* itself it seems that he further sought to cultivate their political allegiances by advocating for the power of the ministerial class, as he made one of his primary objects of historical investigation the political merits of an independent judiciary. Given the historical circumstances, this must have seemed like the surest of ways to win the appointment to the Morning Chair of Civil Law. At the time Vico embarked on canvassing for the Chair, the judiciary had just enjoyed a high point in its autonomy as a political force within the Kingdom. In the summer of 1719, there had elapsed an unusually long four-week interlude between viceroyal governments while the Kingdom awaited the arrival of a new viceroy, Cardinal Wolfgang Hannibal von Schrattenbach, during which time an "enlarged" (*allargato*) Collaterale most ably ruled the land alone, asserting its constitutional right to represent and govern the Kingdom in the absence of a royal designee.[50] Among the regents of that ruling organ had numbered Gaetano Argento, who, with the title of "vice decano," ranked second therein and who then was at the very height of his prestige and power, having served as the foremost advocate of the state in its ongoing battle for jurisdiction over ecclesiastical lands and privileges for over a decade.[51] Moreover, it was Argento who especially prided himself on the interregnum rule of the Collaterale and took umbrage at the ceremonious termination of its extraordinary powers.[52] Even after the arrival of Schrattenbach and the termination of the Collaterale's extraordinary powers, both Argento and Ventura remained especially well placed within the courts to enjoy a certain amount of intellectual latitude in their rulings.

While a regent of the Consiglio Collaterale (since 1709), Argento also served as president of the Sacro Regio Consiglio (since 1714), which possessed the royal prerogative of ruling *contra legem,* that is, against the letter of the law, which enabled it to provide what it deemed fair solutions to vexing jurisdictional questions. Among the counselors (*consiglieri*) of the Sacro Regio Consiglio since 1717 had figured Francesco Ventura, Argento's nephew, whom Vico especially lauded in the Prologue to *De uno* as a most astute judge of cases concerning "equity," which, for Vico, denoted disputes where the norms of natural jurisprudence were employed to adjudicate an outcome preferable to the public welfare. Although Vico could not be sure of it at this time, Ventura would make a career of advocating equity and of facilitating the centralization of the state at the cost of feudal interests,[53] first by promoting the Banco di San Carlo (ideated in 1720 but only created in 1725),[54] whose primary responsibility was to repurchase benefices alienated from the royal domain, and second by promoting and presiding over the tribunal of the Supremo Magistrato del Commercio, which expressly was created in 1739 to expedite the adjudication of commercial disputes.[55] In canvassing for the Chair, then, Vico both targeted and wrote to an audience of jurists who specifically enjoyed, if not cherished, a certain amount of political autonomy within the Kingdom thanks both to their status and to their jurisprudential prerogative of ruling *contra legem,* which in their opinions they often wrapped in the idiom of natural law.[56] As I shall discuss, in one sense the *Diritto universale* represented a manifesto for the autonomy of the judiciary, making Vico's candidacy, for those who would read and understand his treatise, the one that was most clamorously aligned with the political ambitions of the ministerial class.

With his vigorous canvassing, Vico seems to have earned both respect and notoriety among his contemporaries, however. For his strategy of self-promotion not only publicized his talents but also gave cause to his rivals and tested the loyalties of his friends. In July 1720 Vico printed (without license) at the press of his friend Felice Mosca a prospectus of his legal treatise, which he then eagerly distributed among scholars, both local and international, provoking debate about his work before the final product was in hand. In the untitled prospectus, generally known as the *Sinopsi,* Vico confidently announced his plans to publish a two-volume legal treatise in Latin and tersely stated the recondite argument of the same, which he crammed into four pages of text formatted in double columns and printed with miniscule type.[57] With hindsight, it is clear that the decision to produce and circulate the *Sinopsi* was misguided, if not rash, and its consequences undesirable, as it not only elicited a fierce debate that undercut the reception of the actual publication of the *Diritto universale* but also tried the goodwill of Vico's friends both lay and ecclesiastical. From Vico's own comments, it seems that the publication of the *Sinopsi* provoked near scandal. As he wrote to his dear friend Father Bernardo Maria Giacco, a Capuchin preacher, the *Sinopsi* had caused "great commotion in both parts of this city" because, as he explained, "it has found favor among the most learned of men, as the powerful are always generous, just as the poor are always envious."[58] The glibness of Vico's remarks notwithstanding, his printing and distribution of the *Sinopsi* evidently put him on the defensive, so much so indeed that some five years later when he drafted the first part of the *Autobiografia* the sting of criticism was still pungent. Therein, Vico would note both with some resentment and deprecation the objections made to the *Sinopsi*. "Some gave unfavorable opinions of it," he remarked, "but since they did not maintain these opinions when the work later appeared adorned with very complimentary opinions of learned scholars, whose praises weighed in its favor, they are hardly worth mentioning here."[59]

Although Vico did not name the names of his detractors either here or in any of his extant letters, it is assumed that the *Sinopsi* brought him the public criticism of his future opponents in the university competition, Domenico Gentile and Pietro de Turris, as well as the foremost member of the law faculty, Nicola Capasso.[60] While it was predictable that his future rivals would exploit the occasion to their own advantage, unfortunately for Vico, the debate that ensued the printing of the *Sinopsi* also alienated some of his closest friends and divided the allegiances of their intellectual companions, creating rifts among his peers from which his reputation may never have recovered. For example, Matteo Egizio—who was a close friend of Vico and, then, the leading antiquarian in Naples—apparently read the *Sinopsi* as a polemic directed against himself; and his coterie seems to have divided over the positions put forth in the same, so that Vico became an object of controversy and was estranged from one of the most respected scholars of his native city.[61] As for the opinion of the famous lawyer Pietro Giannone— who had been a close friend of Vico from their youths, a protégé of Argento, and the author of the then forthcoming and notoriously anti-ecclesiastical *Storia civile del Regno di Napoli* (1723)—the sources provide few clues beyond a curious silence, which many have interpreted as evidence of Giannone's disapproval of his former companion's endeavors in law.[62] The "commotion" was not limited to Naples, moreover. The effective distribution of the *Sinopsi* also had occasioned the debate and intellectual censor of the Italian community in Vienna, where Vico's former patron, Apostolo Zeno, was engaged as the court librettist. From correspondence between Apostolo Zeno and his brother, Pier Caterino, in Venice, it is evident that Apostolo not only had read the *Sinopsi* some "three times" but also severely disapproved of it as a most obscure and eclectic work ravaged by mere *sofisticherie,* or vain pretensions.[63] To the extent that there was any truth in Vico's famous declaration of isolation in the *Autobiografia,* then, it was partly the unintended consequence of his own overly zealous attempt to win allies both in Naples as well as abroad.

However intense, all the uproar occasioned by the *Sinopsi* was perfectly premature as Vico awaited the final permissions requisite to publish his treatise with all the customary approvals, which he clearly had every intention of obtaining. In order to publish the *Diritto universale* in conformance with all the pertinent regulations, Vico had to receive the imprimatur of both the local ecclesiastical and civil authorities, which he eventually did, although not without some significant difficulties and delays.[64] From the extant evidence, it seems that he first sought to obtain the ecclesiastical imprimatur, which in Naples typically was granted by the Vicar General of the Curia of the Archbishop after the review and approval of a manuscript by one of its trusted censors.[65] From the actual imprimaturs registered in the first volume of the *Diritto universale,* we know that Vico submitted the text of *De uno* to the Neapolitan Curia for review by 6 February 1720, and that he already had secured from the ecclesiastical censor, Giulio Nicola Torno, a long report recommending its publication by the first day of March 1720.[66] According to the *Sinopsi,* sometime in March 1720 Vico then submitted the entire manuscript of the *Diritto universale,* that is, both *De uno* and *De constantia iurisprudentis,* to the press of Felice Mosca, presumably for typesetting.[67] Therewith, it would have been customary for either Vico or Mosca to seek from the viceroy the civil license to print, whose issuance at that time was governed by the Consiglio Collaterale.[68] Precisely when the request for the civil license was made to the viceroy and how the viceroy and the Collaterale proceeded to process that request remains unknown, as the extant documentation in the Archivio di Stato di Napoli has yet to yield any clues.[69] Be that as it may, from the civil license issued, it is plain that the Collaterale did not submit *De uno* for review to the approving civil censor until midsummer, that is, until 19 July 1720, when that work was given to Nicola Galizia, a most learned man who then held the Morning Chair of Canon Law at the university (since 1718) and who presumably was considered favorable to Vico. Once

Galizia was engaged, the civil license to print *De uno* was granted by the Collaterale not long thereafter on 19 August 1720, after its having received and reviewed his report dated 14 August 1720. Immediately thereafter, the official imprimatur of the Neapolitan diocese was released on 17 August 1720, that is, nearly six months after the ecclesiastical censor, Giulio Nicola Torno, had made his recommendation to the Curia to permit the publication of *De uno*.

Temporally viewed, the course of the ecclesiastical censorship had punctuated both the beginning and near end of the entire process of application for the imprimaturs, which altogether had taken several months. While it was customary to request the ecclesiastical imprimatur first, the great length of time that elapsed between Torno's recommendation to the Curia (on 1 March) and the actual release of the ecclesiastical imprimatur (on 17 August) does suggest that something was afoot in the interim. So does the late date (19 July) of the Collaterale's engagement of Galizia as civil censor. That these delays were due to more than the pace with which the machinery of early modern institutions ground forward, furthermore, is evidenced by the correspondence between Apostolo and Pier Caterino Zeno concerning *De uno*.

As Apostolo noted in a letter to his brother, according to Sebastiano Paoli, Vico had run up against a powerful glitch, namely, "Father De Miro, the President of the Cas[s]inesi," who reportedly had objected to the content of *De uno* and hence refused to recommend its publication.[70] The historiography either has dismissed these remarks as "adorned with details that are more or less fantastic,"[71] or it has interpreted them as evidence that Vico had had difficulty obtaining the civil license to publish.[72] Given his profile, it is plausible that De Miro's credentials had in fact led the Collaterale to first engage him as the civil censor. For the job of civil censor, Father Giambattista De Miro was eminently well qualified: at the time, he was resident in Naples as abbot of the Benedictine Monastery of San Severino and Sossio, and, more important, he had a personal connection to the Consiglio Collaterale, namely, his brother, Vincenzo De Miro, who was one of its regents.[73] What is more, Giambattista had a track record as a referee of legal works: in particular, he had reviewed and approved of Gravina's *Origines iuris civilis* (1708), which in Naples would be reprinted with De Miro's review by Vico's own publisher Felice Mosca in 1713.[74] Thus, De Miro was not only well connected and qualified for the review of *De uno,* but, given his high opinion of Gravina, it is even plausible that he was considered to be a potentially favorable reviewer of Vico's work. Yet, if it were the case that the Collaterale had first engaged De Miro to review *De uno,* then it is also true that his same personal profile potentially could have unleashed problems for Vico that went well beyond the delay of the approval of *De uno* by the civil authorities. For Giambattista De Miro was also a consultant for the Roman Index and for the Roman Inquisition.[75] If what Zeno reported was true, then in De Miro Vico had encountered a most formidable critic, whose misgivings about *De uno* not only had held up the civil license of that work but also must have given Vico reason for concern, as the mere prospect of De Miro denouncing *De uno* to higher authorities in Rome must have been a most daunting one indeed and may help to account for Vico's most dogged avowal of orthodoxy.

Regardless of this most formidable of glitches, from the documentation held in the Archive of the Congregation for the Doctrine of the Faith we know that *De uno* was neither prohibited nor even discussed by the Congregation of the Index, which reviewed, and censored, published books suspected of heterodoxy.[76] Similarly, it seems that the same held true for the Congregation of the Inquisition, whose competencies at this time evidently included the review of manuscripts, both suspect and delicate, referred to the Congregation for licensing as well as the scrutiny of published books (and their authors) denounced on the count of heresy.[77] That *De uno* evaded the scrutiny of these organs is not surprising, however, as it seems that De Miro's association with these Roman Congregations was effectively titular,[78] and, more important, that the disapproval of De Miro—and of any other contemporaries for that matter—largely could have had consequences of the sort that were most jealously regulated by the Archbishopric of Naples itself.[79] Put somewhat differently, to the extent that Vico's work demanded it, *De uno* evidently was protected from the scrutiny of Roman authorities by historical circumstance: at the time, it was shielded both by the intransigent independence of the Neapolitan Curia vis-à-vis Rome and by the sympathy and good fortune of Vico's ecclesiastical censor, Giulio Nicola Torno. From the documentation in the Archive of the Congregation for the Doctrine of the Faith, it is clear that in the second decade of the eighteenth century the Neapolitan Curia was able to maintain a large degree of autonomy as regarded the censorship of books. Whereas the ecclesiastical authorities of many Italian states referred the review and approval of books containing questionable doctrines to the Congregation of the Roman Inquisition, the Neapolitan Curia did not.[80] Rather, like the Inquisition in Naples so too was the ecclesiastical censorship of manuscripts a local affair that was conducted under the auspices of the Neapolitan Curia itself, whose decisions were in practice definitive.[81] What is more, the interest of the Roman Index in Neapolitan books came in waves and largely—although not exclusively— pertained to works regarding the jurisdiction of the Holy See over and in the Kingdom.[82]

Consequently, it seems that the censure of Neapolitan works by the Roman Congregations primarily targeted the most scandalous of anti-ecclesiastical examples, which, in their turn, were tacticly prohibited by the Congregations at what were opportune moments for the Holy See in its battles with the Kingdom of Naples. What is more, the career of Giulio Nicola Torno within the Neapolitan Curia further protected Vico. For Torno was evidently the most valued of collaborators with the Curia and, more important, would shortly be awarded the position of consultant of the Neapolitan Inquisition (in 1725),[83] which put him in the strongest of positions to guide and defend his friend against the scrutiny of other (and less sympathetic) ecclesiastics.[84] Whether or not this would prove necessary, it is evident that for the publication of *De uno* Vico had duly followed the regulations governing printed matter, just as was customary for the university professoriate at the time,[85] and that he had benefitted from the contingencies of local circumstances. Indeed, the very first attempt to reprint one of his philosophical works outside the Kingdom—the proposed Paduan edition of the *Scienza nuova* (1725)—immediately brought the censure of the Roman Inquisition.[86]

On obtaining the imprimaturs, Vico immediately published *De uno* at the printing house of his friend Felice Mosca and began to disseminate copies. The volume was published in quarto, and it is assumed that the print run amounted to one thousand copies, as was usual at the time.[87] As this publication had cost Vico a handsome investment of his time and money, he tirelessly worked to promote the final product, which he presumably hoped would bring him not only glory but also qualification for promotion. By custom, it was expected that Vico donate copies of his publication to the regents of the Collaterale and the supreme magistrates of the tribunals, which we can only imagine he most gladly did, given not only their importance but also their role as judges of the university competitions in law.[88] Vico also sent copies of *De uno* to other potential patrons, colleagues, and friends, whose support he especially sought and needed at this crossroads. As Vico had hoped, a number of prominent jurists did respond favorably to *De uno,* namely, Francesco Ventura, to whom the work had been dedicated; Muzio di Majo, who along with Ventura was among the most distinguished counselors of the Sacro Regio Consiglio at the time; and Aniello Spagnuolo, a lawyer who was better known for his literary talents.[89] However, in the immediate wake of the scandal around the *Sinopsi,* it seems that most minds were less receptive to *De uno* on its publication and that the number of them to weigh in negatively on Vico's work would make its publication a Pyrrhic victory for its author. For what was most notable about the reception of Vico's recondite work was its triviality and slander. As Vico related to his friend and correspondent Padre Giacco, his detractors had made their opinions known after what was no more than a hasty reading of the *Sinopsi,* and then they held to them steadfastly after the publication of *De uno.* The most benign critics pronounced that the work was simply unintelligible; as Vico's friend Sebastiano Paoli ungenerously penned in his complimentary copy of *De uno:* "Culpa mea est si non capio tua dicta./ Culpa tua est nemo si tua dicta capit." (It is my fault if I do not understand your text. But it is your fault if no one understands your text.)[90] The more dogmatic took the high ground of the classical authorities and, with some reason, accused Vico of having misrepresented the views of the ancients. At worst, the verdict of Vico's critics bordered on public condemnation: for it apparently accused Vico of the most grave charge of irreligion, reviving suspicions concerning the "weaknesses and errors" of his early youth, when he admittedly had kept company with men investigated and imprisoned for atheism by the Inquisition.[91] Thus, Vico noted, it was only right that "Religion itself would serve me as a shield," by arming him with the written commendation of Padre Giacco, which he reportedly touted around Naples in his self-defense as evidence of the falsity of his critics.[92] Contrary to the intentions of his well-laid plans, then, Vico's endeavors had brought on him the most damaging of charges, namely, the suspicion of heterodoxy, casting the darkest of shadows on his erudite publication and making him vulnerable to the vicissitudes of ecclesiastical politics within the Kingdom.

Despite the criticisms of his detractors, Vico persevered and published the second volume of the *Diritto universale, De constantia iurisprudentis,* approximately one year later in the late summer of 1721. From the front matter of *De constantia,* it seems that the path to publication was not any smoother for the second volume of the *Diritto universale* than it had been for the first. As had been the case with *De uno,* so too with *De constantia* did the acquisition of the imprimaturs take a long time, some as long as several months.[93] Even more curiously, the front matter suggested that the concession of the imprimaturs for *De constantia* had not followed procedure.[94] Specifically, the front matter recorded that the Curia and Collaterale both had granted their imprimaturs for the second volume before the receipt of the reports from their respective censors, suggesting that those authorities effectively had taken it on themselves to grant the customary approvals without the benefit of the very peer reviews they had commissioned.[95] As this decision would have violated the procedural rules governing the concession of imprimaturs that those same authorities were designated to uphold, it is probable that the dates of the censors' reports were falsified for the front matter. Indeed, the letter that Vico composed to accompany his gift of *De constantia* to Padre Giacco, his foremost supporter within greater Naples, predated the published dates of the censors' reports.[96] Whatever the exact reasons for their falsification, the dates of the reports suggest that they were calculated to diffuse criticism of the publication and its censors: for they effectively shifted the burden of responsibility for the authorization of *De constantia* to the supreme authorities of the Kingdom from its censors, who were and would remain among Vico's most faithful friends.[97]

That Vico was defensive about the assessment of his work is illustrated by his inclusion of an appendix to *De constantia* containing "clarissimorum virorum censurae extra ordinem" (uncommissioned reviews of most illustrious men), which published for a broader public select correspondence concerning the merits of the *Diritto universale* penned by colleagues, friends, and a few Italian scholars of peninsular reputation.[98] Beyond the actual content of its letters, what was most interesting about this appendix was the evident priority Vico gave to the reception of his work by Neapolitan colleagues, such as Vicenzo Vidania, the rector of the university, and Giovanni Chiaiese, then professor of Papal Decretal Law, whose letters were the most substantive, and the ones by individuals bearing the imprimatur of university affiliation.

The evident difficulties Vico faced with both the publication and reception of his legal treatise seems only to have emboldened him to promote the completed work to the best of his abilities among international luminaries of the Republic of Letters. As Vico remarked with both disappointment and pride, he henceforth would write only for "the most excellent of learned men," and it seems that he now sought them out with a determination equal to his disillusion.[99] In the past, Vico largely had limited his campaign for self-promotion to the Italian peninsula, to whose most eminent men of letters he had donated copies of his work. The best-known recipient of *De uno,* for example, was Anton Maria Salvini (1653–1729), the Tuscan classicist and contributor to the famous fourth edition of the *Vocabolario della Crusca,* who received his copy along with an accompanying note from the obliging Marquis Alessandro Rinuccini (1686–1758), a Florentine scholar and friend of Vico resident in Naples, to whom Salvini responded with thanks in turn.[100]

Now, Vico more ambitiously set his sights on international arbiters of taste. In his tireless campaign for recognition, he disseminated copies of *De constantia* among inhabitants of Naples who were integrated into the international circuit of letters, rallying the local resources at his disposal for the strategic placement of his work in the hands of select patrons and critics of scholarship throughout Europe. In Rome, Vienna, and Amsterdam, Vico aimed high. In the Eternal City, Vico made a donation of *De constantia* to the Biblioteca Casanatense alla Minerva, an extraordinary public library that hosted an international cohort of scholars in their rounds of books on the Grand Tour.[101] In Vienna, Vico similarly targeted one of the richest libraries and its most influential patron. Via his friend Biagio Garofalo in Rome, Vico arranged for copies of *De uno* and *De constantia* to travel the long road to Vienna, where they were destined for the renowned collection of Prince Eugene von Savoy, who after a distinguished career on the battlefield had settled down in the Habsburg capital to become a patron of the arts, letters, and, no less, controversial ideas amid the comforts of his grand palace, the Schloss Belvedere.[102] With all the due respect, Vico sent Eugene exemplars of the legal works that were printed on superior paper with large margins, presenting his texts to the prince in a format that appeared worthy of their most dignified recipient and his magnificent library. Finally, in Amsterdam Vico worked to place his legal treatise in the hands of one of the greatest living critics of literature, the prodigious Jean Le Clerc, editor of the *Bibliothèque ancienne et moderne,* which was then among the foremost literature reviews in Europe. On his departure from Naples for northern Europe, the young Count von Waldenstein was saddled by Vico with copies of *De uno* and *De constantia* equal to those given to Eugene for the receipt of Le Clerc, to whom Waldenstein faithfully delivered them in Amsterdam.[103] Much to Vico's delight, Le Clerc responded with a warm letter communicating his favorable impressions of the treatise, which he promised to review.[104] For Vico, Le Clerc's letter was a triumph on which he immediately sought to capitalize in Naples, where he touted it much as he had Giacco's the previous year, further stirring the animosity and envy of his rivals.[105] More famously, Vico's efforts did bear the fruit of a favorable review from Le Clerc in the *Bibliothèque* (1722),[106] from which he would quote with pride in the *Autobiografia* as evidence of his international recognition and reputation.[107]

If Vico had set his sights high among the arbiters of taste, then he also selected his judges well, as he rightly identified in both Eugene von Savoy and Jean Le Clerc tough critics who would favor his novel ideas. Indeed, it is not at all surprising that Le Clerc would be receptive to the legal treatise, as Vico evidently had taken his fair share of inspiration from Le Clerc's own literary method and arguments. As one of the leading protagonists of the art of historico-critical exegesis, Le Clerc especially valued Vico's philological method, which apparently investigated and historicized the great texts of history and poetry much as Le Clerc had the Bible. In his review of the *Diritto universale,* Le Clerc specifically noted with approval that Vico had "revealed a great quantity of vulgar errors" concerning ancient history, and that he had contradicted the false assumptions regarding the language of ancient poetry, which literary critics had misunderstood as the art of refined authors rather than as the locutions of primitive peoples.[108] What is more, in Vico's treatise Le Clerc found confirmation of his own religious commitments, that is, of his belief in a rational Christianity and of his refutation of skepticism. In particular, Le Clerc commended Vico for his claims regarding the latent reasonableness of humans and the truth of Christian metaphysics. As Le Clerc paraphrased Vico with approbation: "He supposes that men have the seeds [*semences*] of the sciences in their souls"; "he next remarks that one must banish skepticism from all the sciences, and especially the doctrine of morals," and "he sustains, with justice, that Christian metaphysics is veritable, in that it teaches us that there is a God whose knowledge, power, and will are infinite."[109] In other words, in Vico's legal works what Le Clerc happily found was an espousal of his own credo: a simplification of Christian beliefs to a few articles of faith about God and a historical approach to the doctrines of Christianity and to humanity that affirmed a correspondence between reason and belief. In like manner, in Le Clerc Vico had identified a natural intellectual ally of international fame. What Vico reasonably had hoped to gain from the endorsement of such an ally is unclear, however.[110] While Le Clerc was highly regarded in Naples, it was also true that his reputation was marred by the charges of heterodoxy and that his *Bibliothèque universelle et historique* itself notoriously had figured on the Index of Prohibited Books (1691–92). Needless to say, Le Clerc's review of the *Diritto universale* was an honor but not necessarily the best of credentials for promotion within a royal institution, especially at a time when the relationship of the Kingdom with the Church was fraught with tension.

By contrast, in Eugene von Savoy Vico had identified a natural intellectual ally, who in Vico's own mind indubitably figured as the most powerful of potential patrons, given the celebrated influence of Eugene at the Habsburg court in Vienna. If Vico's religious ideas appealed to Le Clerc, then we can only imagine that Eugene, whose library famously hosted discussions of radical ideas from deism to pantheism, was intrigued by Vico's texts and inclined to his personal favor.[111] Indeed, the only surviving piece of correspondence from Eugene to Vico, dated September 1724, suggests that the prince had been pleased by the gift of the *Diritto universale* and was predisposed to lend Vico his support, where appropriate, in the future.[112] Be that as it may, in the short run it seems that Eugene had most politicly refused Vico his support and that Vico himself had been amiss in his judgment of the powers that Eugene presently could exercise within the cultural politics of the Kingdom of Naples. For in June of 1722, there arrived in Naples Cardinal Friedrich Michael von Althann, who as the new viceroy of the

Kingdom would preside over the university competitions. Although it seems that Althann was at least partially indebted to Eugene for his cardinalate,[113] we also know that the relationship between the two had soured.[114] Even if this had not been the case, there were ample political reasons for the prince to decline to recommend Vico: as will become apparent, Vico's hard-earned reputation as an original thinker had been trumped by the political exigencies of the new viceroyal regime in 1723, whose directives had been set by the Emperor Charles VI himself, and whose challenges had been complicated by the inconveniences of a brewing controversy with the Church.

Whereas Vico's transalpine critics had taken a keen interest in the method and religious tenets of the *Diritto universale,* his Neapolitan colleagues especially noted its unique contribution to the canon of natural law. As Vico's dear friend Aniello Spagnuolo enthusiastically wrote after reading *De constantia:* "O Signor Giovan Battista, you should pride yourself on not only having rendered useless the investigation of natural law by Boecler, Willem Grotius, Selden, Pufendorf, and others, but also in having furnished that great work that Hugo Grotius adumbrated and tried to accomplish in his treatise *De iure belli, et pacis.*"[115] Penned out of his gratitude for the book and frustration of repeatedly missing the author at home, Spagnuolo's letter is not only coincidental but also serendipitous, as it constitutes one of the few records of the reception of the *Diritto universale* in Naples. As letters of this sort were also intended as public documents for the reading and discussion of both intellectual friends and foes, Spagnuolo's enthusiastic reaction to Vico's work certainly also revealed the interests and aspirations of the coterie around Vico in Naples as well as the themes that Spagnuolo believed warranted defense against Vico's detractors. First, with its comparison of Vico to his transalpine predecessors, the letter acknowledged that the Neapolitan and his local interlocutors both valued the great Protestant theorists of natural law and, no less, sought to regain for Italy the pride of first place within the field of natural jurisprudence. In Spagnuolo's estimation, indeed, Vico had done just that, and splendidly, as he effectively had competed with Grotius in terms of method and outshone him in terms of metaphysics. As concerned his method, like Grotius, Vico had applied the art of criticism to the gamut of humanistic sources, from which he consequently had uncovered empirical evidence of the past and data illustrative of those natural laws governing human society. Vico's reconstruction of the past was so faithful, Spagnuolo added, that the reader of his work "could vaunt having clearly seen many intriguing facts from the most ancient times without having been subjected to the ravages of the years."[116]

Second, Spagnuolo's praise of *De constantia* squarely defended Vico's meta-physics, which he asserted had made "human doctrine the servant of the Catholic faith."[117] However, Spagnuolo's evidence for this assertion was not anything contemporaries would have recognized as post-Tridentine dogma-tism, but rather Vico's unusual proof of God, namely, his argument for the existence of a supreme deity from the intelligent design of human society. For contemporaries, the argument from intelligent design presumed that the existence of God was self-evident from the nature of the physical universe: it likened to a humanmade machine the order, structure, and harmony of creation, which, by inference, the argument ran, must have a primary cause, or creator, that was both similar to and more perfect than the nature of humans themselves. As Spagnuolo himself explained, whereas theologians and metaphysicians had demonstrated the existence of God from the order of the physical world (*le sostanze*), Vico had done the same from the demon-strable order governing the formation and development of moral entities. Specifically, Vico had found *aposteriori* evidence for an "order to make mani-fest that infinite order, which is God" in "the ideas and actions (*fatti*) of those who founded the ancient unions, republics, empires, and laws" and the "indifferent modifications" to which those same moral entities were subject. And with this evidence, Spagnuolo concluded, Vico had established with "incontrovertible clarity the fundamental truths of Religion" and, likewise, had "vanquished atheism."[118] From the regularity of societal affairs, in other words, Vico had inferred the existence of God and his unique attributes, refuting disbelief and skepticism. Although Spagnuolo did not specify the atheists refuted by Vico, we can assume with some certainty that his contem-poraries would have borne in mind natural law theorists such as Grotius and Hobbes, both of whom had argued for the absolute independence of human morality from divine governance, as well as the Dutch philosopher Spinoza, with whom at the time both materialism and necessitarianism (the belief that things are as they must and should be) were associated, however unfairly.[119] In the *Diritto universale,* Spagnuolo thus discerned both that which posterity would grant Vico as his greatest innovation, that is, his fundamentally histori-cal approach to the genesis and development of society and law, or "histori-cism," as well as that which most would deny Vico as a tenable position in his texts, that is, a theism that was grounded in the argument from intelligent design, or what is usually called deism.

Whether or not Spagnuolo had done justice to Vico's precepts of belief, it is clear that with his defense of Vico's faith that he did identify both one of the greatest innovations as well as one of the most vexing ambiguities of the *Diritto universale.* On the one hand, Spagnuolo grasped that Vico's inquiry

into the genesis and development of society and law had posited an analogy between these subjects of morality and the ones of natural philosophy.
Unlike Le Clerc, in other words, Spagnuolo keenly understood that Vico had
made natural law itself an object of science, fundamentally challenging its
traditional epistemological status. As discussed earlier, natural law long had
enjoyed the status of a body of universal principles: since antiquity, it had
been associated with the immutable prescriptions and injunctions of right
reason, whether that reason be thought to derive from the minds of superior
judges or the consensus of nations. With his reconstruction of Vico's argument from design and its analogy between the worlds of morality and natural
philosophy, however, Spagnuolo made plain that Vico had treated natural
law not as an immutable source of moral principles but rather as a historical object that was itself subject to physical laws. Put another way, in Vico's
argument from intelligent design, Spagnuolo keenly discerned that Vico had
crafted what we would call a social science, or what contemporaries would
dub a "human science," that is, an analysis of the causes and a prognosis of the
effects of the institutions of society and its forms of group behavior. At the
same time, Spagnuolo also apprehended in Vico's legal treatise precisely that
theme that would prove so very vexing for both his contemporary and later
critics: the precise role that God played in the origins and development of
society. And it was precisely this theme and the resemblance of Vico's solution to necessitarianism that the one other substantive letter dedicated to the
Diritto universale by a contemporary Neapolitan most centrally addressed.

Penned within a few days of Spagnuolo's own, this epistle was authored
by Giovanni Chiaiese, who at the time held the Chair in Papal Decretal
Law at the University of Naples and shortly would participate in the competition for the Morning Chair of Civil Law. A colleague of Vico's at the
university, Chiaiese apparently also shared interests with him. As Chiaiese
pronounced in the very preface to his letter, he had written a book of his
own on the genesis of ancient law, which apparently was not published, and
congratulated himself on having explored the same topic as Vico, whom he
enthusiastically praised as a "great man."[120] Beyond the fine reputation Vico
had earned as a pedagogue at the university, according to Chiaiese, with this
project Vico now additionally had assumed the mantle of Cicero. As had
Cicero in *De legibus,* so too had Vico in the *Diritto universale* searched for
the ultimate source of justice and the universal principles of its laws. Indeed,
with some faithfulness to the aims of Vico's project, Chiaiese reconstructed
his treatise as an affirmative response to the Ciceronian query quoted in the
front matter of *De uno:* "Then you do not think that the science of law is
to be derived from the praetor's edict, as the majority do now, or from the

Twelve Tables, as people used to think, but from the deepest mysteries of philosophy?"[121] However lengthy his affirmative response, Vico's neoclassicism importantly did not end here for Chiaiese. For more than the heir to Cicero, Vico was also the successor to the greatest Stoic cosmopolitans, and the motivations for Vico's search for the source and laws of natural justice were best understood, according to Chiaiese, precisely in the context of his cosmopolitanism. Indeed, Chiaiese compared Vico to the foremost representative and symbol of Stoic cosmopolitanism for contemporaries, Seneca. Like Seneca, Vico was supremely cognizant of the duality of his citizenship, and most nobly had contemplated the laws of that polity bounded by the universe, or what the Roman had called "the path of the sun."[122] Consequently, Vico had understood the relativity of Roman law and opposed the formalism of those jurists who had advocated the enforcement of its letter, regardless of circumstance. If a proponent of cosmopolitanism, then Vico was also an advocate of natural law jurisprudence, according to Chiaiese.

While Chiaiese had derived Vico's natural law theory from a cosmopolitan awareness, he also claimed that this awareness further reflected the more profound cosmic sensibility of the professor of Rhetoric. In other words, Vico shared not only the political convictions but also the cosmological beliefs of the ancient Stoics, who famously had hypothesized the oneness of the universe and the immanence of divine Reason.[123] Indeed, over the course of his letter Chiaiese painted an intellectual portrait of Vico that depicted him among a gallery of ancient cosmologists. Thus, Vico resembled Manilius (first century CE), the didactic poet and ancient author of the *Astronomica* (ca. 17–24 CE), who had recognized that there was nothing more wonderful in this cosmic mass than Reason itself and the certainty of its laws.[124] And he was comparable to the legendary Scipio, who in a dream famously had beheld the universe and from his illuminating vantage point had apprehended not only the retributive system of the cosmos but also its fundamental unity and primary cause, from which all things evidently derived, be they the elements of physical nature or the lesser laws of the human world.[125] Waxing hyperbolic, Chiaiese concluded his series of portraits with the iconic comparison of Vico to Saint John the Apostle, who, Chiaiese added, had uniquely traced the origins of the Judeo-Christian tradition to "Logos," overlaying this emblem of Christianity with a distinctly Pre-Socratic vision of the cosmos. In the context of likening Vico to the Stoics, this oblique reference to the Pre-Socratics was not inappropriate, as the Pre-Socratic ideas of *Logos* and of the cosmos had constituted an important legacy for Stoic cosmological beliefs. An immediate precursor to the Stoic idea of "divine Reason" and its cosmic attributes, *Logos* had denoted for the Pre-Socratics that lawlike principle indistinctly governing both the physical domain of the universe and the moral domain of humans, which together were understood as a self-regulating cosmic order bearing an intelligent plan. With his likening of Vico to St. John the Apostle, what Chiaiese suggested, in other words, was that Vico had embedded in the core beliefs of Christianity those esoteric beliefs of Hellenism regarding the great unity and rationality of the cosmos. With his gallery of portraits, Chiaiese most artfully pictured Vico as bearing a striking resemblance to those ancients who had hypothesized the existence of a singular and lawlike spirit animating a holistic cosmos. If by way of arcane analogy, Chiaiese suggested that Vico had made his mark within the canon of Neo-Stoic authors and that his political convictions specifically had entailed not only a global vision of society but also an understanding of the universe itself that made a rational God the active principle of the physical and moral worlds alike.

However enthusiastic Chiaiese may have been, the association of Vico with Stoic cosmology was replete with implications that were potentially damaging. For this association implicitly raised questions about Vico's precise conceptions of the nature of God and of the role of human agency in the moral world, regardless of Chiaiese's own intentions. Although the Stoics had pictured the world order as divine, unlike the Christian God, the Stoic divinity was neither anthropomorphic nor transcendent; indeed, the common view among the Stoics was that a singular god was both immanent to and identical with the cosmos, a view that is often considered pantheist.[126] Needless to say, the association of Vico with Stoic cosmology tacitly imputed a sort of cosmic naturalism to the framework of his inquiry that did not contradict but rather could lend support to a charge of heterodoxy. It implied that the role Vico attributed to divine Reason in the moral world ran counter to the dogmas of post-Tridentine theology, by laying claim to a determinism that limited humans in their exercise of free will. Specifically, Chiaiese most subtly intimated that Vico's account of the origins of society and law relied on the Stoic notion of fate, which as commonly understood had minimized the role of human agency in the execution of the divine plan.[127] For the Stoics, fate first and foremost had denoted the action of a singular divinity on matter according to the inexorable design of its supreme reason.[128] Similarly, for the heirs (and critics) of the Stoics this account of fate further connoted both a certain necessitarianism and a unitarian determinism that posited a singular God as the primary cause of creation and at the nexus of a lawlike sequence of causes, from which the world as known developed.[129] Significantly, in the Stoic worldview this causal determinism applied not only to the physical but also to the moral realm; in other words, determinism was not only of cosmic but also of ethical import.[130] With his analogy of Vico to the Stoic cosmologists, then, Chiaiese intimated that the notion of fate structured Vico's account of the moral world as well. Indeed, among the moderns Chiaiese applauded Vico for uniquely having identified in divine Reason the first principle and efficient cause of the seeds of society, or what was the potentiality of humankind for growth. However reconcilable this Stoic notion of fate may have been with the Christian notion of Providence in Chiaiese's own mind, he nonetheless did not bother to strip it of its cosmic naturalism in his single most pointed reference to Vico's vision of the origins and development of society. Although many had proposed that the "natural instincts and impulses" of humans had formed the "germs" of societal institutions, Chiaiese declared, Vico astutely had comprehended that they rather stemmed from a "Paramount Nature," or [from] "God," which syntactically figured as identical in Chiaiese's reconstruction of Vico's vision of divinity.[131]

If a bit overwrought by artfulness, the implications of Chiaiese's interpretation of the *Diritto universale* were clear. On the one hand, this interpretation of the *Diritto universale* made a strong case for its challenge to those moderns who had viewed humanity and society as bereft of God and of his benevolent intervention: it argued for the distinctiveness of Vico's natural law theory from that of modern predecessors, such as Hobbes, Pufendorf, and Locke, who famously had posited the human instinct for self-preservation and the contingencies of human needs as the efficient causes for the union of humans and the creation of political society. In other words, according to Chiaiese, Vico importantly had restored the volition and design of God to the picture natural law drew of the origins and purposes of human society. On the other hand, Chiaiese's interpretation implicitly posed the hard question of what role, if any, human volition could play in the unfolding of divine plan in Vico's schema. In other words, its Stoic lens also raised the specter of fatalism, or the charge that there was no place for the operation of free will therein. From his own comments in the *Sinopsi* and *Diritto universale,* it seems that Vico had anticipated the criticism of fatalism and parried it in advance with his own repeated denouncements of the commonly received notion of Stoic fate.[132] Indeed, it seems that Vico expressly had wished to embed modern ideas about the nature of humans and the purpose of society within a framework of Stoic beliefs about the physical laws of the cosmos without advocating fatalism. To be fair to Vico, it bears mentioning here that the effective reconciliation of modern ideas about human autonomy with Stoic core beliefs about the divinity and immutability of the cosmic laws was the tallest of philosophical tasks and that Vico's solution seems to have confused contemporaries no less than the Stoics themselves had when they confronted an analogous problem in antiquity. In fact, Cicero, who was a great synthesizer of Hellenism and empathetic to the Stoic view, seems to have had such difficulty with the ancient Stoic subtleties concerning the mechanics of causation among individuals[133] that he was charged by posterity for obscuring those provisions the Stoic system had made for human agency and moral responsibility.[134] That said, the abstrusity of the solution that Vico found evidently lent itself to the criticism of Stoic fatalism and, by implication and what was worse, its heterodox modern variant, Spinozism, which denounced the concept of human freedom as illusory.[135]

Like the meaning of all texts, so was that of the *Diritto universale* determined by the reception of its contemporary audience. From its reception, it seems that the *Diritto universale* most notably fell prey to Vico's own remarkable versatility and heady ambitions. Because its component ideas and methods were extraordinarily diverse and, as such, recognizable to the broadest spectrum of contemporary readers, the message of the *Diritto universale* seems to have lain in the eyes of its learned beholders, who could find their own beliefs within this text and disregard the rest, including the distinctiveness of its political vision. Indeed, regardless of its political topicality, it is plain that for its foremost critics the legal treatise struck its boldest chord with the burning religious debates of the period, reminding us of just how central the question of belief was to the early Enlightenment, especially in the Catholic lands.[136] As seen earlier, for them the greatest strengths and weaknesses of the *Diritto universale* lay in its claims about the nature and role of God in the moral realm, claims that lent themselves to identification with a number of competing Enlightenment doctrines, namely, that of a rational Christianity (Le Clerc), the argument from intelligent design (Spagnuolo), and that of a holistic universe governed by a rational God (Chiaiese). If none of those doctrines conformed to post-Tridentine theology by anyone's account, the last one most certainly was a particularly dangerous, if not incriminating, attribution, however. For Chiaiese's letter came shockingly close to interpreting Vico's proof of the Judeo-Christian God as proof of a monistic One,[137] which was a belief that not only had deep roots in Stoicism but also was associated with Spinoza, who for contemporaries was a sort of code word for the heresies of materialism and atheism, as the contemporary trials of the Inquisition in Naples make plain.[138]

Precisely what Chiaiese's motivations and intentions were we cannot know. Whether his interpretation was a veiled form of condemnation by a competitor or an instance of genuine praise reserved for a restricted coterie is impossible to determine from the source itself. That Vico did recognize

his own ideas in Chiaiese's interpretation was made manifest by his decision to publish the letter in the appendix to *De constantia* which printed for
the public select criticism regarding the *Diritto universale.* However, it would
be imprudent, I believe, to assign an unambiguously positive bottom line to
the letter merely on the basis of its inclusion in the appendix to *De constantia,*
if not because Vico oftentimes proved to be a poor judge of his own circumstances, then because the letter itself had reproduced (rather than resolved) so
many of the ambiguities of Vico's own text, as if it were an airing of Vico's
doctrinal elusiveness for both his proponents and detractors alike. Be that
as it may, it seems that Chiaiese's letter was received by the authorities as an
endorsement of the *Diritto universale,* as the professor of Canon Law would
be asked by the Collaterale in the not too distant year of 1725 to furnish a
report on the first edition of the *Scienza nuova* for the issuance of its civil
imprimatur, a request to which Chiaiese acquiesced and which he executed
with some brevity and in the affirmative.[139] Regardless of the intentions and
reception of Chiaiese's letter, in any case, it is certain that it underscored how
very indebted Vico's thought was to Stoic cosmopolitanism, and, similarly,
how very concerned Vico was to individuate the epistemological grounds
for the commonalities among humans and their societal institutions. In a
sense, then, Chiaiese's letter can be said to have accomplished two important things: first, it highlighted that cosmopolitan theory of natural rights
and duties that Vico had been developing since the post-1701 orations; and,
second, it inquired about the basis of those same rights and duties, by posing
the open-ended question of whether they derived from the injunctions of
a Judeo-Christian God or from the natural imperatives of a holistic cosmos
governed by a rational force. Although not perfectly faithful to the legal
treatise, Chiaiese nonetheless captured well both the commitments and elusiveness of Vico's Stoic cosmopolitanism. Yet, what Stoicism could not begin
to explain in Vico's work was his insistence on the city as the condition of
possibility for the developmental course of individual societies and, no less,
for human freedom.

III. A New Theory of Natural Law and Society: Vico's History of the City and Citizen Rights

Toward a Definition and Ontology of Natural Law

The reception of his text notwithstanding, Vico plainly had advertised the
nature of his ambitions for the legal treatise in its very title. And his ambitions were grand. If with provocative audacity, in the titles and headings of

the individual volumes of the *Diritto universale* Vico boldly pronounced his intention to revisit the concept of *ius* ("law" or "right," depending on usage) and to identify that legal source of political wisdom for a world presumably characterized by social instability and change. In other words, Vico pronounced that he would revisit the theme of the relationship between law and political civilization, a promise that he duly honored.

While the actual content of Vico's treatise most closely resembled that of humanistic tracts, whose authors had studied Roman law in order to contextualize the rulings of the *Corpus iuris* and to analyze their validity for contemporary society,[140] Vico squarely positioned his own work as a contribution to the school of natural law, which since ancient times had sought to identify those principles of justice common to all peoples, be they ideal or conventional. That Vico understood his work as a contribution to the canon of natural law was made manifest by the title of the first volume of the legal treatise, that is, *De universi iuris uno principio et fine uno* (*The One Principle and One End of Universal Right;* or my translation: The one principle and one end of universal law), which with its reference to "universal law" distinctly recalled that (original) Stoic idea of a supreme law rooted in nature. While Vico already had cited the Stoic notion of natural law in his earliest orations, in *De uno* he labored to give that concept further political meaning, which his contemporaries would have understood as programmatic.

Much as he had in the inaugural addresses, in the *Diritto universale* Vico invoked the Stoic rubric of universal law and of the sage to lend authority to his own program for the contemporary judiciary. As discussed earlier, the Stoic notion of universal law had proposed the existence of a single law for all of humanity, whose prescriptions and injunctions Cicero famously had identified with the "right reason" of divinelike sages in the *Laws*. Similarly, in the *Diritto universale* Vico assumed that the norms of universal law were intrinsically reasonable and that reason itself was most fully developed in the conscience of sages. In contrast to Stoic doctrine, however, Vico considered the sages to be more than cultivated individuals who had learned to master their passions to the profit of their minds; much as they implicitly had in the *Orationes,* in the *Diritto universale* the sages explicitly figured as an institutional caste with a discrete administrative role in society. Recalling his old rallying cries and promises to the students of law from the podium of the inaugural addresses, Vico pronounced that in exemplary Rome the "jurisconsults" had enjoyed the status and prerogatives of "sages" and that their "wisdom" was both exercised and articulated in their practice of "jurisprudence."[141] Indeed, the kind of wisdom the jurist presumably possessed and its significance for the governance of the polity were encoded in the title of the second volume of the *Diritto universale, De constantia iurisprudentis* (*The Constancy of the Jurist*), which attributed to the jurist the virtue of "constancy," or *apatheia,* a virtue that according to Stoics and Neo-Stoics alike made possible the cognition of truth and, in particular, the tenets of universal law.[142] Needless to say, by force of its exemplarity, the profile of the Roman jurist offered a model for the contemporary judiciary in the *Diritto universale.* As he had earlier in his university career, so now did Vico emphatically identify the judiciary as a candidate for the administration of the contemporary polity and, in particular, for the enforcement of universal law as it applied to the contingencies of society. The *Diritto universale* represented, in other words, what was a manifesto for the centrality of the judiciary, and jurisprudence, in the governance of the political community. To the extent that it is proper to speak of a science of policy in the *Diritto universale,* then, the jurisprudence of universal law figured as such, as it purportedly held out both the knowledge of and tools necessary for the betterment of the human condition in community.

Similarly, in the *Diritto universale* the notion of universal law itself bore a contemporary political significance that made it more than a mere citation of Stoic doctrine. Rather than that recondite conversation and philosophical glory with which his work is regularly associated, what was at stake for Vico in his definition of universal law was a recommendation for the kind of justice that the law rendered to the political community. Indeed, it is fair to say that in the *Diritto universale* Vico staunchly and, no less, patently presented universal law as an instrument of social justice like nowhere else in his oeuvre. According to the *Diritto universale,* the purview of universal law far surpassed that of the common Roman notion of the *ius,* or law, as it had been defined by classical jurists and codified in the *Corpus iuris.* Per the tradition of Roman law, it was the role of the *ius* to render justice, which most commonly was understood as the great classical jurist Ulpian had defined it: as *ius suum cuique tribuere,* or to render to each his own right.[143] Significantly for the Romans and their heirs, this expression originally had denoted the restitution of one's personal property, or rightful possessions, which is also why the single greatest part of the *Corpus iuris* had consisted of private law and had addressed property rights. In contrast to the emphasis of Roman law on the restitution of property to its formal owner, universal law held out the grander prospect of the restoration of a natural sort of justice to the community in the *Diritto universale.* Therein, he made the strongest of cases for universal law as an instrument for the safeguarding of the common good and, furthermore, for the reform of society.

Making good on the promises of his title, in *De uno* Vico first expounded what he meant by the principle and end of universal law in his respective definitions of "justice" and "society," wherein he clearly stated his expectations for the judiciary and for universal jurisprudence at what was the very outset of his treatise. As Vico most pithily put it in his chapter "On Justice" in *De uno,* the commands of the "human reason" embodies "justice" (*iustitia*) when they "direct and equalize utilities" (*utilitates*), or what we might call useful things, an action that, Vico specified, comprised the "single principle and single end of universal law (*ius universum*)."[144] If a somewhat convoluted formulation, this definition nonetheless stated in what were unambiguous juridical terms for his readership that the purpose of universal law (*ius universum*) was to enforce the principle of equity. Defined as such, Vico thus presented universal law in what was a normative cast and assigned it the most thorny of political competencies. For this particular definition of universal law effectively construed it as a corrective to positive law of a higher moral order and made it responsible for the more equitable allocation of resources among the persons of the community. Put somewhat differently, Vico therewith assigned to the court of universal law the knotty ethical question of material justice and encharged the legal profession with the political task of advancing the equality of things among the members of the community, or what we would call distributive justice.[145] Within Vico's own oeuvre, this position importantly built on the one that he had assumed regarding the principle and end of law in *De ratione.* As discussed earlier, in *De ratione* Vico already had endorsed the equity ruling of the courts and their regard for the common good; therein, he had made an example of the forensic custom (*usus fori*) of the Sacro Regio Consiglio, the supreme court of Naples, which was known for its prerogative of ruling against the law, a prerogative that the court exercised in the idiom of natural law and, according to Vico, in favor of "aequitas civilis," or public welfare. If in the *Diritto universale* Vico confirmed his decade-old endorsement of equity ruling, then he also stipulated with unprecedented clarity that its directive was to further equality, which his subsequent discussion of "society" would suggest had marked the original condition of the human community.

Although the enforcement of universal law undisputedly was the competency of the judiciary, in the *Diritto universale* the juridical principle of equity more importantly derived its authority and legitimacy from the people. The discretionary powers of the judiciary notwithstanding, Vico sought to show that the court of universal law effectively pursued an agenda that had been set by the conscience of the people and that had remained compelling for their successors, regardless of their historical circumstances. In addition, Vico showed that historically the principle of equity more narrowly denoted an isometric form of equality. In those chapters immediately following "On

Justice," discussed above, Vico first began to evidence humanity's natural sense of equality by hypothesizing how individual humans had lived in what the modern tradition of natural law had called a state of nature and by conjecturing about how that aboriginal state had influenced the terms on which their original union was formed.

Although Vico preferred the semantic categories of Roman law to the historical ones of his contemporaries, he sought to reconstruct the condition of people before the advent of the political community and, more important, those ground rules, or laws (*iura*), that had naturally governed their behavior in that pre-civil state. The ground rules that most concerned Vico were those governing the just division of the fruits and resources of nature, and his assumptions regarding those particular rules evidently were borrowed from the tradition of natural law regarding property. According to that tradition, in the state of nature individuals had enjoyed a natural right (*ius*) to property in those things that they had appropriated with their labor, and they were subject to a natural limitation on the same that capped individual possession at the amount equal to one's personal consumption.[146] For Vico, these rules importantly evidenced humanity's natural sense of justice precisely because they illustrated that people instinctually chose to distribute things among individuals equally, be it in a state of nature or in an unencumbered community. As Vico affirmed in his chapter entitled "The Law (*Ius*) Is in Nature," the human experience had shown that the "equality" (*aequalitas*) of "ephemeral (and ever cyclical) utilities" (*fluxae utilitates*)—an expression that connoted the goods of nature—had what was a universal purchase, or validity, among all humans.[147] What was more, the purchase of this form of equality had borne the test of time, according to Vico, as it had come to bear on the customary practices and laws of the originary community. To document that bearing of equality on the community, Vico cited the juridical language that had been used to describe and legitimate the selection of equality in ancient times. Lending the authority and exemplarity of Roman civilization to the principle of equality, Vico noted that this natural sense of justice had been codified by the Romans in their legal concept of the *aequum bonum*—or equal good—which he highlighted in the place of the legal concept of *aequitas*—or equity proper—to pointedly argue that the equality of things had numbered among the precepts and practices of ancient Roman law. As Vico specified: "what the jurists call the *aequum bonum*, which is the source of all natural law (*ius naturale*), is the useful in nature made equal by an eternal measurement," establishing an inexorable link between equality and universal law.[148]

If any institution illustrated the naturalness and validity of equality in the *Diritto universale*, then that institution was the original union of humans in community, or what Vico specifically called "society." To the extent that the legal treatise had what was a motto, the resounding theme of the *Diritto universale* could be said to have been Vico's declaration in the *Sinopsi* that man's natural sociability predisposed him to the formation of society and, once therein, to the just provision for all its members: "On account of their nature there is among men a society of true justice, in which society all humans always convene (*convengono*) and which is that of the *aequum bonum,* or of equal utilities, in which consists the *ius naturale immutabile* (immutable natural law)," or what was Vico's alternative expression for universal law.[149] As evidence for the equality of this "society," or original community, furthermore, Vico proffered both his moral convictions as well as the most antique customs of ancient Rome, in which he believed to have found the (etymological) remnants of that earliest form of human community.

Conspicuously, Vico's proof of an early communal arrangement among individuals rested on his personal convictions about the nature of humans. In the first place, Vico affirmed as an unquestionable truth that the sociability of humans had yielded not only their union but also their sharing, or pooling, of their material things (*utilitates*) with one another. "Human beings," Vico conjectured, were naturally suited for "the sharing of utilities with others according to the principle of the equal good (*ex aequo bono*)," and as a matter of consequence, the formation of "society" necessarily entailed "the community (*communio*) of those utilities."[150] Beyond the force of strong opinion, as evidence for that original community of things and interests Vico further combed the historical record for what was presumably known about the most ancient forms of society.

While Vico often generalized from historical particulars in support of his argument, he had a strong preference for historical evidence that was derived from the most arcane of philological work, both here and in his subsequent works. In what was his inimitable fashion, then, Vico suggested that the nature of the most ancient *societas* could also be known from the etymological study of its cognates and their etymons, whose meaning presumably would illuminate the origins of "society" itself. As a cognate of *societas,* Vico proposed the Latin word *sodalitas,* or sodality, which, he insisted, derived from the etymon *sodes* and what was the expression *si audes,* "that you do as you please," an expression that he uniquely interpreted for his reader as evidence of the liberty of the individual within the original society.[151] However idiosyncratic his proof may have been, it is uncontestable that by "society" Vico intended an original community of people and goods, or what was a moral entity whose members enjoyed a condition of both natural justice and perfect liberty, and that with this intention Vico vociferously contested the politics of the modern tradition of natural law on what were its own neoclassical terms.

In the *Diritto universale,* the formation of "society" had especial significance, as it not only gave content to that sense of justice Vico attributed to humans but also represented one of his most fundamental points of contention with the tradition of natural law. If in the later orations Vico derived the idea of "society" from the ancient tradition of natural law, then in the legal treatise Vico more specifically understood and explicitly presented his particular exposition of the same as a rejoinder to the conjectures and, more important, core values of the modern tradition of natural law. In the modern tradition of natural law and its successor science of society, the human instinct for self-preservation and the circumstantial condition of unsatisfied needs together had provided the efficient cause for the formation of society, and irreversibly had marked the purpose of the human union.[152] As most moderns would tell it, in other words, the history of civilization essentially had its origins and developments in self-interest. Consequently, it was in sharp polemic with this story of civilization that Vico proposed his own, which cast the occasion for human society in terms of the exigencies and ends of natural justice.

In his own story of civilization, Vico subordinated the history of human needs and instincts to that of justice and the edifying rewards that justice conferred on its beneficiaries. Making justice and the edification of humanity the quintessential purpose of their union, Vico presented his vision of the origins of society as a rebuttal to the utilitarianism of the philosophers from Epicurus to the early Enlightenment. Objecting to the mean self-interestedness those philosophers had ascribed to humans, Vico first asserted that humans were sociable by nature and that this sociability predisposed them to the abandonment of a state of nature for life in community. Further taking issue with the utilitarian purpose those philosophers had attributed to the human union, Vico insisted that the practical occasion for the formation of society was not to be conflated with its cause and end. At the crux of Vico's objection to the natural law tradition in the *Diritto universale* was his conviction that the human instinct for self-preservation was not an end in itself that motivated all of human behavior. "Utility (*utilitas*)," Vico objected, was "not the mother of law (*ius*) and human society," as his predecessors "Epicurus, Machiavelli, Hobbes, Spinoza and Bayle asserted," but rather was the "occasion by which human beings...were drawn to cultivate society or rather to live in accord with their social nature."[153] And what Vico indubitably intended by living "in accord with their social nature" was living by the laws of equality. As he more grandiloquently had painted the origins of society in the

Sinopsi: "Utility is the occasion upon which is awakened in the mind of the human the idea of equality (*ugualità*), which is the eternal motive (*cagione*) of justice."[154] In contradistinction to the tradition of natural law and that of Enlightenment social science, in other words, Vico fiercely argued that human needs had been mistaken as the efficient cause and end of "society," when they merely had prompted humans to overcome that separation from one another born of original sin so as to live by their distinctive social nature and equitable principles. Although Vico did agree with his interlocutors that needs had drawn humans into community, he took umbrage at their conclusion that the purpose of society was simply to enable the satisfaction of those same needs. In passionate defense of the sociability and justice of humanity, Vico objected that "society" had been formed because humans had needs and because it was natural to humans to provide equally for them. As will be shown, the originary "society," or community, was that means by which humanity organized itself once it had outgrown the provisions for justice rendered by an abundant and unpoliticized nature.

Although Vico had expressed his differences with the modern tradition of natural law in the form of trenchant objections, he rather engaged his differences with the Roman tradition in what was undoubtedly the most creative of ways. If he found some corroboration of his convictions in ancient history, then he also acknowledged and, more important, artfully interpreted the most prestigious Roman evidence to the contrary, which he travailed to subsume within the argument of his own work. However uncompromising Vico's beliefs about the nature of society and law may have been, the Neapolitan neither shied from nor dismissed the complexities posed to them by the prevailing Roman models for the same. From its very inception, indeed, the methodology of the *Diritto universale* could be characterized as a painstaking essay by Vico to ingeniously craft a fit between his political imagination and the prevailing models of "society" (*societas*) and "law" (*ius*), especially as those models were known to contemporaries from the canon of Roman philosophy and the corpus of Roman law. And an ingenious fit was crafted by Vico through a narrative of the course of human history, whose development progressed in step with the advent of new Roman legal institutions, and whose origins and ends bore the unmistakable imprint of his own ethico-political tenets. Vico availed himself of history to make sense of the plethora of legal institutions and jurisprudential models offered by Roman civilization and to advocate his own ideals as natural to humans and as befitting of a mature political civilization such as his own.

In the case of the Roman record, indeed, there was ample evidence to the contrary of what Vico wished to prove about the nature of humans and the norms, or laws, of their originary community, which forced the Neapolitan to confront and reevaluate the most revered examples of the law (*ius*) of that ancient society. As could be suspected, the first major stumbling block posed by the Roman tradition for Vico was that of the ancient ius gentium, which had offered boilerplate norms for the regulation of the commerce, and thus conduct, of humans in "society" since (at least) the time of Cicero. Indeed, it was Cicero himself who in *De officiis* famously identified what he specifically called the principles (*ratio*) for the conservation of the "society of humans" (*societas hominum*) and the "community of life" (*communitas vitae*), a set of minimalist philosophical precepts that he immediately identified with the prescription against harming others and the injunction to respect property, be it of the common stock or of private individuals.[155] To these two precepts Cicero also added the injunction to act in good faith, which he lauded as the foundation of justice.[156] Making of the Ciceronian interpretation of the ancient ius gentium a lasting legacy for European legal civilization, these same precepts of justice were later codified for posterity by the great classical jurist Ulpian, who is cited in the *Digest* as having defined the principles of "law and justice" as "to live honestly, not to harm any other person and to render to each his own."[157] Needless to say, in comparison to the ethical minimalism of these Roman precepts the emphasis that Vico placed on the egalitarianism of the law (*ius*) of human "society" offered a marked contrast to the Roman norm. And it was this marked contrast that Vico both recognized and sought to explain, before embarking on his unique historical account of society and law in the *Diritto universale*.

As a sort of preface to that account, Vico first reclassified those Roman precepts of *ius* as *leges*, which squarely contested their status as the timeless principles of the human community and, in light of tradition, defiantly argued for their historicity.[158] Per Roman history, the *leges* were not norms per se but what we would call statutes, or legislative acts, and thus were born of specific historical conjunctures. Second, Vico suggested that these specific *leges* had pertained to distinct forms of "society," one composed of equals and another composed of unequals. Whereas the prescription against harm had obliged (and adequately regulated) the members of a society founded on equality, the injunction to restore to each his own had pertained to one based on inequality.[159] Clearly, within the legal treatise, the immediate importance of this reclassification of these *iura* as *leges* was to dismiss the acquired association of the ius gentium with "natural law" so that Vico could attach his own (egalitarian) principles to that latter renowned category. At the same time, this reclassification had important consequences for how Vico assessed the legacy of Roman law and the relationship between law and society for his contemporary world. However unassuming the reclassification may have seemed, it debunked the idea that the ius gentium, in particular, and the corpus of Roman law, in general, contained eternal rules of universal application, and it maintained that that this was true because society was dynamic and because society and law mutually shaped each other over time. In light of the fact that Roman law long had been considered the *ius commune,* or common law, of Europe and, especially, of the Italian peninsula, Vico's insistence on the historicity and dynamism of law blatantly undercut the very scaffolding of the legal system of contemporary Europe and made meaningful a historical reconstruction of the relationship between Roman law and society that reevaluated the landmarks of legal history and jurisprudence from the viewpoint of the present. While Vico undoubtedly was indebted to the legal humanism of the Renaissance for his insight into the historicity of Roman law, as it was articulated in the legal treatise this insight also anticipated the current of Enlightenment thought that would propose legal evolution as the backbone of historical progress[160] and shared in the spirit of those legal reformers who sought to produce national codes melding the best of Roman law with customary and natural law.[161] If Vico had staked and would defend his claims about the "society of true justice" and its "natural law" (*ius naturale*), then he also acknowledged that the phenomenon of law (*ius*), like the society that created it, nonetheless was subject to change, if not conscientious revision. And it was the reason for this change and its historical outcomes that Vico would analyze in the greatest of detail over the course of the remainder of the *Diritto universale.*

If Vico's exposition of natural law was revisionist, then his revisionism most notably was informed by a political sensibility that was at once imbued with a passion for justice and sobered by respect for forms of authority.[162] For the content that Vico gave to natural law betrayed a keen sense that the behavior of humans was both principled and yet constrained by externalities whose forces were beyond their immediate control. Among the referents of what Vico called natural law, without further qualification, were those forms of human behavior that were both inspired by humanity's natural sense of justice and shaped by the forces of circumstance. As Vico pronounced in his definition of *ius naturale,* "natural law" followed from humanity's instinctual "election of the good that is known to be equal,"[163] and yet its very elections, or good choices, were circumscribed by systemic conditions and subject to the changes investing the same. As Vico most tersely put it in what immediately followed his definition of *ius naturale:* "And if it seems that this law sometimes changes; then it is not the law but the facts that change."[164] Although the principles of natural law remained constant over time, the exhibited phenomena of natural law evidently were determined by "facts," with which terminology Vico referred to the mutable conventions of society and of political authority in the *Diritto universale*. What Vico uniquely argued here was that natural law was at once a singular standard of conduct and an impetus to a plurality of contingent forms of behavior. Delving into the ontology of law, in other words, Vico presented natural law as if it were both a first cause and an effect of the social order. If this read like a paradoxical mixing and matching of both legal and physical associations with natural law for contemporaries, then for Vico this hybridization of associations with natural law was perfectly tactical.[165] For it was construed to account for the ostensible paradox that the singular behavior of humans manifested itself in a plurality of ways over historical time. If the principle of equality compelled human behavior over the course of its history, as it did in his history of Rome, then the behavioral manifestations of that principle were themselves diverse because conditioned and limited by the "facts" of historical circumstance. That Vico himself assessed his ontology of law as a departure from tradition was betrayed in his discussion of the *ratio legis,* or reason of the law. Vico noted with some disdain that the *ratio legis* oftentimes had been conflated by his Renaissance predecessors with the *mens legis,* or will of the legislator, when it rather concerned the particulars of the law, or *leges,* or what were the objects of the principled historical development of the *ius.*[166]

To codify the phenomena of natural law, Vico additionally made novel use of extant juridical categories with which he could convey the singularity of purpose and dynamism of forms inherent to human behavior and could sharply distinguish between those behavioral forms natural to humans at what was the beginning and culmination of their history, namely, the categories of the *ius naturale prius* (primary natural law) and the *ius naturale posterius* (posterior natural law). As the original philosophical source of these juridical categories and their arcane nomenclature, Vico identified Stoic doctrine, which, he further claimed, analogously had employed the terms *prima naturae* (first *iura* of nature) and *naturae consequentia* (consequent *iura* of nature). Whether or not the ancient Stoics had set this precedent, Vico clearly legitimated, if not arrived at, his own conclusions about the behavior of humanity by applying the Stoic idea of cultivation to the entire species of humans. Like the individual undergoing a personal course of cultivation, according to Vico, so did humanity pass from a stage in which needs and desires shaped behavior to one where the dictates and spirituality of reason ruled both the mind and the body. Pertaining to the outset of history and human development, the *ius naturale prius* thus denoted human behavior that was characterized by the mere "tutelage of the senses" and by the unrestrained "liberty of the emotions," while the *ius naturale posterius,* by contrast, signified cultivated behavior and customs, and was marked by the "dominion of reason, the equilibrium of the emotions and the tutelage of personal decisions."[167]

Although a familiar distinction for his contemporaries, applied to the condition of humanity this was highly innovative on at least two counts. In the first place, it provided more conceptual fodder for the assault on the modern tradition of natural law, as it further historicized and belittled the human instinct of self-preservation per the usage of that tradition. In the above rendition of natural law, the instinct of self-preservation specifically constituted the *prima [iura] naturae,* which according to Vico were those brutish claims on nature that humans shared with the animals, namely, the right to life in the broadest sense of the word.[168] Interpreted as a brutish claim, self-preservation was dismissed by Vico as the hallowed foundation of political civilization and its law; he thus controverted the very premises of the political union according to Hobbes and, more generally, challenged the purported ends of natural law within the modern tradition.[169] In response to the physics of Hobbes and his successors, furthermore, Vico objected to the notion that the instinct of self-preservation constituted the law of social physics among fallen humanity, reminding his reader that within his own metaphysics, *conatus,* or motion, was a property of the mind alone, which was moved toward truth by the remnants it possessed of reason.[170]

Second, Vico's distinction between the *ius naturale prius* and *ius naturale posterius* posited an intrinsic correspondence between natural law and natural right, for which there was little precedence in the tradition of political thought. In his elaboration of the distinction between the *ius naturale prius* and the *ius naturale posterius,* Vico explained that the difference between the two was nothing more than one of the form and content of natural law.[171] As he had clarified that difference in the *Sinopsi,* the *ius naturale posterius* denoted the principles, or form, of "eternal reason," while the *ius naturale prius* signified that substance, or content, given to that *ius* by the "human will," which consisted in what we would call the historical rights of "liberty, dominium and tutelage."[172] In other words, if the *ius naturale posterius* was that principled form animating human behavior, then the *ius naturale prius* was its actual content—or what were the entitlements of humans—at any given historical time as specifically concerned the above designated rights. Put somewhat differently, for Vico the rights of humans in political civilization were historically contingent; and they both followed from the principles of natural law and ever more perfectly conformed to those principles over time.

Within the legal treatise, the force of Vico's analogy between natural law and right was somewhat blunted by his use of the Latin language, which with the term *ius* could denote both concepts. Nonetheless, Vico's analogy stood apart from tradition. In the tradition of classical political thought, the concept of *ius naturale* was dualistic: it had been employed to connote either the injunctions governing behavior or the entitlements of humans qua humans in the extrapolitical world, depending on the context of its usage. And within the modern tradition, where an intrinsic correspondence had been posited between natural law and right, such as in the thought of Hobbes and Pufendorf, that correspondence made a singular principle (i.e., of self-preservation) the basis of natural right, and it subordinated the exercise of one's natural right to the rule of natural law, which made peace (Hobbes), or sociality (Pufendorf), its priority.[173] Thus, Vico's qualification of *ius* and analogy of its concepts uniquely prioritized rights by arguing for their necessity, potentiality, and for the lawlike nature of their taking. By the same token, Vico's qualification also suggested that there were historical limitations on rights that derived from the social relations of their subjects. As noted above, if rights were natural to humans, then their forms were also highly contingent for Vico. For this reason, it would not be meaningful, I believe, to speak of the *Diritto universale* as an early instance of a theory of inalienable rights.[174] Rather, as crafted in the *Diritto universale,* the correspondence between natural law and rights begged a history of rights that embedded them in their larger sociocultural context and that made their progressive acquisition both the milestones and victories of humanity's ever-evolving second nature. In other words, Vico's distinction between the *ius naturale prius* and *ius naturale posterius* necessitated a historical conceptualization and treatment of rights that presumed that humans were impelled to innovation by their intrinsic sense of justice and showed that the outcome of their instinctual claims was conditioned by circumstance. And it was this historical conceptualization of rights that Vico subsequently documented in his history of the civic forms of Roman justice in the *Diritto universale.*

Before reconstructing that history, it bears mentioning a few caveats. In the first place, Vico's history of Rome was not told in the form of a perfectly seamless and chronologically ordered narrative in the *Diritto universale.* Rather, it was presented in a piecemeal way over a series of thematically structured chapters, which built upon one another in sometimes predictable and sometimes unusual ways. As concerns the specific themes and placement of those chapters in the legal treatise, generally speaking it is fair to say that the second part of *De uno* outlined that history of Roman institutions to which Vico gave considerably more content in *De constantia,* and that the final sections of *De uno* and, to a lesser extent, *De constantia* both thematized and evaluated the most famous schools and practices of Roman jurisprudence for their value as models for the present-day judiciary.

Second, it is undeniable that Vico's history of Rome in the legal treatise would have been utterly unrecognizable as a neoclassical narrative—indeed, it defied both the conventions and content of the annalist tradition to which it was so indebted. From the style and content of the *Coniuratio,* it is clear that Vico was a most capable, if not formidable, epigone of classical history, when it suited his purposes. In the case of the *Diritto universale,* however, his narrative exhibited few of the telltale signs of a classical history of Rome: the logic of its narrative was subordinated to the illustration of axioms and its language was peppered with legal jargon; its chronology dispensed with the formality of the foundational myth of Rome, that is, the legend of Romulus and Remus, as well as the usual epochal divisions marked by the rule of Rome's kings and consuls; its topics were selectively culled from Livy, with whom Vico inexorably quibbled about the dates and precise nature of events; and finally, and most conspicuously perhaps, its evidence was drawn from the presumed data of etymology rather than the historical record.[175] It was, in other words, an unusual and tendentious history of Rome, whose aim was to set the record straight regarding not only Rome itself but also, as it turned out, world history. Whereas Vico's Roman history dispensed with the formalities of classicism, the organization of its narrative, and, more important, the universalism of its claims certainly bore a strong resemblance to those landmark histories of the Enlightenment, which shortly would be penned by his younger contemporaries.

Indeed, Vico's Roman history is probably best understood as a transitional example of the contemporary genre of universal history between its baroque incarnation, which had embedded a pluralistic history of world peoples within the sacral time of biblical chronology, and its Enlightenment one, which would posit the singular history of Europe outside of sacral time and present it as the generalizable experience of the greater world.[176] As a transitional example, Vico's history distinctly shared a number of features with baroque universal history. In particular, it made numerous references to the legends and customs of diverse ancient peoples and, most notably, essayed to preserve, and rework, biblical chronology as the frame for its own narrative.[177] Regardless of its baroque features, in the *Diritto universale* Vico's history of Rome adumbrated a claim that he would more fully articulate in the *Scienza nuova* and that was typical of Enlightenment historiography, namely, the notion that the legends, customs, sciences, and experiences of the most diverse world peoples bore a morphological resemblance to one another over time. In this sense, in the *Diritto universale* the history of Rome already was more than the history of that particular civic polity, for it exemplified a pattern of social developments and cultural forms through which Vico could view and assess those of other peoples. And in this sense, Vico's history of Rome anticipated the Enlightenment claim, most fully articulated in the stage theory of society, that all peoples partook of a singular path of development and that this path had most fully been traversed by European civilization.[178] Yet, as much as Vico anticipated the Enlightenment claim about the universality of the European experience and its culture, the emphases of his history of Rome were distinct from the Enlightenment's stage theory of society on a number of counts. What evidently distinguished Vico's own history from that particular genre were the nature of that lawlike force compelling societal development, the kind of progress won by the agents of historical change and, no less, the bases for the alleged universality of the Roman experience. For Vico's history above all was the chronicle of the acquisition by humanity of justice, by which he meant equity. Consequently, what mattered to Vico in his reconstruction of Rome was the pattern and forms of justice that the history of the *urbs orbis* exemplified. Indeed, if there was anything distinctive about Vico's history of Rome, it was his contentious demonstration that this particular urban space had contained within itself a history of those rights that were particular to political civilization and that ideally pertained to all peoples of the globe. And it was the reasons for the global exemplarity of that urban space and the nature of the rights that it exhibited that I shall now consider.

From Natural Law to Historically Grounded Social Theory: Vico's Revisionist History of Rome and Civic Rights

In the *Diritto universale,* the exemplarity of Roman history lay in its illustration of the singular form and pluralistic content of natural law. In defiance of conventional political wisdom,[179] Vico hypothesized that Rome provided a model of constitutional change whose beginning and culmination were marked by distinct species of natural law. In other words, he patently reconstructed Roman history in light of his prior distinction between the *ius naturale prius* and *ius naturale posterius.* Abandoning those specific terms for more conventional ones, however, Vico specifically claimed that the course of Roman history had been a passage from the rule of an ancient ius gentium, by which he meant the law of war, to the rule of an *ius gentium naturale,* by which he denoted a supreme law common to all peoples. What was more, Vico painstakingly showed that both rules were manifested in the content that the rights of dominium, liberty, and tutelage assumed in the respective epochs he examined. At the heart of Vico's history, in other words, was an examination of the natural right to the property of oneself and of one's things, as evidenced by the Roman example.

The reasons for Vico's choice of Rome for his history of law and its species of rights were, on the one hand, indebted to a number of time-honored associations with Roman civilization and, on the other, predetermined by his own philosophical and, more important, political convictions. First, in Vico's own time Roman civilization was recognized as the undisputed progenitor and codifier of European law, making it the most obvious subject for his history in the eyes of contemporaries. Second, it bears mentioning that Vico viewed Rome as (literally) illustrative of ancient civilization, if not because of its great antiquity per se then because of its value as a treasure trove of information about the most ancient customs and practices of peoples predating the Romans. In his philosophical work *De antiquissima* (1710), Vico already had asserted the great antiquity of Italic civilization—that is, of the Etruscans and Ionians of ancient Italy—and had argued for the importance of the legacy of Italic civilization for the Romans, in whose language the "wisdom" of the ancient Italians presumably lay reposited. Similarly, in the *Diritto universale,* Vico assiduously maintained that the Latins were the heirs of the most ancient cultures of the Italian peninsula, and that the Latin language provided an incontrovertible source of evidence about the originary state of their polities. Put somewhat differently, it was Vico's philosophical conviction that the political culture of the Romans and their Latin language held the keys to the realities of a prehistory, which heretofore had been clouded by the legends of mythology.[180]

Yet, the inheritance of Rome was but one of the purported reasons for its exemplarity. For Vico supplemented this philosophical assertion with the political one that the foundation of the Roman polity had replicated, and most fully dramatized, those institutions that typically had marked the origins of ancient polities worldwide. Indeed, what made Rome an icon of universal history for Vico was the typicality of the institution by which Romulus reputedly had grown the city: the establishment of a sacred asylum. What was typical, and thus important, about that particular institution in Vico's own mind was its ability not only to diversify the community de facto but also to forge it anew out of two essentially unequal groups de jure. In the inequality of Rome's constituent groups, in other words, Vico found a famous example of what he believed to be the common origins and aporia of political civilization. In his history, Vico thus placed an especial emphasis both on the foundation of Rome and on its so-called conflict of the orders, because he believed that they were emblematic of the political nature and dynamic animating all civic communities and, more important, the historical development of the entire globe. If the greatest originality of Vico's history lay not in his etymological evidence, then it is was in his observation that the struggle for rights was not only inherent to the foundation of all individual political civilizations but also a struggle of truly global proportions. However neoclassical his idiom and ancient his metaphysics, then, Vico provided what was the most pointed of critiques of political civilization and an account of what we would call the process of globalization *avant la lettre*.

In the *Diritto universale,* the origins of political civilization lay in warfare. As Vico recounted it, the foundation of the polity, its institutions, and, no less, the nature of its constituency all were the outcomes of originary acts of violence. If humans naturally formed just "societies," as Vico claimed in the first section of *De uno,* then those communities had been characteristic of the earliest epoch of human history and were alien to the institutions of the civic polity. According to Vico, the history of what he called "dark time" had been composed of five epochs,[181] and it was only during the first epoch, when humankind purportedly had been governed by a "theocratic" regime and the basic unit of society was the family, that all domestic utilities were held in common.[182] Furthermore, the stability of that community of goods was contingent on the maintenance of an external peace that proved fragile at best. What most distinctly interested Vico about the history of early humanity, therefore, was the occasion for warfare, which he identified with the institution of an inequality of things and, more important, of persons. Like a number of ancient and modern natural law theorists, Vico conjectured that prior to the civil state all humans had enjoyed a natural right of possession to the fruits of nature,[183] which he likened to their occupation of a seat in the theater, implicitly citing Cicero.[184] And Vico too hypothesized that the advent of scarcity had brought an end to that golden age of natural possession and instituted conventional forms of property, as had Grotius and Locke before him.[185] However, in contradistinction to his predecessors and in anticipation of Rousseau, Vico associated the institution of conventional property with the advent of a form of inequality among men that was quintessentially unnatural, because more than an inequality of things it also entailed a form of slavery.[186]

Vico explicitly accounted for this conjuncture of property and inequality with the hypothesis that in the state of scarcity the predations of the strong had made the law of war apply universally, creating among its victims both victors and vanquished of necessarily unequal status. In other words, Vico proposed that the ius gentium, or the law of war, which especially had pertained to nations in the work of Grotius, had in the most ancient of times also determined the relationships among individuals and, what was more, ineluctably influenced the bases for creation of the first civic polities. As Vico recounted the events, the usurpation of the natural fruits belonging to the weak by the strong had forced the weak to seek refuge among those humans who had been able to defend themselves from the predations, and who allegedly were known as either "Optimates" for their excellence and great strength or *viri* for their reputed virtues or *inclyti* for the splendor of their victory.[187] The Optimates who received the weak and offered them protection, furthermore, purportedly had been living in family units constituting established settlements and had maintained their lives by cultivating tracts of land, which they marked off by borders.[188] And it was in those cultivated tracts of land that the refugees of war took asylum, exercising the hallowed corollary of humanity's natural right to self-preservation, namely, the right to asylum.[189] However, per the law of war, in exchange for asylum, the refugees literally were indebted for their lives to the Optimates, to whom they consequently owed perpetual servitude. As Vico specifically explained, the refugees were obliged to acknowledge their debt and to accept the real condition of subjugation that it entailed by honoring and compensating their patrons with their perpetual and uncompensated labor.[190] Thus, the first *civitas,* or city, was born and founded on the wartime customs associated with victory and defeat.[191] Composed of the patrons and clients of the asylum, the first city was sustained by the governance of the former and the unconditional labor of the latter. The single most important consequence of this form of clientelism for Vico was that the city was predicated on the appropriation by the Optimates of the refugees' natural rights of personal liberty, self-tutelage, and dominion, which divided the civic polity from its very inception into those who possessed full natural rights and those who possessed none.[192] As Vico repeatedly made plain, the origins of the city thus presented the most uncanny of political paradoxes: for the singular civic community henceforth would be composed of two distinct "body politics," making the distinguishing feature of the *civitas* the division of its intramural population and the unnatural alienation of the rights of one group by the other.[193]

To formalize this arrangement, the Optimates made their own prerogative the so-called *ius nexi,* which, according to Vico, literally made "bondsmen" of the clients, by enforcing their labor by the threat, if not means, of corporeal restraint.[194] What was more, the Optimates closed ranks among themselves and established an "order," or defensive league, that bolstered the power wielded by its individual members with the force of the whole.[195] Per Vico's own analysis, then, the Optimates literally ruled the civic community by the norms of the ius gentium, making proper to the political culture of the civic polity the customary practices and laws of war.[196] Consequently, the subjugation of their clients made the patrons of the civic polity not only the masters of non-agnatic groups but also the sole rights-bearing subjects of the community and, as such, the sole ministers and beneficiaries of the rites of worship, the exclusive custodians of the laws, and, no less, the proprietors of the lands. If there was a single political paradox that Vico's conjectural history dramatized, in other words, it was that the scarcity of resources had made self-enslavement a consensual arrangement and that the enforcement of this consensual agreement had set the members of the incipient polity on a (collision) course demarcated by the clients' vindication of their rights to liberty, (self-)tutelage, and dominion.

It was analogously to this conjectural history that Vico uniquely reinterpreted the origins and history of Rome.[197] Indeed, Vico went to some lengths to maintain that the foundation of Rome had reproduced the same conditions and institutions as those intrinsic to the originary city of Optimates, although its foundation was relatively recent by Vico's own calculation and had been documented otherwise by the annalistic tradition.[198] In defiance of classical tradition, in other words, Vico took pains to show that Rome similarly had been shaped by the norms and customs of the ius gentium and that the same had been of lasting significance for the Roman polity. To this end, Vico most conspicuously engaged in polemic with Livy regarding the origins and early history of Rome. As Livy had narrated it, the early history of Rome had been a history of its individual leaders and the succession of its political forms. According to the conventional wisdom codified by Livy, the city had been founded and then ruled by kings for the first 250 years of its history before the oppressive tyranny of Tarquinius Superbus had compelled the people of Rome to alter their constitution and to found what would be known as the Roman Republic.[199] In sharp contradistinction to this authoritative view of Roman history, Vico quibbled with Livy regarding the origins of Rome, the exploits of its individual leaders, the reputed constitution of its polity, and, most important perhaps, the institutions promoting its demographic growth, trouncing the annals of political tradition in favor of his singular systemic view of human history.

In the first place, Vico utterly dispensed with the legends surrounding the foundation of Rome—most notably, the legend of Romulus and Remus and the rape of the Sabines—to impose on Roman history the schema for what he called the "origin and succession of universal (profane) history."[200] For Vico, the city of Rome had been neither founded by Romulus and Remus nor inaugurated by the former's infamous slaying of the latter, legends about the origins and kingship of Rome that he did not even bother to contest. In the place of these legends, Vico offered instead a caricature of Romulus that literally subordinated his persona and individual agency to the logic of the larger social structures that he helped to put in place, defying traditional views about his right to the kingship and the constitution of the incipient Roman polity.[201] First, Vico asserted that Romulus had founded the city with a number of companions, who together constituted an order of fathers and who elected Romulus king from among themselves.[202] In Vico's account of Rome, in other words, the kingship was elective and not the uncontested prize of the preeminent warrior. What was more, the political institution of the kingship was of less importance than the familism of the founders, which, as Vico most thoroughly showed, inexorably structured Roman society and set the effectual parameters within which its constituents found their delimited roles and demanded their natural rights.

Beyond his quibbles with Livy over the legendary beginnings of Rome, Vico construed a number of distinct parallels between the supposed social structure of early humanity and that of the incipient Roman polity. Under the cover of analogy, Vico broached the age-old question of the origins of the patrician and plebeian orders of the city, to which he offered a most original response that contrasted with that of his ancient predecessors.[203] Most important for Vico, like that of the originary city, the constituency of early Rome was the by-product of warfare and was composed of the same two distinct and antagonistic classes: the victors and refugees of warfare. In the first place, Vico sought to evidence that the patriciate uniformly descended from a formidable class of warriors. According to him, the companions of Romulus had been warriors, proof of which he identified in the etymology of their appellation "Quirites," which allegedly derived from the ancient Sabine word for their spear, *quir*, and not from the toponym Cures as Livy had speculated.[204] And as warriors, Vico emphasized, Romulus and the Roman fathers had adopted asylum-seeking clienteles, with whom they necessarily populated the civic community, and from whom the plebeians would descend in their turn.[205] In addition, Vico claimed that the deliberate policy of Romulus caused the ranks of the clienteles to swell. For Romulus purportedly extended a strategic invitation to other well-known Latin families, who settled in Rome with their war-born clienteles as well,[206] and established a sacred asylum for aggrieved and displaced persons that was of lasting importance for the rejuvenation of the Roman community, giving especial significance to an institution that Livy had mentioned in passing.[207]

In sum, Vico both reinterpreted the historical record and fabricated it anew in the utmost detail to argue that Rome, like the originary city, had adopted the norms of the ius gentium and had replicated the social relations among the victors and their vanquished. As in the originary city, so in Rome the law of war had generated the community's patrons and clients, and it had determined the constituent relationships among them. Vico explicitly retold the legendary beginnings of Rome, in other words, so that the origins of the plebeians were identified with the vicissitudes and slavery born of warfare. However plausible, or even familiar, this account might sound, it was polemical, as the tradition surrounding the origins of the plebeians was cloudy, at best, and the classical sources themselves had made a distinction between the plebeians and the clients of war.[208] As more narrowly concerned the Roman constitution, furthermore, the upshot of Vico's novel history for his analysis of the polity was to give overwhelming precedence to the social structure of Rome over that of its political forms. In short, Vico posited clientelism as the distinguishing feature of Rome, and it was in terms of that particular form of social organization that he would recast the political history of the Roman community, anticipating the objects and insights characteristic of a modern social science such as social anthropology.[209] As Vico wrote, it was the existence of two distinct orders, that is, the so-called patricians and plebeians, within the body of a single city that had inaugurated and would propel the long course of Roman history, which was marked by the successive struggle by the plebeians for their full natural rights.[210]

The most striking difference of Vico's history from the classical tradition, indeed, was his interpretation of the succession of political forms as a succession of the forms of natural rights.[211] Whereas Vico had dispensed with the legends concerning the origins of Roman history, he did recount the watershed events known from tradition, which, according to Livy, had altered the political constitution of Rome irreversibly. However, to those same events Vico gave considerably different significance than had the ancients. Rather than identify in them a change in the political structure of Rome, as had Livy, Vico found in those events the occasions for a change in the legal regime of the Roman polity. For Vico, each legal regime inflected and institutionalized the new nature of the relationship among the patrons and clients of Rome. Consequently, to each period in the history of Rome belonged its own law, which expressly was articulated in those sets of rights respectively assigned to the patrons and clients of the polity. Thus, in Vico's narrative the legal history of the Roman polity proceeded in step with the conflicts and resolutions of the orders. More specifically, the outcomes of those conflicts purportedly regarded the liberty, tutelage, and dominion of both the Roman patrons and, in particular, their clients, the so-called plebeians, who gradually advanced the cause of their rights at their patrons' expense. In contrast to Livy, then, Vico retold the history of Rome so that the stadial acquisition of political gains achieved by the plebeians was reconfigured as their graduated reconquest of natural rights. Indeed, one could say that Vico retold the history of Rome as the history of the plebeians' gradual enforcement of their natural right to postliminy, which per the ius gentium entitled them to the full restoration of their legal personality and civic rights on the cessation of the state and conditions of war.[212]

Of the episodes of Roman history Vico rehearsed in the *Diritto universale,* perhaps the most distinctive was his account of the infamous secessions of the plebs from the city of Rome. According to the classical tradition, those secessions had achieved new political rights for the plebeians and had contributed to the inception and reinforcement of institutions synonymous with the Roman Republic. In particular, Livy had related that the first revolt of the plebs had won for them the critical political concession of their own magistracies, namely, the plebeian tribunes, whose office was inviolable and whose purpose was to aid the plebeians in their defense against the consuls.[213] Similarly, Livy had narrated how the second secession of the plebs had both restored the lapsed tribunate and provided the plebeians with the requisite leverage to enact a number of statutes that increased the instruments of political power at their disposal.[214] If Livy had identified the results of the plebeian secessions with political gains, then Vico associated the same with the victories of the plebeians as humans qua humans, which first and foremost comprehended the legal acknowledgement of the plebeians' natural right to possession of themselves, of their volition, and of their labor—or property, as it were. Indeed, Vico explicitly referred to the legislation that followed the plebeian secessions as "agrarian laws," imputing to these events a reallocation of property and transfer of ownership that only occurred in later times per the historical record.[215] According to Vico, in response to the plebeian revolts, the patrician "fathers" sought to lure the plebeians back to the polity with the concession of more "equitable" conditions. More specifically, those concessions successively awarded the plebeians superior rights to the lands they tilled; and they greatly diminished the powers of guardianship to which they were subject by Roman clientelism. As Vico specifically recounted it, the first secession was organized by the *nexi* and wrested from the patricians the rights of personal liberty and of *dominium bonitarium,* which effectively accorded them the natural possession of the fields they cultivated in exchange for the exaction of a tribute.[216] At the same time, the patricians purportedly preserved the *ius optimum* over the same fields and the *ius nexi* over their clients in case of their delinquency in the payment of the tribute,[217] making the legal gains of the first secession ones that both furthered and tantalized their exponents with the prospect of justice. Consequently, from this secession the order of "plebeians" allegedly was born, making of the once disparate group of refugees (and their descendents) a cohort that was desirous of "new things" and "whose proper characteristic is to struggle for innovations," as Vico put it.[218]

In reaction to subsequent retractions of their gains, the "plebeians" once again seceded from the polity and, this time, additionally acquired the *ius optimum,* or optimal right to the fields they naturally possessed, achieving at last full possession of their own property and of themselves. The application of the *ius nexi* therewith would apply only to the debtors of usury, which Vico identified as the new instrument of power exercised by the patricians over the plebeians of the republic.[219] In Vico's history of Rome, finally, the crowning achievement of the plebeians' victories was the Poetelian Law (Lex Poetelia, 326 BCE), which, Vico noted, had outlawed the commutation of one's person for the repayment of a loan, bringing to an end the possibility of the bondage of plebeians for debt within the Roman polity.[220] In other words, the secessions gradually had lessened the severity of the debt owed by the refugees of war and their descendants until the plebeians had achieved their full personal freedom. For Vico, the secessions had dismantled those inequalities born of war and formalized by the laws to regain for the plebeians their right to the possession of themselves and the fruits of their labor. They had made of the plebeians, in other words, full personal and economic subjects, whose participation in the marketplace henceforth would be unfettered by the tyrannical privileges of the patriciate.

What Vico's history of early Rome illustrated, in sum, was the transformation of the plebeians into full legal persons, whose chief right to self-possession was both recognized and protected by the polity. And what his history importantly argued, furthermore, was that this transformation had taken place under the auspices of natural law, and not under those of the civil law. In polemic with the Renaissance idea of the *civitas* as a place literally immune from the law of war, then, Vico contended that there had been no categorical break between the so-called state of nature and that of the civic polity, or between their respective genera of law.[221] Indeed, Vico's evidence purposively contradicted the notion that the state of war had been temporally anterior to the foundation of the civic polity, and it disproved that the latter was distinguished from the former both for its peace and for the coextensiveness of the law with its community. As the Roman community per received tradition had above all been defined by its common personality and rights at civil law, Vico's model of a divided city boldly challenged the historical record and was an oxymoron, at best.[222] For Vico's model of the Roman polity captured well the political condition of a city where the supposed legal basis of the civic community was belied by the sheer diversity of its legal persons, and where the operative norms of the same, therefore, were guided by natural law. What Vico's history effectively dramatized, in other words, was the political paradox of the metropolis, both ancient and modern:

it controverted the hallowed ideas of the freedom and justice of the city; and it depicted the emergence of a polity that was defined by the commonality of natural proprietary rights rather than the reciprocity of civic duties. It made Rome the supreme example of the anachronism of Renaissance civism, of the metapolitical nature of the city, and, consequently, the necessity of extracivic norms and rights as the basis for the moral guidance and personal protection of a metropolitan constituency.[223] What was more, Vico's model of the Roman polity undeniably accorded new meaning to what it meant to be a full participant in the civic community. For more than the enjoyment of full legal personality, in the *Diritto universale* what could be called citizenship in the Roman polity demonstratively entailed legal possession of oneself and one's natural property. In other words, Vico clothed the notion of citizenship in its juridical terms, so that the citizen was a rights bearer and proprietor, and, analogously, the civic polity was a guarantor of his proprietary rights per natural jurisprudence.[224] Put somewhat differently, Vico both embraced and transformed the juridical definition of citizenship so that it was inclusive and, more specifically, could make both intelligible and actionable within the political territory of the city the natural rights of the entire community regardless of their original provenance.

Vico's Critique of the Roman Constitution and of the Paradoxes of Metropolitan Society, Ancient and Modern

If Vico interpreted anew the events of early Rome, then he also gave novel content to the constitutional forms of the Roman polity and the order of their succession.[225] Just as his interpretation of the events of Roman history highlighted their importance for the relationship of the orders, so did his definition of the constitutional forms of Rome especially draw attention to the parameters governing the interaction between the patricians and the plebeians. Since antiquity, the succession of the constitutional forms of Rome had been associated with the foundation and passage of the polity from the state of monarchical to republican rule. To the extent that Vico maintained the semantics of this political tradition, the meaning of these terms was utterly transformed by his keen speculation about what we would call the systemic nature of the constitutional forms described. In the first place, Vico gave an entirely new connotation to the very notion of the city, or *civitas*. As already described, Vico identified the foundation of the *civitas* with that asylum that Rome had provided for the refugees of war. At the same time, according to Vico, the *civitas* also had internalized the law of violence and its system of justice to administer the refugees, who therewith were deprived of all that was proper to them, including their personal liberty. Needless to say, the notion of a city ruled by the customs and implements of war was nothing less than the strangest of paradoxes for contemporaries, since in the Italian tradition the Roman *civitas* long had been associated with the citizen community, its system of participatory politics, and the rule of law. Indeed, by legal definition, the *civitas* was "citra vim habitas," or literally an inhabited space that repelled acts of violence and their related customs.[226] Similarly, Vico attributed to the Roman "republic," or *respublica,* a meaning that was antithetical to its primary usage. Rather than denote a mixed constitution, which authors from Polybius to Machiavelli had praised for its invincible stability,[227] Vico used the term *respublica* to signify the *societas omnium bonorum,* or what had been the Roman consortium of goods among non-agnatic individuals.[228] As Vico recounted it, *respublica* quite literally meant the public holding of the aggregate property of its members; for the accommodation of wartime refugees had behooved the fathers to secure their own persons, things, and privileges by uniting in a military order that was not only organized for their self-defense but also for the pooling of their resources.

For contemporaries, this usage of *respublica* certainly involved misattribution on at least two counts. In the first place, and most conspicuously, it prematurely dated the advent of the republic to that period when Rome presumably had been ruled by monarchs, conflating two distinct political periods in its history. Second and more important, Vico's usage of the term *respublica* gutted it of its hallmark political connotation to locate the defining characteristics of the republic in its structural organization of property holdings. Indeed, Vico brought an analogous interpretation of the Roman polity to bear on the reign of Servius Tullius, a sixth-century king of Rome who was famous for favoring the plebs and instituting the census, which Vico uniquely viewed as the foundation of what he called the *respublica democratica.*[229] According to Livy, the census had proved instrumental in the preparation for warfare, as it assigned to distinct classes of men different obligations for the provision of the military forces.[230] By contrast, Vico spoke of the census as a measure for land reform that specifically granted clients the right of usufruct over their cultivated plots, radically reinterpreting what had been a military initiative as one that concerned the legal right of possession.[231] In contradistinction to both his ancient and Renaissance predecessors, then, Vico put stock in Roman history not for its lessons in governance but rather for its presumed disclosures about the material origins of the Roman constitution.

Although property had not been an important feature of the political identity of Rome—it was neither a qualification for nor a hallmark of citizenship in the Roman polity—Vico contended that the defining characteristic of each form of the Roman constitution had been its respective system of property holding. Indeed, Vico reconstructed the constitutional forms of Rome as if they were both determined and permeated by the respective rights of the Roman orders to the legal possession of property. More than a curious reinterpretation of the Roman constitution, then, Vico's history of Rome mounted an argument for the centrality of the legal definition of property to the political structures of the civic community. In other words, Vico's analysis of Roman history maintained that the political institutions of the *urbs* were inseparable from property relations, arguing for the larger significance of property to the political culture of the community long before the advent of Marxist sociology.[232] Indeed, it was in light of the legal system of property holding that Vico also believed he could account for the hallmark customs of each polity as well as the very legends that each harbored about the past, as his discussion of the popular literature and legal culture of Rome made plain.

While Vico believed that the Roman constitution was predicated on the property relations of its orders, he also maintained that the cultural manifestations of those relations were manifold, as humans naturally had told stories about the institutional beginnings of their history and, in particular, most tenaciously had maintained the very forms of their prior institutions as symbols. Like many of his medieval predecessors and early modern contemporaries, such as Bacon, Vico believed that fables contained veiled truths about the past.[233] Consequently, in the *Diritto universale* Vico allocated some space to the interpretation of mythology and popular legends, in which he specifically found evidence for the experience of early humanity.[234] Indeed, Vico claimed that the first mythologists, or "poets," had been "political theologians,"[235] whose stories had made famous the universal customs of the earliest societies, all of which Vico made corroborate the pattern he had established for the foundation and progress of cities.[236] In Vico's interpretation of the pantheon of the gods, for example, Mercury, the swift-footed messenger of the gods and deity of trade, represented the delegation sent by the fathers to the plebs for the deliverance of the first agrarian law; and Ceres, the goddess of grains, was also known as Legifera, or [to] lay down the law, as a symbolic reminder that the agrarian law simultaneously had marked the first act of legislation.[237] What was more, Vico similarly interpreted Aeneas, the protagonist in the canonical epic by Vergil, as representative of the types of men who first founded and ruled over humanity;[238] and, in his *Notae* to the *Diritto universale,* his third volume of the legal treatise (consisting of notes to the prior ones), Vico interpreted the poems of Homer, as (jumbled) narrations of the universal history of the dark time.[239] As further evidence for the universality of the Roman pattern of history, Vico similarly read the Greek myth of Theseus, the legendary founder and king of Athens—who famously had vanquished the symbols of Cretan power over the Athenians, the Marathon Bull and Cretan Minotaur, and single-handedly had united the peoples of Attica under his rule—as a metaphorical tale about the freeing of the Athenian plebeians from their rule by the Optimates and subjection to the *nexus*, which, Vico added, had established Athens as a "popular state" and refuge for the plebeians from the country-side of Attica.[240] In other words, for Vico the figures of mythology were verisimilar characters, who bore testimony to the experience of humanity during its preliterate times. The figures of myth were, in sum, typological emblems of the protagonists of human history and, more important, their stories were allegories of its grandest developments, as Vico had ascertained them. As much as Vico's interpretation of myth and epic legend were also interesting for the novel conclusions they reached regarding the primitive-ness of the first poets and the dating of their legends, it is incontrovertible that Vico first took an interest in myth and epic for the same reasons he had in etymology, that is, for their value as data for his conjectural history of the originary city.[241]

If Vico took an interest in legend, then he also applied his hermeneutics to the cultural practices of law, in which he further found symbols of what he conjectured had been the actual prior customs of humanity. More than a change in legal regime, Vico argued, the passage from one age of history to the next also entailed a transformation of customary practices into sym-bols of themselves.[242] At the root of this notion was Vico's observation that the violence of the earliest civic communities was preserved in a number of those rituals mediating the transactions of a more civil society.[243] To give but one example, Vico spoke of the ritual accompanying the formal conveyance of land as literally reenacting the manumission of the *nexi*. As Vico described it, the Roman ritual of land conveyance required the surrender of a literal *nexus,* which Vico identified as a knot emblematic of the former condition of the clients. This act of surrender ostensibly symbolized the assent of the patrons to the conveyance of their property by way of analogy, as the land, like its cultivators, once had been their exclusive right and had been kept by the use of force.[244] Subsequent to the secessions of the plebs, in other words, legal rituals imitated the violence that previously had enforced the propri-etary rights of the Optimates. For those rituals were mediated by emblems that were at once a reminder and supercession of those forms of authority that had governed the relationship among the orders. While it is not evident why Vico so insisted on this emblematic continuity of forms, I would hazard the guess that the reason for his conviction derived, in part at least, from his generalization of the equity practices of the praetors, who were believed to have transferred the traditional legitimacy of certain legal categories to non-pertinent objects by way of fictitious analogies.[245] As Vico himself held the conviction that the process of history entailed the progressive application of equity, it is easy to imagine that his cultural hermeneutics derived from the assumption that the historical process similarly involved the regular use of fictitious analogies, be they verbal or emblematic, to more extensively render justice. Be that as it may, whereas generations had found in the Roman legal corpus standards of justice, therein Vico more specifically found forms of justice for all those whose inclusion in the civic polity was physical rather than politico-moral.

Still, Vico's history was anything but a call to arms. Rather, it was a most sophisticated diagnosis of the wrongs inherent to the metropolitan community that was intended to rally the judiciary to the cause of social justice. While Vico's conjectural history evidently was formulated as a contribution to natural law, unlike other contributions to the same, Vico's was neither an endorsement nor a scurrilous critique of a single political constitution. Whereas Hobbes and (the late) Grotius both had endorsed a monarchical form of government, and Rousseau scathingly would depict the same, Vico distinctively criticized political civilization per se and uniquely identified its panacea not in any particular constitution but in a form of justice. Indeed, Vico explicitly censured Grotius's justification of self-enslavement precisely because he understood that it had arisen not out of consensus, as Grotius had believed, but out of necessity.[246] Put somewhat differently, the novelty of Vico's history lay not in its political but social analysis: Vico employed history not to justify a particular political form but rather to account for the genesis and development of political forms over time, an account that subordinated the importance of any particular constitution per se to what we would call the social reasons for its existence. And it was Vico's emphasis on the significance of social relations and processes that both distinguished his work from that of his chosen interlocutors and made his work difficult, if not uncanny, I believe, for his contemporaries.

Be that as it may, if there was a constitution Vico criticized,[247] then it was the one Vico and his contemporaries associated with the fief and the institutions of feudal law, whose historical origins he assigned to the most ancient law of war and to the most ancient customs of clientelism.[248] Unveiling the dominions and privileges of the European nobility as remnants of the ius gentium and as proper to a state anterior to the rule of civil law, that is, the *ius romanum,* this ostensibly historical observation clearly lodged derisive criticism at what was a contemporary institution for Vico. For it presented the fief, feudal law, and, no less, the baronage itself as residua of a less-civilized past, or what were anachronisms in the present, articulating the sharpest of polemics against the persistence of feudal prerogative and, in this sense, anticipating the sensibility of the Kingdom's greatest reformers during the age of Enlightenment.[249] At the same time, and more significantly, Vico substantiated the anachronism of feudal law in the present by way of analogy with the Roman past: specifically, he posited feudalism as analogous to the clientelism of archaic Rome, which, he further argued, had permeated the city in both archaic and republican times.[250] While this claim about the clientelism of ancient Rome was not entirely novel in Vico's day, the lessons that Vico took from it were unusual and provided the bridge between his civic and world histories in both the *Diritto universale* and the first edition of the *Scienza nuova*.

As has already been noted by his critics, Vico's description of the clientelism of ancient Rome recalled the debate about the origins and customs of feudalism carried on by the greatest protagonists of legal Humanism: indeed, it bore some resemblance to the arguments of sixteenth-century scholars such as Budé, Alciato, Zasius, and Cujas, who had argued for the origins of the fief and feudal law in the Roman system of clientelism.[251] However, the resemblance that Vico's argument bore to the Romanism of those Humanists was complicated both by Vico's own characteristic eclecticism—which mixed and matched the evidence for what had been two irreconcilable positions in the sixteenth century, namely, that of the Romanists and that of the Germanists—and by his curious emphasis on the persistence of feudalism internal to the civic culture of Rome itself.[252]

In the works of the Humanists, the patron-client relations of Rome had literally marked the origin of feudal custom and its law—indeed, they had represented the social institution by which the Romans subjected, and effectively incorporated, new peoples into its empire.[253] However, the precise link between the institutions of Rome and those of the conquered territories is what interested Vico least about the analogy between the two. By contrast, what interested Vico about the analogy between ancient Rome and post-Roman Europe was the evidence both cases independently provided for the resilience and transmutation of the institutions born of the law of war. What the resemblances between ancient Rome and post-Roman Europe made plain was that "feudal law" was born of war and yet survived well beyond the peace, regardless of the contingencies of space and time. In *De constantia*, for example, Vico went to some lengths to show that although the law of war had been superseded by the institutions of the Roman Republic, the relations among the orders still maintained forms and rituals that were coeval to the ancient ius gentium, such as the retinue, the *cena,* and the *sportulae.*[254] In other words, the customs of war had endured long beyond their relevance to the constitution of the city of Rome, so that even the "free" republic was populated by armies of clients who publicly rendered obsequiousness in return for customary gifts, partaking of an older, and arguably atavistic, economy of exchange. And this observation was by no means meant to be of antiquarian interest but rather the basis for unlocking the complexity of the contemporary world, where, Vico noted, there was a similar persistence of anachronism.

In conjunction with his discussion of medieval feudal practices, for instance, Vico also noted examples of their survival in his present day, making plain to his reader the actuality of his historical inquiry.[255] As had been the case in his account of the originary polity, so in his discussion of the origins of feudal law what was at stake for Vico was the typology of civic society. If the Humanists had fought over the fief as a way to assess the applicability of Roman law to the French legal system, then Vico rather drew on their evidence to reinforce his standing argument about the ontology of the Roman community and of its law. Vico was willfully eclectic precisely because he did not share the political concerns of the legal Humanists: the origins of the fief was not the test case for the validity of Roman law per se but was more evidence for the noncontemporaneity of social forms in the metropolis and, consequently, the incongruousness of civic society with its written law. To the extent that the Humanist debate about the origins of the fief struck a contemporary chord for Vico, it was because of what it implied about the nature and enduring legacy of the originary civic community. Indeed, as chapter 4 shows, Vico would argue for the persistence of clientelism as a world-historical phenomenon, making the Romanist thesis the key to understanding not only the metropolis but also the global permutations of the civic order.

As a diagnosis of the civic community, Vico's Romanism was the flip side of his programmatic vision of the endpoint of the history of law and of jurisprudence. For Vico's interests in the history of law and society not only included the tensions between the two but also concerned the role of the judiciary and its jurisprudence in the accommodation of extant laws, be they Roman or customary, to the exigencies of the present. And it is to Vico's treatment of the role of the judiciary and its jurisprudence in contemporary society and, in particular, their significance for the personal liberty, self-determination, and material autonomy of the civic community that I now turn.

Vico's History of Roman Jurisprudence and Exhortation of the Judiciary to Reform

Although Vico's interest in the grand events of Rome was largely limited to the period of its monarchical rule, his interest in the legal institutions of Rome regarded a broader period in its history. Indeed, much of the third section of *De uno* was devoted to pinpointing the emergence and function of the different sources of the law during what is properly called the Roman Republic, namely, the Law of the Twelve Tables, the *Senatus consulta,* the *leges* of the Roman assemblies (or *comitia*), the plebiscites, and, most important for Vico, praetorian law.[256] At the same time, Vico took an even keener interest in how those sources of law furthered the larger pattern of historical development he had sketched in his treatment of early Rome, that is, the history of the restitution of natural rights to the membership of the civic polity. Consequently, Vico focused his attention on the spirit of those institutions and their laws to underscore the role that they played in equalizing and enforcing the rights among the members of the Roman metropolis.

With his analysis, Vico first argued that the spirit of Roman law both instantiated and protected the interests of the polity's dominant groups. Specifically, he showed that both law and jurisprudence were tools of the powerful, and that both changed with the modification of the hierarchy and power bases of the Roman orders. For Vico, the trajectories of Roman law and jurisprudence went hand in hand: they commenced with the "arcane jurisprudence" of the patriciate and the codification of the Twelve Tables, and they culminated in the "benevolent jurisprudence" of the emperor's class of professional jurists and the *ius civile* of the Empire. Like so many of his categorical claims about the Roman world, this typology of jurisprudence too was original, and it too presumed that the raison d'être of these respective types was uniquely determined by the social upheavals of the civic community.

In what he called the *respublica,* for example, Vico reminded his reader that the power base of the Optimates greatly had been undercut by the census, which not only had redistributed land but also had destabilized the categories of "patrician" and "plebeian" by making wealth, as opposed to lineage, the basis for one's classification within the polity and access to its magistracies.[257] Consequently, this fluidity of the orders had spurred the so-called patricians by lineage to develop new strategies to maintain the exclusivity of their rank and its concomitant powers, strategies that Vico identified in their practice of usury,[258] and, more centrally, in their jealous guarding of the laws and practice of an arcane jurisprudence.[259] According to Vico, the jurisprudence of the patricians by lineage had derived from that of their ancestors, the Optimates, whose jurisprudence had been arcane, because it employed a recondite poetic language (based on similitude) to which they alone were privy,[260] and rigorous, because it enforced the letter of the law.[261] In the *respublica democratica* this arcane jurisprudence was tactically employed to stymie the new social mobility and institutional gains won by the plebeians. In particular, it was renewed and deployed to countervail the equity and transparency of the Twelve Tables, that first body of written laws whose codification, Vico reported, had been demanded by the plebeians themselves.[262] In this institutional way, Vico insisted, the patriciate thus sought to stave off the erosion of their power by the democratization of the political institutions and honors of the civic community. Be that as it may, for Vico the plebeians' natural sense of equity would challenge the patrician stranglehold on the provision of justice through the compensatory powers of its own magistracy, that is, the tribunate. And the very codification of the Twelve Tables themselves, appropriately enough, would aid the plebeians to discredit the art of patrician jurisprudence, as the new "facts" of subsequent times would make evident that disconnect between the letter of the law and the reality it was intended to serve, undercutting the formalism of patrician legal science and calling for its remedy.

   In his history of law, Vico's systematic correlation between the changing power base of the polity and its legal institutions was least rigorous and methodological as it concerned the period that transpired between the secessions of the plebs and the emergence of the Roman Empire. In other words, Vico had conspicuously little to say about the dynamic between society and law during what is properly called the Republic, although he provided an outline of the legislative institutions available to the polity as a result of its form of government.[263] Consequently, the many conflicts and groundbreaking legal changes that occurred between the monarchs and emperors of Rome and the crucial political gains that they won for the plebeians were virtually neglected, save for Vico's observations about the nature of the laws that the Roman consuls, Senate, and tribunes were capable of enacting respectively.[264] That said, the outcomes of this period were epochal for Vico, for they supplemented the extant legislative bodies of Rome with one that would indelibly shape the destiny of Roman law. If the patriciate had sought to maintain its power through the exercise of jurisprudence, then the plebeians, those men desirous of "new things," not only responded in kind with the promulgation of tribunitial laws,[265] which, Vico singularly argued, helped to further the property rights of the plebs, but also with their recourse to the newly established magistracy of the praetor, in which Vico identified the source of an equitable law. For Vico, in sum, it was the creation of the praetors that irreversibly changed the nature of Roman law and jurisprudence by displacing the formalism of the old with natural forms of the new that could accommodate the law to the facts and restore to the plebeians their full rights.

Although the rigor of the law had had what was a civilizing function within the earliest civic community,[266] what made Rome exemplary, if not truly cosmopolitan, for Vico was its institutional provision for a natural law that could adjudicate cases among the most diverse legal persons. What Vico recognized as the greatest strength of Roman law, in other words, was the ability it developed to adapt to the changing social fabric of the burgeoning metropolitan community and to equitably determine the disputes of all of its effective members. While Vico had neglected to recount much of the crucial legal history of the republican period, he did highlight the creation and evolution of the republican magistracy of the praetor and of its edicts, the *ius praetorium,* which supplemented the *ius civile* by addressing the legal needs of all those whose causes traditionally had been excluded from the purview of Roman civil law. However, in this case, as in all others, Vico mixed the recorded facts with fictions to encode his own politics and to embed them in his history as if they were a naturally occurring teleology, or directive.

Traditionally, the *ius praetorium* had been defined by the classical jurists as "that which in the public interest the praetors have introduced in aid or supplementation or correction of the *ius civile.*"[267] In other words, according to classical tradition, the praetors remedied the *ius civile* by accommodating the diversity of legal persons and by facilitating, or granting, just entitlements that were not conceivable by the norms and rules of the extant civil law. Consequently, the *ius praetorium* generally has been recognized and upheld as that vehicle by which equity rulings were introduced into the corpus of Roman law. As has been seen, the primary instruments of this magistracy for the remedy of the *ius civile* was its flexible formulary system of justice, that is, its granting of formulae for causes of action that were not possible under the constraints of the civil law, and, most important, its employment of equitable principles to conceive those same formulae, principles that immortalized the praetors as the "viva vox" of the Law of the Twelve Tables in the mind of the ancients and moderns, such as Vico himself.[268] Yet, for Vico the *viva vox* of the praetors and their equitable principles were more narrowly conceived than they had been in ancient times. For the praetors and the *ius praetorium* most prominently left their mark on Roman law as the final source for the restitution of the natural rights of possession to the plebs, bringing the course of the history of the plebeian struggle for rights to a felicitous close.

As Vico recounted it, the creation of the magistracy of the praetors in the fourth and third centuries BCE (367 and 242 BCE) marked the last of the groundbreaking concessions that the patriciate granted the plebeians as a result of the conflict of the orders.[269] For Vico it was, in other words, the last and most critical episode in the conflict-based institutional innovation of Rome prior to the Lex Poetelia and the advent of the Principate. More important, Vico contended that the specific role of the praetors was to exercise authority (on behalf of the citizenry) in matters of private (i.e., property) law,[270] and, in so doing, to not only enforce the extant forms of action where they applied but also to aid in the implementation of natural law where a just cause presented a reasonable exception to the extant rules.[271] From Vico's discussion, the most reasonable exceptions to the extant rules concerned possession, which, he reminded his readers, had been denied the plebeians by the Optimates, as full property rights quite literally constituted their powers vis-à-vis their clients.[272] Thus the praetors remedied the law of property in causes that were provided for neither by the Law of the Twelve Tables nor by the juridical art of interpretation (pontifical *interpretatio*).[273] As an example of such Vico provided the praetorian interdicts protective of natural possession, which were in fact among the most far-reaching of praetorian remedies and had served the "police function" of upholding the rights of the natural possessor until ownership could be determined in court.[274] Indeed, the praetorian interdicts made possible what was called "bonitary ownership," a category of natural possession that preceded usucapion, and which Vico had identified as the first critical right wrested from the patricians by the plebeians.[275]

In sum, Vico recognized the praetors as the advocates of the plebeian rights of possession and lauded praetorian law as the consummate source of the *ius naturale:* it was, as he put it, "the *ius naturale* itself under the personal guise and in the image of the *ius civile.*"[276] What was more, this praetorian *ius naturale* formed the basis of what was the ultimate and supreme form of jurisprudence in the *Diritto universale,* namely, "benevolent jurisprudence," which purportedly was well suited to "free republics" because it advocated the supremely equitable and did so in the language of "common sense."[277] Simply put, then, the development of praetorian law marked one of the last institutional steps in the progressive formation of legal "persons" from "men"—a Roman legal distinction that Vico had made his own. For praetorian law overruled the inequities of civil law to honor and restore to the expropriated their natural possessions, or what Vico considered the fullest form of their natural rights.[278]

Despite the actual centrality of praetorian law to the innovation of Roman law, it is both curious and telling, I believe, that Vico chose to discuss it in relationship to the conflict of the orders. For the greatest innovation of this magistracy was not associated with its resolution of proprietary conflicts among the citizens of Rome but between citizens and foreigners. In other words, Vico treated praetorian law as if its significance for the noncitizen residents of Rome had applied to the plebeians themselves, which he therewith, and most explicitly, posited as alien to the purview of the civil law. Vico's treatment of praetorian law made plain, in other words, what was his most polemical contention of all: that the Roman plebeians were alien to the Roman *civitas* and, as aliens, noncitizens possessive of nothing more than natural rights. It both underscored and resolved what Vico heretofore had described as the political conundrum intrinsic to the city, namely, its composition out of two alien, and yet mutually dependent, populations, whose conflicts had been extrinsic to the letter of the law.

Curiously, to date the critics of Vico's Roman history largely have neglected his reconstruction of praetorian law and, more important, the political paradox that reconstruction formulated. Even more curiously, the value of Vico's reconstruction of praetorian law as a model for the legal instruments and material ends of social justice too has been overlooked, despite the very centrality of the *ius praetorium* to Vico's story in the *Diritto universale* about the plebeians' reacquisition of their rights.[279] Be that as it may, it is indubitable that Vico's choice to highlight the advent of the praetors and praetorian law was purposive and meant to offer a model of justice for a diverse community. Within the history of rights exemplified by Rome, the profile of the praetor provided an institutional model for the advancement of social justice precisely because the competency of the praetor was to judge a cause based on its natural merits, rather than by the letter of the law and, where just, to provide a form of remedy that circumvented the strictures of formalism. As Vico described it, in other words, the flexible, common sensical approach of the praetor to justice unequivocally provided the most effective of panaceas for the problems endemic to a civic community characterized by both diversity and dynamism while constrained by the norms of an exclusive and revered legal tradition.

What was more, the equitable principles of praetorian law also corroborated Vico's own vision of those tenets governing a just "society," which, as he had defined it at the very outset of *De uno,* comprised a community of utilities. In his own words, Vico affirmed that the *ius praetorium* was "benevolent" and, as such, exemplary because it not only protected natural "possession" but also helped to "equalize utilities" among the members of the civic community, adjudicating what people naturally would have chosen in a "society" unencumbered by the fetters of historical circumstance.[280] In short,

Vico declared that the *ius praetorium* had ushered in that golden Roman era of "benevolent jurisprudence," which he identified with the *ars aequi boni*,[281] and which he defined as "the art of equalizing utilities without regard to either the *ius, leges* or *formulae* that would propose the unequal."[282] And given what we know about the constitution of the Kingdom of Naples, which permitted its highest-ranking tribunal to decide its most vexed cases by the dictates of "natural law" and which granted that same tribunal's decisions the force of law, what Vico found praiseworthy about ancient jurisprudence had the plainest points of comparison in his own modern world. Indeed, one of the very judicial prerogatives of the Sacro Regio Consiglio was referred to as "praetorian" and provides evidence for the actuality of that Roman institution in the minds of Neapolitan contemporaries. The popular wisdom of the Roman praetor too had its obvious modern equivalent. As has been discussed, Vico himself had exhorted the university's students of law to prepare themselves for their future obligations by cultivating their "common sense," which he viewed as the norm of all prudence and the foundation of the future jurist's eloquence.[283] However Roman an institution, in the mind of Vico and his contemporaries, the praetor and praetorian law had their equivalents in the modern world, and it was those equivalents and their policies that Vico evidently endorsed in his highly tendentious history of Roman law and society.

That Vico considered natural jurisprudence the hallmark policy of the most enlightened monarchs was made manifest by way of the greatest Roman historical examples in *De uno*. Whereas Vico largely neglected the legal history of the Republic, he captured that of the Principate and Empire in some detail, especially as it concerned the developments of praetorian law and jurisprudence. As regarded the first, Vico's history documented the most important innovations of praetorian law,[284] the waning independence of the praetors by the creation of new offices of judicial authority,[285] and, most important, the codification of praetorian principles of equity with the publication of the Perpetual Edict under Hadrian.[286] Interestingly enough, these bold strokes captured the trends in Roman legal history under the Empire with what was unusual faithfulness for Vico. However faithful those strokes may have been to the historical record, Vico did take some liberty with his representation of the predominant schools of jurisprudence under the Empire. In Vico's depiction of its history, Roman jurisprudence would reach its perfection under the Principate, when it would make natural equity its rule.[287] The reason Vico gave for this trajectory first and foremost was a systemic one, as he viewed the Principate, like all mixed forms of monarchy, as adverse to the rule of the nobility and beholden to the support of the people, whom it sought to satisfy with more "popular," or democratic, forms of jurisprudence and law.[288]

Additionally, the very codification of the Perpetual Edict reportedly facilitated the study of and commentary on those principles of natural equity embodied in praetorian law, spawning a new and prolific body of legal literature that made natural justice its primary concern.[289] For these reasons there arose and flourished what Vico called the "new jurisprudence" of the Empire, which he associated with the systemization of the longstanding Roman tradition of equitable decisions, and whose champion he made the Proculian School of jurisprudence founded by the legendary jurist M. Antistius Labeo.[290] In the *Diritto universale,* the "new jurisprudence" figured, in other words, as the culmination of the Roman legal tradition of natural law and, in particular, the crowning achievement of the legal policy of the enlightened *princeps* of the Roman state. Therefore, the "new jurisprudence" was a good example of how a monarchy could advance the equality and well-being of its people while tempering the self-interests of its nobility. At the same time, it seems that the "new jurisprudence" was an invention of Vico, who evidently overstated what was a rhetorical contrast in Tacitus concerning the political differences between Labeo and the head of the rival school, Capito, to differentiate the doctrine of the former from that of the latter and their predecessors.[291] If Vico portrayed Labeo as an indomitable proponent of natural equity, it was because Labeo evidently could provide what was the most illustrious of precedents for Vico's own sanctioning of natural jurisprudence and its equitable ends.

Within Vico's history of Rome, the "new jurisprudence" reached its apogee during the Empire under Christianity, and its grand outcome was its codification of what Vico alternatively called the *ius civile commune* and the *ius naturale gentium,* that is, a natural law for the governance of humanity.[292]

Although Vico believed that the law achieved its fullest and most just expression under the reign of Constantine and his Christian successors, he devoted curiously little room to a discussion of how Judeo-Christian beliefs affected Roman legal norms. As those beliefs generally are thought to have infused the Roman legal system with precepts that Vico himself prized—such as, greater "humanitas"—his oversight is significant indeed. By contrast, the endpoint of Vico's narrative was more simply posited as proof of the circularity of history, which, he explained, culminated where it had began, that is, with the worship of God.[293] What is more, the "humanity" won by the plebeians was associated with their acquisition of their full rights of possession. Indeed, Vico went so far as to pronounce in his introductory material to *De constantia* that "suitas"—an early modern neologism that had been employed by the

French Humanists to signify both one's proper right (*droit*) and self-possession (*propre personne*)—promoted both commerce and, ultimately, "humanity,"[294] prefacing his history of the *urbs orbis* in that second volume with a profession of his faith in the civilizing powers of possession and exchange.

Conclusion

It is certainly easy to imagine that the caricature of Rome Vico offered in the *Diritto universale* was a metaphor for the state of the contemporary capital city of Naples, as Naples itself famously possessed a number of those features Vico labored to ascribe to the ancient city. As I have noted, clientelism had formed the bedrock of the social landscape of early modern Naples, as the transplantation of the feudal barons of the Kingdom to the capital city had replicated the domestic structures of the feudal countryside. What was more, the overwhelming foreignness of the capital's lowest orders was not only epic but also notorious. The very attractiveness of the capital city relative to the countryside notedly drew scores of persons from the periphery of the Kingdom to Naples—some ambitious and, more conspicuously, many abject—so that in contemporary accounts the capital literally seemed an asylum for persons displaced by the vicissitudes of life in the early modern Kingdom. Not only did the hospitals and charities provide aid and sustenance for the destitute but so did the open-air piazzas and waterfront enclaves of the city provide makeshift shelter for countless persons, whose telltale signs of provenance all betrayed their extraneousness to the community of the capital. The extraneous nature of Naples' demographic growth, indeed, was already legendary at the time of Vico and became increasingly topical among its authorities, as the many decrees from the Austrian viceroy regarding the containment, employment, and resettlement of the capital's army of vagrants make plain.[295]

Whether or not Vico intended his work as a metaphor for modern Partenope, it is plain that he reconstructed ancient Rome as if it had been beset by and had resolved the very same problems that were stereotypical of burgeoning European capitals like Naples. In other words, Vico most evidently retold the history of Rome as if it were an ancient model of the metropolis and metropolitan forms of governance. For Vico's history of Rome most prominently thematized the condition of a city whose urban community vastly outstripped the confines of its citizenry and municipal forms of governance. If there was anything unusual and, as such, polemical about Vico's history of the origins of Rome, then it was his contention that the Roman community was incommensurable with its *civitas* because the rule of law did not unify but rather divided and antagonized the same. Furthermore, this contention not only betrayed time-honored notions about the constituency and foundation of the Roman *civitas,* but it also entailed an origins story about the plebeians that challenged the historical record and introduced a new set of problems as those intrinsic to the city and, by analogy, political civilization. In the *Diritto universale,* then, Vico represented Rome as the classical model of a metropolitan community that was defined by the exclusivity of its citizenship and animated by the quest of its outsiders for their full recognition and rights per natural law. And in so doing, he debunked as legendary the hallowed notions that the originary city had constituted a political community of equals and that the rule of civil law had provided the basis for its civilization. In Rome, then, Vico found an illustrious precedent for those paradoxes of urban civilization that so plagued his contemporary world, as well as a model of instruction for how to reconcile the uncanny differences among men whose political resemblances arguably were limited to those of humanity.

What was more, Vico represented Rome as the classical model of how a judicial system accommodated a diversity of legal persons internal to its jurisdiction and rendered justice to causes that were at once reasonable and incompatible with the extant categories of law. That this representation of Rome was meant to be prescriptive was made plain by Vico's depiction of natural jurisprudence as the exemplary instrument of justice and the endpoint of the history of political civilization in the *urbs orbis.* At the same time, the solution to the shortcomings of the contemporary judicial system for Vico's contemporaries would be to codify the laws of the nation, borrowing from the best of Roman, natural, and customary law to produce uniform legal codes for the governance of the polity. Certainly, it would not be far-fetched to find in Vico's historicization of Roman law and in his praise for the Empire's codification of praetorian law a call to standardize the laws of the Kingdom so that the decisional literature of the supreme court of Naples, the Sacro Regio Consiglio, could provide a core set of legal principles and rules by which to judge all the subjects of the Kingdom. Indeed, at the time, nations such as France and Spain had designated the customary laws of their respective capitals as national standards, and Charles VI of Austria had begun to draw up uniform rules for particular legal practices, setting the stage for the creation of an Austrian national code. However, if this is what Vico's judicial audience understood from his treatise, then it is no wonder that his text fell on deaf ears, since just as in ancient so in modern times the standardization of law was a means by which to limit the independence of the courts and the discretionary powers of their judiciary, making the *Diritto universale* a most bitter pill for the presidents of the Kingdom's tribunals to swallow.

❧ CHAPTER 4

From Social Theory to Philosophy

*Vico's Disillusions with the Neapolitan Magistracy
and the New Frontier of Philosophy*

I. Introduction: The Politics of the Kingdom
and the Untimeliness of the *Diritto universale*

To date, the political postures of Vico's texts have been neglected by most scholars and pondered by others with notable frustration. As one critic of the *Scienza nuova* has admitted with some dismay: "Vico's writing is frustratingly vague as to its connections and application for his own time. Commentators are even uncertain as to whether he saw himself as living at the end of the heroic age, possibly entering a period of democracy, or as writing in the last phase of monarchy just before a time of renewed barbarism."[1] And the reasons for their uncertainty derive from Vico's texts themselves. For in his best-known work, the *Scienza nuova* (1725) and its revised editions (1733, 1744), Vico increasingly overlaid his narration of Roman history with polemic regarding the nature of his evidence, therewith altering the exemplarity of the *urbs orbis* for his readership. After the prospects of his career as a professor of Civil Law had been dashed by the outcome of the *concorso* of 1723, it was philosophy that purportedly interested him and guided his drafting and revision of his most famous text, in which, as the critical literature has amply shown, he most fully elaborated his singular contributions to a number of preexistent scholarly debates.

Be that as it may, the political lessons of Roman history in the *Diritto universale* had been plain and suggest why Vico had embarked on a reconsideration of Rome in the first place. What is more, the failure of those political lessons in his bid for political patronage helps to explain why Rome became less an exemplum of Vico's contemporary world and more a figure for the historical development of culture in the *Scienza nuova*. Indeed, it seems undeniable that the political lessons of the *Diritto universale* most effectively alienated Vico from his patrons and endangered his candidacy for the Morning Chair of Civil Law. As we have seen, in the *Diritto universale* Vico's reconstruction of Rome had mounted what were two (most unusual) interpretations of the Roman historical record, which together recast the *urbs orbis* as an exemplum of the modern metropolis. In the first place, Vico represented Rome as if the history of its political conflicts and progress all had derived from a single ineluctable feature of the originary city: its composition out of an indigenous population with rights at the law and foreign clients wanting the very same. In other words, Vico had advanced the thesis that the Roman community had comprised both citizens and noncitizens alike, from whom the patricians and plebeians, respectively, derived, and that this dualism of the city had represented both the juggernaut and force of its subsequent historical development. Second, Vico had interpreted the history of Roman law and society in the *Diritto universale* as if the natural law of the praetors had offered the judicial remedy for the unintelligibility of disputes among the patricians and plebeians per the civil law (*ius civile*). In particular, Vico had put his rhetorical weight behind the Perpetual Edict—the imperial initiative that had codified praetorian law for the Empire and made it the standard of Roman jurisprudence—unambiguously endorsing a historical example of monarchical policy to codify and make applicable to all legal persons the equitable principles of a single, central magistracy. On the counts of the history of the Roman community and of its law, in sum, Vico had staked the unusual claim that the plebeians of Rome had been extraneous to the *civitas* and that the history of Roman law thus documented the plebeian struggle for the acquisition of full legal personality, or what was admission to the citizenry of Rome.

It seems plain that Vico's history of Rome in the *Diritto universale* was first and foremost a history of the gradual acquisition of rights by the plebeians and, as full legal members of the civic community, their accession to the Roman citizenry. Indeed, this is the way that Vico was read by his most faithful eighteenth-century epigone, Emmanuele Duni, who in imitation of Vico penned *Origine, e progressi del cittadino e del governo civile di Roma* (Rome, 1763–63).[2] What is more, if there was anything that the first edition of the

Scienza nuova clarified for Vico's readership, then it was his understanding of the political nature of the plebs in archaic Rome, who, as he put it, were "a completely different nation from the order of nobles" and, so, "a multitude lacking citizenship."[3]

Yet, there were a few instructive ambiguities about Vico's tale of citizenship in the *Diritto universale* that suggest "citizenship" would have been a misnomer for the rights Vico believed full legal personality conferred on its subjects and, consequently, that the juridical model of citizenship was of heuristic value not for its political but social import in Vico's eyes. In the first place, although Vico called the originary city of Rome a *civitas* and scrupulously enumerated the components of its constituency, he never employed nor formally defined the word *civis* (citizen) in the *Diritto universale,* so that his idea of citizenship was predicated on the painstaking negation of what he construed as alien to the civil law. More important, his painstaking negation proposed a history whose high points were distinct from those any lay reader would have associated with the traditional history of citizenship in ancient Rome. For example, in the *Diritto universale* Vico omitted any mention of the watershed Antonine constitution, which was a natural endpoint for a history of political citizenship, as in 212 CE it had granted such to virtually all the free males of the Empire, making Rome what was truly the city of the world (*urbs orbis*). Finally, what the progress of history obviated, according to Vico, was the expropriation of the plebeian's person, which granted the plebeian the right to the possession of himself and of his property. While self-possession and property were *iura,* or rights, stipulated and protected by the civil law, they were by no means the hallmark prerogatives of Roman citizenship itself but just two of the many rights associated with it, which notably included a number of public entitlements and duties.[4] In other words, Vico exclusively underscored the private rights and duties that accrued to the citizen, severing the juridical condition of citizenship from its political one. In the *Diritto universale,* in sum, Vico depicted the telos of incorporation into the civic community as the acquisition of a form of *libertas* that made of its beneficiaries autonomous agents with equal rights at private law.[5] And, by the same token, with his unique focus on the *libertas* of the citizen, Vico belittled, if not outright dismissed, the significance of the civic forms of governance for the livelihood of the community, while valorizing the activity and contribution of free agents to the public welfare.

In light of the peculiarities of Vico's Roman history, the question remains as to what inspired Vico to reinterpret the Roman record so. This same question has been posed before, but its answer has foundered, I believe, on precisely what was unique to Vico's history of Rome in the first place. In his illuminating study of Vico's historical method and narrative, Arnaldo Momigliano famously maintained that unique to Vico's history of Rome was his interpretation of the Servian constitution and the Twelve Tables as agrarian laws, and he consequently asked what, if any, changes in the contemporary Kingdom of Naples might have lent themselves to the fabrication of such an ancient exemplum.[6] Whereas Momigliano shied from responding to his own question, his younger contemporary Giuseppe Giarrizzo speculated that, in his history of Rome, Vico was literally describing contemporary peasant revolts, which, as he noted, were common throughout the European Continent at the time.[7] If these were indeed the source of inspiration for the particularities of Vico's Roman history, however, then it also bears mentioning that there were in the Kingdom of Naples numerous occupations of lands by peasants, who therewith reclaimed by force expropriated holdings, asserting both their customary and natural rights to possession.[8] Indeed, the peasant revolts of Calabria in 1721 are a case in point.[9] What was more, the cases of grievances brought by *università* against the baronage in the courts, grievances that await their study, further suggests that the prerogatives of feudalism were under siege, however resilient the power of their practitioners.[10]

Yet, the framing of this question about Vico's inquiry into feudalism circumscribes the particularities of his Roman history in ways that misrepresent, I believe, both the occasion and the breadth of his political concerns. For, if we may assume that Vico's Rome was a metaphor for the contemporary Kingdom of Naples, then it is important to note that feudalism was intrinsic to the city, according to Vico. As he posed it in the *Diritto universale,* feudalism was an urban problem, and its most conspicuous presence in the *urbs* made pressing not agrarian reform per se but, and more generally, the full entitlement of the plebeians to "property" so that they could extricate themselves from the limitations of clientelism and become mercenaries of the marketplace of exchange, or what we would call economic actors. Indeed, it was presumably for that same reason that Vico identified the culmination of Roman history in the Poetelian Law, which, as we have seen, he had interpreted as the freeing of the plebeians from the *ius nexum,* or law of bondage, an interpretation that underscored not only the prohibition of their enslavement but also the right of the plebeians to unfettered participation in the labor market. Agrarian reform was understood, in other words, as an instrument for the supercession of that older economy of exchange—which had traded obsequiousness for sustenance—and as a precondition for the application of one's labor to things. It was a panacea for the ills of the capital city, both swollen and taxed by the "multitude" of plebeians, whose persons were extraneous to the marketplace of exchange. Indeed, in the first edition of the *Scienza nuova,* Vico most thunderously concluded his treatment of the Roman agrarian laws with a poignant reflection on the miserable social conditions of the *urbs* during the Republic, when, he lamented, the conquests of Rome had so increased the number of poor in the city that it had become "necessary to unburden the city of the poor, who were a source of shame, fear and trouble to the nobles, and turn them into [sources of] strength in the provinces by setting them up comfortably in their own fields."[11] That this picture of Rome would have conjured the ills of Naples in the minds of contemporaries seems doubtless, especially as the relocation of the urban poor to farming communities of the Kingdom was one of the urban policy initiatives most famously debated on multiple occasions in the eighteenth century.[12] In short, then, Vico's curious reconstruction of the agrarian laws was not an end in itself but evidently subordinate to his larger concern about the destitution of the capital city and about the rights and things due to humans because necessary for their full participation in what Vico himself had called "society."[13]

If the conundrum of the capital had behooved Vico to imagine social change in Rome the way he uniquely did, then the question remains as to why Vico's vision not only failed to win the support he sought from the viceroy and presidents of the Kingdom's tribunals but also seems to have marginalized him from them, thwarting his advancement and sealing his university career in the Chair of Rhetoric. As we shall see, the reasons for Vico's failure were evidently political, as the viceroy would make plain that he strongly favored the candidacy of another, and as the selection committee would split their own votes between the viceroy's candidate and one of Vico's other adversaries. In other words, despite his international renown, it seems that Vico was not considered for the appointment and that his dogged canvassing effectively had disqualified him for the Morning Chair of Civil Law.

To the extent that the politics of the *Diritto universale* contributed to this mishap, it is not difficult to imagine why, in that a conjuncture of older traditions and new events evidently made the lessons of the *Diritto universale* a poor fit with the conceptual framework and political aims of its target audience. In the first place, Vico's history of Rome challenged long-standing assumptions about the origins and political culture of that city, which had been utterly integral to the historical reconstruction of Naples itself. For Vico's interpretation of Roman history not only deviated from Livy but also from a long tradition of local writing about the political nature of the Roman Republic and the import of republican institutions for the municipality of Naples. Whether accepted or vociferously rejected as a model for Naples itself, the idea of Roman Naples as a community of citizens composed of and ruled by the *Ordo et Populus* (nobility and people) had long held purchase as the example against which to assess the contemporary relationship among the Neapolitan orders, namely, between the so-called civic patriciate and the Popolo. Throughout the seventeenth century, in particular, histories of Naples had relied on that construct of Rome for their evaluation of the division of political labor within the contemporary municipality.[14] And regardless of their respective evaluations, the municipal histories all implicitly had understood the Roman orders as distinct social entities that were distinguished by their political rights and privileges.

Given the political terms on which the municipal historiography had understood the relationship among the orders, then, Vico's conceptualization of the Roman orders as social entities that were distinguished by their rights of possession and subject to historical development probably baffled most of his contemporaries. For Vico's Romanism redefined the orders so that they no longer pertained to longstanding debates about the relative political powers of the municipal constituencies but rather were relevant to a discussion of the relative economic rights and personal qualities of the same. Put somewhat differently, for an audience well schooled in arguing about the political implications of the Greco-Roman origins of the municipality, Vico's ancient history of rights shifted the ground of the political debate about Rome onto what was novel, if not unintelligible, terrain indeed.

Second, if Vico's categories baffled some, then his construal of the civic patriciate of Rome as atavistic barons must have outright irked others. For that category connoted anything but an anachronism for those numerous individuals who either possessed or sought patrician citizenship within the municipality of Naples. It is noteworthy that among the most ambitious members of the capital's administrative class accession to patrician citizenship was anything but discredited and dishonored under Austrian Habsburg rule. Rather, it is remarkable just how coveted the title of "patrician and citizen of the City of Naples" remained in that age of state building and of the venality of feudal title. Indeed, in the State Archive in Vienna there is ample evidence of the municipality's zealous defense of its right to control the process of admission to the patrician *piazze,* and of the keen contest for accession to the same.[15] For example, one of the causes célèbres of the early 1720s was the attempt by Vienna to obtain the award of Neapolitan citizenship for its most able envoy to the Kingdom, Count Fleischman, who had been entrusted with a program of reform and ended as the object of most bitter contention between the Habsburg administration, Neapolitan magistracy, and the *piazze* of Naples, which sternly refused the naturalization of Fleischman as a transgression of their customary liberties and prerogatives.[16]

As this controversy made perfectly plain, the distinction and powers of the civic patriciate certainly remained coveted by some and zealously defended by others, few of whom would have empathized with Vico's plebeian vision of citizenship and historical progress.

Third, although Vico's diagnosis of the Roman metropolis as plagued by the destitution of the multitude struck a contemporary chord, his vision for its cure certainly suggested a transformation of the social order that was profound in ways that most of his contemporaries would neither have imagined nor desired. One of the striking features of the Austrian period of Habsburg rule is the attention it paid to the ills plaguing the capital city of Naples. Yet, despite the intentions of the regime, there was a conspicuous gap between its diagnosis of the capital and its policy of reform, which foundered on the limitations of its instruments for change and the lack of collaboration by the municipality itself.[17] Among the directives of the memorandum issued in the name of the Habsburg sovereign for the guidance of Viceroy Althann, for example, were the condemnation of the "otioseness" of the Neapolitan plebs and of their avidity for "new things" as well as the recommendation that they employ their forces in "useful activities" designated by the Collaterale and the tribunals.[18] However, the ad hoc initiatives undertaken by the viceroy and his advisory council fell short of the task at hand,[19] and the *prammatiche* (edicts) issued in the name of the sovereign were largely unenforceable and piecemeal remedies aimed at the containment of the plebs. What was more, it seems that both the Collaterale and tribunals of the Kingdom were ill-equipped to deal with the problems of the metropolis: indeed, among the *consulte* of the Collaterale conserved from this period there is not a single one that frontally addresses the metropolitan question.[20]

Finally, the modest initiatives undertaken relied on older static notions of the difference between the plebs and the other orders of society, making for what was hardly a practical political counterpart to Vico's exhortation to transform them by way of their societal incorporation. Indeed, perhaps the unconventionality of Vico's vision is best captured by the contrast it offered to that of his contemporary and good friend Paolo Mattia Doria, who too had famously contemplated the ideal structure and governance of the civic polity in his tract *La vita civile* (1709), which Doria published just shortly after the Austrian Habsburg conquest of the Kingdom and evidently intended as a sort of manifesto on how to govern Naples.[21] Like Vico in the *Diritto universale,* in *La vita civile* Doria primarily had been concerned about how to integrate into "civil life," or civic society, the plebs, who he most vividly described as an unedified mob ruled by the basest of the senses and passions. While Vico's descriptions of the archaic plebs would echo Doria's own, his solution to the duality of the city Doria had described would not. For Doria had proposed that the plebs be made to accept a productive form of dependency on the civic patriciate. In other words, the imagery of the plebs as an unedified mob had provided the basis for what was a static model of their natural inferiority and strict tutelage by superiors in Doria's much-discussed work. By contrast, for Vico the patrician tutelage of the plebs was not a solution to the duality of the city but rather the unjust outcome of its origins, whose very supercession Vico had been so concerned to hypothesize. In comparison to the work of his friend Doria, who was close to the Austrian authorities and whose advice was solicited by them, Vico's vision of the nature of the social order of the city and the historical mission of the plebs were unconventional to say the least.

Finally, and most important, in the *Diritto universale* Vico's recommendations for the reform of the judicial system arguably threatened the interests of the very people whose votes he sought in the *concorso* of 1723. For his recommendations challenged both the judicial agenda of the Habsburg viceroy and the vested interests of the Neapolitan judiciary. As we have seen, Vico's history of Roman jurisprudence had at once endorsed natural jurisprudence, which underpinned the autonomy of the Neapolitan judiciary, and supported the standardization of the same in the form of a national code, which would have undercut the judiciary's famed discretionary powers. Beyond the mixed signals these endorsements presumably sent to his target audience, there was clearly something for everyone to dislike about them, and as a consequence they may have contributed to the disfavor with which the candidacy of Vico was viewed by the viceroy and the representatives of the Kingdom's tribunals. On the one hand, by the time of the *concorso* of 1723, the autonomy of the Neapolitan judiciary was under siege by the Habsburg authorities: with the change in regime that had taken place in 1722, there also was a change in the political directive from Vienna regarding the powers of the Neapolitan tribunals. In the same memorandum that identified the "otioseness" of the plebs as a pressing problem, so did the emperor make plain to Viceroy Althann that the autonomy of the judiciary was to be curbed at all costs.[22] Similarly, secret reports conserved in the State Archive of Vienna on the members and politics of the Kingdom's tribunals make plain that the discretionary decisions and *consulte* of the leading Neapolitan jurists were being closely watched, and with notable apprehension.[23] As one report remarked of Gaetano Argento—who then still was considered the maverick of jurisdictionalism in the Kingdom and occupied the offices of regent of the Collaterale and president of the Sacro Consiglio and of the Reale Giurisdizione, an organ of the king that advised him on matters with the Church especially pertaining to his jurisdiction over lands and offices—the jurist was not only power hungry and presumptuous but also neglectful of the letter of the law.[24] In light of Habsburg concerns about the autonomy of the Neapolitan judiciary, it is no wonder that Vico's candidacy ran afoul of the viceroy. For Vico's endorsement of natural jurisprudence—which as we have seen had so empowered the Sacro Regio Consiglio—would now find its legitimacy strongly questioned. By the same token, Vico's historical endorsement of the codification of natural law would not have ingratiated him with the magistrates of the Kingdom's tribunals either, as the codification of the law would have curbed their powers, just as the viceroy had wished. However benevolent and interesting the lessons of Vico's history of Roman jurisprudence, they clearly were a poor advertisement for his candidacy for the Morning Chair of Civil Law.

If this all were not enough to disqualify Vico, then it further seems that luck simply was not on his side either. To try to tip the balance in his favor, Vico had solicited—and indeed pinned his hopes on—the patronage of the powerful Prince Eugene von Savoy, who apparently had and would intervene in the cultural politics of the Kingdom on behalf of his Neapolitan clients.[25] As we have already noted, Vico had sent luxurious and annotated copies of the *Diritto universale* to Eugene via his Italian representative, Biagio Garofalo, who was a Neapolitan acquaintance of Vico and intellectual ally.[26] On the very day of the death of the former proprietor of the Morning Chair of Civil Law, Vico hastened to write directly to Eugene to make known his intention to publicly compete for that chair and, more important, to request that Eugene "promote" his candidacy for the same with Viceroy Althann.[27] To dispel any fears Eugene might harbor regarding the delicacy of such a recommendation, Vico further assured the prince that Althann was predisposed to favor Vico, as the viceroy "of all my readers particularly has expressed his respect for my arguments."[28] However, this expression of Eugene's gratitude and favor would not additionally translate into the form of patronage Vico had sought from the prince, that is, his recommendation to Viceroy Althann, who had himself fallen out of favor with Eugene. Despite Vico's sense of being on the side of political power, it seems that Eugene politely neglected to honor Vico's request, as there is no trace of correspondence between Eugene and Althann concerning the *concorso* and, given the nature of their contemporary relationship, little reason to suspect as much. What is more, the brewing controversy around the publication of *Istoria civile del Regno di Napoli* by Pietro Giannone and his imminent excommunication would not have helped matters either, as it would have made the Neapolitan authorities all the more cautious as regarded their relationship with the Church and also would have made Giannone's cause the more pressing one for the cohort of Neapolitan ministers and intellectuals who supported cultural innovation.[29] If Vico had impressed Eugene and the latter's expression of favor was indeed sincere, then it seems that the circumstances did not help Vico procure the support he so needed to promote his candidacy for the Morning Chair of Civil Law, which was destined for another.

II. From Law to "Philosophy": The University Competition of 1723

After a long illness, on 12 December 1722, the proprietor of the Morning Chair of Civil Law at the University of Naples, Domenico Campanile, died, leaving the Chair vacant and subject to award by competition. At the time, the Morning Chair of Civil Law was a highly prestigious position at the University of Naples. Within the Faculty of Law, it was one of just four "perpetual" positions—the other seven being contractual and subject to reappointment—and it paid the handsome salary of six hundred ducats, a salary that was second only to the one paid to the Afternoon Chair of Civil Law, which was then occupied by the middle-aged Nicola Capasso.[30] On the death of Campanile, arrangements were scrupulously made for an interim substitution and for a public competition that would attract the very best candidates for the Chair and award it to the most meritorious of them. Indeed, from the correspondence of the administrator of the university, Cappellano Maggiore Vincenzo Vidania, it is evident that he was determined to insure the best of outcomes for the university by holding a public competition that strictly adhered to the procedure of the university's statutes.

In accordance with procedure, in mid-January an edict was issued announcing the competition for the Morning Chair, and aspirants were given a few weeks to register for it.[31] On 24 January, the first aspirant to register was Vico himself, and by the time of the closing date for the competition there were some fifteen applicants, six of whom already held contractual positions within the Faculty of Law at the university. On 12 February, Vidania tallied the candidates for the competition in an official memorandum that briefly informed the viceroy how the competition would proceed, making plain not only the rules but also his intention to abide by them.[32]

However, Vidania's intention to hold the competition in accordance with procedure repeatedly was challenged by the candidates themselves and by the Kingdom's highest-ranking authorities. Once the competition had closed, Vidania's office apparently was flooded by a spate of petitions from candidates requesting what amounted to special consideration for the Chair as well as other lesser positions. In his correspondence with the viceroy, Vidania politely restated these requests and unambiguously expressed his indignation. Paolo de Mercurio, professor of Civil Institutions, for example, had implored the viceroy for his vote, which, Vidania carefully explained, would only be necessary in the case of an actual tie, when it was customary for the viceroy to determine the winner.[33] And even more presumptuously, the professor of Decretal Law, Giovanni Chiaiese—who in a letter had passed his judgment on the *Diritto universale*—implored the viceroy to suspend the vote on the candidates and award him the Chair on the basis of his seniority and length of service to the university. While Vidania was most respectful of Chiaiese's qualifications, which were indeed significant, he rebuked Chiaiese's demands by pointedly underscoring both the lawfulness and great benefits of a system that maintained and awarded its "perpetual" chairs to its most meritorious applicants.[34]

Despite the intentions of Vidania, it seems that the actual competition for the Morning Chair of Civil Law had begun long before the death of Campanile and that its outcome would be decided behind closed doors. And, ironically, Vidania himself had played a role in laying the groundwork for the outcome that he least desired. For Vidania had first promoted the candidacy of the individual who eventually would replace Campanile: in 1717, Vidania arranged for the retirement of Campanile and nominated as his substitute Domenico Gentile,[35] whose interim appointment to the Chair of Civil Law he then enthusiastically recommended to Viceroy Althann on its vacancy in December 1722.[36] What was more, Vidania evidently failed to foresee the consequences of his endorsement: Gentile's expectation that he would be awarded the Morning Chair and his formal qualification for it. On 14 January 1723, Vidania related to the viceroy how Gentile impudently had demanded the entire salary and honors of the Morning Chair of Civil Law, a demand that Vidania found to be perfectly "unreasonable." Indeed, Vidania doubted whether Gentile could win the competition for the Chair, which he suspected would be awarded to one of the "more qualified and mature" candidates of the competition.[37] Be that as it may, Gentile did indeed emerge the victor of the competition for the Morning Chair of Civil Law, beating his rival by a hair's breadth with a single vote.

While the doubts that Vidania had expressed were surely justified, they had the very opposite effect of what he had hoped. For the viceroy did indeed adopt Gentile as his candidate for the Morning Chair of Civil Law. Consequently, the outcome of the competition was as much a victory for Viceroy Althann as it was for Gentile, as it effectively represented the power that the viceroy could wield to implement his political will, however arbitrary, on the

Kingdom of Naples. Indeed, it was a public triumph for the viceroy in his contest with local authorities at the outset of his career in Naples. Viewed from the norms of the time, the outcome of the competition was nothing less than an upset. In the first place, the victory of Gentile marked the defeat of the candidate of the Neapolitan judiciary, namely, Pietro Antonio (de) Turris, who at the time held the perpetual Afternoon Chair of Canon Law.

Second, it overturned Vidania's own evaluation and ranking of the candidates, which apparently conformed to the university's standards and was of some significance for the actual procedure of the competition. Most important, Vidania's seeding of the candidates had structured the competition itself, as it determined the order in which the candidates delivered their talks, commencing with the least and culminating with the most qualified aspirants to the Chair.[38] What was more, Vidania's evaluation and ranking of the candidates ought to have been of untold importance for the decision of the selection committee, which, it seems, not long before their final meeting was served with a dossier on the candidates prepared by Vidania himself. Regardless of its importance for the final decision, that same dossier is of some interest for what it reveals about the criteria brought to bear on the assessment of the candidates. For it contained not only a list of the candidates for the Morning Chair in order of their rank but also a short bio on each that briefly summarized and reviewed their credentials independently of their talk.[39]

Vidania's assessment of the candidates was at once traditional and scrupulous: it first and foremost let the rank of the current positions held by the candidates determine their pecking order, while detailing all the titles previously held and years of service paid by them to the university. Consequently, the members of the Faculty of Law were ranked most highly for the Morning Chair. And, in keeping with this logic, it was the single candidate possessing a perpetual chair of law, Pietro Antonio Turris, who occupied the pride of first place in the pecking order of the contestants and who received the honor of delivering his talk last. Following Turris, in second place was Gentile, who was then the interim appointee to the Morning Chair of Civil Law. It was only after another four professors of law with full-time appointments, then, that Giambattista Vico, professor of Rhetoric, appeared in Vidania's list of candidates, occupying a most modest seventh place among the grand total of fourteen contestants.

Although the criteria for the ranking of the candidates clearly disadvantaged Vico, it nonetheless is unclear just how long a shot the Morning Chair of Civil Law was for the professor of Rhetoric. In the first place, the ranking of the candidates reproduced what were formal divisions within the university, which valued the Faculty of Law above all others. As a consequence, on

account of their faculty affiliation the ranking system formally gave preference to professors of law with the same rank as Vico, regardless of their intellectual merits. Thus, it is hard to assess just how meaningful the divide was
between Vico and his colleagues in law who officially ranked above him.
Second, the question concerning the meaningfulness of this divide becomes
even more pressing if one considers that Vico's colleagues in law were all
bound by custom to participate in the competition, which was obligatory for
their reappointment to their own current positions, and that not a single one
of them actually received a vote for the Morning Chair of Civil Law. In other
words, their participation in the competition was somewhat perfunctory, and
their formal ranking above the members of external faculties was surely also
a way to recognize their supreme qualification for their own jobs. Indeed,
the four professors of law ranking above Vico were all formally nominated
and reelected to their own positions by consensus at the final meeting of the
selection committee.

If Vico stood a chance to win the Morning Chair of Civil Law, then the
professor of Rhetoric's single credential for the job was indeed his legal treatise. In fact, one of the surprising aspects of the documentation relating to the
competition is just how precious little Vidania found to say in the candidates'
bios about his esteemed colleague Giambattista Vico, whom we know he
admired. Unlike all of the candidates, both young and old, Vico had never
before participated in a competition within the Faculty of Law and, consequently, did not have any experience whatsoever in the instruction of law,
not even as a substitute. Nor had Vico tutored students of law privately, as
had his younger rival Francesco Rapolla, who was then only twenty-eight
and who handily won one of the two open contractual positions in Canonical Institutions. Furthermore, it is dubious that Vico even possessed the title
of "Doctor of Law," as did all the successful members of the competition
except for the ecclesiast Nicola Pandolfelli, who had been born into a family
of high-profile jurists. Although Vidania prefaced Vico's name with the title
"Doctor," there is no actual evidence that Vico ever obtained his doctorate.[40]
Indeed, in the *Autobiografia,* Vico relates that he once had decided to apply
for admission to the courts, but he never told the outcome of this decision, which could only have been successful had the Collegio dei Dottori
of Naples waived the five-year attendance requirement for the aspirant, as
he admittedly had not attended the university.[41] What was more, if he had
in fact obtained the doctorate, then it would have befitted his aims to sign
the volumes of the legal treatise, the *Diritto universale,* with the title "Doctor of Law" to help establish his authority on his subject matter, as was usual
at the time. Consequently, it is plain that the potential for success of Vico's

candidacy rested in large part on the reception of the *Diritto universale* by his judges, as his legal tract was most probably his sole qualification for the Chair beyond his service to the university as a superb practitioner and instructor of oratory.

On 9 April 1723, Vico delivered his talk before the selection committee for the Morning Chair of Civil Law in the auditorium of the College of St. Thomas Aquinas in the center of Naples. As was customary, Vico enjoyed the right to choose the topic for his talk from one of three laws that were picked by means of random selection from the *Digest*. From among those three, Vico evidently chose the first law from "Actions Using Prescribed Words," which was an opinion from book 8 of the *Questions* by the so-called prince of classical jurists, Papinian.[42] According to the *Autobiografia*, Vico chose this passage because "it was taken from Papinian who of all jurisconsults had the loftiest faculties, and had to do with the definition of legal terms, which in jurisprudence is the hardest task to carry out well."[43] Given his choice of topic and method of exposition, it is easy to imagine that Vico portrayed himself in that lecture as carrying on the grand tradition of legal Humanism and as the worthy heir of its most renowned protagonists. In the first place, his choice of topic perfectly coincided with the most celebrated interests of the Humanists. For the terms of the *Digest* had indeed been among the pet topics of the greatest exponents of legal Humanism since the sixteenth century, and their exposition had helped to secure the international reputation of the same. It is likely that Vico was familiar with Alciati's lectures "De verborum significatione" ("On the Significance of Legal Terms"), regarding title 16 of book 50 of the *Digest,* with which the founding figure of the French school of legal Humanism had won his fame and sealed his career as the most sought-after (and highly remunerated) professor of law in his own time. And as Vico himself purposively noted in the *Autobiografia,* Alciati's heir and leading figure of the French school, Jacques Cujas, too had expounded on the legal terms of the *Digest* in his famous work, *Paratitla* (*Paratitles*). Second, Vico's method in his lecture evidently resembled that of the legal Humanists. Like them, he purportedly employed exegesis to the end of capturing the historical sense, or principle, of the law under consideration. According to the *Autobiografia,* Vico literally interpreted the words of the law "one by one," and "from the interpretation of the words he elicited the sense of Papinian's definition."[44] Finally, it is plain that Vico engaged the well-known debate among the Germanists and Romanists of the French school by defending Cujas against Favre and neglecting Hotman, which in the eyes of his contemporaries squarely would have aligned him with the historical vision and politics of the Romanists.[45]

Retrospectively, Vico would claim that his talk had been well received by its jury: indeed, the very next day he purportedly bothered to write out his talk for distribution among friends, and the "general applause" it earned him allegedly heightened his expectations of winning the Morning Chair.[46] Although it is hard to imagine that Vico's talk was anything less than superlative, there is reason to believe that it was not received as much by his judges.[47] At the very least, it seems that his dazzling erudition was marred by his unrivaled presumption. Not only had Vico presented himself as assuming the mantle of the legal Humanists, but he also had peppered his talk with Greek technical terms and expressions, which he apparently pronounced with some difficulty and resulted in at least one noteworthy moment of pregnant silence during his delivery.[48] What was more, with his choice of topic it seems that Vico openly courted disqualification. For one of the cardinal rules of the competition apparently was that the candidates refrain from interpreting Roman law through the lens of their own work, and with his selection Vico had chosen to speak about a law from the *Digest* that provided superb evidence for his personal vision of the development and ends of jurisprudence.[49] Indeed, the *actio praescriptis verbis* referred to a broad category of actions that extended the normative duties and obligations of civil law contracts to nontypical circumstances by way of analogy. Historically speaking, in other words, this sort of *actio* was the descendent of praetorian law, whose principle of equity it adapted and generalized for a wider set of circumstances, providing an excellent example of that trend in Roman jurisprudence that Vico had not only described but also praised in the *Diritto universale.*

Needless to say, Vico was utterly indignant over the outcome of the competition for the Morning Chair of Civil Law, and rightfully so. For the Morning Chair would in the end be awarded on the basis of political allegiance rather than demonstrable merit. In the *Autobiografia,* Vico wrote that he withdrew from the competition shortly after the delivery of his lecture on the advice of his friend Domenico Caravita, a lawyer and the son of Nicola, who, if the *Autobiografia* is to be trusted, apparently had informed Vico that the finalists for the Morning Chair had been chosen in advance and that he was not among them. However, from the documentation concerning the competition it rather seems that Vico remained in the contest to its bitter end, when he suffered the blow of being altogether overlooked for the position that he had so desired.

On 3 July 1723, the final meeting of the selection committee for the Morning Chair of Civil Law convened in the College of St. Thomas, and it comprised University Prefect Vidania, twelve senior members of the university's professoriate, twelve leading members of the Neapolitan judiciary, and the heads of four religious orders in Naples.[50] According to the documentation, the purpose of the meeting was manifold: the committee was charged with not only awarding the Morning Chair of Civil Law but also in the confirmation of the contractual appointments to the Faculty of Law and the assignment of the three lesser vacant positions there that paid a modest salary of sixty ducats per year. By the time of their meeting, the candidates for the Morning Chair apparently had been narrowed to fourteen, as four of the registered candidates had withdrawn from the competition, and their ranking had remained unchanged, with Vico frozen at seventh place. However, of these fourteen only two were actually considered for the position: Gentile, its interim appointee, and Turris, who was the most senior candidate for the Morning Chair and already held the Afternoon Chair of Canon Law. Despite the unequivocal qualifications of these two candidates for the Morning Chair, what transpired in the College of St. Thomas that day clearly was the last act in a sorry piece of political theater, which largely had been staged and managed by the viceroy himself. For the actual voting would best illustrate the schism between the new viceroy and the Neapolitan judiciary, and the lengths to which Althann would go to control this important educational institution.

Before the talks of the last two candidates in late spring 1723, there was a month-long hiatus in the actual schedule of the talks—coinciding with the controversy over the publication of the *Istoria civile* by Giannone—during which time Althann evidently arranged to make manifest his political will and favoritism. In two pieces of correspondence addressed to Vidania, the viceroy had his nephew make known to the university prefect that he was "resolved to intervene in the competition" on behalf of Domenico Gentile and that the appropriate arrangements should be made for the viceroy's attendance at Gentile's lecture.[51] When Vidania balked at the prospect of such a display of partiality for one of the candidates, Em(m)anuele Althann explained that the viceroy had no intention of publicly presiding over that event and ordered that a private balcony be made available to him for the occasion.[52] Needless to say, be he seated in a private balcony or among the committee itself the imposing presence of the viceroy at Gentile's talk made eminently well known his strong preference for that candidate and his willingness to take unconventional measures to ensure his success. Among those unconventional measures was the viceroy's order in June that two members of the professoriate be banned from the final vote: Cherubino Romano, a professor of Theology; and Giacomo Poeta, a professor of Medicine, whose allegiances were presumably suspect and whose public disgrace could only serve to intimidate the rest into submission. Indeed, it is probable that the browbeating did not end there. For on the day of the final vote the committee split into two blocks along institutional lines with the representatives of the religious orders dividing their votes. For Turris, who was undisputedly the more qualified candidate of the two, the twelve members of the judiciary voted en masse, while all thirteen employees of the royal university cast their votes for the lesser-qualified candidate, Gentile, who consequently was awarded the Chair. Surprisingly, among the professoriate to tow the viceroy's line numbered Vidania himself, who had already objected to the pretensions of Gentile and doubted the sufficiency of his credentials to prevail in the competition. Evidently, for Althann the competition for the Morning Chair of Civil Law had been a test of his political will to defeat the independence of the judiciary; and of that test he evidently had won what was a shameless public victory.

Given the circumstances governing the process of selection for the Morning Chair, it is plain that Vico's candidacy was not tenable. In the first place, the viceroy had destined for the prize of the Morning Chair the least accomplished of the formally qualified candidates, that is, someone who would incur a debt of allegiance to the viceroy with his appointment. By the same token, the interests of the judiciary clearly were best served by fielding a consensus candidate whose credentials were not only honorable but also above the least bit of contention—a bill that Vico clearly did not fit especially given the mixed messages and controversial reception of the *Diritto universale*. It is thus not difficult to understand why the Neapolitan judiciary chose Turris as their candidate, and in light of the unanimous support he received from the Neapolitan magistracy it is fair to say that he had served their purposes well in spite of defeat. However transparent the politics of the competition must have been to contemporaries, Vico seems to have taken his loss to heart and experienced it as a betrayal by the judiciary, whose interests he evidently felt he had long served and cultivated, be it as the professor of Rhetoric or as a theorist of natural jurisprudence in the *Diritto universale*. Given the circumstances, it seems that Vico's expectations were unreasonable. They not only had failed to take into account the politics of the university competition but also had underestimated, I believe, the unconventionality of his ideas about the orders of the city and the impracticality of his implicit political recommendations. As the documentation from the period suggests, the Neapolitan judiciary was neither able nor interested in taking on the sort of projects that Vico had advocated, if only because it was hamstrung by the limits of its jurisdictional powers. Consequently, it is hard to imagine that in even less combative circumstances the judiciary would have mustered an adequate number of votes to elect to the Morning Chair the professor of Rhetoric whose views were at once so very unorthodox and prescriptive.

In any case, it was this bitter defeat that Vico would cite as the reason for his abandonment of law for philosophy and the undertaking of his next intellectual enterprise, the *Scienza nuova*. As Vico reflected on the publication of the first edition of the *Scienza nuova* (1725) in a famous letter to his friend Bernardo Maria Giacco: "All the other poor works of my mind I owe to myself, because they were devised for my own ends, with a view to winning an honorable station in my native city; but since our university has considered me unworthy of one, I assuredly owe this work entirely to it, for its unwillingness to have me occupied in expounding paragraphs (from the *Pandects*) has left me the leisure to compose it."[53]

Although Vico's failure in the university competition of 1723 purportedly had freed him to draft the *Scienza nuova*, the road to its completion and actual publication was rocky indeed. Over the course of 1724, Vico drafted what later would be called the "new science in negative form,"[54] a large manuscript for which he consequently sought patronage. As usual, for patronage Vico aimed high, namely, the powerful Cardinal Corsini, who shortly would be elected Pope Clement XII. And he did so with the aid of friends, such as the Abate Garofalo, whose canvassing for Vico among powerful clergy apparently helped him to secure success. On 18 November 1724, Vico wrote to Filippo Monti, a high-ranking ecclesiastic of Bologna, to thank him for his help in soliciting the patronage of Cardinal Corsini and to describe the argument of his work, which, he insisted, derived its principles of natural law from the Sacred Scripture and confuted the doctrines of the Stoics, Epicureans, and moderns (i.e., Hobbes, Spinoza, Pierre Bayle, and Locke) alike.[55] Vico's solicitation evidently was a success. By Christmas 1724, he had won a commitment for patronage from Cardinal Corsini, to whom he sent obsequious thanks along with the promise to emblazon the cardinal's name on the title page of his work.[56] It is easy to imagine just how much Vico must have reveled in his success and how quickly the news must have spread that the powerful Cardinal Corsini had agreed to lend his name and financial support to Vico's upcoming publication. However, and sadly for Vico, the cardinal's commitment was fleeting, as he politely withdrew his offer in July 1725 with the excuse of unforeseen and exorbitant expenditures recently incurred in the Diocese of Frascati.[57] The humiliation this caused Vico must have been immense. As he wrote in the *Autobiografia:* "By a stroke of bad luck he [Vico] found himself in such straits that he could not afford to print the work and yet felt only too obliged to do so as a matter of honor, since he had promised its publication."[58] Although his pride was deeply wounded, Vico's determination did not lapse, and he "bent all his faculties toward finding, by intense meditation, a positive method (of exposition) which would be more concise and thus more efficacious."[59]

Given the humiliating circumstances, in other words, it seems that Vico chose to shorten his text to a length that he could afford to publish at his own cost. In summer 1725, he evidently recomposed a "more concise and thus more efficacious one," which he then published in October 1725 with the press of his good friend Felice Mosca after having obtained the imprimaturs of both the ecclesiastical and civil authorities of the Kingdom.[60] The publication of that same text was self-financed and cost Vico a precious ring inlaid with a diamond—but it was the price of glory.[61]

The "more concise" text Vico published bore the title *Principii di una scienza nuova intorno alla natura delle nazioni per la quale si ritruovano i principii di altro sistema del diritto naturale delle genti,* and it constituted what is more generally known as the first edition of the *Scienza nuova.* In so many ways, the first edition of the *Scienza nuova* was less a break with Vico's scholarly past than the title would imply. Indeed, it principally represented a synthesis and simplification of the cardinal ideas of the *Diritto universale,* which had been so disparately presented throughout that text. In this sense, the first edition of the *Scienza nuova* can be thought of as a popularization of Vico's vision of society and law, however uncanny his ideas remained for his contemporaries. In the first place, it was written in the vernacular; it was shorter, and, from a conceptual point of view, it was brilliantly incisive. What was more, the *Scienza nuova* (1725) eliminated a number of themes that had figured prominently in the *Diritto universale,* making room for Vico's first round of clarification and elaboration of what would become known as the hallmark ideas of his magnum opus, the *Principii di scienza nuova d'intorno alla commune natura delle nazioni* (1744), the third edition of the *Scienza nuova.* As this clarification and elaboration occurred at the expense of other themes, however, it is important to acknowledge the change in emphasis that the *Scienza nuova* (1725) marked for Vico's treatment of law and society. Despite their many similarities, there were also important differences between the *Diritto universale* and the first edition of the *Scienza nuova,* which, however predictable, would shape the reputation of Vico for posterity.

The reasons for these differences cannot be distinguished, I believe, from the differences between the audiences that Vico targeted for his respective works. And those respective audiences were quite diverse indeed. If Vico had sought to cultivate the political protagonists of the Kingdom with the *Diritto universale,* he rather imagined the *Scienza nuova* as a platform from which to make an appeal to the literati and scholars of the "academies of Europe in this enlightened age."[62] However histrionic this might have sounded, the difference that this change in target audience made for his work was more than rhetorical. In fact, it would give Vico cause to abstract the findings of the *Diritto universale* and re-present them as a "science of the nature of the nations," or what we might call a science of humanity.

III. Vico and the Social Sciences: Toward a Conjectural History of Humanity

For the literati and scholars of the "academies of Europe in this enlightened age," Vico proposed a "science" that he vaunted as utterly novel, namely, a "science of the nature of the nations," or what he alternatively called a "philosophy of humanity." The central claim of this "new science" was that the "origins and progress" of all nations were "constant," by which Vico meant identical among and repeatable by all peoples throughout the world regardless of "the times in which they arose and began."[63] In other words, Vico's "new science" of "humanity" hypothesized that there were laws governing the formation and experience of peoples and that those laws were not only regular but also universal and, as such, had predictable outcomes over space and time. The obvious analogy Vico posited between his "science of the nature of the nations" and the physical sciences of the natural world would not have escaped his contemporaries and is noteworthy. Indeed, as is well known, the very idea of a "new science" had been coined by Galileo to represent (the novelty of) his endeavors in the study of mechanics.[64] Thus, Vico's employment of the term "new science" indubitably was meant to present his work as a contribution to the field of knowledge about naturally occurring phenomena; and his work itself arguably demonstrated that the Galilean "book of nature" included the human experience in general and that of peoples in particular. In this sense, the first edition of the *Scienza nuova* clearly articulated an early contribution to Enlightenment social science: for it formulated a "science" of the origins and development of human unions whose basis and telos were suprapolitical, or social, and whose phenomena demonstratively conformed to laws of nature. In particular, it articulated a conjectural history of humanity that hypothesized that the origins of all peoples derived from the same causes and that their histories exhibited the same effects. As Vico himself plainly put it at the outset of his final book of the *Scienza nuova* (1725): "With the aid of the foregoing necessary discoveries, this Science becomes a philosophy of humanity in virtue of the series of causes it provides, and a universal history of the nations in virtue of the sequence of effects it traces."[65] Furthermore, as concerned Vico's own career, the first edition of the *Scienza nuova* piloted that very theory of history that is generally thought to be the hallmark of its revised third edition, that is, the theory of the three ages of humanity (the ages of the gods, heroes, and men) and the three types of languages, customs, and laws characteristic of them.[66] As Vico presented it, then, the *Scienza nuova* (1725) marked a distinct break from the interests of his earlier career and the beginning of a new oeuvre, on which, as it turned out, he (obsessively) would work until his death.

If the first edition of the *Scienza nuova* made an important early contribution to Enlightenment social science, then it did so by repackaging for a broader scholarly audience the most basic tenets of the *Diritto universale*. As regarded their most fundamental hypotheses, the differences between the *Scienza nuova* (1725) and the *Diritto universale* were differences of degree rather than kind. For the literati and scholars of the "academies of Europe in this enlightened age" Vico evidently draped the assumptions that had shaped his contribution to natural law in the language of contemporary science. Indeed, with Vico's earlier contribution to natural law the "new science" shared the same object, method, and objectives of inquiry. Generally speaking, in other words, it is fair to say that in the *Scienza nuova* Vico took a body of knowledge that he had produced for the Neapolitan judiciary and systematized it for an audience with a distinct scientific idiom and a different relationship to demonstrable human behavior. Similarly, it can be said that the most notable innovations of the *Scienza nuova* had their origins in Vico's concern to address the scientific debates and interests of the "academies of Europe in this enlightened age," however idiosyncratic his own novelties may have been.

While those innovations were important per se, they did not significantly alter either the premises or the prognosis of Vico's contribution to social theory as it had been formulated for the *Diritto universale*. In what were often-times the most interesting of ways, they supplemented the extant historical evidence for Vico's foundational claim that civic polities universally were subject to a course of development that was at once akin to the Stoic progression to cultivation and marked by the incremental equalization of rights among the members of the polity. What was so fascinating about the *Scienza nuova,* in other words, were the protean and imaginative additions, or corollaries, that Vico amassed to further substantiate and refine his overarching argument about the experience of humanity. Still, it is these same additions that make the *Scienza nuova* less meaningful for, or pertinent to, an account of the emergence of social theory, such as mine, as they primarily substantiate Vico's singular contributions to recondite debates that were auxiliary to his laws of social change. In other words, as regards Vico's social theory, the subtleties of his elaborations per se are of less interest to me than the reasons for and meaning of his engaging in those subtleties.

If Vico's revisions of his text first and foremost supplemented his social theory, the knotty question nonetheless remains as to how Vico's painstaking elaboration and systematization of his prior ideas affected the purpose and moral authority of his social science. On the one hand, in the *Scienza nuova* (1725) Vico simply restated his prior object, method, and objectives of inquiry with unprecedented clarity and reordered the presentation of his evidence accordingly. On the other, Vico also trimmed and reevaluated his extant material in ways that had less bearing on its content than they did its message. While he expanded the purview of his argument on a number of counts in the *Scienza nuova,* he also limited it on others; and those same limitations were consequential for the moral imperatives of his social science.

As concerned its objectives of inquiry, first, the *Scienza nuova* (1725) not only corroborated but also clarified how Vico understood his contribution to natural law. Like the legal treatise, the *Scienza nuova* (1725) responded to and trounced the origins stories told by the ancient and modern proponents of natural law. It too began with a virulent denouncement of the views of human nature and of the originary city proposed by Hobbes, John Selden, Pufendorf, and their ignominious ancient predecessors, the Epicureans. And it too retold the history of peoples as if the beginnings and ends of their union all uniformly had been marked by distinct forms, one violent and one benevolent, of the ius gentium, that is, by the laws of war and by those of equity, respectively. In sum, it too adopted and historicized the competing notions of natural law to conjecture a model for the history of world nations that laid claim to universality. What was more, though, in the *Scienza nuova* (1725) Vico presented this model with unprecedented incisiveness and elaborated on it in an argumentative way. In the first place, in the *Scienza nuova* (1725) he better communicated that his differences with seventeenth-century theorists of natural law concerned not only their respective understandings of human nature and of the originary city but also the supposed universality of natural law. For Vico made explicit in his prefatory remarks to the *Scienza nuova* (1725) that the universality of natural law applied not only to the originary condition of humankind, as his predecessors had believed, but also to its experience over historical time. As Vico understood it, one of the shortcomings of his seventeenth-century predecessors was that they had overlooked that "natural law might have arisen with the customs of nations and yet be eternal." Moreover, Vico plainly articulated the upshot of the eternal nature of natural law for conjectural history with the hypothesis that in all nations natural law proceeded through the same "stages" (*gradi*)—or what Vico admitted the jurisconsults had called "sects of times"—before attaining "perfection."[67] In other words, it was in the *Scienza nuova* (1725) that Vico manifestly stated the implications of his polemical understanding of natural law for his vision of history. It was therein that he first formulated in patent

terms what he so painstakingly had evidenced in the *Diritto universale* and that
would now figure as the central contention of his work, namely, his claim for
"the uniformity of the course that humanity takes among nations."[68]

As concerned his sources and method, second, Vico expanded his purview to more emphatically convey his sense that at any given time the life
of a nation was replete with signs, both old and new, that encoded not only
its power relations but also the mental world of its people. As he had in the
Diritto universale, so in the *Scienza nuova* (1725) did Vico take the language,
mythology, poetry, and histories of the most ancient nations as his sources for
the evidence of the human experience. And so did he bring to bear on those
sources a hermeneutics that presumed that both words and symbols—be they
poetic or iconic—had their origins in concrete things and practices and, as
such, were verisimilitudes of an ancient past that—with the passage of time
and change in customs—had been transmuted into allegories. However, for
this principle Vico provided considerably more evidence in the *Scienza nuova*
(1725), devoting an entire book to "The Principles of This Science concerning Language." Herein Vico more explicitly formulated and elaborated on his
theory of "natural signification," wherewith he held that the earliest forms
of human expression had a natural relation to the ideas they were employed
to signify.[69] Herein he more boldly stated his prior assessment of etymology
and mythology by defining the first as "true speech" and the second as "true
narration,"[70] and complicated the latter by evincing its instability as a mirror
of the nation's mind. And herein he adumbrated his hallmark concept of
"poetic wisdom" by tentatively offering physical explanations for the origins
of language and verse,[71] and for the anthropomorphism of the earliest fables
of humanity and its figures of speech, which he viewed as both fantastic and
sublime.[72] Together, these insights constituted the guidelines of what Vico
now explicitly called "a new critical art," which made possible the discern-
ment of "what is true in all the gentile histories," and famously provided a
key to the historical literature of tradition in an age that tended to view it
with the utmost skepticism.[73]

As concerned its specific object of inquiry, furthermore, the *Scienza nuova*
(1725) also took Rome as its primary example of "the uniformity of the
course that humanity takes among nations." And it clarified Vico's interpretation of Roman history on a number of points that had been vexed—if
not outright contradictory—in the *Diritto universale,* while giving renewed
emphasis to others. For example, in the first edition of the *Scienza nuova,*
Vico made plainer that the origins of the Roman clienteles, and consequently
feudalism, had lain in the "surrender" of the weak and their acceptance
of asylum from the strong.[74] Furthermore, Vico stated with unprecedented

clarity that the Roman plebeians were noncitizen members of the civic polity.[75] And, consequently, he more markedly argued that the history of Rome
was tantamount to the history of their acquisition of rights, or what Vico
here called "liberties," which, as he clearly emphasized, culminated in the
Poetelian Law under which the plebeians were formally freed of the *nexus*
and admitted to the full political rights of the civic polity.[76] As he put it:

> Thus under Romulus' bond, the Roman plebs waged war for the life
> that he saved them in his asylum. Then, under Servius Tullius' bond,
> it waged war for the natural liberty that it had gained through natural
> ownership of the fields under the census, but of which it would have
> been deprived through slavery. Thus, it waged war most obstinately
> for life and liberty. Finally, under the bond of the Law of the Twelve
> Tables, in which the fathers had ceded optimum ownership of the
> fields to the plebs but confined the public auspices within their own
> order, it waged war for civil liberty.[77]

What was more, Vico resolved the contradiction that had arisen in the *Diritto
universale* regarding the dates and the nature of the agrarian laws by identifying the census of Servius Tullius as the first agrarian law and the land
reform of Spurius Cassius as the second.[78] And he floated for the first time
his hallmark claim about the Twelve Tables: that this Roman code was not
a Greek cultural import by a Roman embassy but rather was "simply the
wholly native customs of the heroic peoples of Latium," or the archaic laws
of the Romans themselves.[79]

Finally, and most important, in the first edition of the *Scienza nuova,* Vico
placed renewed emphasis on the cosmopolitanism of Rome, in particular,
and the historical process, in general. Indeed, he literally spoke about the
community that the historical process invested as the "great city of man-
kind."[80] However, herein cosmopolitanism was born of neither the rationality
of the sage nor the commonalities of enterprise but rather from the shared
experiences of warfare. For Vico claimed that it was by way of warfare and
imperialism that Rome literally had imposed a uniformity of development
on the world. According to Vico, the progress of Roman expansion had
displaced those social discrepancies and conflicts that had once characterized
the Roman polity onto the geographical space of its conquests, establishing
a differential between the metropole and its periphery that could be understood in terms of developmental time.[81] Indeed, Vico literally asserted that
the distance from the imperial center neatly correlated with the sequence
of temporally anterior epochs of Roman history, so that the status and rights
of the individual regions of the Empire corresponded to the succession of

rights bearers characteristic of the history of the city of Rome. In other words, the geography of the Empire constituted, for Vico, what was a recapitulation of the history of the Roman struggle of the orders. It re-presented the conundrum of the metropolis on a global scale and offered a prognosis for its resolution: the recognition of natural ownership and the right to property transfer among all members of the world order.[82] As Vico understood the order of things in the Roman Empire:

> The people of Latium, with their municipalities, came to be like an order of knights... the people of Italy came to be like the Roman plebs after the Law of the Twelve Tables... the people of the docile provinces came to be like the Roman plebs in the times of Servius Tullius, with natural ownership of the fields, for which they paid a levy... and the people of the ferocious provinces came to be like the Roman plebs in the times of Romulus.[83]

In the *Scienza nuova,* the history of Rome, in sum, was paradigmatic for the history of the world.

Yet, despite the genealogical relationship between the *Diritto universale* and the first edition of the *Scienza nuova* (1725), it is plain that the exemplarity of "Rome" in the latter work had changed dramatically, and that this dramatic change was of the utmost significance for the purpose and moral authority of Vico's project. Rome no longer figured as an example of the import of property relations for the rights, both personal and societal, of the respective orders of the originary polity and its successor states. Rather, in the first and subsequent editions of the *Scienza nuova,* Rome increasingly figured as an example of the physio-moral development of world peoples, as Vico's initial delvings into the early language and poetry of archaic peoples made plain. More important, though, if Rome had enjoyed the purchase of an account of and prescription for the contemporary metropolitan world in the *Diritto universale,* then in the *Scienza nuova* (1725) it became a placeholder for world processes that knew no bounds and recalled no finite remedies. And, in this sense, the universality of Rome in the *Scienza nuova* had left the *urbs orbis* bereft of the imperatives of "Romanism," which had not only legitimated but made morally binding the application of Roman law. In other words, the exemplarity of Rome in the *Scienza nuova* invoked a brand of cosmopolitanism that curiously wanted a vocation: it was a call to legal theory without praxis. The significance of this difference between the *Diritto universale* and the *Scienza nuova* is perhaps best captured by the treatment of Roman jurisprudence in those respective works. Whereas the discussion of Roman jurisprudence in the *Diritto universale* had been tied to that work's lessons about the history and instruments of equity ruling, in the *Scienza nuova* the history of jurisprudence primarily was treated as what Vico called "a science of the mind of man."[84] Jurisprudence primarily interested Vico for what it revealed about the spirit of the law, or *mens legis*. It yielded knowledge about a people without the imperative of application. In fact, Vico's treatment of praetorian law in the *Scienza nuova* (1725) was not included in his short discourse on the history of jurisprudence per se, but was relegated to his book on language, where it not only evidenced the importance of the praetorian edicts for the introduction of equity principles into Roman law but also, and more important, revealed the importance of the pattern of linguistic development associated with the innovation of law for the advent of the fictions of the praetors.[85]

In his conclusion to a most suggestive essay on what he called the philosophical significance of Renaissance jurisprudence, Donald R. Kelley once remarked: "Comte said that metaphysics is the ghost of dead theologies. From the perspective of more anthropological-minded thinkers like Vico it might be said with equal justice that social philosophy is the ghost of dead jurisprudence. Unfortunately, this is a transformation that has not even begun to be understood."[86] I cite this quote because I strongly believe that there is perhaps no better way to characterize the first edition of the *Scienza nuova* than as "the ghost of dead jurisprudence," as Kelley so insightfully put it. If there was anything distinctive about the first edition of the *Scienza nuova,* indeed, then it was the lapse of Vico's commitment to natural jurisprudence as the appropriate remedy for the renovation of society. If the laws of social behavior were, like the free will of its human agents, semiautonomous in the *Scienza nuova,* then it was because those laws were no longer coupled with a jurisprudential program that was meant to provide their practical counterpart. In other words, within Vico's own intellectual career it is clear that the advent of a theory of history that so singularly described the behavior of social types had something to do with the decoupling of his description of legal persons from the prescription of jurisprudential remedies for their observed condition. Unhinged from the very political culture from which its categories were generated, Vico's laws of social change constituted a discrete field of knowledge in the *Scienza nuova* as they previously had not in his work, making that "concise and more efficacious" text what was less a diagnosis than a prognosis of group behavior within the ever-expanding cosmos of the civic polity.

My interest in Vico similarly ends here. And that is not because what followed was not equally interesting, but because as a project the *Scienza nuova* was so very different from the earlier texts that Vico had written. For the literati and scholars of the "academies of Europe in this enlightened age"

the *Scienza nuova* strayed ever more from the investigation of historical phenomena with presumed bearing on the present of Vico's own world. And by
the same token it delved ever more deeply into a series of recondite debates
surrounding the chronology and evidence of history as well as the nature and
signs of language, which—although adumbrated in his prior writings—had
not had the same sort of purchase in the early works. Consequently, the sorts
of questions that the subsequent editions of the *Scienza nuova* raise are different than the ones posed by the earlier works. They more exclusively pose
questions about the resemblances and differences of Vico's ideas to tradition,
and, similarly, they also confront the critic with the hard task of assessing the
curious afterlife of the figures of Romanism bereft of their juridical prescription, or what were the ghosts of jurisprudence indeed.

❧ Note on References and Translations

Throughout this book my citation of sources chiefly has followed the norms of others.

Although this work is intended primarily for an Anglophone audience, throughout my text and notes I refer to Vico's works by their original-language titles. For the sake of stylistic consistency with the reference-literature on Vico as well as economy, furthermore, I have adopted the convention of modernizing (the capitalization and spelling) and abbreviating those original-language titles. The only exception to this rule is my occasional reference to the *Diritto universale,* which is the conventional title for the three-book legal study whose volumes Vico published individually—and with distinct titles—but he considered part of a single project.

Similarly, I have adopted the Italian norm of modernizing the capitalization and spelling of the titles of all books published in the Italian language prior to 1800. I have also modernized the capitalization and spelling of the titles of all Latin books, both ancient and early modern. However, I have chosen to maintain the original capitalization and spelling of all the manuscripts referenced by this book.

So that this book serves both specialists and students of Vico alike, where available I reference both the modern original- and English-language editions of Vico's works. Fortunately, the English-language editions of Vico's works maintain the system of identifying numbers proper to their modern original-language counterparts. Consequently, in each note I cite the uniform identifying number(s) of the referenced passage and page numbers upon which it appears in both the modern original- and English-language editions of Vico's work. In each reference to a work by Vico, in other words, I have provided: the conventional abbreviation of the original title; the conventional identifying number(s) of the passage quoted, or paraphrased; and the page numbers of that same passage in the modern original- and English-language editions of Vico's works, respectively. For example, subsequent to its first full reference I cite the twenty-first paragraph of the PRINCIPJ/ DI UNA SCIENZA NUOVA/ INTORNO/ ALLA NATURA DELLE

NAZIONI/ PER LA QUALE/ si ritruovano/ I PRINCIPJ/ DI ALTRO SISTEMA/ DEL DIRITTO NATURALE/ DELLE GENTI, which is known in English as *The First New Science: Scienza nuova* (1725), para. 21: Battistini edit., 989; Pompa edit., 17.

In my references to the classics I cite modern editions throughout this book. As a consequence, I have also chosen to maintain the names of the classical authors and the titles of their works as they appear on the title page of the modern editions I cite. Fortunately, among the modern editions of the classics the system of identifying numbers largely remains the same. Thus, just as I do in my references to Vico's works, in my references to ancient Greek and Latin texts I cite the uniform identifying numbers of the passages referenced in my text. However, it bears mentioning that I have always reproduced the numerical conventions of the modern editions employed without further modernization. For example, subsequent to its first full reference I cite the second book, second section and fifth paragraph of the Loeb edition of Marcus Tullius Cicero's *On Duties* as: Cicero, *De officiis,* Loeb Classical Library, II.ii.5. The only exception to this rule is my citation of the *Digest,* which follows the more modern convention of using Arabic numerals throughout to signify its successive subdivisions.

Wherever possible, I have quoted from standard English-language translations of foreign-language works. However, I sometimes have modified those translations somewhat. Wherever I have employed a translation word for word I have acknowledged as much parenthetically in my notes. Wherever I have adapted a translation, I have not. For example, where my English-language quotations from *De uno* and *De constantia* employ the translation of Giorgio Pinton and Margaret Diehl word for word I have inserted at the end of my reference the following parenthetical notation: (Pinton and Diehl trans.). Where my quotations do not employ their translation literally, I do not. However, it bears mentioning that my modification of the Pinton and Diehl translation is oftentimes minor, if not limited to my substitution of their uniform translation of the Latin word *ius* as "right" with other words that better capture Vico's interpretation of the nature of Roman law in the period under consideration.

All other translations are my own.

✒ ABBREVIATIONS

References to foreign libraries and archives employ the following abbreviations:

ACDF   Archivio della Congregazione per la Dottrina della Fede
ASDN   Archivio storico diocesano di Napoli
ASN   Archivio di Stato di Napoli
ASV   Archivio Segreto Vaticano
BNN   Biblioteca Nazionale di Napoli
ONB   Österreichische Nationalbibliothek
SAW   Haus-, Hof- und Staatsarchiv, Wien
SNSP   Società Napoletana di Storia Patria

Where it remains standard, I have cited and abbreviated the following critical edition of Vico's works as:

Opere   Vico, Giambattista. *Opere*. Edited by Fausto Nicolini with Benedetto Croce and Giovanni Gentile. 8 vols. Bari: Laterza, 1911–1941. Unless noted otherwise references cite the first edition of the volumes of this work.

References to Vico's individual writings listed below employ the following abbreviations and cite the following standard modern original-language editions and English-language translations, respectively:

Autobiografia   *Vita di Giambattista Vico scritta da se medesimo* (first published 1728).

In the original Italian: Vico, Giambattista. *Vita di Giambattista Vico scritta da se medesimo*. In Vico, Giambattista. *Opere*. Vol. 5: *L'autobiografia, il carteggio e le poesie varie*. Edited by Benedetto Croce and Fausto Nicolini. Second edition, revised and enlarged. Bari: Laterza, 1929.

And in the English language: Vico, Giambattista. *The Autobiography of Giambattista Vico*. Translated by Max Harold

Fisch and Thomas Goddard Bergin. First edition. Ithaca: Cornell University Press, 1944.

Coniuratio *Principum Neapolitanorum coniuratio* (written circa 1703–4).

In the original Latin and Italian translation: Vico, Giambattista. *La congiura dei principi napoletani.* Edited by Claudia Pandolfi. Naples: Morano, 1992.

De constantia *Liber alter qui est de constantia iurisprudentis* (first published 1721).

In the original Latin and Italian translation: Vico, Giambattista. *De constantia iurisprudentis.* In Vico, Giambattista. *Opere giuridiche.* Edited by Paolo Cristofolini. Florence: Sansoni, 1974.

And in the English language: Vico, Giambattista. *The Constancy of the Jurist.* In Vico, Giambattista. *Universal Right.* Translated from the Latin and edited by Giorgio Pinton and Margaret Diehl. Amsterdam: Rodopi, 2000.

Epistole Vico, Giambattista. *Epistole.* Edited by Manuela Sanna. Naples: Morano, 1992.

Institutiones *Institutionum oratoriarum liber unus* (written circa 1711–41).

In the original Latin and Italian translation: Vico, Giambattista. *Institutiones oratoriae.* Edited by Giuliano Crifò. Naples: Istituto Suor Orsola Benincasa, 1989.

And in the English language: Vico, Giambattista. *The Art of Rhetoric (Institutiones Oratoriae, 1711–41).* Edited and translated by Giorgio A. Pinton and Arthur W. Shippee (from the Crifò edition). Amsterdam: Rodopi, 1996.

Minora Vico, Giambattista. *Minora: Scritti latini, storici e d'occasione.* Edited by Gian Galeazzo Visconti. Naples: Guida, 2000.

Oratio, no. *Orationes: I–VI* (written 1699–1707).

In the original Latin and Italian translation: Vico, Giambattista. *Le orazioni inaugurali, I–VI.* Edited by Gian Galeazzo Visconti. Bologna: Il Mulino, 1982.

And in the English language: Vico, Giambattista. *On Humanistic Education (Six Inaugural Orations, 1699–1707).* Translated by Giorgio A. Pinton and Arthur W. Shippee from the Visconti edition. Ithaca: Cornell University Press, 1993.

De ratione *De nostri temporis studiorum ratione* (first published 1709).

In the original Latin: Vico, Giambattista. *De nostri temporis studiorum ratione.* In Vico, Giambattista. *Opere.* Vol. 1:

Le orazioni inaugurali, Il De Italorum sapientia *e le polemiche.* Edited by Giovanni Gentile and Fausto Nicolini. Bari: Laterza, 1914.

And in the English language: Vico, Giambattista. *On the Study Methods of Our Time.* Translated and with an Introduction and Notes by Elio Gianturco. Ithaca: Cornell University Press, 1990.

De rebus gestis   *De rebus gestis Antonii Caraphaei* (first published 1716).

In the original Latin and Italian translation: Vico, Giambattista. *Le gesta di Antonio Carafa.* Edited by Manuela Sanna. Naples: Guida, 1997.

Scienza nuova   *Principii di una scienza nuova intorno alla natura delle nazioni*
(1725)   *per la quale si ritruovano i principii di altro sistema del diritto naturale delle genti* (first published 1725).

In the original Italian: Vico, Giambattista. *Princìpi Di Una Scienza Nuova....*In Vico, Giambattista. *Opere.* Edited by Andrea Battistini. Milano: Mondadori, 1990.

And in the English language: Vico, Giambattista. *The First New Science.* Edited and translated by Leon Pompa (from the Battistini edition). New York: Cambridge University Press, 2002.

Scienza nuova   *Principii di scienza nuova d'intorno alla comune natura delle*
(1744)   *nazioni in questa terza impressione dal medesimo autore in un gran numero di luoghi corretta, schiarita, e notabilmente accresciuta* (first published 1744).

In the original Italian: Vico, Giambattista. *Principi di scienza nuova.* In Vico, Giambattista. *Opere.* Vol. 4: *La scienza nuova.* Edited by Fausto Nicolini. Bari: Laterza, 1928.

And in the English language: Vico, Giambattista. *The New Science.* Unabridged translation of the third edition (1744) by Thomas Goddard Bergin and Max Harold Fisch. First edition. Ithaca: Cornell University Press, 1948.

Sinopsi   Untitled Book Prospectus (first published 1720).

In the original Italian: Vico, Giambattista. *Sinopsi del diritto universale.* In Vico, Giambattista. *Opere giuridiche.* Edited by Paolo Cristofolini. Florence: Sansoni, 1974.

And in the English language: Vico, Giambattista. "The Synopsis of *Universal Right.*" In Vico, Giambattista. *Universal Right.* Translated from the Latin and edited by Giorgio Pinton and Margaret Diehl. Amsterdam: Rodopi, 2000.

De uno   *De universi iuris uno principio, et fine uno liber unus* (first pub-
                  lished 1721).

                  In the original Latin and Italian translation: Vico, Giam-
                  battista. *De universi iuris uno principio et fine uno.* In Vico,
                  Giambattista. *Opere giuridiche.* Edited by Paolo Cristofolini.
                  Florence: Sansoni, 1974.

                  And in the English language: Vico, Giambattista. *The
                  One Principle and One End of Universal Right.* In Vico,
                  Giambattista. *Universal Right.* Translated from the Latin and
                  edited by Giorgio Pinton and Margaret Diehl. Amsterdam:
                  Rodopi, 2000. [NB: I have translated this title as *The One
                  Principle and One End of Universal Law.*]

References to the *Bibliografia Vichiana* employ the following abbreviation and
cite the following edition:

Bibliografia   Croce, Benedetto. *Bibliografia Vichiana.* Revised and enlarged
  Vichiana   by Fausto Nicolini. 2 vols. Naples: Ricciardi, 1947.

References to the *Digest* of Justinian employ the following abbreviation and
cite the following edition:

Digest   *The Digest of Justinian.* Edited by Theodor Mommsen with
                  the aid of Paul Krueger and English translation edited by
                  Alan Watson. Philadelphia: University of Pennsylvania Press,
                  1985.

The following standard abbreviations denote:

DBI   *Dizionario Biografico degli Italiani.* Rome: Istituto della Enci-
                  clopedia Italiana, 1960–.
RSI   *Rivista Storica Italiana.* Naples: Edizioni Scientifiche Ital-
                  iane, 1884–.

❧ Notes

Introduction

1. The historiography on Vico is immense and cannot be cataloged here. However, for evidence of the appropriation of Vico by historians of modern disciplines, see the contributions by social scientists and others to the series of monumental conference proceedings edited by Giorgio Tagliacozzo between 1968 and 1981: Giorgio Tagliacozzo and Hayden V. White, eds., *Giambattista Vico: An International Symposium* (Baltimore: Johns Hopkins University Press, 1969); Giorgio Tagliacozzo and Donald Philip Verene, eds., *Giambattista Vico's Science of Humanity* (Baltimore: Johns Hopkins University Press, 1976); and Giorgio Tagliacozzo, ed., *Vico, Past and Present* (Atlantic Highlands, NJ: Humanities Press, 1981).

2. In particular, see Benedetto Croce, *The Philosophy of Giambattista Vico* (1913; repr., Brunswick, NJ: Transaction, 2002) or any of Fausto Nicolini's numerous contributions regarding the "a-politicalness" of Vico, such as his articles in *Atti dell'Accademia Pontaniana* 5 (1955): "Fu il Vico uomo di partito?" 289–98; "Ancora dell'apoliticità del Vico," 299–317; and "Sempre sull'apoliticità del Vico," 403–6.

3. See the *Vita di Giambattista Vico scritta da se medesimo,* cited by the specialty literature in Italian as the *Autobiografia* in Giambattista Vico, *Opere,* vol. 5, *L'autobiografia, il carteggio e le poesie varie,* ed. Benedetto Croce and Fausto Nicolini, 2nd ed., rev. and enl. (Bari: Laterza, 1929), 20 and 42; and, in English, Giambattista Vico, *The Autobiography,* trans. Max Harold Fisch and Thomas Goddard Bergin (Ithaca: Cornell University Press, 1944), esp. 132 and 158. Henceforth, this work will be referred to as the *Autobiografia* and my citations of its above editions will be abbreviated. The Nicolini edition of Vico's works will be abbreviated as *Opere.*

4. Among Italian scholars, the most brilliant exposés of this interpretation have been offered by Nicola Badaloni, *Introduzione a G. B. Vico* (Milan: Feltrinelli, 1961); Eugenio Garin, "Da Campanella a Vico," in *Dal Rinascimento all'Illuminismo* (Pisa: Nistri-Lischi, 1970); and Paolo Rossi, *I segni del tempo: Storia della terra e storia delle nazioni da Hooke a Vico* (Milan: Feltrinelli, 1979). In the Anglo-American world, this backward-looking approach to Vico has been embraced and intelligently pursued by Nancy Struever and Donald Kelley in their numerous conference contributions, as well as by Michael Mooney in his *Vico in the Tradition of Rhetoric* (Princeton: Princeton University Press, 1985) and Giuseppe Mazzotta in his *The New Map of the World: The Poetic Philosophy of Giambattista Vico* (Princeton: Princeton University Press, 1999).

5. See the fine studies by Harold Samuel Stone, *Vico's Cultural History: The Production and Transmission of Ideas in Naples, 1685–1750* (New York: Brill, 1997) and John

Robertson, *The Case for the Enlightenment: Scotland and Naples 1680–1760* (Cambridge: Cambridge University Press, 2005).

6. See Isaiah Berlin, *Vico and Herder: Two Studies in the History of Ideas* (New York: Viking Press, 1976); Donald Kelley, "Vico's Road: From Rhetoric to Jurisprudence and Back," in Tagliacozzo and Verene, *Science of Humanity;* Donald Kelley, "The Pre-history of Sociology: Montesquieu, Vico, and the Legal Tradition," *History of the Behavioral Sciences* 16, no. 2 (1980): 133–44; and Mark Lilla, *Vico: The Making of an Anti-Modern* (Cambridge: Harvard University Press, 1993). Lilla has indicated the centrality of Vico's legal texts for his social theory and emphasized its providential design and, thus, theodicy. A number of Italian scholars have analyzed Vico's approach to law in reference to both the metaphysical and philosophical traditions available to him. In particular, see Dino Pasini, *Diritto, società e stato in Vico* (Naples: Jovene, 1970); Guido Fassò, *Vico e Grozio* (Naples: Guida, 1971); Guido Fassò, "The Problem of Law and the Historical Origin of the *New Science*," in Tagliacozzo and Verene, *Science of Humanity;* and Santo Mazzarino, *Vico, l'annalistica e il diritto* (Naples: Guida, 1971).

7. J. G. A. Pocock, "The Ideal of Citizenship since Classical Times," repr. in Ronald Beiner, ed., *Theorizing Citizenship* (Albany: SUNY, 1995), 29–52, esp. 35 and 43.

8. While some have considered the political theory of Vico's works, few have contextualized it in the concerns and factions of his contemporaries. On select political topoi in Vico's work Enrico Nuzzo has written a number of learned essays, the last appearing in Lorenzo Bianchi, ed., *Cosmopolitismo* (Naples: Liguori, 2004). An astute reading of the political theory of Vico's oeuvre is Riccardo Caporali's *Heroes Gentium: Sapienza e politica in Vico* (Bologna: Il Mulino, 1992). Nonetheless, Caporali does little to contextualize Vico's political ideas in the Italy of his day. Before his untimely death, Eluggero Pii sought to recover the importance of Vico's political theory for midcentury Neapolitan philosophes by underscoring some of the themes in Vico that would recur in Genovesi and his school. See Eluggero Pii, "L'utile e le forme di governo nel Vico politico," *Il pensiero politico* 23 (1997): 105–34. Exceptionally, Giuseppe Giarrizzo's work has provided some valuable insights into the contemporary politics of Vico's legal theory in Naples that have long been worthy of further consideration and exploration. See Giuseppe Giarrizzo, *Vico, la politica e la storia* (Naples: Guida, 1981). The one sustained postwar debate about the politics of Vico in his Neapolitan context was conducted among Raffaele Ajello, Giuseppe Giarrizzo, and Giuseppe Galasso, which somewhat foundered on Ajello's infelicitous insistence on the conservatism of Vico, which he anachronistically has contrasted with the liberalism of contemporary advocates of economic reform. In particular, see Raffaele Ajello, *Arcana Juris: Diritto e politica nel Settecento italiano* (Naples: Jovene, 1976); and for their pointed exchange, see Giuseppe Giarrizzo "Giannone, Vico e i loro interpreti recenti," *Bollettino del Centro di Studi Vichiani* 11 (1981): 173–84; Raffaele Ajello, "Dal *facere* al *factum*," *Bollettino del Centro di Studi Vichiani* 12–13 (1982–83): 343–59; and Giuseppe Galasso, "Il Vico di Giarrizzo e un itinerario alternativo," *Bollettino del Centro di Studi Vichiani* 12–13 (1982–83): 359–75. In English, see Frederick Vaughan, *The Political Philosophy of Giambattista Vico* (The Hague: Martinus Nijhoff, 1972); B. A. Haddock, *Vico's Political Thought* (Swansea, Wales: Mortlake Press, 1986); and Lilla, *Vico.*

9. Compare the excellent studies of the usage of the word "society" in Keith Michael Baker, "Enlightenment and the Institution of Society: Notes for a Conceptual History," in *Main Trends in Cultural History*, ed. Willem Melching and Wyger Velema (Amsterdam: Rodopi, 1994) and Daniel Gordon, *Citizens without Sovereignty: Equality and Sociability in French Thought, 1670–1789* (Princeton: Princeton University Press, 1994), esp. 51–54.

10. Here I am thinking of the magisterial work (and school) of Quentin Skinner and, in particular, his *Liberty before Liberalism* (New York: Cambridge University Press, 1998). Among his many classics, also see *The Foundations of Modern Political Thought*, 2 vols. (New York: Cambridge University Press, 1980); *Machiavelli* (New York: Oxford University Press, 1981); *Reason and Rhetoric in the Philosophy of Hobbes* (New York: Cambridge University Press, 1996); *Visions of Politics*, 3 vols. (New York: Cambridge University Press, 2002); and *Hobbes and Republican Liberty* (New York: Cambridge University Press, 2008). Skinner has also edited a number of books specifically dedicated to the history of republicanism, in which he has argued for the importance of that tradition beyond the traditional scope of the Renaissance. See Gisela Bock, Quentin Skinner, and Maurizio Viroli, eds., *Machiavelli and Republicanism* (New York: Cambridge University Press, 1980) and Martin van Gelderen and Quentin Skinner, eds., *Republicanism: A Shared European Heritage*, 2 vols. (New York: Cambridge University Press, 2002). Skinner has also served as the editor of the Cambridge series Ideas in Contexts, which has published a number of exemplary contextualizations of the work of Enlightenment authors, including James Tully, *An Approach to Political Philosophy: Locke in Contexts* (New York: Cambridge University Press, 1993) and Helena Rosenblatt, *Rousseau and Geneva: From the* First Discourse *to the* Social Contract, *1749–62* (New York: Cambridge University Press, 1997).

11. The political critique of Skinner's work has been significant, as have been his erudite responses. For a fine first overview of this debate, see Kari Palonen, *Quentin Skinner: History, Politics, Rhetoric* (Cambridge: Polity Press, 2003).

12. Here I am thinking of the work of Richard Tuck and the studies that work has inspired. In particular, see his classic *Natural Rights Theories: Their Origin and Development* (New York: Cambridge University Press, 1979). A number of scholars have further explored natural law and rights over the course of the Middle Ages. For two fine examples, see Brian Tierney, *The Idea of Natural Rights* (Atlanta: Scholars Press, 1997) and Annabel S. Brett, *Liberty, Right, and Nature: Individual Rights in Later Scholastic Thought* (New York: Cambridge University Press, 1997).

13. Here I am thinking of the collections of essays by Istvan Hont and by J. G. A. Pocock. In particular, see Istvan Hont, *Jealousy of Trade: International Competition and the Nation-State in Historical Perspective* (Cambridge: Harvard University Press, 2005) and J. G. A. Pocock, *Virtue, Commerce, and History: Essays on Political Thought and History, Chiefly in the Eighteenth Century* (New York: Cambridge University Press, 1985).

14. Quentin Skinner, "Meaning and Understanding in the History of Ideas," *History and Theory* 8, no. 1 (1969): 3–53.

15. Much of the career of Donald R. Kelley has been dedicated to exploring this theme. In particular, see *The Human Measure: Social Thought in the Western Legal Tradition* (Cambridge: Harvard University Press, 1990).

16. This metaphor most famously is contained in a memoir written by Pietro Contegna entitled "Alcune riflessioni intorno al presente governo del Regno di

Napoli sotto l'Augustissimo Imperatore Carlo VI" (1733) in SNSP MS XXI.A.7, f. 90v, and has been cited on a number of occasions in the historiography on Naples. For example, see Cesare De Seta, *Storia della città di Napoli* (Naples: Laterza, 1973), 323. However, in my own research I have found usage of this image in earlier texts, and it is a commonplace throughout the eighteenth century. Also see Giuseppe Maria Galanti, *Breve descrizione della Città di Napoli e del suo contorno* (Naples: Gabinetto Letterario, 1792), 14.

17. This fact is well known and has been tabulated in a number sources, whose findings have been reproduced in Peter Clark and Bernard Lepetit, eds., *Capital Cities and Their Hinterlands in Early Modern Europe* (Brookfield, VT: Ashgate, 1996), 30–31. It is noteworthy that around 1600 the metropolitan area of Naples contained the largest population in all of Europe. What is more, it was only after the devastating plague of 1656–57—which more than halved its population—that Naples was reduced to the third-largest city of Europe, a rank that it would hold through 1800. Traditionally, the historiography has identified the census figures of 1742 as evidence of the city's full recovery and supercession of its preplague population. See Claudia Petraccone, *Napoli moderna e contemporanea* (Naples: Guida, 1981), 55. More generally, on the urbanization of Naples in the early modern period, see her *Napoli dal Cinquecento all'Ottocento: Problemi di storia demografica e sociale* (Naples: Guida, 1974). Brigitte Marin has sought to offer a summary and reassessment of the historiography concerning the political and social history of the capital in a number of fine articles. See her "Mythes ou Mystification," in Collette Vallat, Brigitte Marin, and Gennaro Biondi, *Naples: Démythier la ville* (Paris: L'Harmattan, 1998); "Naples: Capital of the Enlightenment," in Clark and Lepetit, *Capital Cities and Their Hinterlands;* and "Town and Country in the Kingdom of Naples, 1500–1800," in *Town and Country in Europe, 1300–1800,* ed. S. R. Epstein (New York: Cambridge University Press, 2001). On the demographic history of the Kingdom, also see Gerard Delille, "Demografia," in *Storia del Mezzogiorno,* Giuseppe Galasso and Rosario Romeo, eds., vol. 8 (Naples: Edizioni del Sole, 1991) and the studies of Pasquale Villani, such as his *Documenti e orientamenti per la storia demografica del Regno di Napoli nel settecento* (Rome: Istituto Storico Italiano per l'età moderna e contemporanea, 1968) and "Territorio e popolazione: Orientamenti per la storia demografica," in his *Mezzogiorno tra riforme e rivoluzione,* 2nd rev. ed. (Rome: Laterza, 1973).

18. On the importance of immigration for the demographic growth of early modern capitals, such as Naples, especially see Paul M. Hohenberg and Lynn Hollen Lees, "Urban Systems and Economic Growth: Town Populations in Metropolitan Hinterlands, 1600–1800," in Clark and Lepetit, *Capital Cities and Their Hinterlands.*

19. "Metropolitan question" is my term. However, it is a variation on a number of similar terms employed in the contemporary historical literature. Brigitte Marin has aptly used the term "la question de la capitale" to refer to the debate about Naples that took place in its eighteenth-century public sphere. See Marin, "Mythes ou Mystification" in Vallat, Marin, and Biondi, *Naples,* 85. Historians have also used analogous terms to describe and generalize about the phenomenon of metropolitan growth in the early modern period. On the "metropolitan effect," see Clark and Lepetit, *Capital Cities and Their Hinterlands,* 2. (Compare S. R. Epstein, *Town and Country.*)

20. Ibid., 7 (citing 31) and 12.

21. Michael Reed, "London and Its Hinterland 1600–1800: The View from the Provinces," in Clark and Lepetit, *Capital Cities and Their Hinterlands,* 52.

22. Villani, *Mezzogiorno tra riforme e rivoluzione,* 4.

23. Based on the famous work of Paul Bairoch and Jan de Vries, these trends have been tabulated by Hohenberg and Lees in their essay "Urban Systems and Economic Growth: Town Populations in Metropolitan Hinterlands, 1600–1800," in *Capital Cities and Their Hinterlands,* ed. Clark and Lepetit, 31. Therein they note, for example, that the population of Benevento increased from 7,000 in 1600 to 8,000 in 1700 and then 10,000 in 1750, while the population of Salerno actually declined from 11,000 in 1600 to 8,000 in 1700 and remained at that figure through 1750. Salerno, like Naples, most certainly was affected by the plague of 1656. However, without the postplague figures it is hard to assess whether or not there was any real growth between 1657 and 1700. Be that as it may, it is evident that the population of Salerno stagnated throughout the first half of the century as Naples grew.

24. Villani, *Mezzogiorno tra riforme e rivoluzione,* 95. This stunning fact often has been cited by Brigitte Marin.

25. The population of Naples in 1798 numbered 435,930 inhabitants, and in 1804 it numbered 449,519, according to the official statistics of the court. Petraccone, *Napoli dal Cinquecento,* 138.

26. Both Petraccone and Marin have insisted on the role that the peripheries of the city played in the accommodation of newcomers to the capital and territory of Naples. On the new axis of demographic growth characteristic of the first half of the eighteenth century, see Petraccone, *Napoli dal Cinquecento,* 135–36. On the growth of the *casali,* see Marin, "Mythes ou Mystification," in *Naples,* ed. Vallat, Marin, and Biondi, 98–104.

27. Aristotle, *Politics,* ed. Stephen Everson and trans. Jonathan Barnes (New York: Cambridge University Press, 1996), esp. I.1–2, III.1, and III.6.

28. For the former sense, see Cicero, *De legibus,* trans. C. W. Keyes, Loeb Classical Library (1928; repr., Cambridge: Harvard University Press, 2000), II.ii.5; and for the latter, see Cicero's *De re publica,* trans. C. W. Keyes, Loeb Classical Library (1928; repr., Cambridge: Harvard University Press, 2000), VI.xiii.13 and I.xxvi.41.

29. As per the rhetoric of the imperial *civitas,* I am especially thinking of the famous panegyric on Rome by Aristides. For a general history of Roman citizenship, see A. N. Sherwin-White, *The Roman Citizenship* (Oxford: Clarendon Press, 1939), which has been reprinted on a few occasions; and for the Republic, see Claude Nicolet, *The World of the Citizen in Republican Rome,* trans. P. S. Falla (Berkeley: University of California Press, 1980).

30. For Cicero's description of the degrees of fellowship within "human society," or the world *civitas,* see Cicero, *De officiis,* trans. Walter Miller, Loeb Classical Library (1913; repr., Cambridge: Harvard University Press, 2005), I.xvii.53.

31. This idea was expressed by Ulpian in his book of *Edicts.* See *The Digest of Justinian,* ed. Theodor Mommsen with the aid of Paul Krueger and English translation ed. Alan Watson (Philadelphia: University of Pennsylvania Press, 1985): 1.5.17. Henceforth all my citations of passages from the *Digest* will refer to the above edition and employ its identifying numbers. For contemporary opposing views on the actual significance of this grant, see Tony Honoré, "Roman Law AD 200–400: From Cosmopolis to Rechstaat" and Peter Garnsey, "Roman Citizenship and Roman Law

in the Late Empire," both in *Approaching Late Antiquity,* ed. Simon Swain and Mark Edwards (New York: Oxford University Press, 2004).

32. Giulio Cesare Capaccio, *Il forastiero,* 3 vols. (1634; repr., Naples: Lucca Torre, 1989), esp. 276 and 466–67.

33. A famous eighteenth-century example of this usage is the one by Pietro Giannone in his *Istoria civile del Regno di Napoli,* ed. Antonio Marongiu, vol. 6, chap. 3 (Naples, 1723; repr., Milan: Marzorati, 1972), 23.

34. See Aristotle, *Politics,* esp. book 3, where the criteria for citizenship are treated.

35. See, for example, Jean Bodin, *The Republic,* book. 6, chap. 1, and Jean-Jacques Rousseau, *The Social Contract.* In the case of early modern Spain, the discussion of the appropriate criteria for and meaning of national citizenship has been identified in the legal case literature concerning the naturalization of foreigners by Spanish municipalities: see Tamar Herzog, *Defining Nations: Immigrants and Citizens in Early Modern Spain and Spanish America* (New Haven: Yale University Press, 2003). For the case of France, where the naturalization of foreigners was rather the prerogative of the court, see Peter Sahlins, *Unnaturally French: Foreign Citizens in the Old Regime and After* (Ithaca: Cornell University Press, 2004).

36. Among the best treatments of the history of citizenship in early modern Italy remain, in chronological order: William Bowsky, "Medieval Citizenship: The Individual and the State in the Commune of Siena, 1287–1355," *Studies in Medieval and Renaissance History,* ed. William Bowsky, vol. 4 (Lincoln: University of Nebraska Press, 1967); Peter Riesenberg, "Civism and Roman Law in Fourteenth-Century Italian Society," *Explorations in Economic History* 7, no. 1–2 (1969): 237–54; Julius Kirshner, "*Civitas Sibi Faciat Civem:* Bartolus of Sassoferrato's Doctrine on the Making of a Citizen," *Speculum* 48, no. 4 (1973): 694–713; Julius Kirshner, "*Ars Imitatur Naturam:* A Consilium of Baldus on Naturalization in Florence," *Viator* 5 (1974): 289–331; and Julius Kirshner, "Between Nature and Culture: An Opinion of Baldus of Perugia on Venetian Citizenship as Second Nature," *Journal of Medieval and Renaissance Studies* 9, no. 2 (1979): 179–208.

37. I am synthesizing material from Kirshner, "*Civitas Sibi Faciat Civem,*" esp. 695, and Bowsky, "Medieval Citizenship," esp. 198 and 203.

38. This has been shown most sophisticatedly in Julius Kirshner's "*Ars Imitatur Naturam*" and "Between Nature and Culture."

39. My own discussion of the privileges of and requirements for citizenship in early modern Naples is indebted to the pioneering work of Piero Ventura, on whose following articles I have drawn to provide my own short overview of the topic in this paragraph and the next: "Le ambiguità di un privilegio: la cittadinanza napoletana tra Cinque e Seicento," *Quaderni storici* 89, no. 2 (1995): 385–416, and "Privilegio di cittadinanza, mobilità sociale e istituzioni statali a Napoli tra Cinque e Seicento," in *Disuguaglianze: stratificazione e mobilità sociale nelle popolazioni italiane (dal secolo XIV agli inizi del secolo XX),* ed. Società Italiana di Demografia Storica, vol. 2 (Bologna: Clueb, 1997), 515–30. On the possibility of "naturalization" for Spaniards in Italy and the delicate question of nationality more generally in the Spanish Empire, see Mireille Peytavin, "Espanoles y italianos en Sicilia, Nápoles y Mílan durante los siglos XVI y XVII: Sobre la oportunidad de ser 'nacional' o 'natural,'" *Relaciones* 19, no. 73 (1998): 87–114.

40. Ventura, "Le ambiguità," 387–88.

41. Ibid., 390.

42. From the documentation analyzed by Ventura, it seems that birthright was the first criterion for citizenship in Naples, a criterion that essentially distinguished Naples from other early modern Italian cities, where typically residency of as little as ten years was satisfactory. For the Sommaria, successful aspirants documented either their own or their wife's birth or conception in the City of Naples. Additionally, the property requirement in Naples was proof of home ownership, which effectively meant that the masses of laborers who flocked to the capital for work were excluded from the prospect of citizenship. Ventura, "Le ambiguità," esp. 404, and Ventura, "Privilegio di cittadinanza," esp. 518.

43. Ventura, "Le ambiguità," 407.

44. For the identification of and speculation about the reasons for this trend, see Ventura, "Le ambiguità," 385, and Ventura, "Privilegio di cittadinanza," 515.

45. Here, I am drawing on Bartolommeo Capasso, *Sulla circoscrizione civile ed ecclesiastica e sulla popolazione della città di Napoli dalla fine del secolo XIII fino al 1809* (Naples: Tipografia della Regia Università, 1882). If Capasso is correct, then it seems that the physical enlargement of the city only translated into an enlargement of the political jurisdiction of the municipality with some temporal delay, if not territorial unevenness. *Sulla circoscrizione civile ed ecclesiastica,* esp. 34–45. More important, the *casali* were never fully brought into the administrative fold of the city, although their residents had the right to Neapolitan citizenship. As he summarized: "The *casali* had the same privileges as the City of Naples, and they governed themselves by the same customary laws. Beyond that they had their own mayors, or elected officials, who administered the local government in an entirely independent way. The only jurisdiction that the government of the City [of Naples] had over them consisted in the administration of the food supply and of taxes." Ibid., 39–40.

46. On the creation and success of a legal corps with a distinct identity, see Salvo Mastellone, *Pensiero politico e vita culturale a Napoli nella seconda metà del Seicento* (Messina: Casa Editrice D'Anna, 1965) and Salvo Mastellone, *Francesco D'Andrea politico e giurista (1648–1698): L'ascesa del ceto civile* (Florence: Olschki, 1969).

47. Francesco D'Andrea, *Avvertimenti ai nipoti,* ed. Imma Ascione (Naples: Jovene, 1990), 141. Also cited in Ventura, "Le ambiguità," 385.

48. For examples of the usage of "civiltà" in the works of the *illuministi,* see Antonio Genovesi, *Lezioni di commercio, o sia di economia civile,* 2nd ed., 2 vols. (Naples: Simoniana, 1768–70) and Giuseppe Maria Galanti "Diverse classi della nazione e loro costumi," in his *Della descrizione geografica e politica delle Sicilie,* ed. F. Assante and D. Demarco, vol. 1. (Naples: Edizioni Scientifiche Italiane, 1969), 272. For its usage in guides, see Domenico Antonio Parrino, *Napoli, città nobilissima, antica e fedelissima esposta a gli occhi e alla mente de'curiosi* (Naples: Parrino, 1700), 57. Also see "Civiltà," in *Vocabolario degli Accademici della Crusca,* rev. Neapolitan ed. (Naples: Giovanni di Simone, 1746), where interestingly it additionally denotes *humanitas.*

49. This trope resonates throughout the early modern guides to the city of Naples. For example, see Parrino, *Napoli città nobilissima, antica e fedelissima,* in which he introduces Naples as "la più gentil Città dell'Europa" in his (unpaginated) preface.

50. For a typological overview of the types of nobility in the Kingdom, see Giovanni Muto, "Problemi di stratificazione nobiliare nell'Italia spagnola," in *Dimenticare*

Croce? Studi e orientamenti di storia del Mezzogiorno, ed. Aurelio Musi (Naples: Edizioni Scientifiche Italiane, 1991); Giovanni Muto, "I segni d'honore: Rappresentazioni delle dinamiche nobiliari a Napoli in età moderna," in *Signori, patrizi, cavalieri in Italia centro-meridionale nell'Età moderna,* ed. Maria Antonietta Visceglia (Rome: Laterza, 1992), esp. 174–78; and Maria Antonietta Visceglia, "Composizione nominativa, rappresentazioni e autorappresentazione della nobiltà," in *Identità sociali: La nobiltà napoletana nella prima età moderna* (Milan: Edizioni Unicopli, 1998).

51. This claim is tabulated and asserted by Visceglia for the sixteenth century in her "Composizione nominativa," 114. The concentration of feudal powers in the hands of the civic patriciate in the eighteenth century is further documented by Angelo Massafra in his "Nota sulla geografia feudale del Regno di Napoli alla fine del XVIII secolo," in *Le mappe della storia,* ed. Giuseppe Giarrizzo and Enrico Iachello (Milan: FrancoAngeli, 2002), 28.

52. Based on her synthesis of work on the nobility, Visceglia has surmised this trend in her *Identità sociali,* esp. 19–29. Also see Tommasso Astarita, *The Continuity of Feudal Power: The Caracciolo of Brienza in Spanish Naples* (New York: Cambridge University Press, 1992), 119–31.

53. For an important example of this usage, see "Del sistema feudale," the first section of chapter 4 of book 1 in Galanti's *Della descrizione geografica e politica delle Sicile,* 126.

54. See José Miguel López García and Santos Madrazo Madrazo, "A Capital City in the Feudal Order: Madrid from the Sixteenth to the Eighteenth Century," in *Capital Cities and Their Hinterlands,* ed. Clark and Lepetit.

55. See Gerard Labrot, *Baroni in città: Residenze e comportamenti dell'aristocrazia napoletana, 1530–1734* (Naples: Società editrice napoletana, 1979).

56. On the importance of this trend for the religious fabric of Naples, see among other works that of Helen Hills, *Invisible City: The Architecture of Devotion in Seventeenth-Century Neapolitan Convents* (New York: Oxford University Press, 2005); and for its importance concerning religious rituals, see Visceglia, "Nobiltà, città, rituali religiosi," in her *Identità sociali.*

57. On the competition to enter the *piazze* and the effective closing of them in the early modern period, see Giovanni Muto, "Gestione politica e controllo sociale nella Napoli spagnola," in *Le città capitali,* ed. Cesare De Seta (Rome: Laterza, 1985).

58. Petraccone, *Napoli dal Cinquecento all'Ottocento,* esp. 90–93 and 123, where the percentage of immigrants employed in domestic services was calculated at 64.6% for the second half of the seventeenth century. Concerning their origins, Petraccone has speculated: "Inoltre gli adetti ai servizi seguivano spesso i feudatari del loro paese, quando essi si venivano a stabilire a Napoli." (Those individuals suited for domestic service often followed their local feudal barons, when the latter relocated to Naples.) Ibid., 124.

59. Astarita, *Continuity of Feudal Power,* 129.

60. Galanti, *Breve descrizione della Città di Napoli,* 266–67.

Chapter 1

1. Vico's elegy, "In funere excellentissimae Catharinae Aragoniae Segorbiensis ducis, etc. Oratio a Io[h]anne Baptista a Vico, cive neapolitano" was published in *Pompe funerali celebrate in Napoli per l'eccellentissima signora donna Caterina d'Aragona...*(Naples:

Giuseppe Roselli, 1697[but 1699]). See Benedetto Croce, *Bibiliografia vichiana,* rev. and enl. by Fausto Nicolini, vol. 1 (Naples: Ricciardi, 1947), 94. This latter reference work henceforth will be abbreviated as *Bibiliografia vichiana.*

2. For information regarding the ancestry of Vico, see the Annotazioni to the *Autobiografia* in *Opere,* vol. 5, 2nd ed., 105. Similarly, for information regarding his own family, see ibid., 129. On the ruling caste of the village of Maddaloni in the early modern period, see Alfred van Reumont, *The Carafas of Maddaloni: Naples under Spanish Dominion* (London: H. G. Bohn, 1854).

3. I owe this insight to Anna Maria Rao, who has noted how in the eighteenth century the old norm of the constitutions of Frederick II barring persons born under feudal jurisdiction from administrative offices of the crown was still enforced, however partially. See Anna Maria Rao, "Nel Settecento napoletano: La questione feudale," in *Cultura, intellettuali e circolazione delle idee nel '700,* ed. Renato Pasta (Milan: Franco Angeli, 1990), 102–3. Further research on the application of this norm would be required to know if, and when, this custom pertained to the candidates for positions at the university, which was a royal institution.

4. See *Autobiografia:* Croce and Nicolini edit., 24; Fisch and Bergin trans., 136; and Annotazioni to the *Autobiografia* in *Opere,* vol. 5, 2nd ed., 112.

5. According to the *Autobiografia,* Vico competed for this position in 1697. See *Autobiografia:* Croce and Nicolini edit., 24; Fisch and Bergin trans., 136. However, based on documentation in the ASN, his actual competition and assumption of that post has been dated by specialists to October 1698 and January 1699, respectively. See Annotazioni to the *Autobiografia* in *Opere,* vol. 5, 2nd ed., 112, where January 1699 is provided as the date for his election by the committee and official nomination by Viceroy Medinaceli. Also see Benedetto Croce, "I due concorsi universitari di G. B. Vico," *La critica* 6 (1908), 306–8, and Fausto Nicolini, *La giovinezza di Giambattista Vico (1668–1700)* 2nd rev. ed. (Bari: Laterza, 1932), 188–91. Contrast Vico's own pronouncements, where he indicates that he held the Chair from 1700, in Vico, "Catalogo che accompagna una supplica dell'anno 1734," in *Opere,* vol. 5, 2nd ed., 93. In 1735 his son Gennaro was designated as his successor to the position in Rhetoric, and assumed it in 1741.

6. For a published copy of Vico's manuscript lessons, see Giambattista Vico, *Institutiones oratoriae,* ed. Giuliano Crifò (Naples: Istituto Suor Orsola Benincasa, 1989). This work will herewith be cited as the *Institutiones.*

7. Indeed, in terms of rank, the position in Rhetoric was second from the bottom. Furthermore, it was not a "perpetual" chair but a "quadriennale," that is, a lectureship offering a four-year contract with the possibility of renewal. Materially, it bore the modest annual stipend of one hundred ducats, the lowest on the university's pay scale for academic employees. As a point of comparison, the highest-paid position, the Afternoon Chair of Civil Law, paid the handsome annual salary of eight hundred ducats, while the two university janitors were allocated sixty ducats each. See Gian Giuseppe Origlia, *Istoria dello Studio di Napoli,* vol. 2 (Naples: Giovanni di Simone, 1754), 234–36. Compare ASN Cappellano Maggiore, Affari Diversi, 718 II, 366r for a petition signed by the university professoriate that lists the titleholders of positions in terms of rank.

8. Benavides served as viceroy of the Kingdom of Naples from 1688 until 1696, when he was succeeded by Luigi de la Cerda, Duke of Medinaceli. His departure from

office took place in March 1696, when de la Cerda succeeded him. See Giuseppe Coniglio, *I viceré spagnoli di Napoli* (Naples: Fausto Fiorentino, 1967), 322–36. For information about the festivities marking the departure of Benavides, see Giuseppe Galasso, "Napoli nel viceregno spagnolo (1696–1707)," in *Storia di Napoli,* vol. 6, *Fra Spagna e Austria* (Naples: Edizioni Scientifiche Italiane, 1970), 95. Domenico Antonio Parrino dedicated to Benavides his *Teatro eroico, e politico de'governi de'viceré del Regno di Napoli dal tempo del re Ferdinando il Cattolico fino al presente,* 3 vols. (Naples: Nella nuova stampa del Parrino, e del Mutii, 1692–94).

9. See *Varii componimenti in lode dell'eccellentissimo signore don Francesco Benavides conte di S. Stefano…raccolti da don Nicolò Caravita* (Naples: Giuseppe Roselli, 1696). Although trained as a jurist, Caravita (1647–1717) first gained renown as a man of letters. Additionally, Caravita wrote a number of groundbreaking legal tracts in favor of limiting the jurisdiction of the Church in the Kingdom of Naples, which squarely established him as a spokesperson for the interests of the state. See, especially, the memorandum *Ragioni a pro' della fedelissima Città e Regno di Napoli contr'al procedimento straordinario nelle cause del Sant'Officio* (1695) and *Nullum ius Pontificis maximi in Regno Neapolitano* (Alethopoli [but Naples]: n.p. and n.d. [but 1707]; repr., 1788; Italian edit., 1790]). Later in life, he held a number of prestigious public positions, from the Fiscal Counselor of the Junta of Royal Jurisdiction (from 1702) and the Presidency of the Regia Camera della Sommaria (from 1702) to Chair of Feudal Law at the University of Naples (1708–13). Above I am drawing on S. Fodale, "Nicola Caravita," in *Dizionario Biografico degli Italiani* (Rome: Istituto dell'Enciclopedia Italiana, 1976), herewith cited as DBI, and Lorenzo Giustiniani, *Memorie istoriche degli scrittori legali del Regno di Napoli,* vol. 1 (Naples: Stamperia Simoniana, 1787), 218–19. On the Caravita edition, see *Bibliografia vichiana,* vol. 1, 92–93.

10. *Autobiografia:* Croce and Nicolini edit., 23–24; Fisch and Bergin trans., 135–36. In light of the local politics of the period, Imma Ascione has persuasively hypothesized why the profile of Vico would have fit so well with the Chair of Rhetoric and, similarly, why Caravita presumably could have endorsed his candidacy. See Imma Ascione, *Seminarium doctrinarum: L'Università di Napoli nei documenti del '700* (Naples: Edizioni Scientifiche Italiane, 1997), 34–36.

11. See *Componimenti recitati nell'accademia a' dì 4 di novembre anno 1696 ragunata nel real palagio in Napoli per la ricuperata salute di Carlo II re di Spagna, di Napoli, ec.* (Naples: Nella nuova Stampa di Domenico Antonio Parrino, 1697) and the *Pompe funerali celebrate in Napoli per l'eccellentissima signora donna Caterina d'Aragona…,* which Nicolini claims was not edited by Caravita but rather Federico Pappacoda. *Bibliografia vichiana,* vol. 1, 94.

12. Vico's lecture was delivered on his admission to the Accademia; and it was entitled "Delle Cene sontuose de'Romani." A manuscript copy of this lecture is contained in the proceedings of the Accademia entitled *Delle/ Lezioni Accade-/ miche/ De' Diversi Valentuo-/mini de' Nostri Tempi/ Recitate Avanti/ L'Eccellentissimo Signore/ Duca di Medina-Coeli/ Vice-Re, che fù del Regno di Napoli. Parte III.* In Italy it is conserved in the BNN with the call number MS XIII.B.73(1). Another copy is conserved in the Biblioteca Nacional de Madrid, ms. 9110, and has been studied by Michele Rak, whose work is cited below. I have consulted Vico's lecture in BNN MS XIII.B.73(1, pp. 1r–6v. Another copy reportedly is contained in BNN MS XII.G.58. See *Bibliografia vichiana,* vol. 1, 83. This lecture was published by

Nicolini in *Opere,* vol. 6, 389–400. For Vico's participation in the academic gatherings at both the viceroyal palace as well as the home of Caravita, see *Autobiografia:* Croce and Nicolini edit., 24; Fisch and Bergin trans., 137–38. For an overview of both, see C. Minieri Riccio, *Cenno storico delle accademie fiorite nella città di Napoli* (Naples: Francesco Giannini, 1879). On the Accademia Medinaceli, in English see Stone, *Vico's Cultural History,* 93–110, and in Italian, Guido Rispoli, *L'Accademia Palatina del Medinaceli* (Naples: Nuovo Cultura, 1924). More recently, the lessons of the Accademia Medinaceli have been published by Michele Rak, a student of the Academy and Neapolitan literature more generally, who has also written an essay on its manuscript tradition and activities. See Michele Rak, ed., *Lezioni dell'Accademia di Palazzo del duca di Medinaceli,* 5 vols. (Naples: Istituto Italiano per gli Studi Filosofici, 2000–5); and for the lesson by Vico, see vol. 4, 47–55. For classical studies of the Academy that also consider its importance for Giannone, see Giuseppe Ricuperati, "La prima formazione di Pietro Giannone: L'Accademia Medina-Coeli e Domenico Aulisio," in *Saggi e ricerche sul Settecento* (Naples: Istituto Italiano per gli Studi Storici, 1968) and Giuseppe Ricuperati, "A proposito dell'Accademia Medina Coeli," *RSI* 84 (1972): 57–79.

13. The choice of Philip, Duke of Anjou and grandson of Louis XIV, as the successor to Charles II, the heirless Habsburg king of Spain, frustrated the ambitions in the Spanish lands of the Austrian Habsburgs, who thus led an offensive against the armies of Louis XIV, which devolved into the intestine pan-European War of the Spanish Succession, whose eventual outcome brought the Austrian Habsburgs to power in the Kingdom of Naples (1707) and finally recognized Philip V as the king of Spain (1720).

14. In 1701 a coup d'état threatened to topple the regime of Medinaceli and install the Austrian Habsburg Archduke Charles as his successor.

15. See Vico, *Panegyricus Philippo V Hispaniarum, Indiarumque, utriusque Siciliae potentissimo regi* (Naples: Felice Mosca, 1702), which is one of his rarest works. On that edition, see *Bibliografia vichiana,* vol. 1, 94–95. In his discussion, Nicolini is drawing on information offered in a manuscript catalogue of Vico's work purportedly drafted by the philosopher to accompany a demand made in 1734. See *Opere,* vol. 5, 2nd ed., 92–93. This catalogue presumably accompanied Vico's request to the Bourbon King Charles for the position of Royal Historiographer in a letter from July 1734, the original copy of which was destroyed by fire but which has been published on a number of occasions. For its publication in the critical edition of Vico's letters, see Giambattista Vico, *Epistole,* ed. Manuela Sanna (Naples: Morano, 1992), 174–76. Herewith this work will be referred to as the *Epistole.* Compare *Autobiografia:* Croce and Nicolini edit., 56; Fisch and Bergin trans., 174, where Vico limits his discussion of that work to information about its viceroyal commission and quick execution. I draw on the catalogue reprinted in the *Opere,* vol. 5, 2nd ed.

16. This document was the first in a series concerning the nomination of Vico to the post of Royal Historiographer, which he obtained in 1735. The original had been addressed to the Secretary of State and was conserved in its archive in the ASN; a copy thereof was held in the SNSP XXI.A.10 and reprinted in Benedetto Croce, *Bibliografia vichiana,* 1st. ed. (Naples: Alfonso Tessitore & Figlio, 1904), 84–85.

17. According to Nicolini, the title of the definitive version of this history— which is missing from its manuscript-copy conserved in the SNSP with the call

number XXVI.D.1—originally must have been *J. B. VICI PRINCIPUM NEAPOL-ITANORUM CONIURATIONIS ANNI MDCCI HISTORIA,* which he apparently surmised from the extant (but damaged and fragmentary?) title embossed on the manuscript's spine: i.e., PRINCIPUM NEAPOLITANORUM CONIURA-TIO. For a summary of Nicolini's findings concerning the commission, manuscript tradition, and divergent titles of this work, see *Bibliografia vichiana,* vol. 1, 79–81, which elaborates on the *Nota* to the history published by the same in *Opere,* vol. 6, 437–39. For further information on the manuscript tradition, also see Fausto Nicolini, "Vicende e codici della *Principum neapolitanorum coniuratio* di Giambattista Vico," in *Atti della Reale Accademia Pontaniana di Scienze Morali e Politiche* 59 (1938): 122–63 and, more recently, the philological study by Claudia Pandolfi, *Per l'edizione critica della* Principum neapolitanorum coniurationis anni MDCCI historia *di G. Vico* (Naples: Guida, 1988). Claudia Pandolfi subsequently executed the critical edition of this work for the Centro di Studi Vichiani, which contains—side by side—both an earlier draft and the definitive version of Vico's history, which she has distinguished with the epithets *Scriptura prior* and *Scriptura altera* respectively. It is her critical edition of this latter and definitive version of Vico's history that I herewith employ and cite. See Giambattista Vico, *La congiura dei principi napoletani, 1701 (Prima e seconda stesura),* ed. Claudia Pandolfi (Naples: Morano, 1992). For the title of the latter and definitive version of Vico's history, the *Scriptura altera,* Pandolfi maintained the one that had been visible to Nicolini on the spine of the manuscript conserved in the SNSP. However, for her edition Pandolfi further chose to modernize the Latin syntax of that same title and adopted the following minor variation on it: namely, CONIURATIO PRINCIPUM NEAPOLITANORUM. Consequently, and henceforth, this work will be cited as *Coniuratio,* and each citation will indicate the identifying numbers of the passage(s) referenced. It bears noting that this edition of the *Coniuratio* contains not only the original-language text but also its translation into modern Italian, and that the system of identifying numbers employed by Pandolfi is consistent throughout both the original- and modern-language texts of the *Coniuratio.*

18. Quoted from Francesco Antonio Soria, *Memorie storico-critiche degli storici napoletani,* vol. 2 (Naples: Stamperia Simoniana, 1781–82), 381. Also cited in Nicolini, "Vicende e codici della *Principum neapolitanorum coniuratio* di Giambattista Vico" as well as by Benedetto Croce in his *Uomini e cose della vecchia Italia,* 2nd rev. ed., vol. 1 (Bari: Laterza, 1943), 241–42. Although Soria does not name the two authors to whose histories of the failed coup this judgment pertained, both Nicolini and Croce have argued that Vico first and foremost was implied. On the censorship of the *Coniuratio,* documentation in the Archivio del Vicerè of the ASN may yield further evidence about the political objections to its publication.

19. As concerns his epistolary, see Vico's letter to Antonio Coppola, dated 3 September 1703 in *Epistole,* 75–76. In this letter, Vico passionately defends the content of the political tract by Serafino Biscardi in defense of the succession of the Bourbon Duke Philip to the Spanish throne, entitled *Epistola pro augusto Hispaniarum monarcha Philippo V, qua & ius ei assertum successionis universae monarchiae, et omnia confutantur, quae pro investitura Regni Neapolitani, & pro caeteris regnis a Germanis scripta sunt* (Naples: Giuseppe Roselli, 1703). At the time, Serafino Biscardi was one of the highest-ranking magistrates of the Kingdom as regent of the Consiglio Collaterale. See G. Ricuperati,

"Serafino Biscardi," in DBI and, for additional detail, Dario Luongo, *Serafino Biscardi: Mediazione ministeriale e ideologia economica* (Naples: Jovene, 1993).

20. In the literature on Renaissance historiography, it is commonly held that the invasion of Italy by Charles VIII in 1494 marked a watershed in both the history of Italy and the history of historiography, as the so-called Italian Wars that followed rendered the older humanist model of municipal historiography inadequate to the times and ushered in a genre of "national history," which was attuned to the place of the peninsula in the ambitions and power politics of larger European nation-states. The canonical example of this new genre is Guicciardini, *Storia d'Italia,* which was penned in the 1530s and thematized the Italian states' loss of self-determination. The studies on Guicciardini are numerous. For a classic discussion of the new genre of "national history" and, in particular, Guicciardini, see Eric Cochrane, *Historians and Historiography in the Italian Renaissance* (Chicago: University of Chicago Press, 1981), 295–305. Of the many calamities that struck Italy in the fifteenth and sixteenth centuries, perhaps the most shocking was the brutal sack of Rome by imperial forces, whose significance for the genre of Italian historiography has been studied by Kenneth Gouwens in *Remembering the Renaissance: Humanist Narratives of the Sack of Rome* (London: Brill, 1998). Vico evidently shared the political sensibility and concerns of this genre, and they distinguish the focus and lessons of his work from that of the earliest humanist historiography produced by and about the Kingdom of Naples, which had adopted the ancient model of the "life and deeds" to write instructive biographies of the Kingdom's foremost rulers. Contrast the historical literature produced by the academy of the fifteenth-century Neapolitan humanist Giovanni Pontano, which in English has been studied by Jerry H. Bentley in *Politics and Culture in Renaissance Naples* (Princeton: Princeton University Press, 1987).

21. Patricia J. Osmond, "*Princeps Historiae Romanae:* Sallust in Roman Political Thought," *Memoirs of the American Academy in Rome* 40 (1995): 103. On the reception of classical histories in the Renaissance more generally, see the following classics: Peter Burke, "A Survey of the Popularity of Ancient Historians, 1450–1700," *History and Theory* 52, no. 2 (1966): 135–52, and Arnaldo Momigliano, *The Classical Foundations of Modern Historiography* (Berkeley: University of California Press, 1990).

22. Osmond, "*Princeps Historiae Romanae,*" 113 and 126, respectively. Among other things, the Florentine patrician Bernardo Rucellai was the author of *De bello italico,* for which he won the praise of Erasmus as being another Sallust. See Cochrane, *Historians and Historiography,* 30. On the use of Sallust made by Rucellai in *De bello italico,* see William McCuaig, "Bernardo Rucellai and Sallust," *Rinascimento* 32 (1982): 75–98; and on the life and times of Rucellai during the composition of this work, see Felix Gilbert, "Bernardo Rucellai and the Orti Oricellari: A Study on the Origin of Modern Political Thought," *Journal of the Warburg and Courtauld Institutes* 12 (1949), 101–31, esp. 124. Ben Johnson composed and staged *Catiline* in 1611.

23. Osmond, *Princeps Historiae Romanae,* 102.

24. Interestingly, the *Congiura* by Camillo Porzio was first printed by Paolo Manuzio of Rome in 1565 and reprinted twice in Naples during the eighteenth century, once in 1724 and by Giovanni Gravier in 1769. On Porzio, see Soria, *Memorie storico-critiche degli storici napoletani,* vol. 2, 500–502. More recently, on the career of Porzio, see Ernesto Pontieri, *Camillo Porzio storico* (Naples: Società Napoletana di Storia Patria, 1958).

25. On the Ciceronian epithet "historia magistra vitae," see Reinhart Koselleck, "Historia Magistra Vitae: The Dissolution of the Topos into the Perspective of a Modernized Historical Process," in his *Futures Past: On the Semantics of Historical Time* (Cambridge: MIT Press, 1985).

26. *Coniuratio,* [11], 5, lines 43–46.

27. Vico's extraordinary descriptions of these characters are in ibid., [11], 7–13, lines 59–172.

28. Ibid., [11], 5, lines 50–56.

29. Specifically, Vico noted with reservation that among the noble conspirators also ranked representatives of the prominent Spinelli, Carafa, and Acquaviva families of the Neapolitan patriciate, for whose unusual alliance with the conspiratorial forces he provided ample excuses. Ibid., [11], 9, lines 86–92. For an account of the relationship between the Spanish and the Kingdom's barons in the second half of the seventeenth century that underscores the efforts of the Spanish to render ineffectual the customary role of the barons as "officers" of the king, among others, see Salvo Mastellone, *Pensiero politico e vita culturale a Napoli nella seconda meta del seicento* (Florence: D'Anna, 1965). Therein, there is also information regarding the increasing competition for political influence between the Neapolitan patriciate and the *ceto civile,* or class of legal professionals, increasingly employed by the Spanish administration in high-ranking positions.

30. Sallust, *The War with Catiline,* trans. J.C. Rolfe, Loeb Classical Library (1921; repr., Cambridge: Harvard University Press, 2005), xxxvii.7–8. (Rolfe trans.)

31. In Rome, Lentulus and other conspirators recruited men for the insurrection from the plebeian citizenry among others. Ibid., xxxix.6.

32. According to plan, the convocation and rousing of the "contio" was supposed to set the stage for the coup. Ibid., xliii.1.

33. Vico introduced the members of the plebs in *Coniuratio,* [18], 8, lines 36–37.

34. Ibid., [18], 9, lines 42–43.

35. On the events of the revolt of Masaniello and, in particular, the fraught relationship between the nobility and the Popolo, see Aurelio Musi, *La rivolta di Masaniello nella scena politica barocca* (Naples: Guida, 1989), esp. chaps. 2 and 6. On the origins of the revolt, see the English translation of the older work by Rosario Villari entitled *The Revolt of Naples* (Cambridge: Polity Press, 1993). On the republicanism of the revolt, as both articulated and practiced, especially see Vittor Ivo Comparato, "From the Crisis of Civil Culture to the Neapolitan Republic of 1647: Republicanism in Italy between the Sixteenth and Seventeenth Centuries," in *Republicanism,* ed. van Gelderen and Skinner; Pier Luigi Rovito, "La rivoluzione costituzionale di Napoli (1647–48)," *RSI,* vol. 98, no. 2 (1986): 367–462; and Vittorio Conti, *Le leggi di una rivoluzione* (Naples: Jovene, 1983). More generally, on the symbolic status of the territory of the city in the course of the revolt and accounts thereof, see Silvana D'Alessio, *Contagi: La rivolta napoletana del 1647–48* (Florence: Centro editoriale toscano, 2003) and the article by Rosario Villari, "Masaniello: Contemporary and Recent Interpretations," *Past and Present,* no. 108 (1985): 117–32, which was a rebuttal to Peter Burke's "The Virgin of the Carmine and the Revolt by Masaniello," *Past and Present* no. 99 (1983): 3–21.

36. *Coniuratio,* [18], 9, lines 43–51, esp. 45–46.

37. Vico uses this expression and variations on it in ibid., [18], 1, line 3; [18], 2, line 5; [18], 13, line 61; [19], 6, lines 33–34, etc.

38. Ibid., [18], 22, lines 101–3.

39. Ibid., lines 105–6.

40. Ibid., lines 106–10.

41. Vico typically used the Latin adjectives "vilis" (vile) and "ima" (base) to qualify the members of the "plebs" who supported the insurrection.

42. See ibid., [18], 23, lines 112–13. Given the track record of the barons, this strikes me as a disingenuous representation that was meant to show some deference to baronial rank and authority while disclosing their vileness.

43. In early modern Naples, it was commonly held that the Popolo of Naples was divided into numerous subgroups, or "popoli" as Giulio Cesare Capaccio, the former Secretary of the City, put it. See the social taxonomy of Capaccio in *Il forastiero,* 468 and 524. However, the "modesti cives" was not an obvious translation of any of the Italian terms usually used to describe the members of the Popolo of Naples, making it an unusual choice. Normally, well-to-do members of the Popolo might be referred to as members of the *popolo grasso,* if distinguished by their assets, or the *ceto civile,* if distinguished by their learning and offices. What is more, the semantic ambiguity of this term's adjective, "modestus," built unique meaning into this new social category. By its usage, "modestus" was made to connote both the moral qualities of restraint and modesty as well as the acquired attribute of wealth. In other words, the usage of "modestus" brilliantly rendered, I believe, Vico's argument that the acquisition of wealth civilized. It is important to note that this sort of evaluation of the middling sort was not unique to Vico at the time in Italy. Later in chapter 2, I discuss the similar sociological language employed by Gian Vincenzo Gravina, who in his contemporary writings identified and noted the great political merits of citizens of middling condition, which he believed provided not only a buffer between the nobles and the plebs but also a source of stability for the polity.

44. As for Vico's specific usage of the term "modesti cives," the first two are most telling of what Vico meant by it and appear in *Coniuratio,* [18], 2, line 6 and [18], 22, line 107 where in both cases he lists the various economic orders of the city of Naples. On the first occasion, he observes that the city is divided into two geographical zones, one high and the other low, which are inhabited by two corresponding social groups, or by the "nobiles modestique cives" ("patrician and modest citizens") on high and by the "ima plebs" ("base plebs") on low. On the second occasion, Vico listed those groups that had a stake in safeguarding their store of goods and possessions during the revolt, namely, the "artifices ac mercatores" ("artisans and shopkeepers"), "modesti cives et quamplurimi privatae fortunae nobiles" ("modest citizens and most of the nobles of private fortune"), as well as the "magistratus ac splendidiores patricii" ("magistracy and illustrious patricians").

45. Ibid., [19], 7, line 36.

46. Ibid., [22], 22, lines 148–49, where Vico explicitly noted that "modesti cives" accompanied the military parade that effected the actual suppression of the revolt. Yet, elsewhere Vico does speak about the political instrumentality of "decuriones plebis," who presumably were the "Consultori del Popolo," or advisers to the Eletto of the Popolo. Ibid., [22], 2, line 6 and [22], 6, line 62.

47. Giuseppe Galasso, "Ai tempi del Vico: Fra il tramonto del viceregno e l'avvento di Carlo di Borbone," in *Napoli capitale,* ed. Giuseppe Galasso (Naples: Electa, 1998), esp. 205. Also see Galasso, Introduction to his *Napoli spagnola dopo Masaniello: Politica, cultura, società,* vol. 1 (Florence: Sansoni, 1982), xii–xiii, where he has estimated that approximately two-thirds of the populace of Naples were not citizens after the last episode of plague in Naples.

48. *Coniuratio,* [18], 20, line 89.

49. Ibid., [20], 1, lines 1–2.

50. In his text, Vico had noted this claim in his discussion of the reaction of the civic patriciate to the unofficial news of the death of King Charles II in 1700, when the patriciate reportedly requested of the viceroy that they be entrusted with the governance of the Kingdom during the interregnum. Ibid., [5], 5, lines 17–30. It was precisely in the context of a virulent dissemination of this political rhetoric that Vico penned the *Coniuratio.*

51. Ibid., [22], 8, lines 75–80 and [22], 23, lines 156–63 describe the popular consensus created by the cavalcades.

52. Ibid., [22], 59–62, lines 358–80.

53. Especially ibid., 59, lines 362–64.

54. See *Conjuratio/ Inita et extincta Neapoli anno MDCCI a Carlo Majello exarata.* I have consulted the manuscript versions of this text conserved by the SNSP with the call numbers MS XXII.B.17(2; MS XXVIII.C.17; and Cuomo MS I.6.21(2, whose texts are essentially identical. A fourth manuscript copy of this text is conserved in the BNN and bears the call number MS XV.F.34. The *Conjuratio/ Inita et extincta* was published with the following bibliographical information: *Conjuratio inita et extincta Neapoli anno MDCCI* (Antverpiae (Antwerp): Typis Ioannis Frik, 1704). According to Soria, it was commissioned by the same viceroyal advisers who had censored Vico's work in the first place. See Soria, *Memorie storico-critiche,* vol. 2, 381. Based on the indications provided by Soria, Croce too claimed that this work was translated into French and published as an original work with the following bibliographical information: J. Claude Viany, trans., *Histoire de la dernière conjuration de Naples* (Paris, 1706). See Croce, *Uomini e cose,* vol. 1, 240. However, the "translator" seems to have been another, and this French text apparently was not a strict translation of that by Maiello. I have only found evidence for Jérôme Du Perier, *Histoire de la dernière conjuration de Naples en 1701* (Paris: Chez Pierre Giffart, 1706), a copy of which is held by the Library of the Istituto per la Storia del Pensiero Filosofico e Scientifico Moderno in Naples and was kindly brought to my attention by Dott. Roberto Mazzola. The Du Perier text must have had a significant circulation in northern Europe, as the other example that I consulted in the BNN was a less expensive edition with smaller type that apparently was sold in Brussels. What is more, the text by Du Perier seems to be a pastiche that drew on the works of both Maielllo and Vico, despite the claim of its author that it was based on a single Latin text by an illustrious literatus who had refused Du Perier permission to credit him. Croce also added that this same work was then translated into Italian by a writer using the pseudonym Garonne Baconcopia. Croce, *Uomini e cose,* vol. 1, 244n1. However, the manuscript history of the coup translated from the French by Baconcopia does not correspond to the manuscript text by Maiello but rather to that of Du Perier, to which it is most faithful. See *Storia dell'ultima congiura di Napoli/ nel 1701./ Versione dal francese di/ Garonne Baconcopia*

conserved in SNSP MS XXI.A.15. Be that as it may, the Maiello text was translated into Italian by an anonymous author, whose translation—*Congiura formata e distrutta in Napoli l'anno 1701*—is conserved as a manuscript in the SNSP where it bears the call number MS XXVI.A.18.

55. Maiello, *Conjuratio/ Inita et extincta Neapoli anno MDCCI,* paras. 19 and 22, where Maiello recounted with especial verve how deft Gambacorta was to "cajole the plebs to tumult" so that he found himself surrounded and indeed supported by a "moltitude of seditioners," who then brazenly carried out his machinations. Contrast *Coniuratio,* [18], 7–9, lines 29–51, discussed earlier, where Vico noted how a number of the plebs balked at the promises of Gambacorta, refusing to partake of the revolt, which was spearheaded by peasants and criminal elements.

56. Maiello, *Conjuratio/ Inita et extincta Neapoli anno MDCCI,* paras. 28–end, where Maiello described the restoration of order effected by Cantelmo's army of "patricians," by which Maiello primarily meant members of the civic patriciate of Naples. It bears noting that Maiello went to some length to suggest that the leading members of the civic patriciate—including kinsmen of the conspirators themselves—came to the aid of the Spanish administration to restore the peace, by listing in an appendix the names of the "patricians" who contributed to the regime's show of force reportedly staged on the 9th and 8th of October. (These dates were erroneous, I believe; and curiously, they postponed the actual dates of the famous parades that restored law and order.) Contrast *Coniuratio,* [22], 22, esp. lines 146–49, where the role of the patriciate in the quelling of the revolt was upstaged by the citizen guards and overshadowed by the presence of the "*modesti cives*" and "foreigners."

57. For an overview of the phenomenon of Tacitism from antiquity through the early modern period, see Peter Burke, "Tacitism," in *Tacitus,* ed. T. A. Dorey (London: Routledge and Paul, 1969) and his "Tacitism, Scepticism and Reason of State," in *The Cambridge History of Political Thought, 1450–1700,* ed. J. H. Burns (New York: Cambridge University Press, 1991); Momigliano, "Tacitus and the Tacitist Tradition," in his *Classical Foundations of Modern Historiography,* 109–31; a number of the contributions to T. James Luce and A. J. Woodman, eds., *Tacitus and the Tacitean Tradition* (Princeton: Princeton University Press, 1993); and, more narrowly on the early modern period, J. H. Whitfield, "Livy > Tacitus," in *Classical Influences on European Culture, AD 1500–1700,* ed. R. R. Bolgar (New York: Cambridge University Press, 1976) as well as Kenneth Schellhase, *Tacitus in Renaissance Political Thought* (Chicago: University of Chicago Press, 1976). On the importance of Tacitus in Renaissance Italy, see Giuseppe Toffanin, *Machiavelli e il Tacitismo* (Padua: Draghi, 1921). In the late sixteenth and seventeenth century, the phenomenon of Tacitism was particularly important in the Netherlands, where Tacitus was popularized by Justus Lipsius. On Lipsius and the (twin) phenomena of Tacitism and Neo-Stoicism there, see Richard Tuck, *Philosophy and Government, 1572–1651* (New York: Cambridge University Press, 1993), esp. chap. 2. On Tacitism in France, see Jacob Soll, "Empirical History and the Transformation of Political Criticism in France from Bodin to Bayle," *Journal of the History of Ideas* 64, no. 3 (2003): esp. 203–7; Jacob Soll, "Amelot de la Houssaye: Annotates Tacitus," *Journal of the History of Ideas* 61, no. 2 (2000): 167–87; and J. H. M. Salmon, "Cicero and Tacitus in Sixteenth-Century France," *American Historical Review* 85, no. 2 (1980): 307–31, esp. 317. On the importance of Tacitism for the work of the Enlightenment historian Edward Gibbon, see J. G. A. Pocock,

Barbarism and Religion, vol. 3, *The First Decline and Fall* (New York: Cambridge University Press, 2003).

58. As the work of Gary Ianziti, James Hankins, and others has shown, it was normal for municipal historians in the humanist tradition to avail themselves of historical documents. For example, see Gary Ianziti, "A Humanist Historian and His Documents: Giovanni Simonetta, Secretary to the Sforzas," *Renaissance Quarterly* 34, no. 4 (1981): 491–516, and the introduction by James Hankins to his edition of Leonardo Bruni, *History of the Florentine People,* vol. 1 (Cambridge: Harvard University Press, 2001). The same held true for the ancients. Among other examples, see Ronald Syme, *Tacitus* (Oxford: Oxford University Press, 1958).

59. Compare the accounts of the emergency meeting of the Consiglio Collaterale on 20 November 1700 in *Coniuratio,* [3], 3–5, and ASN, Collaterale, Consiglio, Notamenti, vol. 101, 114v–118r. This source in the ASN herewith will be abbreviated as ASN, Coll., Con., Notamenti.

60. ASN, Coll., Con., Notamenti, vol. 101, esp. 115v–116r, where the viceroy and his counselors specifically discussed how to best inform the members of the patrician *piazze* of the death of Charles II. In particular, the viceroy insisted that the *piazze* must be informed of the death of Charles immediately, and proposed that they be called to his antechamber, a tactic that he believed could best cultivate their fidelity and avert their "meeting" ("unione di Piazze"). This proposal was seconded by his advisers, who cautioned that the patricians should be called one by one, however.

61. Ibid., 116r.

62. Ibid., 117r.

63. Ibid., 117r–v.

64. Ibid., esp. 118r.

65. *Coniuratio,* [3], 3, lines 46–47.

66. Ibid., [5], 7, line 50.

67. Anonymous, *Succinta Relattione del Tumulto successo/In Napoli il giorno del 23 7bre/ 1701....*SNSP MS XXVI.D.10(3. Although the author refers to the recruits mustered among the commoners as the "Genti dalla Plebe" on ibid., p. 57, he speaks of the insurrectionaries as members of the "Popolo" on ibid., pp. 59–60. Moreover, this author underscored his impression that the constituents of the revolt were numerous and above the fray of civic social divisions, by additionally noting that Gambacorta succeeded at "seducing all sorts of persons (*ogni sorte di persone*)." Ibid., p. 63.

68. Garonne Baconcopia [pseudonym?!], *Storia dell'ultima congiura di Napoli/ nel 1701/ Versione dal francese di/ Garonne Baconcopia.* SNSP MS XXI.A.15, 48 and 55. Baconcopia tended to translate the French word "populace" as "popolaccio," which he twice qualified: one with "più vile" (p. 56) and once with "minuto" (p. 58); in this latter case the French expression was "le petit Peuple." The latter usage occurs in Du Perier, *Histoire de la dernière conjuration de Naples en 1701,* 106.

69. Maiello, *Conjuratio/ Inita et extincta Neapoli anno MDCCI,* esp. para. 22. Compare Anonymous [but Italian translation of Carlo Maiello], *Congiura formata e distrutta in Napoli l'anno 1701.* SNSP MS XXVI.A.18., esp. 9r–v. Contrast the account of the revolt in ASN, Coll., Con., Notamenti, vol. 103, 130v–131r, where the Secretary recorded the news that the "gente di seguito de'detti ribelli non era in molto numero, e gente bassa e vile, conoscendosi fedelissima tutta l'altra." (The people

following those rebels were not many in number, and were lowly, vile people, who made themselves known as other than faithful.)

70. Antonio Bulifon, *Quarant'hore del Principe di Macchia,*…SNSP MS XXVIII. C.12, 65r–v.

71. Ibid., esp. 73r–v.

72. Maiello, *Conjuratio/ Inita et extincta Neapoli anno MDCCI,* para. 22. Compare [Maiello], *Congiura formata e distrutta,* 9r.

73. ASN, Coll., Con., Notamenti, vol. 103, 130v and 131r. Compare the reference to "numerous excellent citizens" ("moltissimi ottimi cittadini"), whom the Secretary of the Collaterale enumerated among the forces constituting the parade of force that was led by Cantelmo and restored law and order to the city. ASN, Coll., Con., Notamenti, vol. 103, 132v.

74. ASN, Coll., Con., Notamenti, vol. 103, 131v. On the role of the *ottine* in the defense of the city of Naples in times of crisis, see Muto, "Gestione politica," in *Le città capitali,* ed. De Seta, 87–88.

75. ASN, Coll., Con., Notamenti, vol. 103, 131v and 132v, where both representatives of the "nobility" and "excellent citizens" are credited with participation in the cavalcade led by Cantelmo to restore peace. Compare *Coniuratio,* [22], 22 where the patrician and modest citizens figure together and, by implication, as if they were equally important—a claim that surely would have offended the civic patriciate's sense of their right of precedence. As Pandolfi has ascertained, the representation of the actual order of this cavalcade varied from one account to the other. Ibid., p. 261n213. Contrast Maiello, *Conjuratio/ Inita et extincta Neapoli anno MDCCI,* para. 28, where the role of the popular, or non-noble, citizenry in this important event is virtually elided.

76. On the publishing history and circulation of those tracts, see Angelo Granito, Principe di Belmonte, *Storia della congiura del Principe di Macchia,* vol. 1 (Naples: Iride, 1861), 180. Granito also reprinted the content of those same tracts in his volumes.

77. These four documents have all been reprinted by Granito in his *Storia della congiura,* vol. 1, from which I shall herewith cite. However, it bears mentioning that while some of these documents were printed internal to his narrative, others were printed in a separately paginated appendix at the back of that volume, entitled "Annotazioni e documenti al primo e secondo libro." From its content, the "Risposta alla risposta" seems to have been penned sometime in May 1702, when Philip V was resident in Naples and seeking both the formal and financial support of the Kingdom.

78. Francesco Spinelli, "Risposta alla risposta data al manifesto di D. Francesco Spinelli duca della Castelluccia," in Granito, *Storia della congiura,* vol. 1, "Annotazioni e documenti al secondo libro," 72. This meticulously crafted objection by Spinelli strategically employed the protean expression *"commune consenso"* (common consensus), which in the minds of his contemporaries probably invoked both the idea of the popular consensus, or will, and of the *consensus gentium,* consensus or agreement (of opinions and practices) among nations, such as the Spanish and Neapolitan.

79. For a discussion of the political symbolism of the civic rituals surrounding the reception of the new head of state in the early modern Kingdom, see my discussion of the cavalcade in Naddeo, "Topographies of Difference: Cartography of the City of Naples, 1629–1798," *Imago Mundi* 56, no. 1 (2004): 23–47.

80. Spinelli, "Risposta alla risposta" in Granito, *Storia della congiura,* vol. 1, "Annotazioni e documenti al secondo libro," 73.

81. Spinelli, "Manifesto" in Granito, *Storia della congiura,* vol. 1, 176 and 178.

82. Bartolomeo Ceva Grimaldi, "Lettera" in Granito, *Storia della congiura,* vol. 1, "Annotazioni e documenti al secondo libro," 81.

83. Compare the demands famously made by the jurist Alessandro Riccardi to the Austrians in 1707. See Giuseppe Ricuperati, "Alessandro Riccardi e le richieste del 'ceto civile' all'Austria nel 1707," *RSI* 81 (1969): 745–77.

84. Spinelli, "Risposta alla risposta" in Granito, *Storia della congiura,* vol. 1, "Annotazioni e documenti al primo e secondo libro," 73–74; and Ceva Grimaldi, "Lettera" in Granito, ed., *Storia della congiura,* vol. 1, "Annotazioni e documenti al primo e secondo libro," 81. Both Spinelli and Ceva Grimaldi were concordant on the points that the archduke would stimulate the Kingdom's commerce and reserve all offices for "nationals" (*nazionali*), rendering the Kingdom prosperous. Not surprisingly, both also insisted that the archduke would respect the privileges and prerogatives of the capital. Ceva Grimaldi additionally noted that the archduke would create a senate, which would presumably consist of the civic patriciate and select barons.

85. Ceva Grimaldi, "Lettera" in Granito, *Storia della congiura,* vol. 1, "Annotazioni e documenti al secondo libro," 80. John Robertson has shown how very topical this discourse about the ignominy of the province-kingdom was throughout this period. Interestingly, however, he has shown how current it was among members of the magisterial class and identified its culmination in the work of Paolo Mattia Doria, whose tracts were posterior to the failed coup of 1701. See Robertson, *Case for Enlightenment,* 147–200.

86. Ceva Grimaldi, "Lettera" in Granito, *Storia della congiura,* vol. 1, "Annotazioni e documenti al secondo libro," 81.

87. The "Protesta stipulata per mano di pubblico notaro in questa città di Napoli segretamente da un gran numero di nobili, ceto civile e fedelissimo popolo dela città e regno di Napoli, e fatta stampare per universale cognizione" has been reprinted in Granito, *Storia della congiura,* vol. 1, 231–33. Granito treats the rituals confirming Philip's rule in his *Storia della congiura* on pages 230–42.

88. These were requested by the acting viceroy, General Daun, in a letter written to Vico on 11 October 1707, reprinted in *Epistole,* 76. The funerary inscriptions themselves have been published in *Opere,* vol. 7, 263–86; and they most recently have been republished in Vico, *Le iscrizioni e le composizioni latine,* ed. Gian Galeazzo Visconti (Naples: Guida, 2004). Vico also penned the introductory text describing the pomp and circumstance of the funeral for the elegant commemorative volume published by Felice Mosca entitled *"Acta Funeris,"* in *Publicum Caroli Sangrii et Josephi Capycii nobilium Neapolitanorum funus a Carolo Austrio III Hispaniarum Indiarumque et Neapolis rege indictum.* (Naples: Felice Mosca, 1708), conserved in the BNN 37. F. 21. This text has been reprinted in *Opere,* vol. 6, 369–88; and it most recently has been reprinted in Vico, *Minora: Scritti latini, storici e d'occasione,* ed. Gian Galeazzo Visconti (Naples: Guida, 2000), 161–85.

89. Vico makes this claim about the occasion of his last oration in the autobiography. See *Autobiografia:* Croce and Nicolini edit., 32; Fisch and Bergin trans., 146. The first part was originally published in Angelo Calogerà, ed., *Raccolta d'opusculi scientifici, e filologici,* vol. 1 (Venice: C. Zane, 1728) and has been reprinted on numerous

occasions. The last oration itself was published in Latin as *De nostri temporis studiorum ratione* (Naples: Felice Mosca, 1709) and has been reprinted on many occasions, including *Opere,* vol. 1, 67–121. It has also been translated into English as *On the Study Methods of our Time,* trans. Elio Gianturco (Ithaca: Cornell University Press, 1990).

Chapter 2

1. Specifically on Stoic cosmopolitanism, see Cheikh Mbacké Gueye, *Late Stoic Cosmopolitanism* (Heidelberg: Universitaetsverlag Winter, 2006). On Stoicism more generally, I have drawn from Brad Inwood, ed., *The Cambridge Companion to the Stoics* (New York: Cambridge University Press, 2003); Christopher Rowe and Malcolm Schofield, eds., *The Cambridge History of Greek and Roman Political Thought* (New York: Cambridge University Press, 2000); and John Sellars, *Stoicism* (Berkeley: University of California Press, 2006), as well as a number of primary sources by classical authors.

2. This famous statement was attributed to Diogenes by Plutarch. As there is no other confirmation of it, the authenticity of this statement remains uncertain. See "Diogenes," in Diogenes Laertius, *Lives of the Eminent Philosophers,* trans. R. D. Hicks, vol. 2, Loeb Classical Library (1925; repr., Cambridge: Harvard University Press, 1970), VI.63. (Hicks trans.)

3. Plutarch, "On the Fortune of Alexander," 329a–b, cited in D. N. Long and A. A. Sedley, *The Hellenistic Philosophers,* vol. 1 (New York: Cambridge University Press, 1987), 429. (Long and Sedley trans.) The exemplarity of this passage for Zeno's thought has been questioned by Malcolm Schofield in *The Stoic Idea of the City* (New York: Cambridge University Press, 1991).

4. This claim reverberates throughout the Stoic tradition from the *Republic* of Zeno to the *Meditations* of Marcus Aurelius. On the early Hellenic ideas of the cosmic city, see Schofield, *Stoic Idea of the City.*

5. For those works on Neo-Stoicism pertaining to its political theory, on the Renaissance and Reformation, see Gerhard Oestreich, *Neostoicism and the Early Modern State,* ed. Brigitta Oestreich and H. G. Koenigsberger, trans. David McLintock (New York: Cambridge University Press, 1982); Guenter Abel, *Stoizismus und fruehe Neuzeit: Zur Entstehungsgeschichte modernen Denkens im Felde von Ethik und Politik* (Berlin: Walter de Gruyter, 1978); J. H. M. Salmon, "Stoicism and the Roman Example: Seneca and Tacitus in Jacobean England," *Journal of the History of Ideas* 50, no. 2 (1989): 199–225; Martin van Gelderen, "The Machiavellian Moment and the Dutch Revolt: The Rise of Neostoicism and Dutch Republicanism," in *Machiavelli and Republicanism,* ed. Gisela Bock, Quentin Skinner, and Maurizio Viroli; Martin van Gelderen, *The Political Thought of the Dutch Revolt, 1555–1590* (New York: Cambridge University Press, 1992), esp. 180–87; and Richard Tuck, *Philosophy and Government, 1572–1651* (New York: Cambridge University Press, 1993). And on the Enlightenment, see Thomas J. Schlereth, *The Cosmopolitan Ideal in Enlightenment Thought* (Notre Dame, IN: University of Notre Dame Press, 1977); Martha C. Nussbaum, "Kant and Stoic Cosmopolitanism," *Journal of Political Philosophy* 5, no. 1 (1997): 1–25; Pauline Kleingeld, "Six Varieties of Cosmopolitanism in Late Eighteenth-Century Germany," *Journal of the History of Ideas* 60, no. 3 (1999); and Gordon, *Citizens without Sovereignty.* Contrast

Margaret C. Jacob, *Strangers Nowhere in the World: The Rise of Cosmopolitanism in Early Modern Europe* (Philadelphia: University of Pennsylvania Press, 2006), which gives cultural content to institutions associated with "cosmopolitanism" without exploring the semantic meaning and intellectual traditions of that word for the same.

6. On the repercussions of the death of Charles II of Spain for the Kingdom, see chapter 1.

7. For example, in his study of the life and times of Nicolas-Claude Fabri de Peiresc, Peter N. Miller has shown that in the seventeenth century the Stoic virtues of constancy and beneficence especially appealed to aristocratic men of learning and informed their ideals of sociability and of conversation. Thus, according to Miller, Peiresc's was a "practical Stoicism" that guided his comportment in scholarly society; the study of philosophy reputedly armed him with that constancy and patience that was needed in even the best of times, and his exemplary beneficence, conversation, and intellectual indefatigability created a model of individual excellence for the European Republic of Letters that rivaled those of old. See Peter N. Miller, *Peiresc's Europe: Learning and Virtue in the Seventeenth Century* (New Haven: Yale University Press, 2000), esp. 39–40 and 51–61, where Miller offers a stimulating discussion of the interpretation of lesser-known Italian pedagogical tracts from the late sixteenth century, which present the art of "civil conversation" as supplanting older ideas about the excellence of the *vita attiva,* or what was the practical training for a life of participatory politics. For a sampling of works on Neo-Stoicism illustrative of its influence on culture, see on geography: Denis Cosgrove, "Globalism and Tolerance in Early Modern Geography," *Annals of the Association of American Geographers* 93, no. 4 (2003): 852–70; on literature: Andrew Shifflet, *Stoicism, Politics, and Literature in the Age of Milton* (New York: Cambridge University Press, 1998); Adriana McCrea, *Constant Minds: Political Virtue and the Lipsian Paradigm in England, 1584–1650* (Toronto: University of Toronto Press, 1997); Geoffrey Miles, *Shakespeare and the Constant Romans* (New York: Oxford University Press, 1996); and Gilles D. Monserrat, *Light from the Porch: Stoicism and English Renaissance Literature* (Paris: Didier-Edition, 1984); on theater: Roland Mayer, "Personata Stoa: Neostoicism and Senecan Tragedy," *Journal of the Warburg and Courtauld Institutes* 57 (1994): 151–74; on opera: Peter N. Miller, "Stoics Who Sing: Lessons on Citizenship from Early Modern Lucca," *Historical Journal* 44, no. 2 (June 2001): 313–39; on baroque art: Mark Morford, *Stoics and Neostoics: Rubens and the Circle of Lipsius* (Princeton: Princeton University Press, 1991).

8. Oestreich, *Neostoicism and the Early Modern State,* esp. 6, 28, 35, and 45. Since its appearance in English, the work by Oestreich has enjoyed wide acclaim and has also received its share of criticism. From early on, Oestreich has been criticized for having made enthusiastic claims for the originality and influence of Lipsius to the fault of eclipsing similarly important Neo-Stoics. See Peter Burke's "Review" of Oestreich's work in *English Historical Review* 100, no. 395 (1985): 403–4. Second, Oestreich has been charged with overstating the resemblances of Lipsius's thought to civic humanism, which purportedly lead him to overlook Lipsius's debt to Machiavelli and to falsely attribute *actio,* or action, to the persona of the citizen. In particular, see van Gelderen, *Political Thought of the Dutch Revolt,* esp. 185–86. Also see Jan Waszink's Introduction to Justus Lipsius, *Politica: Six Books of Politics or Political Instruction,* ed. by Jan Waszink (Assen, Netherlands: Royal Van Gorcum,

2004), esp. 10–15. In light of the fact that Oestreich emphasized the ways in which Lipsius's political theory anticipated theories of absolutism, however, this criticism points up what is a minor inconsistency within Oestreich's own thought. Finally, and most important perhaps, Oestreich has been charged with sociological anachronism, that is, with ascribing contemporary ideas of social disciplining to the reality of early modernity. See Peter N. Miller, "Nazis and Neo-Stoics," *Past and Present* 176 (2002): 144–86, in which Miller contextualizes Oestreich's particular interest in the professionalization of the early modern army and the impact of the same on society within Oestreich's own experience of National Socialism. Be those criticisms as they may, Oestreich's recovery of the importance of Lipsius for his contemporaries and successors; his contextualization of Lipsius's Neo-Stoicism in the atrocities of the religious wars and Dutch Revolt; his astute analysis of the conjuncture of moral and political ideas in Lipsius's companion texts, *De constantia* (1584) and *Politicorum sive civilis doctrinae libri sex* (1589); and his identification of the emergence of an absolutist theory of the polity remain useful.

9. On the manuscript tradition of the *Orationes,* see Salvatore Monti, *Sulla tradizione e sul testo delle orazioni inaugurali di Vico* (Naples: Guida, 1977) and the introduction by Gian Galeazzo Visconti to Giambattista Vico, *Le orazioni inaugurali, I–VI,* ed. Gian Galeazzo Visconti (Bologna: Il Mulino, 1982). Both these accounts draw on and selectively contest that of the *Bibliografia vichiana,* vol. 1, 10–12.

10. As pertains to the above discussion, important is the finding by Monti, confirmed by Visconti, that the "Emendationes" of the first five orations, penned after 18 October 1706 and by the end of 1707, comprised both stylistic and conceptual revisions of the original orations read before the student body. After his incorporation of the "Emendationes" into his original text, Vico apparently continued to revise the manuscript of the orations, although it seems that the subsequent corrections were solely stylistic. Monti, *Sulla tradizione,* 69–90, and Visconti, Introduzione to Vico, *Le orazioni inaugurali,* ed. Visconti, 10.

11. *Autobiografia:* Croce and Nicolini edit., 27–32, esp. 32; Fisch and Bergin trans., 139–47, esp. 146.

12. On the manuscript tradition and publication of *De ratione,* see Biagio De Giovanni, "Il *De nostri temporis studiorum ratione* nella cultura napoletana del primo Settecento," in *Omaggio a Vico,* ed. A. Corsano et al. (Naples: Morano, 1968), 141–92, and *Bibliografia vichiana,* vol. 1, 12–14.

13. See, for example, Cicero, *De officiis,* Loeb Classical Library, esp. I.xvii.53–55; Seneca, "De otio," in his *Moral Essays,* trans. John W. Basore, vol. 2, Loeb Classical Library (1928; repr., Cambridge: Harvard University Press, 1970), IV.1; and Marcus Aurelius, *Meditations,* trans. C. R. Haines, Loeb Classical Library (1916; repr., Cambridge: Harvard University Press, 2003), esp. IV.4.

14. Seneca, "De otio," in his *Moral Essays,* vol. 2, Loeb Classical Library, IV.1. As Seneca therewith added: "Some yield service to both commonwealths at the same time—to the greater and to the lesser—some only to the lesser, some only to the greater. This greater commonwealth we are able to serve even in leisure—nay, I am inclined to think even better in leisure—so that we may inquire what virtue is...." (Basore trans.)

15. See Gordon, *Citizens without Sovereignty* and Nussbaum, "Kant and Stoic Cosmopolitanism."

16. This was especially true of the Hierocles fragment cited by the late-antique scholar Stobaeus in his *Florilegium*, which specifically employed the image of a series of concentric circles to describe man's potential for world fellowship. As Hierocles advised: "Once these have all been surveyed, it is the task of a well tempered man, in his proper treatment of each group, to draw the circles together somehow towards the center, and to keep zealously transferring those from the enclosing circles into the enclosed ones." (Long and Sedley trans.) See Hierocles in Long and Sedley, *Hellenistic Philosophers,* vol. 1, 349–50. It bears mentioning that the *Florilegium* itself survived in the form of an epitome, which was translated into Latin and published on numerous occasions over the course of the sixteenth and early seventeenth centuries. Also, Cicero had first sketched this same image when contemplating the nature and extent of human fellowship. See Cicero, *De finibus,* trans. H. Rackham, Loeb Classical Library (1914; repr., Cambridge: Harvard University Press, 1961), III.xix.62–III.xx.68 and esp. Cicero, *De officiis,* Loeb Classical Library, I.xvii.53–55.

17. While the connotations of *oikeiosis* are many, Malcolm Schofield has translated *oikeiosis* into English as "affinity" in his article on "Stoic Ethics" in Inwood, *Cambridge Companion to the Stoics,* 243. It bears noting that the more usual translation of *oikeiosis* is "self-preservation."

18. I am drawing here on the discussion of *oikeiosis* by Christopher Gill in "Stoic Writers of the Imperial Era," in *Cambridge History of Greek and Roman Political Thought,* ed. Rowe and Schofield, esp. 608.

19. See Donald Philip Verene, Introduction to Giambattista Vico, *On Humanistic Education (Six Inaugural Orations, 1699–1707),* trans. Giorgio A. Pinton and Arthur W. Shippee (Ithaca: Cornell University Press, 1993), 14.

20. Vico, *Oratio I,* para. 13, lines 275–76 in Vico, *Le orazioni inaugurali, I–VI,* ed. Visconti, 90, and Vico, *On Humanistic Education,* trans. Pinton and Shippee, 49. (Pinton and Shippee trans.) It bears mentioning that Pinton and Shippee translated from Visconti's critical edition of the original Latin text by Vico. Consequently, the identifying numbers of the orations and their paragraphs are consistent throughout the Visconti edition and Pinton and Shippee translation, although only the paragraphs of the Latin text edited by Visconti (additionally) bear line numbers. Thus, and henceforth, I will cite the *Orationes* by providing for each of the passages referenced in my text: the number of its *Oratio,* paragraph and, lines followed by the page number on which the same passage appears in each of the above editions. It also bears mentioning that the Visconti edition of the *Orationes* contains not only the original-language text but also its translation into modern Italian. Similarly, Vico would add at the very outset of the second oration: "Men are lovers of truth but surrounded by errors; they are gifted with reason but subservient to passions." (Pinton and Shippee trans.) *Oratio II,* para. 1, lines 18–20: Visconti edit., 96; Pinton and Shippee trans., 55.

21. *Oratio I,* para. 4, lines 76–103: Visconti edit., 76 and 78; Pinton and Shippee trans., 38–39. (Pinton and Shippee trans.) Vico not only makes an oblique reference here to Epictetus as well as to a number of Plato's dialogues, including *Charmides* 164e–165a, but also explicitly cites Cicero. See Cicero, *Tusculan Disputations,* trans. J. E. King, Loeb Classical Library (1927; repr., Cambridge: Harvard University Press, 2001), I.xxii.52. Indeed, it is probable that Vico primarily derived his ideas about Stoicism from Cicero's representation of them, on which he most evidently draws throughout the *Orationes.*

22. *Oratio I*, para. 5, lines 110–11: Visconti edit., 78; Pinton and Shippee trans., 40. (Pinton and Shippee trans.)

23. *Oratio I*, para. 12, lines 268–74: Visconti edit., 90; Pinton and Shippee trans., 48. (Pinton and Shippee trans.) Compare *Oratio I*, para. 13, lines 303–4: Visconti edit., 92; Pinton and Shippee trans., 50.

24. *Oratio I*, para. 14, lines 310–14: Visconti edit., 92; Pinton and Shippee trans., 51.

25. Ibid.

26. This tenet was especially characteristic of the works of Marcus Aurelius, for whom cosmopolitanism was first and foremost an inner freedom. See, for examples, Marcus, *Meditations*, The Loeb Classical Library, II.16; III.2 and 11; IV.3–4, 29, and 40; V.21 and 30; VI.36; VII.9; VIII.5–7. For my discussion of this Stoic notion of wisdom and of *apatheia*, I primarily have drawn from Tad Brennan, "Stoic Moral Psychology" in Inwood, *Cambridge Companion to the Stoics;* and Sellars, "The Stoic System" and "Stoic Ethics" in his *Stoicism*, as well as a number of primary sources by the classical authors cited. See esp. Cicero, *Tusculan Disputations*.

27. *Oratio II*, para. 12, lines 296–98: Visconti edit., 116; Pinton and Shippee trans., 69. (Pinton and Shippee trans.)

28. *Oratio II*, para. 8, lines 153–55: Visconti edit., 106; Pinton and Shippee trans., 61–62. (Pinton and Shippee trans.)

29. *Oratio II*, para. 11, lines 262–66: Visconti edit., 114; Pinton and Shippee trans., 67. (Pinton and Shippee trans.)

30. *Oratio I*, para. 14, lines 326–29: Visconti edit., 94; Pinton and Shippee trans., 51–52. In contrast to Pinton and Shippee, but like Visconti, I have translated "magistratus" not as "masters" but as "magistrates," whom Vico indeed could have expected among his audience. Similarly, I have translated "honor" not as "authority" but as "offices," as Vico specifically wished to address the payoff of diligent study here.

31. The doctorate of law was requisite for the appointment to the position of "togato," or judge, and also for all of the highest-ranking judicial positions within the Kingdom's tribunals. See Vittor Ivo Comparato, *Uffici e società a Napoli (1600–1647): Aspetti dell'ideologia del magistrato nell'età moderna* (Florence: Olschki, 1974), esp. 88–92, and, more generally, Ileana del Bagno, *Legum doctores: La formazione del ceto giuridico a Napoli tra Cinque e Seicento* (Naples: Jovene, 1993).

32. On the foundation of the University of Naples and its function, see Origlia, *Istoria dello Studio di Napoli*, vol. 1, book 1 and especially book 2, chaps. 1 and 4, and Francesco Torraca, "Le origini: L'età sveva," in *Storia della Università di Napoli*, ed. Francesco Torraca et al. (Naples: Riccardo Ricciardi, 1924), 1–17. As Torraca therein asserted, the primary reason for the foundation of the university by Frederick II was "to form for the Kingdom a cadre of cultivated and capable individuals, who would be useful to the government, to the administration and to the judicial system." Ibid., 3. Consequently, as Torraca also noted, the most prestigious appointments were made to the faculty in law.

33. Nino Cortese, "L'età spagnola," in *Storia della Università di Napoli*, ed. Torraca et al., esp. 213–14, although his entire book-length article essentially is devoted to evidencing this thesis.

34. For documentation of the faculty of the university and their instruction of jurisprudence in the sixteenth and seventeenth centuries, see Nino Cortese, "L'età

spagnola," in *Storia della Università di Napoli,* ed. Torraca et al., esp. 316–57, where Cortese listed the *cattedre,* or chairs, of the university as well as their docents. For a celebratory narrative of the university's Faculty (and instruction) of Law, see Origlia, *Istoria dello Studio di Napoli,* esp. vol. 2, books 5–6, where he offered short biographies of the outstanding instructors and graduates of the university from the sixteenth and seventeenth centuries. As concerned the student body of the university during that same period, Del Bagno has generated the numbers for "doctors" of law and of medicine, and further provided information about the social profile of both groups. Del Bagno, *Legum doctores,* 27–42. In particular, her book has evidenced the great popularity and status of the doctorate of law relative to medicine.

35. While the University of Naples offered instruction in jurisprudence, the actual degree of law, i.e., the doctorate of law, was conferred by the Neapolitan Collegio dei Dottori [of Law], a corporate body and tribunal largely made up of Neapolitan members of the ministerial class. Thus, the Collegio was responsible for the enforcement of qualification for the license of advocate in the Kingdom. In the first place, it was supposed to review the credentials of individuals seeking the doctorate of law before admitting them to candidacy, among which numbered the certification of five years of attendance at the university. Furthermore, the Collegio presided over the examination of doctoral candidates, and with the utmost ceremony it then awarded the title of *doctor in utroque jure* to the successful ones. For an overview of the three *collegii* and their functions, see Cortese, "L'età spagnola," esp. 358–406. On the Collegio dei Dottori [of Law], see Del Bagno, *Legum doctores* and her *Il Collegio napoletano dei dottori: Privilegi, decreti, decisioni* (Naples: Jovene, 2000).

36. Ileana del Bagno has shown that the majority of the "doctors of law" were non-nobles (87.6%) and hailed from the provinces of the Kingdom (72.89%), although the single largest contingent was from Naples itself (27.11%). See Del Bagno, *Legum doctores,* 12–27. These figures are by no means surprising, given that the University of Naples virtually had a royal monopoly on the public instruction of law within the Kingdom. Similarly, a foreign degree of law had to be recognized by the Collegio dei Dottori before an individual could practice in the Kingdom. Cortese, "L'età spagnola" and Del Bagno, *Collegio.*

37. Discourse about the dignity of the doctorate of law dated back to the Middle Ages and had been ascendant throughout the early modern period in the Kingdom. For example, see Carlo De Frede, *Studenti e uomini di legge a Napoli nel Rinascimento* (Naples: L'arte tipografica, 1957) and Del Bagno, *Legum doctores.* Yet, the same by no means excluded the attractiveness of feudal title for the doctor of law. See Comparato, *Uffici e società,* esp. 99–126.

38. Niccolo Toppi, "Praeludium Primum" to his *De origine omnium tribunalium nunc in castro Capuano fidelissimae Civitatis Neapolis existentium, pt. 1* (Naples: Onofrio Savio, 1655), esp. para. 13. Cited in Comparato, *Uffici e società,* 89. Compare the reflections about the value of the doctorate contained in Giovanni Battista De Luca, *Il Dottor volgare, overo il compendio di tutta la legge civile, canonica, feudale, e municipale, nelle cose piu ricevute in pratica* (Rome: Giuseppe Corvo, 1673).

39. In the BNN and other Italian libraries, there are numerous copies of D'Andrea's memoir, the sheer multiplicity of which is indicative of the great popularity and circulation of this text at the outset of the eighteenth century. For an excellent treatment of the manuscript tradition of D'Andrea's letter, which introduces a critical

edition of the text, see the second prefatory essay by Imma Ascione to D'Andrea, *Avvertimenti ai nipoti,* ed. Ascione.

40. D'Andrea, *Avvertimenti ai nipoti,* ed. Ascione, 156.

41. Ibid., 141.

42. As Comparato has indicated, the purchase of a noble title was indeed for the seventeenth-century jurist "the terminus of the process of social climbing." Comparato, *Uffici e società,* 102. What is more, from the study of Comparato it is also clear that in the first half of the seventeenth century the possession of aristocratic credentials gave an individual competitive advantage in the selection process for the highest judicial offices of the Kingdom.

43. It was only toward the climax of the Enlightenment in the Kingdom that the publicist Lorenzo Giustiniani canonized the idea that merit distinguished while feudal title traduced in his *Memorie istoriche degli scrittori legali,* a three-volume work dedicated to the biographies of early modern jurists, which on its publication in 1787 already was regarded as a reference work of immense authority and long thereafter was considered the definitive prosopography of the Neapolitan judiciary. See Lorenzo Giustiniani, *Memorie istoriche degli scrittori legali,* 3 vols. (Naples: Stamperia Simoniana, 1787).

44. In particular, see *Notizie/ di Alcune famiglie Popolari/ Della Città e Regno di Napoli/ Che per ricchezze, e dignità sono divenute/ nobili, e riguardevoli* (1693), BNN MS X.A.15, which comprises seventy-eight entries regarding distinct Neapolitan families and is 144 pages in length. Interestingly, of this work there are multiple manuscript copies with annotations. In the BNN alone there also exists MS X.A.14 (without title, author, or date), which seems to be a later and updated text of the one cited above, as well as MS I.D.5, *Notitiae/ D'Alcune famiglie Popolari/ Della Città, e Regno/ di Napoli./ Divenute riguardevoli per causa/ di Ricchezze, ò Dignitadi./ Opera del fù Domenico Conforto./ Con le note marginali/ Del Dottor Domenico Bertelli./ L'autore scrive circa il 1693; e/ poco appresso./ E le note son fatte dal 1706 in avanti.* In the SNSP there are another two manuscripts bearing this title: MS XX.B.28 and MS XXIV.D.2. Similarly, the companion piece to that work by Confuorto documented the same phenomenon by uncovering the humble origins of a number of the Kingdom's most honored noble families and by recording the vicissitudes to which the great fortunes of others had been subjected. Domenico Confuorto, *Il/ Torto, Òvero Il/ Dritto della Nobilità Napo-/litana/ Esposta al/ Vetro della Verità./ Del Dr. Domenico/ Confuorto.* BNN MS X.A.25. This same text evidently was based upon the Italian translation of the (infamous) fifteenth-century tract on the Neapolitan nobility penned by the Humanist Francesco Elio Marchese, which circulated in manuscript copy through the seventeenth century. Among the seventeenth-century manuscripts of Marchese in the BNN, see: *Esame/ Della Nobiltà Napolitana/ distribuita/ Nei cinque Seggi, cioè/ Capuano, Montagna, Nido, Porto, e Portanova/ Trattenimento dispassionato/ d'Incerto Autore del 1695./ In fine il trattato dell'Origine delle/ Nobili Famiglie della Città di Napoli di Elio Marchese.* BNN MS X.B.72. On Marchese, see: Croce, *Uomini e cose,* vol. 1, 26–45 and C. Bianca, "Francesco Elio Marchese" in DBI.

45. Roberto Bizzocchi has written about this phenomenon more generally in relation to the early modern Italian peninsula in his *Genealogie incredibili: Scritti di storia nell'Europa moderna* (Bologna: Il Mulino, 1995).

46. To cite just two famous seventeenth-century examples given by Giustiniani, the otherwise exemplary Biagio Aldimari (1641–1713), the compiler and editor of

the important *Pragmaticae, edicta, decreta, regiaeque sanctiones Regni Neapolitani,* 1st ed. (Naples: Giacomo Raillard, 1682) and Caporuota of the Vicaria Criminale from 1690 onward, reportedly had been overcome by "fanaticism" (*fanatismo*) to obtain a declaration of his descent from the noble Altimari family of Florence in 1681 as well as to pen under the false name of Carlo de Lellis a genealogy of his family not long thereafter. See "Biagio Aldimari," in Giustiniani's *Memorie istoriche.* While the "fanaticism" of Aldimari did not deter his career, that of his contemporary Andrea Gizio would, abetting him to dedicate most of his energies to genealogical work, which took him to Vienna, where according to Giustiniani he relentlessly vaunted the feigned nobility of his family and died a "madman" (*matto*). See "Andrea Giuseppe Gizio," in ibid. A number of manuscripts concerning the nobility of the Kingdom by Gizio are held in the BNN, including *Prerogative, Genealogie e discorsi di / diverse famiglie / con varie cose notabili e singolari.* BNN MS Branc. IV.D.1.

47. Biscardi wrote in favor of the succession of Philip V to the Spanish throne in his *Epistola pro augusto Hispaniarum Monarcha Philippo quinto...;* and he penned a number of vociferous attacks on the attempt to try individuals accused of heresy by the *via straordinaria* of the Roman Inquisition within the political confines of the Kingdom. BNN MS. XV.B.3 and BNN MS. XI.C.1. For a summary of this battle against the Inquisition in English, see Stone, *Vico's Cultural History,* 28–45. Both Harold Stone and John Robertson have further considered the debate about modern philosophy waged in the wake of the controversy over the Inquisition. See ibid., 46–71, and Robertson, *Case for Enlightenment,* 94–101. Riccardi made a famous contribution to the criticism of the Papacy's allocation of ecclesiastical benefices within the Kingdom to non-nationals. See Alessandro Riccardi, *Ragioni del Regno di Napoli nella causa de' suoi beneficii ecclesiastici* (n.p., n.d. [but Naples, 1708 circa]) and his *Considerazioni sopra al nuovo libro intitolato* Regni Neapolitani....(Cologne: Pier Martello, 1709 [but Naples, 1709]). For a summary of this dispute over benefices, see Stone, *Vico's Cultural History,* 144–52. Information about the noble aspirations of both can be found in the articles devoted to the respective men in Giustiniani, *Memorie istoriche.*

48. Indeed, the *reggente,* or regent, of the Vicaria, the civil and criminal court of Naples, as well as the positions of *preside,* or president, of the provincial *udienze,* or courts, were reserved for members of the civic patriciate of Naples. See Anna Maria Rao, "The Feudal Question, Judicial Systems and the Enlightenment," in *Naples in the Eighteenth Century,* ed. Girolamo Imbruglia (New York: Cambridge University Press, 2000), 96, and Comparato, *Uffici e società,* 44–69. As the work by Comparato more generally has shown, the patricians who studied law had a competitive edge in the competition for the highest of judicial positions throughout the first half of the seventeenth century. However, since the time of the plague (1656), which decimated not only the population of Naples but also the staff of its tribunals, nonpatrician jurists had fared far better in appointment to the highest magistracies of the tribunals, gradually substituting the patriciate in the composition and direction of the judiciary. For an account of the impact of the plague on the staffing of the Kingdom's tribunals, see Carlo Francesco Riaco, *Il giudicio di Napoli: Discorso del passato contaggio, rassomigliato al Giudicio Universale, in cui si specificano le qualità, e numeri de'morti, con tutti gl'accidenti intervenuti.* (Perugia: Pietro di Tomasio, 1658). For an overview of the shift in power from the patriciate to the "ceto civile," or corps of university-trained jurists, see Mastellone, *Pensiero politico e vita culturale a Napoli,* which includes evidence

regarding the modernization of the criteria for the award of office by the Spanish. For an empirical study of the staff and magistrates of the various Neapolitan courts over the course of the seventeenth century, see the more recent work by Gaetana Intorcia, *Magistrature del Regno di Napoli* (Naples: Jovene, 1987). Nonetheless, the sense remained that the gains of the nonpatrician jurists had been as steady as they were vulnerable to the politics of the Spanish in the Kingdom, whose appointments were part of a larger strategy of alliances that cultivated the loyalties of leading members of the Popolo, or commoners. As D'Andrea importantly remarked with both pride and reservation, since the time of the infamous revolt of Masaniello (1647) appointments to the most honorific of vacant offices, the magistracies of the tribunals and regencies of the Consiglio Collaterale, largely had been awarded to nonpatrician "doctors of law" instead of the Neapolitan nobility, whose own marginalization from the axes of power delighted him. See D'Andrea, *Avvertimenti,* 154–57.

49. For in Naples the title of "doctor of law" was conferred by a collegiate body independent of the university, the Collegio dei Dottori, which apparently closed one eye to the (proper) certification of university attendance, especially in its review of the credentials of patricians.

50. Mastellone, *Pensiero politico e vita culturale a Napoli,* 25.

51. This trend did not go untheorized by contemporary philosophers of law and politics well known to Vico, such as the famed Neapolitan jurist Gian Vincenzo Gravina, who had begun to advocate on behalf of the "citizens of a middling condition"—that social order that he located between the titled "nobility" and "plebs" and which he described as "noble" by the nature of its cultivated mind and customs. Gravina believed that this order could best govern a state committed to rule by law. See, especially, Gian Vincenzo Gravina, *Originum iuris civilis libri tres,* vol. 3 (Naples: Felice Mosca, 1713). As Scipione Maffei summarized Gravina's positive views on oligarchy: "Ottimo dunque sarà questo modo di governo, dove non siano affatto esclusi dagli onori quelli, che solamente per ingegno e per costumi son nobili, benche per condizion plebei. È da porre singolar cura in accrescere i cittadini di condizion mezzana; perche essendo per lo più i nobili disposti a insolontire, ed i plebei d'animo abietto o tumultoso, quest'ordine di persone sarà come interposto fra questi e quelli, e si unirà alla nobiltà nelle sedizioni del popolo, ed al popolo nell'insuperbi della nobilità." (In English: The following form of government thus would be optimal: one wherein those people who are noble only on account of their mind and customs would not be excluded from honors and offices, even if they were of plebeian origin. It is desirable that the citizens of the middling sort grow; because this order of persons would be placed between the nobles—who are disposed to insolence—and the plebs—who are of an abject and tumultuous spirit—and because this order would unite with the nobility against the seditions of the people and with the people against the arrogance of the nobility.) Scipione Maffei, ed., *De origine iuris civilis* (Naples: Gennaro Matarazzo, 1822), 78–79. On Gravina's politics, see Carlo Ghisalberti, *Gian Vincenzo Gravina: Giurista e storico* (Milan: Giuffrè, 1962); and, on his literary works, see Amodeo Quondam, *Cultura e ideologia di Gianvincezo Gravina* (Milan: Murisa, 1968).

52. In times of political transition it was customary for a coalition of the Consiglio Collaterale and the heads of the Kingdom's leading tribunals to claim and exercise the right to rule, a practice that was often challenged by the municipality of

Naples. For example, see chapter 1 concerning the question of interim rule on the death of Charles II.

53. This was especially the case in the fourth oration.

54. Contrary to much of the historiography, my own reading of Vico's social theory interprets it as part of the modern school. Contrast Lilla, *Vico.*

55. This idea derived from the Aristotelian notion that man was a political animal. See Aristotle, *Politics,* III, 6: "Man is by nature a political animal. And, therefore, even when they do not require one another's help, they desire to live together; not but that they are also brought together by their common interests in so far as they each attain to any measure of well-being. This is certainly the chief end, both of individuals and of states." (Jonathan Barnes trans.) As we shall see, it also restated with new emphasis the central belief of the Stoics and their Roman spokesperson, Cicero, that humans were sociable by nature. See Cicero, *De finibus,* Loeb Classical Library, III.xix.62–68 for an extended treatment of this topic.

56. For the term "commercial cosmopolitanism" I am partly indebted to Pauline Kleingeld, who in her article "Six Varieties of Cosmopolitanism" uses the terms "economic" and "market" "cosmopolitanism" to refer to the advocacy of a free global marketplace. Also see Gordon, *Citizens without Sovereignty,* where he employs the term "self-centered cosmopolitanism," and his "Citizenship," in *The Encyclopedia of the Enlightenment,* ed. Alan Kors (Oxford: Oxford University Press, 2005).

57. The historiography on the eighteenth century's variety of commercial cosmopolitanism typically has glossed over the specific context and meaning of its program. While both Pauline Kleingeld and Daniel Gordon have brilliantly reconstructed the ideas associated with the German and French examples of commercial cosmopolitanism, they have done less to show the practical relevance of those ideas in the mid-eighteenth century. See Kleingeld, "Six Varieties of Cosmopolitanism," esp. 518–21 and Gordon, *Citizens without Sovereignty,* esp., 72–77. Contrast Amalia Kessler, *A Revolution in Commerce* (New Haven: Yale University Press, 2007), which suggests just how central the ad hoc decisions of the Merchant's Court of Paris were to the innovation of both commercial practices as well as the ideas about the role of commerce in the civilization of society.

58. *Oratio II,* para. 2, lines 48–55: Visconti edit., 98–100; Pinton and Shippee trans., 57–58. Compare this passage in Vico to Cicero, *De legibus,* Loeb Classical Library, I.vi.18–19, I.xii.33 and I.vii.23.

59. On moral realism versus moral nonrealism in the tradition of natural law, especially, see James Tully, Introduction to Samuel Pufendorf, *On the Duty of Man and Citizen,* trans. Michael Silverthorne (New York: Cambridge University Press, 1991), xvii, whose lucid definition of the term I am employing.

60. This point was forcefully argued by Cicero in *De finibus,* Loeb Classical Library, III.xix.62–68, where he postulated that natural justice followed from the directives of natural sociability. This famous passage is also cited in Long and Sedley, *The Hellenistic Philosophers,* vol. 1, 348–49. As Cicero put it: "Hence it follows that mutual attraction between men is also something natural. . . . We are therefore suited to form unions, societies, and states. . . . From this it is a natural consequence that we prefer the common advantage to our own. . . . Furthermore we are driven by nature to desire to benefit as many people as possible." (Long and Sedley trans.) Similarly, Cicero condemned the pursuit of self-interest per se in the *De legibus,* Loeb Classical

Library, I.xviii.49, where he stated: "In addition, if it be true that virtue is sought for the sake of other benefits and not for its own sake, there will be only one virtue, which will most properly be called a vice. For in proportion as anyone makes his own advantage absolutely the sole standard of all his actions, to that extent he is absolutely not a good man." (Keyes trans.)

61. The influence of Hobbes in Naples is testified by both the library holdings from that period as well as the interpretation of natural law proffered by contemporary proponents of the reason of state. For example, at the outset of the eighteenth century the Biblioteca Brancacciana, which in the early modern period was a private library open to the literary public, held the first edition of the *Elementa philosophica de cive* (Amsterdam: [Daniel Elzevir], 1642) by Hobbes. This edition is listed in the manuscript catalogue of prohibited books held in the Bibliotecca Brancacciana, which was apparently drafted in 1725—the most recent publication date listed. See *Inventario/ De' Libri/ Prohibiti/ Della/ Libraria/ Brancaccio* conserved in the BNN with the following call number: MS II.G.14. Over the course of the eighteenth century, the Biblioteca Brancacciana then very likely acquired a number of the following seventeenth-century editions of Hobbes's works held in its present-day collection: *Opera philosophica* (Amsterdam: [Johannes Blaeu], 1668); *Elementa philosophica de cive* (Amsterdam: [H. and Th. Boom], 1696); and *Leviathan* (Amsterdam: [Johannes Blaeu], 1670). For evidence of a public endorsement of natural law theory that was derived from Hobbesian political philosophy, see the lesson delivered by Nicola Capasso in front of the Accademia Medinaceli entitled "Se la Ragion di Stato possa derogare alla legge Naturale," conserved in the BNN with the following call number MS XIII.B.73(5, 23r–28r and reprinted in Rak, *Lezioni dell'Accademia di Palazzo del duca di Medinaceli,* vol. 4, 82–90.

62. For my treatment of Cicero's notion of natural law in this paragraph, and particularly on the latter two points, I am drawing on the insights of E. M. Atkins in his article on "Cicero" for Rowe and Schofield, *Cambridge History of Greek and Roman Political Thought,* esp. 500.

63. *Oratio III,* para. 2, lines 38–39: Visconti edit., 124; Pinton and Shippee trans., 75 (Pinton and Shippee trans.), and *Oratio III,* para. 2, lines 42–43: Visconti edit., 124; Pinton and Shippee trans., 75. (Pinton and Shippee trans.)

64. *Oratio III,* para. 4, lines 64–68: Visconti edit., 126; Pinton and Shippee trans., 76. "Indeed, there is such a great and powerful force inherent in the soul of man which leads him to associate and join together with others, that no person, however wicked or treacherous or wretched, can be found to exist without it. There is none, though he be so depraved, who does not hold and nurture some sense of the just like a glowing cinder concealed by the ashes." (Pinton and Shippee trans.) Compare Cicero's adamancy regarding the natural benevolence and philanthropy of humans and the significance of such as the foundation for the union of humans and success of their communities. See especially Cicero, *De finibus,* Loeb Classical Library, III.xix.62–68.

65. There is a wealth of studies on the so-called Republic of Letters. Among the finer studies in English, see Anne Goldgar, *Impolite Learning: Conduct and Community in the Republic of Letters, 1680–1750* (New Haven: Yale University Press, 1995) and Dena Goodman, *The Republic of Letters: A Cultural History of the French Enlightenment* (Ithaca: Cornell University Press, 1994). In French, see Hans Bot and Françoise Wacquet, *La République des Lettres* (Paris: Belin, 1997).

66. *Oratio III,* para. 4, lines 73–76 and esp. 75: Visconti edit., 126; Pinton and Shippee trans., 77.

67. *Oratio III,* para. 5, lines 77–78: Visconti edit., 128; Pinton and Shippee trans., 77. (Pinton and Shippee trans.) Importantly, here Vico is employing the customary Roman legal definition of the partner of an association, or commercial corporation.

68. *Oratio III,* paras. 3, 6, and 10: Visconti edit., 126, 130, and 138; Pinton and Shippee trans., 76, 79, and 85.

69. *Oratio III,* para. 6, lines 117–19: Visconti edit., 130; Pinton and Shippee trans., 79–80. (Pinton and Shippee trans.)

70. *Oratio III,* para. 7, line 70: Visconti edit., 134; Pinton and Shippee trans., 82. This expression recurs in Cicero, *De officiis.*

71. In French language sources from the era, it typically was employed to refer to either corporations or associations of friends engaged in cultural activities, such as conversation. See Johan Heilbron, *The Rise of Social Theory,* trans. Sheila Gogol (Minneapolis: University of Minnesota Press, 1995); Gordon, *Citizens without Sovereignty,* 51; and Baker, "Enlightenment and the Institution of Society," in *Main Trends in Cultural History,* ed. Melching and Velema, 95–100.

72. Here I am citing Heilbron, *Rise of Social Theory,* esp. 86–88. For Heilbron, Montesquieu initiated the new intellectual genre of "social theory" with the *Spirit of the Laws* (1748), although, as he notes, it was only Montesquieu's successor Rousseau who would first employ the terms "society" and "social" in their more modern senses. This trend has been corroborated with a broader field of linguistic evidence by both Daniel Gordon in his *Citizens without Sovereignty,* esp. 53–54 and 65, and by Keith Michael Baker, "Enlightenment and the Institution of Society," in *Main Trends in Cultural History,* ed. Melching and Velema, 100–105, with his insightful discussion of the *Encyclopédie.* However, the precedence for the globalization of the idea of "society" was already set by Cicero in *De officiis.*

73. It seems likely that Vico had drawn this example from a section of Cicero's *De officiis,* where the latter argued for the normativeness of commercial principles among strangers. See Cicero, *De officiis,* Loeb Classical Library, III.xii–xvii, where the author discusses the moral obligations of sellers and speaks of the principles of equity and good faith as those of universal law. Therein, on the obligations imposed by equity and good faith see, especially, III.xvii.69–70. Vico is citing III. xiii.55.

74. "Praetor," in Adolf Berger, *Encyclopedic Dictionary of Roman Law* (Philadelphia: American Philosophical Society, 1953).

75. Peter Stein, "Equitable Principles in Roman Law," in his *Character and Influence of Roman Civil Law* (London: Hambledon Press, 1988), 19.

76. H. F. Jolowicz and Barry Nicholas, *Historical Introduction to the Study of Roman Law* (Cambridge: Cambridge University Press, 1972), 103.

77. Fritz Schulz, *Classical Roman Law* (Oxford: Clarendon Press, 1954), 524–25. Compare Barry Nicholas, *An Introduction to Roman Law* (Oxford: Oxford University Press, 1979), esp. 163n5.

78. Stein, "Equitable Principles," in *Character and Influence,* 25.

79. See "Ius naturale," in *Dictionary of Roman Law.* Gaius was cited in the *Digest* (I.1.9) thusly: "All peoples who are governed under laws and customs observe in part their own special law and in part a law common to all men. Now that law which

each nation has set up as a law unto itself is special to that particular *civitas* and is called *jus civile,* civil law, as being that which is proper to the particular civil society (*civitas*). By contrast, that law which natural reason has established among all human beings is among all observed in equal measure and is called *jus gentium,* as being the law which all nations observe." (Watson trans.)

80. Hans Julius Wolff, *Roman Law: An Historical Introduction* (Norman: University of Oklahoma Press, 1951), 82.

81. He primarily located these in the offices of justice and the obligations of good faith. Cicero, *De officiis,* Loeb Classical Library, I.vii.23; III.v.23.

82. Ibid., III.xv.61; III.xvii.70.

83. While it is hard to parse Vico's similarities to Pufendorf from his similarities to Cicero, it is also true that Pufendorf and Vico had common interests in Cicero's texts and that they both differed from Cicero on a number of the same points, such as his unflinching commitment to the moral realism of *oikeiosis.* For moderns, Pufendorf famously had made the standard Roman legal definition of the *societas* that of human association, and, what is more, had used that definition as evidence for his hallmark principle of *socialitas,* which recognized self-preservation as the impetus for human association while acknowledging the sociability of its members' exchange as a secondary source of their attachment to the same association. However, for Pufendorf, *socialitas* did not render association perfectly self-regulating, as both the passions and free will of humans threatened the moral order of their "society"; consequently, *socialitas* necessitated the creation of the state, or "civitas," and the imposition of moral rules, or natural law duties, on that political community by a superior, whose decrees were self-evidently beneficial and enforceable. For an abbreviated statement of Pufendorf's views on these subjects, see Pufendorf, *On the Duty of Citizen and Man,* esp. book 1, chap. 3, "On Natural Law"; book 2, chap. 5, "On the Impulsive Cause of Constituting the State"; and book 2, chap. 12, "On Civil Laws in Particular." Compare Pufendorf, *De iure naturae et gentium,* book 2, chap. 3; book 7, chap. 1; and book 8, chap. 1. For my definition and conclusions regarding Pufendorf's concept of *socialitas* here, I particularly am indebted to both Istvan Hont, "The Language of Sociability and Commerce: Samuel Pufendorf and the Theoretical Foundations of the 'Four-Stages' Theory," in his *Jealousy of Trade,* 159–84, and James Tully, Introduction to Pufendorf, *On the Duty of Man and Citizen,* esp. xxiv–xxix. In light of the fundamental differences between Hont and Tully in their emphasis, it bears noting that I have reiterated Hont's great appreciation for the societal benefits of *socialitas,* while taking Tully's point that Pufendorf saw political order and authority as indispensable to the proper functioning of *socialitas.* Of relevance to my discussion here are also the insights of T. J. Hochstrasser, *Natural Law Theories in the Early Enlightenment* (New York: Cambridge University Press, 2000), 60–65, and Knud Haakonssen, *Natural Law and Moral Philosophy* (New York: Cambridge University Press, 1996), 37–43.

84. Indeed, it was on the very day before Vico's oration that the regent "protector" of the university presented his program for university reform to the Consiglio Collaterale. On the university reform of 1702–4, see Ascione, *Seminarium doctrinarum,* 47–74, and Cortese, "L'età spagnola," 267–71.

85. Capasso, "Se la Ragion di Stato possa derogare alla legge Naturale," BNN MS XIII.B.73(5, 23v.

86. On the emergence of a "reason of state" doctrine in Italy, see Maurizio Viroli, *From Politics to Reason of State: The Acquisition and Transformation of the Language of Politics (1250–1600)* (New York: Cambridge University Press, 1992).

87. Paraphrasing Hobbes, in his lecture Capasso had hypothesized that the circumstances of the state of nature, which he saw as marked by both want and war, had made it intrinsically reasonable for humans to form a political community governed by a prince, to whom they alienated and transferred their "ius naturale," and who consequently embodied the natural reason of law. See Capasso, "Se la Ragion di Stato possa derogare alla legge Naturale," BNN MS XIII.B.73(5, esp. 24v–25r. Compare Hobbes on the "lex naturalis" and the "common-wealth," respectively, in *Leviathan*, part 1, chap. xiv (New York: Cambridge University Press, 1991), esp. pp. 91–92 and ibid., part 2, chaps. xvii–xviii, pp. 117–29. I herewith cite this edition. As Capasso importantly concluded, the "ius naturale" thus could not be invoked to challenge the will of the sovereign on behalf of any individual person: "Quindi è che non compete il 'ius naturale' della defensione a chi è stato dal principe proscritto, o, come diciamo noi, forgiudicato; nè mai la ragion di stato fa ingiuria ad alcuno, quando il principe per regola di governo deroga alla ragione naturale, della quale esso è concessionario." (In English: Thus the *ius naturale*, or natural law, does not defend him who has been proscribed by the prince; nor does the reason of state harm anyone, when the prince for the purpose of government deviates from that natural reason, of which he is the concessionary.) Capasso, "Se la Ragion di Stato possa derogare alla legge Naturale," BNN MS XIII.B.73(5, 25r. Capasso was made the Acting Chair of Canon Law by the grace of a viceroyal recommendation. On this see Ascione, *Seminarium doctrinarum*, 55.

88. On the military trial, torture, and execution of the rebels, see Granito, *Storia della congiura*, 153–57. On the rights of war, see Cicero, *De officiis*, I.xi.34–38, and Hugo Grotius, *De iure belli ac pacis libri tres* (1st edit., Paris, 1625), esp. book 3.

89. On the institution of the *universitas* in the early modern Kingdom, see Giovanni Muto, "Istituzioni dell'*universitas* e ceti dirigenti locali," in *Storia del Mezzogiorno*, ed. Galasso and Romeo, vol. 9, *Aspetti e problemi del medievo e dell'età moderna*, part 2 (Naples: Edizioni del Sole, 1991), 17–67.

90. Although Vico claimed to have delivered this particular oration in 1705, study of the manuscript tradition suggests otherwise. See *Autobiografia:* Croce and Nicolini edit., 29; Fisch and Bergin trans., 142. Contrast Monti, *Sulla tradizione*, 28 and 57–62. Compare *Bibliografia vichiana*, vol. 1, 9–12.

91. *Oratio IV,* para. 1, lines 7–14: Visconti edit., 146; Pinton and Shippee trans., 92, and *Oratio IV,* para. 4, lines 47–49: Visconti edit., 148; Pinton and Shippee trans., 94. On the university reform, see Origlia, *Istoria*, vol. 2, 232 and following. More recently, see Ascione, *Seminarium doctrinarum*, 47–74, and Cortese, "L'età spagnola," 267–71.

92. Cortese, "L'età spagnuola," 304.

93. *Oratio IV.* The themes of this oration evidently were meant to recall those of Cicero's *De officiis.* Indeed, Vico's equivalence of the honest and the useful explicitly derives from Cicero, *De officiis*, book 3.

94. The theme of the relative importance and prestige of the literary and military arts was a common one during the Renaissance, which, as Visconti has noted, famously was initiated by Bernardo da Siena (1380–1444) in comments he published

on the works of Petrarch. For studies of this debate, see the contributions by Lucia Gualdo Rosa and Francesco Tateo to Luisa Avellini, ed. *Sapere e/è potere: Forme e oggetti della disputa delle arti* (Bologna: Istituto per la Storia di Bologna, 1990). As more specifically concerns the idea of nobility in Naples, there are several excellent studies by Giovanni Muto that make plain just how normative and fictional the exaltation of the military prowess of the nobility remained for the Mezzogiorno over the course of the sixteenth and seventeenth centuries. See among others Giovanni Muto, "I trattati napoletani cinquecenteschi in tema di nobilità," in *Sapere e/è potere: Dalle discipline ai ruoli sociali,* ed. Angela De Benedictis (Bologna: Istituto per la Storia di Bologna, 1991) and "I segni d'Honore. Rappresentazioni delle dinamiche nobiliari a Napoli in Età moderna," in *Signori, patrizi, cavalieri,* ed. Visceglia, 171–92.

95. *Oratio V,* para. 7, line 62: Visconti edit., 176; Pinton and Shippee trans., 117. As Vico put it: "Wars are courts of law."

96. Seneca, "De otio," in *Moral Essays,* vol. 2, IV.1.

97. *Oratio V,* para. 7, lines 63–71: Visconti edit., 176 and 178; Pinton and Shippee trans., 117.

98. *Oratio V,* para. 8, lines 82–85: Visconti edit., 178; Pinton and Shippee trans., 118. (Pinton and Shippee trans.)

99. *Oratio V,* para. 7, lines 66 and 71: Visconti edit., 178; Pinton and Shippee trans., 117.

100. Cicero, *De officiis,* Loeb Classical Library, I.xi.

101. See Francisco de Vitoria, *De Indis* and *De Indis Relectio Posterior, sive de iure belli,* both available in translation in Vitoria, *Political Writings,* ed. Anthony Pagden (Cambridge: Cambridge University Press, 1991) and Hugo Grotius, *Mare liberum* (1st ed., Leiden: Elsevier, 1609) and *De iure belli ac pacis,* both available in translation in the Liberty Fund series.

102. *Autobiografia:* Croce and Nicolini edit., 113; Fisch and Bergin trans., 146.

103. Felice Mosca would publish all of Vico's subsequent work written before his death in 1744.

104. *Bibliografia vichiana,* vol. 1, 13–14.

105. *De ratione,* section 1: Gentile and Nicolini edit., 77; Gianturco edit., 5. (Gianturco trans.)

106. See *Oratio VI,* para. 2, esp. lines 45–46: Visconti edit., 190; Pinton and Shippee trans., 127.

107. See *Oratio VI,* para. 4, esp. lines 91–96: Visconti edit., 194; Pinton and Shippee trans., 129. "Moreover, self-love, as its own tormentor, makes use of these wicked plagues and tortures. Because basic human nature has been changed by original sin, assemblies of men may appear to be societies, but the truth is that isolation of spirits is greatest where many bodies come together. Even more it is like the crowded inmates of a prison." (Pinton and Shippee trans.)

108. At this time, there was ample reason for Vico to tread carefully when dealing with theological issues, given the still recent imprisonment and trial of "atheists" by the Inquisition in the Kingdom of Naples. See Stone, *Vico's Cultural History,* 28–34; Robertson, *Case for Enlightenment,* 94–101.

109. It bears noting that Vico's dogmatism did serve to position him on the side of orthodoxy within the theological debate on grace and free will as it concerned pedagogy. For example, the Protestant-like Jansenists of the Port-Royal

school urged study on their pupils in their search for grace, while the Jesuits believed that it behooved men to exercise their own free will to try to win their salvation.

110. See *Oratio VI,* para. 6, esp. lines 127–33: Visconti edit., 196; Pinton and Shippee trans., 131. "Orpheus and Amphion…have led isolated man into union, that is, from love of self to the fostering of human community, from sluggishness to purposeful activity, from unrestrained license to compliance with law and by conferring equal rights united those unbridled in their strength with the weak." (Pinton and Shippee trans.)

111. See *Oratio VI,* para. 14, esp. line 313: Visconti edit., 206; Pinton and Shippee trans., 138. (Pinton and Shippee trans.)

112. There was some cultural precedent for this pedagogical theory in that of the Humanists, especially as elaborated in the fifteenth century. Compare the pedagogical theory of a Renaissance proponent of the *studia humanitatis* such as Pier Paolo Vergerio. See Vergerio, "De ingenuis moribus et liberalis studiis adulescentiae" (1403) partially reprinted in Eugenio Garin, ed., *Il pensiero pedagogico dello umanesimo* (Florence: Editrice Universitaria, 1958) and printed in its entirety in modern translation in Garin, *Educazione umanistica in Italia* (Bari: Laterza, 1949). More recently, on the innovation of Vergerio's pedagogy, see Benjamin G. Kohl, "Humanism and Education," in *Renaissance Humanism,* vol. 3, *Humanism and the Disciplines,* ed. Albert Rabil (Philadelphia: University of Pennsylvania Press, 1988), where Kohl shows that the novelty of Vergerio's method lay in his proposition that the curriculum of study be tailored to the natural abilities of the individual child and that a single subject be taught at a time.

113. The literature on Jesuit pedagogy is enormous and largely superfluous to the argument made here. For a brief overview of the predominance of the Jesuit curriculum in Catholic Europe, see Bowen, *A History,* vol. 3, 22–32.

114. The Port-Royal tracts on education in actuality were more diverse in their emphases than the *Logique.* Compare the more holistic approach of Pierre Coustel, *Les règles de l'éducation des enfants* (1687). However, in the Kingdom the Port-Royal school was associated with the *Logique,* and it was indeed this same text that Vico would cite and criticize in the *De ratione.* See *De ratione,* section 3: Gentile and Nicolini edit., 84; Gianturco edit., 20.

115. Especially see *Oratio VI,* paras. 12–14: Visconti edit., 202–8 (even pages); Pinton and Shippee trans., 135–39; and *De ratione,* section 3: Gentile and Nicolini edit., 83–84; Gianturco edit., 19.

116. For further discussion of Vico's defense of the *ars topica,* which was one of the rhetorical arts, see Donald Verene, *Knowledge of Things Human and Divine* (New Haven: Yale University Press, 2003), esp. 83–84.

117. For the first mention of Cartesian method, see *De ratione,* section 1: Gentile and Nicolini edit., 78; Gianturco edit., 6 (Gianturco trans.)

118. On the importance of common sense for Vico, see *De ratione,* section 3: Gentile and Nicolini edit., 81; Gianturco edit., 13.

119. For Vico's opinion on physics, see *De ratione,* section 4: Gentile and Nicolini edit., 84; Gianturco edit., 22.

120. Here I am paraphrasing *De ratione,* section 7: Gentile and Nicolini edit., esp. 90; Gianturco edit., esp. 33.

121. Francis Bacon, "Of the Dignity and Advancement of Learning" (*De dignitate et de augmentis scientiarum*), in *The Works of Francis Bacon,* ed. James Spedding, vol. 4: *Translations of the Philosophical Works,* vol. 1 (London: Longmans and Co., 1875) 290 and 275. (Spedding trans.)

122. *De ratione,* section 1: Gentile and Nicolini edit., 76–77; Gianturco edit., 3–4. It is worth noting that this critique of Bacon was not entirely fair to his positions in the *De augmentis* (1623), especially as he had been a proponent of those same human sciences that Vico would laud in *De ratione* and had anticipated Vico's own thoughts about the importance of an age-appropriate curriculum as well. See Bacon's introduction to book 2 of *De augmentis.* Nonetheless, it is true that Bacon primarily was associated with the advancement of the natural sciences in the eighteenth-century Kingdom, which, as we have seen, Vico subordinated to ethics and politics. For the reception of Bacon in the Kingdom, see Vincenzo Ferrone, *Scienza natura religione* (Naples: Jovene, 1982).

123. *De ratione,* section 11: Gentile and Nicolini edit., 102; Gianturco edit., 51. (Gianturco trans.)

124. *De ratione,* section 11: Gentile and Nicolini edit., 105 and 103; Gianturco edit., 56 and 53.

125. *De ratione,* section 11: Gentile and Nicolini edit., 104; Gianturco edit., 54–5.

126. *De ratione,* section 11: Gentile and Nicolini edit., 104; Gianturco edit., 55.

127. *De ratione,* section 11: Gentile and Nicolini edit., 113; Gianturco edit., 69.

128. For this contrast between the past and present, see *De ratione,* section 11: Gentile and Nicolini edit., 106–7; Gianturco edit., 58–59. It bears mentioning here that Vico's critique of his contemporaries repeated many of the criticisms he had already vented against the Roman praetors, although he evidently wished to establish that the jurisprudence of his own day was even more damaging to the public welfare than that of the Roman Empire.

129. *De ratione,* section 11: Gentile and Nicolini edit., 111; Gianturco edit., 66.

130. *De ratione,* section 11: Gentile and Nicolini edit., 111; Gianturco edit., 67. (Gianturco trans.)

131. The literature on *scientia civilis* is huge and cannot be summarized here. For a brief but rich overview of its centrality to the Renaissance, see Viroli, *From Politics to Reason of State.*

132. Roberta Colussi, "Diritto, istituzioni, amministrazione della giustizia nel Mezzogiorno vicereale. I: La struttura regalistica," in Galasso and Romeo, eds., *Storia del Mezzogiorno,* vol. 9, *Aspetti e problemi del medioevo e dell'età moderna,* part 2 (Naples: Edizioni del Sole, 1991), 33; and Giancarlo Vallone, "Il pensiero giuridico meridionale," in Galasso and Romeo, eds., *Storia del Mezzogiorno,* vol. 10, *Aspetti e problemi del medioevo e dell'età moderna,* part 3 (Naples: Edizioni del Sole, 1991), 317.

133. According to Peter Stein, the Sacro Consiglio of Naples was the first European court to publish a collection of its decisions, setting a precedent for the codification of forensic custom, or what was known as the *usus fori.* See Matthaeus de Afflictis, *Decisiones* (1499) and, subsequently, Vincenzio de Franchis, *Decisiones Sacri Regii Consilii Neapolitani* (1580). The importance of the *decisiones* of this court for other European powers has been noted with some detail in Marco Nicola Miletti, *Tra equità e dottrina: Il Sacro Regio Consiglio e le «decisiones» di V. de Franchis* (Naples: Jovene,

1995), 153–54, and treated by the same author at greater length in his *Stylus judicandi: Le raccolte di 'decisiones' del Regno di Napoli in età moderna* (Naples: Jovene, 1998).

134. Colussi, "Diritto, istituzioni, amministrazione," 34, and Miletti, *Tra equità e dottrina,* 156–57.

135. Ibid.

136. Colussi, "Diritto, istituzioni, amministrazione," 37, and Miletti, *Tra equità e dottrina,* 151.

137. Colussi, "Diritto, istituzioni, amministrazione," 34, and Miletti, *Tra equità e dottrina,* 153.

138. *De ratione,* section 11: Gentile and Nicolini edit., 113; Gianturco edit., 69–70. Vico used the expression "ex doctrina civili" here.

139. *De ratione,* section 11: Gentile and Nicolini edit., 113; Gianturco edit., 70. It is noteworthy that the formula was simply "ex causis" and that Vico had reinforced it rhetorically.

140. Ibid.

141. Colussi, "Diritto, istituzioni, amministrazione," 36.

142. For an unambiguous expression of the hopes that the Neapolitan intelligentsia pinned on the advent of the Austrians and the changes they implemented in its tribunals, see Pietro Giannone, *La vita di Pietro Giannone,* ed. Sergio Bertelli, vol. 1 (Turin: Einaudi, 1977), esp. 50–57.

143. For example, an investigation of the abuses perpetrated by the Count of Conversano in his feudal lands was apparently undertaken by Francesco Gascon, a counselor of the Sacro Consiglio, on the request of Viceroy Benavides in 1688. See Mastellone, *Pensiero politico e vita culturale a Napoli,* 52–53, and, at greater length, Raffaele Colapietra, *Vita pubblica e classi politiche del viceregno napoletano (1656–1734)* (Rome: Edizioni di storia e letteratura, 1961), 1–8. The original documentation relating to that case is conserved in BNN MS. XI.D.32, 49–57. Interestingly, this Spanish-language document speaks of the abuses of the count as being against the "ius naturale" (*derecho naturale*). However, this investigation seems to be one of the exceptions that proved the rule in the early modern period, as the Court seems to have largely functioned as a place of recourse for the powerful, a fact made particularly plain by the (however partial) inventory of cases assumed by the SRC that was compiled by Zeni. Indeed, for the last several years of Spanish rule, specifically 1700–1707, there is only one example of a case brought by a *università* with a grievance against its local lord among the many trials inventoried for those same years in the catalogue of the ASN entitled Processi Antichi, Sacro Regio Consiglio, Ordinamento Zeni, vol. 792. It bears noting that for the first decade of Austrian rule the same catalogue lists several examples of *università,* whose grievances against their feudal lords were heard by the Sacro Consiglio. Herewith this source within the ASN will be abbreviated as ASN, SRC, . . .

144. On the career of Gaetano Argento, see Dario Luongo, *Vis jurisprudentiae: Teoria e prassi della moderazione giuridica in Gaetano Argento* (Napoli: Jovene, 2001). Also see Domenico Zangari, *Gaetano Argento: Reggente e Presidente del Sacro Regio Consiglio* (Naples: La Cultura Calabrese, 1922), which explicitly treats Argento's appointment to the Sacro Consiglio on pages 86–89.

145. ASN, SRC, *Consulte,* vols. 625 and 626. While the majority of the *consulte,* or opinions, conserved in these two volumes still treated the usual fare of patrimonial

disputes among barons, among the exceptions are a number of opinions on disputes between the baronage and the state and on the grievances of civic communities against local feudal lords, bearing testimony to the attention the Sacro Consiglio gave to these matters in the first years of Austrian rule. In the first place, the documentation conserved in these volumes suggests that at the very outset of Austrian rule the new cohort of judges constituting the Sacro Consiglio were behooved—oftentimes by the royal court—to both renew their investigation of (long) pending cases and to assume new ones concerning the litigation of the Kingdom's communities with its baronage. Second, the same documentation also suggests that the Sacro Consiglio did (at the very least) formally adopt the royal court's directive of expediting, if not favoring, the justice of communities with cases pending against their local baronage. For example, at the behest of the viceroy, the Sacro Consiglio expedited its decision of a case pending between the citizens of San Giovanni Rotondo and the marquis of S. Marco, duke of San Giovanni Rotondo, which favored the demands of the former. ASN, SRC, *Consulte,* vol. 625, 316r. Similarly, at the behest of the emperor himself, the Sacro Consiglio promised to provide for the justice of Isernia in its litigation with the prince of the Colle d'Anchise, its baron, in a manifesto-like memorandum addressed to the emperor and signed by the entire court on 14 February 1709, which among other things politicly denounced the baron's *"prepotenza"* (tyrannical power) and "the partiality of those ministers who defend him." ASN, SRC, *Consulte,* vol. 625, 317r–v. Third, these volumes make plain that Argento almost immediately assumed a key role in adjudicating disputes with relevance to the persistence and fairness of feudalism. For example, a pending case between the *università* of the Terra d'Eboli and the local baron concerning the usage of enclosures by the citizens of Eboli evidently was assigned to, and assumed by, Argento shortly after his appointment to the SRC in 1708. While Argento's final decision is not evident from this documentation, it bears noting that the first and temporary provision taken by the jurist accommodated the demands of the *università* concerning the contested enclosures. ASN, SRC, *Consulte,* vol. 625, 284r–286v. What is more, it is interesting to note that under his leadership the court would later defend the demand of certain citizens of Tricarico (sp. 2) for the election of new administrators of their *università* without the presence (and threatening surveillance) of the local baron, who apparently sought to control the elections, and whose interests were (momentarily?) protected by the Consiglio Collaterale. ASN, SRC, *Consulte,* vol. 626, 73r–74r. As I have already noted, the tendency of the Court to increasingly assume cases like the ones above in which the grievances of communities were brought against their lords is borne out by the numbers from the second decade of the eighteenth century. However, and just as importantly, the outcomes of most of these cases assumed by the new Austrian Court were not actually decided for years, if not decades, making it difficult to assess the actual significance of the directives of the new Austrian regime for the Court's tactical employment—or neglect, for that matter—of its own technical prerogatives and, more significantly, for its provision of justice for the Kingdom's communities.

146. Although the jurisprudence of the Sacro Consiglio from this particular period remains understudied, from the manuscript volumes held in the Archivio di Stato di Napoli recording the sentences of the Sacro Consiglio it seems that there were decisions made *ex causis* in the first years of Austrian rule. ASN, SRC, *Sentenze,* vols. 252 and 253, as well as ASN, SRC, *Decreti,* vols. 523 and 534. On this

prerogative, also see Antonio Romano Columna, *De praestantia Sacri Regii Consilii* (Naples: Carlo Porsile, 1704), esp. 302.

147. *De ratione,* section 11: Gentile and Nicolini edit., 113; Gianturco edit., 70.

148. Especially see Salvo Mastellone, *Francesco D'Andrea politico e giurista* (Florence: Olschki, 1968), 117–37, and Imma Ascione, *Il governo della prassi: L'esperienza ministeriale di Francesco D'Andrea* (Naples: Jovene, 1994), 295–334.

149. The opinion was entitled: *Iura pro regio Fisco et Regno adversus pedagiorum seu passuum exactiones, quae exercentur a nonnullis Baronibus et Universitatibus eiusdem Regni.* It would later be published in a volume curated by Nicola Gaetano Ageta, *Annotationes pro regio aerario ad supremi regiae Camerae Summariae senatus Regni Neapolis decisiones* (Naples: Raillard, 1692; repr., Naples: Voccola, 1736).

150. *Autobiografia:* Croce and Nicolini edit., 33; Fisch and Bergin trans., 147.

151. Vidania's objection (dated 1709.IV.26) was printed by Vico in an appendix to his *De constantia iurisprudentis* (Naples: Mosca, 1721) and has been reprinted in *Epistole,* on pages 77–80 and, in modern Italian translation, on pages 241–44. Vico publicly replied to Vidania's objection in a footnote to *De universi iuris uno principio et fine uno* (Naples: Mosca, 1720), which has been reprinted in *Epistole,* on pages 80–82 and, in modern Italian translation, on pages 245–46.

152. Croce and Nicolini note these two reviews in their *Annotazioni* to *L'autobiografia,* in *Opere,* vol. 5, 2nd ed., 114.

153. The review of *De ratione* in the *Giornale de' letterati d'Italia* appeared in volume 1 (1710): 321–33. It has been reprinted in Vico, *Le orazioni inaugurali…e le polemiche,* ed. Gentile and Nicolini, in *Opere,* vol. 1, 281–86.

154. See Vico, *De antiquissima Italorum sapientia ex linguae latinae originibus eruenda* (Naples: Felice Mosca, 1710), reprinted in *Opere* and translated into English by L. M. Palmer as *On the Most Ancient Wisdom of the Italians* (Ithaca: Cornell University Press, 1988).

155. From his correspondence with Apostolo Zeno, it seems that Vico not only provided the *Giornale* with copies of *De antiquissima* for review, but also the reviewer, with whom he would so debate. See the letter by Vico to Apostolo Zeno published in *Epistole,* 83–84. The initial review of *De antiquissima* was published in the *Giornale* 5 (1711): 119–30, to which Vico (defensively) responded with his *Risposta del signore Giambattista di Vico nella quale si sciogliono tre gravi opposizioni fatte da dotto signore contro il primo libro* De antiquissima Italorum sapientia, *ovvero della metafisica degli antichissimi filosofi Italiani tratta da' latini parlari* (Naples: Felice Mosca, 1711). An article in response to Vico's defense was then published in the *Giornale* 8 (1711): 309–38. Vico again responded in kind with his *Risposta di Giambattista di Vico all'articolo X del tomo VIII del* Giornale de' letterati d'Italia (Naples: Felice Mosca, 1712).

156. This work was a commissioned biography of the life of Antonio Carafa, a Neapolitan nobleman who had served in the Habsburg army, and was published in Naples by Felice Mosca in 1716. According to Croce and Nicolini, this work was modeled on the *Vita di Andrea Cantelmo* by the Neapolitan scientist Lionardo Di Capua and reviewed by his university colleague D'Aulisio. See their *Annotazioni* to the *Autobiografia,* in *Opere,* vol. 5, 2nd ed., 114. In his autobiography, Vico relates that this commission led him to read and prepare an edition of *De iure belli,* which nonetheless remained unfinished. See *Autobiografia,* Croce and Nicolini edit., 39; Fisch and Bergin trans., 154–55.

Chapter 3

1. *Autobiografia:* Croce and Nicolini edit., 33; Fisch and Bergin trans., 146.

2. *Institutionum/ Oratoriarum/ Liber Unus/ exposuit/ Utriusque Juris Doctor Iohannes Baptista a Vico/ In almo Neapolitano Gymnasio/ Die 24 mensis Aprilis Anno/ 1711.* Manuscript conserved in BNN XIX.42.IV(1. For a description of this manuscript, see Giuliano Crifò, Introduction to Vico, *Institutiones oratoriae,* ed. Crifò, esp. LXXI, and *Bibliografia vichiana,* vol. 1, 111–12.

3. The popularity of Vico's lessons was noted in an untitled memo on proposed university reforms penned by Filippo Caravita, the consultore of the Cappellano Maggiore, on 29 September 1714. See BNN MS.XI.B.17, 282r–289v, and for mention of Vico in particular, 285v. More generally, on the university during this period and the controversy concerning its reform, see Ascione, *Seminarium doctrinarum,* 77–104, and Dario Luongo, ed., *All'alba dell'illuminismo* (Naples: Guida, 1997), esp. 9–75. In his appendix, Luongo has published the memo by Caravita on pages 107–29. For further evidence of the popularity of Vico's lessons and of a coterie of epigones around his persona, see the evidence marshaled by Croce in his *Bibliografia vichiana,* 1st ed. (Naples: Alfonso Tessitore e figlio, 1904), 86–91, and the observations of Fausto Nicolini in *Giambattista Vico nella vita domestica* (1927; repr., Venosa: Edizioni Osanna, 1991), 37–52.

4. Beyond numerous single pieces of poetry composed for the nuptials of leading members of the Neapolitan nobility, for the marriages of his private students Adriano Carafa and Giambattista Filomarino, Vico edited the following celebratory volumes of poetry: *Varii componimenti per le nozze degl'illustrissimi & eccellentissimi signori don Adriano Carafa duca di Traetto, conte del S.R.I., grande di Spagna &c., e donna Teresa Borghesi de' prencipi di Sulmona, di Rossano, &c.* (Naples: Felice Mosca, 1719) and *Varii componimenti per le nozze degli eccellentissimi signori don Giambattista Filomarino prencipe della Rocca &c., e donna Maria Vittoria Caracciolo de'marchesi di Sant'Eramo* (Naples: Felice Mosca, 1721), whose principal composition was Vico's own *Giunone in danza,* which rendered in verse his mythological theories. On these two volumes, see *Bibliografia vichiana,* vol. 1, 106–8.

5. For a list of the single poems, funerary eulogies, and inscriptions composed by Vico over this decade, see "Cronologia degli scritti di Giambattista Vico," in *Bibliografia vichiana,* vol. 1, 154–56.

6. The full citation is Giambattista Vico, *De rebus gestis Antonii Caraphaei libri quatuor, excellentissimo domino Hadriano Caraphaeo, Trajectinorum duci, Forolivensium domino XIII, Sacri Romani Imperii comiti, Hispaniarum magnati amplissimo, inscripti* (Naples: Felice Mosca, 1716). On this edition, see *Bibliografia vichiana,* vol. 1, 77–79. The modern critical edition of this work is Giambattista Vico, *Le gesta di Antonio Carafa,* ed. Manuela Sanna (Naples: Guida, 1997), which I will herewith use and cite as *De rebus gestis.*

7. *Autobiografia:* Croce and Nicolini edit., 38; Fisch and Bergin trans., 154.

8. Ibid.

9. On the domestic life of Vico, see Nicolini, *Giambattista Vico nella vita domestica,* esp. 27–35 and 57–61. For a portrait of the intellectual life of Luisa Vico, see Paula Findlen, "Translating the New Science: Women and the Circulation of Knowledge in Enlightenment Italy," *Configurations* 3, no. 2 (1995): 174–84.

10. *Autobiografia:* Croce and Nicolini edit., 38; Fisch and Bergin trans., 154.

11. Sanna, Introduzione to *De rebus gestis,* 18. For the announcement of *De rebus gestis* in the *Giornale de' letterati d'Italia,* see chapter two.

12. *De rebus gestis* is listed in the manuscript catalogue of books acquired from Riccardi's library by the emperor. See *Index / Librorum, qui ex Riccardiana Bibliotheca, et in Caesaream illati sunt.* ONB Handschriftensammlungen, Cod. 11927.

13. Tuck, *Natural Rights Theories,* 72–81.

14. Hugo Grotius, Prolegomena to *The Rights of War and Peace,* ed. Jean Barbeyrac, trans. John Morrice (London: D. Brown, 1738; repr., Indianapolis: Liberty Fund, 2005), bk. 1, xxvii and xxix. It is this edition that I herewith cite. For the Latin text, I am citing Hugo Grotius, *De iure belli ac pacis libri tres, in quibus ius naturae & gentium, item iuris publici praecipua explicantur* (Amsterdam: Johannes Blaeu, 1646), wherein the Prolegomena is unpaginated.

15. "Hugo Grotius," in Richard Tuck, *The Rights of War and Peace* (New York: Oxford University Press, 1999), 78–108.

16. "Hugo Grotius," in Tuck, *Philosophy and Government,* esp. 199.

17. The rhetoric Carafa employed was often belied by the content of his requests and actions. For example, Carafa's repeated and unusually cruel request for the head of Thököly was justified according to the Neapolitan by the Hungarian's perfidious breach of an international pact, one of the cardinal tenets of the law of nations. *De rebus gestis,* bk. 2, chap. 1, lines 150–200, and bk. 2, chap. 3, lines 1–50.

18. See the Melian Dialogue in Thucydides, *History of the Peloponnesian War,* bk. 5, 85–113.

19. *De rebus gestis,* bk. 2, chap. 7, lines 86–146.

20. Grotius, Prolegomena to *De iure belli ac pacis,* 11, which is known in the historiography as the *etiamsi daremus* passage. In my own comments, I am drawing on the treatment of this passage by Richard Tuck in his Introduction to the Liberty Fund edition of *The Rights of War and Peace,* esp. xxiii–xxiv.

21. On the preface to Vico's presumably lost edition of Grotius, see *Bibliografia vichiana,* vol. 1, 21. This manuscript most recently has been reprinted in Vico, *Varia,* ed. Giangaleazzo Visconti (Naples: Guida, 1996), 20–23. Although Vico cites Grotius with the greatest approval in this document, it is not self-evident that this was a preface to an edition of Grotius's magnum opus rather than intended for an original work.

22. Vico made mention of this project in *Autobiografia:* Croce and Nicolini edit., 39; Fisch and Bergin trans., 155. However, there is no record of Vico ever having undertaken the annotation of *De iure belli* beyond his own pronouncement. See "Commento a Grozio," in *Bibliografia vichiana,* vol. 1, 125–26.

23. At that time, Vico had reason to argue that he had been unfairly treated in the concorso of 1723. What is more, there is ample evidence that knowledge of Grotius was considered fashionable, if not valuable, in Naples in Vico's day. For instance, in 1714 there had indeed been talk by the rector of the University of Naples of establishing a chair in Ius Naturae et Gentium or Diritto Naturale e delle Genti, a chair to which Vico presumably would have aspired. See Ascione, *Seminarium doctrinarum,* 95. In 1717 the Chair of Civil Law became vacant, presenting a new, concrete opportunity for advancement within the university for Vico.

24. Around 1720 the Bibliotecca Brancacciana of Naples, the foremost public library of the city, already held three copies of *De iure belli* as well as a few examples

of Grotius's religious tracts. See *Inventario/ De' Libri/ Prohibiti/ Della/ Libraria/ Brancaccio* BNN MS II.G.14. From my consultation of manuscript library catalogues in Vienna, furthermore, it is evident that *De iure belli ac pacis* was also a standard holding in the eighteenth-century libraries of Habsburg statesmen. See *Index/In Catalogum Librorum Archiepiscopi de Valentia/ defuncti qui in Augustissimam Bibliothecam/ Caesaream traslati sunt.* ONB Handschriftensammlungen, Cod. 11899. Also see *Index/ Librorum, qui ex Riccardiana Bibliotheca, et in Caesaream illati sunt.* ONB Handschriftensammlungen, Cod. 11927.

25. J. M. De Bujanda and Marcella Richter, *Index Librorum Prohibitorum, 1600–1966* (Montreal: Médiaspaul, 2002).

26. Grotius, Prolegomena to *De iure belli ac pacis,* 11. Indeed, in Rome Gravina evidently had been careful to distinguish his own position on the role of God in relation to the existence of natural law from that of Grotius in *Origines iuris civilis* (Leipzig: Johannes Friedrich Gleditsch, 1708). See Antonio Sarubbi, Introduzione to Gianvincenzo Gravina, *Curia romana e Regno di Napoli* (Naples: Guida, 1972), xxix.

27. According to Fisch, the first part, "Part A," of the *Autobiografia* was drafted in late spring 1725. See Fisch and Bergin, Introduction to Vico, *Autobiography,* trans. Fisch and Bergin, 12–13.

28. *Autobiografia:* Croce and Nicolini edit., 39; Fisch and Bergin trans., 155.

29. At the same time, this remark betrays, I believe, just how common it was to read prohibited books in the Naples of Vico's day, and just how much stock certain contemporaries placed in their knowledge of prohibited books. Indeed, the correspondence between the Pontifical Ambassador to Naples and the Roman court makes plain that the circulation of prohibited books gave the Vatican ample cause for concern at that time. See, for example, the letter dated 18 June 1720 in SAV, Segr. Stato, Napoli, vol. 158, 585r–v, which complains of the "scandalous frankness with which prohibited books, and especially those of heretical authors, are introduced and sold in this city" by Neapolitan printers and booksellers. The recidivism of Neapolitan printers and booksellers, and the seeming disinterest of Neapolitan authorities in curbing the circulation of prohibited books in Naples, apparently lead the Vatican later in the 1730s to employ its ambassador in Vienna to exert pressure on the imperial court to intervene in the cultural politics of its southern Italian satellite. This is one of the themes running through the *Carteggio fra la Corte di Roma et il Sig. Card. Passionei…Sulle Materie appartenenti alla Religione et al Tribunale del S. Offitio del Regno di Napoli et di Sicilia* conserved in the ACDF, S.O., St. St. D2-d.

30. *Autobiografia:* Croce and Nicolini edit., 38–39; Fisch and Bergin trans., 154.

31. See Annotazioni to the *Autobiografia* in *Opere,* vol. 5, 2nd ed., 116, wherein Nicolini questions the truth of Vico's claims that the papal court approved of his work.

32. See Hobbes, *Leviathan,* part 2, chap. 17, "Of the Causes, Generation, and Definition of a Common-Wealth"; Locke, *Second Treatise on Government,* chap. 3, "Of the State of War"; and Pufendorf, *On the Duty of Man and Citizen,* bk. 2, chap. 5, "On the Impulsive Cause of Constituting the State."

33. Grotius, *De iure belli,* trans. Morrice, bk. 3, chap. 7, para. I.1–2.

34. For an overview of the Renaissance literature on the city, see Viroli, *From Politics to Reason of State* and Pietro Costa, *Civitas: Storia della cittadinanza in Europa,* vol. 1 (Rome: Laterza, 1999), esp. chap. 1. A classic example of the attribution of

"freedom" to the city is that by Leonardo Bruni in his *Panegyric on Florence,* which was identified by Hans Baron as the quintessential example of how republican Italy understood itself. See Hans Baron, *The Crisis of the Early Italian Renaissance,* rev. ed. (Princeton: Princeton University Press, 1966). Baron's thesis spurred a famous debate, which was initiated by an article by Jerrold Siegel, entitled "'Civic Humanism' or Ciceronian Rhetoric? The Culture of Petrarch and Bruni," *Past and Present* 34 (1966): 3–48. More recently, see James Hankins, "The Baron Thesis after Forty Years and Some Recent Studies of Leonardo Bruni" *Journal of the History of Ideas* 56, no. 2 (1995): 309–38.

35. I am thinking here of Rousseau's celebrated criticism of Grotius in *The Social Contract,* chap. 4, "On Slavery," where Rousseau most eloquently derides the Grotian idea that one could alienate one's liberty without renouncing one's very humanity. In light of Rousseau's eloquence, it bears mentioning that Vico did not anticipate this critique with the rhetorical invective and literary genius of a Rousseau, but rather simply showed with his history that people naturally fought to recover what was proper to themselves, including their self-possession, or humanity.

36. In particular, see Stein, "Equitable Principles in Roman Law," 25.

37. For a broader account of the meaning and associations with natural law that includes the concept of the *lex naturalis,* see Jan Schroder, "The Concept of Natural Law in the Doctrine of Law and Natural Law of the Early Modern Era," in *Natural Laws and Laws of Nature in Early Modern Europe,* ed. Lorraine Daston and Michael Stolleis (Burlington, VT: Ashgate, 2008).

38. This notion resounds throughout the republican texts of the Renaissance. In particular, see Machiavelli's *Discourses on Livy.*

39. Hobbes had defined "liberty" as the "absence of externall Impediments." I am quoting from Hobbes, *Leviathan,* part 1, chap. 14, p. 91. Similarly, Locke had defined "liberty" as the power "to [freely] dispose of his Person or Possessions." However, for Locke the exercise of that power was limited to the "state of nature," wherein the laws of nature, or reason, prohibited "harm [to] another in his Life, Liberty, Health, or Possessions." I am quoting from John Locke, *The Two Treatises on Government,* a critical edition by Peter Laslett, second treatise, chap. 2, para. 6 (New York: Cambridge University Press, 1960; New American Library, 1965), 311. I herewith cite this edition. For a lengthier discussion of the idea of "liberty," see Skinner, *Liberty before Liberalism.*

40. Vico's notion of property as a natural right had an important modern precedent, namely, that of Locke in *The Second Treatise on Government,* chap. 5: "On Property," esp. para. 27. The history of the theme of self-possession in the natural law tradition has been treated by Brian Tierney in "Dominion of Self and Natural Rights before Locke and After" in *Transformations in Medieval and Early-Modern Rights Discourse,* ed. Virpi Maekinen and Petter Korkman (Netherlands: Springer Verlag, 2006): 173–203.

41. For my discussion of legal personality I particularly am drawing on Schulz, *Classical Roman Law,* 71–202; Nicholas, *Introduction to Roman Law,* 60–97; and H. F. Jolowicz, *Roman Foundations of Modern Law* (Oxford: Clarendon Press, 1957), 107–26.

42. Lilla, *Vico,* 108. Throughout his work, Lilla argued that Vico's science accorded a central role to divine volition.

43. Ibid., esp. 59 and 72–73.

44. Ibid., 36.

45. For classic assessments of the Council of Trent for Catholic theology and, in particular, the importance of the assent of the free will to God's grace, see the concise overview by John C. Olin, *Catholic Reform: From Cardinal Ximenes to the Council of Trent* (New York: Fordham University Press, 1990), esp. 28–29, and the classic study by Hubert Jedin, *A History of the Council of Trent,* 2 vols. (St. Louis: B. Herder, 1957–61).

46. Ascione, *Seminarium doctrinarum,* 113–14.

47. The list of candidates who had registered for the competition for the Morning Chair of Civil Law by the first date of its official closure is conserved in ASN, Coll., Con., Affari Diversi, Prima Serie (IV 37), no. 68, unpaginated; it is dated 12 February 1723 and signed by Vidania. More generally, the documents concerning the procedure of the competition for the Morning Chair of Civil Law as well as the profiles of the candidates and the assessment of them are contained in ASN, Cappellano Maggiore, Affari Diversi, 718 III, 272r–273r; 313r–v, and 321r–327r. Henceforth the papers of the Cappellano Maggiore will be cited as C.M. My own history of the competition cites and discusses these documents. To my knowledge, these documents were first referred to by Croce in the first edition (1904) of his *Bibliografia vichiana,* 83–84, where he noted a few of the more pertinent facts about the concorso of 1723 without citing his sources; and they were discussed at some further length in his article on "I due concorsi universitari di G. B. Vico," *La critica* 6 (1908), 306–8. More recently, they have also been studied by Imma Ascione in her *Seminarium doctrinarum,* 115–31. In one of my many attempts to find documentation about Vico's life noted but not cited by Croce and Nicolini, I found these documents in the ASN without prior knowledge of Ascione's excellent study, with which my conclusions largely concur.

48. For Vico's own account of the 1719 oration, see *Autobiografia:* Croce and Nicolini edit., 40; Fisch and Bergin trans., 156. The text of this oration is no longer extant. See *Bibliografia vichiana,* vol. 1, 126–27. It seems that this oration presented the argument of the *Diritto universale.* See Vico, De opera proloquium to *De universi iuris uno principio et fine uno,* in his *Opere giuridiche: Il diritto universale,* ed. Paolo Cristofolini (Florence: Sansoni, 1974), where Vico seems to acknowledge that oration and paraphrase it for his own prologue, as Croce and Nicolini had indicated in the *Bibliografia vichiana.* There are a few fragmentary English translations and one full one of the *Diritto universale.* Herewith, for the convenience of an anglophone audience, I will also cite the full English translation of the *Diritto universale* alongside that of the Italian edition by Cristofolini cited above, which remains the standard one for scholars. In English, see Vico, Prologue to *The One Principle and the One End of Universal Right,* in Giambattista Vico, *Universal Right,* ed. and trans. Giorgio Pinton and Margaret Diehl (Amsterdam: Rodopi, 2000), 3. Henceforth, this first volume of the *Diritto universale* will be cited as *De uno.* It bears mentioning here that the Cristofolini edition contains both the original-language text and its modern Italian translation side by side.

49. Vico, De opera proloquium (Prologue) to *De uno:* Cristofolini edit., 21; Pinton edit., 3. If his representation is faithful, it further seems that Vico himself had gone to solicit Ventura's opinion of his work in the privacy of Ventura's home, which Vico further claimed he often frequented to enjoy the learned conversation so brilliantly

moderated by the young jurist. There is little known information regarding the salon hosted by Ventura. In his own autobiography Giannone noted that Ventura's uncle, Gaetano Argento, had hosted a vibrant salon in his home dedicated to the study and debate of jurisprudence, the Accademia dei Saggi, which followed the procedure of the Sacro Regio Consiglio. See Pietro Giannone, *La vita di Pietro Giannone,* vol. 1, ed. Sergio Bertelli (Turin: Einaudi, 1977), 42–43.

50. On this interim period of rule by the Collaterale, see Heinrich Benedikt, *Das Koenigreich Neapel unter Kaiser Karl VI* (Vienna: Manz Verlag, 1927), 208–11.

51. Much ink has been spilled over what has been called "jurisdictionalism," or regalism, in the Kingdom of Naples. For a recent contribution to Gaetano Argento's role in jurisdictionalism, see Luongo, *Vis jurisprudentiae,* 5–155.

52. Benedikt, *Koenigreich Neapel,* 208–11.

53. On Ventura see *Orazione di Frate Felice Maria di Napoli…*(Naples: Stamperia Simoniana, 1760) and "Francesco Ventura," in Giustiniani, *Memorie storiche.*

54. On the Banco di San Carlo, see Rafaelle Ajello, "Il Banco di San Carlo: Organi di governo e opinione pubblica nel Regno di Napoli di fronte al problema della ricompra dei diritti fiscali," *RSI* 81 (1969): 812–81. Also see on the same Giuseppe Ricuperati, *L'esperienza civile e religiosa di Pietro Giannone* (Milan: Riccardo Ricciardi, 1970), 293–309.

55. For a very fine overview of the creation and competencies of this tribunal, see Anna Maria Rao, *Il Regno di Napoli nel Settecento* (Naples: Guida, 1983), 71–77.

56. Evidence for Argento's invocation of the law of nations in his opinions and decisional literature is ample. For example, see Luongo, *Vis jurisprudentiae,* 242–50 and 347–48.

57. The *Sinopsi* has been reprinted in Vico, *Opere giuridiche,* ed. Cristofolini, and in Vico, *Universal Right,* ed. and trans. Pinton and Diehl.

58. Letter from Vico to Bernardo Maria Giacco dated 14 July 1720 in *Epistole,* 86–87.

59. *Autobiografia:* Croce and Nicolini edit., 41; Fisch and Bergin trans., 157.

60. Annotazioni to the *Autobiografia,* in *Opere,* vol. 5, 2nd ed., 117.

61. Letter from E. Enriquez to Matteo Egizio dated 19 April 1720 in BNN MS XIII.C.91(15. This letter is partially reproduced in Salvatore Ussia, *L'epistolario di Matteo Egizio e la cultura napoletana del primo Settecento* (Naples: Liguori, 1977), 58. I am drawing on Ussia's interpretation of this letter, which identifies the *Sinopsi* as the textual occasion for the scandalous division between Egizio and Vico therein recounted. In the end, it seems that Egizio and Vico did make amends to each other, however. See: Letter from Vico to Matteo Egizio, dated 1720, in *Epistole,* 90, in which Vico most respectfully thanks Egizio for his gift of desserts, themselves presumably a sign of Egizio's recognition of his receipt of *De Uno.*

62. That Giannone disapproved of the *Sinopsi* seems likely, if only because Vico's antiquarianism, as received, ostensibly served a political purpose that was antithetical to Giannone's own. Moreover, the historiography on the period has underscored the poor relations between Giannone and Vico. For instance, Giuseppe Ricuperati has noted that from exile Giannone took it upon himself to criticize, if not defame, Vico's work from his influential position in the court in Vienna. See Giuseppe Ricuperati, *La città terrena di Pietro Giannone* (Florence: Olschki, 2001), 19. Specific examples of that criticism can be found in *Bibliografia vichiana,* vol. 1, 193–94. At the

same time, there is evidence that Giannone and Vico had once admired each other and that the former's animosity toward the latter had been acquired over time. See the verse by Gherardo degli Angioli: "Or tua scorta saranno i brievi e chiari/ .../ di Niccolò de' Caravita arringhi,/ e del Giannon, cui solo Vico udiva./ Sol del Giannon lodar non vo' gl'insani/ modi ond'è la sua dotta istoria offende." (And now your guide will be the brief and clear/ .../ legal addresses of Nicola Caravita/ and of Giannone, to whom only Vico listened./ Of Giannone I only don't want to praise the strange expressions,/ with which he offends his learned history.) Cited in *Minora,* 24. What is more, from the correspondence of Giannone (that Nicolini himself cites in the *Bibliografia vichiana*) it is also evident that the two had held among their closest associates and friends in Naples the same jurists, namely, Francesco Ventura and Muzio di Maio. SNSP XXXI.B.4, vol. 1.

63. Letter from Apostolo Zeno to Pier Caterino Zeno dated Vienna, 27 July 1720, printed in Apostolo Zeno, *Lettere di Apostolo Zeno,* vol. 3, 2nd ed. (Venice: Francesco Sansoni, 1785).

64. For an overview of both the civil and ecclesiastical laws governing the publishing industry at this time in the Kingdom of Naples, see G. M. Monti, "Legislazione statale ed ecclesiastica sulla stampa nel Viceregno austriaco di Napoli," in *Scritti giuridici in onore di Santi Romano* (Padua: Cedam, 1940). The new civil legislation introduced for the better governance of the publishing industry during this period was discussed in Gregorio Grimaldi and Ginesio Grimaldi, *Istoria delle leggi e magistrati del Regno di Napoli,* vol. 11 (Naples: Stamperia de G. di Simone, 1749–74), esp. 264 and 276. The best study of the civil procedures governing the publication of books in the eighteenth-century Kingdom remains Carolina Belli, "I fondi archivistici napoletani e la storia di librai, stampatori e biblioteche," in *Editoria e cultura a Napoli nel XVIII secolo,* ed. Anna Maria Rao (Naples: Liguori, 1998), 829–50. For an introduction to the ecclesiastical procedures governing the publication of books in the early modern Kingdom, see Pasquale Lopez, *Inquisizione, stampa e censura nel Regno di Napoli tra '500 e '600* (Naples: Edizioni del Delfino, 1974). More generally, on the Roman Index and its peripheral Italian collaborators, see Gigliola Fragnito, "The Central and Peripheral Organization of Censorship," in *Church, Censorship, and Culture in Early Modern Italy,* ed. Gigliola Fragnito (New York: Cambridge University Press, 2001), 13–49.

65. It seems that Vico proceeded normatively. From the sample of books published in Naples circa 1720 that I have studied, it evidently was customary in the contemporary Kingdom to request the ecclesiastical imprimatur first. (Indeed, I have to date found only one example circa 1720 where that was not the case.) What is more, the civil authorities of the Kingdom had long maintained that the ecclesiastical approval of texts was subordinate to that of the Collaterale, which was normally approached only after a text already had been approved by an ecclesiastical censor, and which periodically insisted on its right to reject works deemed publishable by the Curia. This tension between the civil and ecclesiastical authorities of the Kingdom regarding their respective jurisdiction over the licensing of publications is a theme that runs throughout Lopez, *Inquisizione, stampa e censura.* At the time the vicar of the Curia of the Archbishop was Onofrio Montesoro, Bishop of Castellaneta, who when publicly challenged proved Draconian: in 1723, he would have both the printer and author of the *Istoria civile* excommunicated for not having sought his imprimatur. See Giannone, *La vita di Pietro Giannone,* vol. 1, ed. Bertelli, 75–76.

66. Both the reports of the ecclesiastical and civil censors as well as the ecclesiastical imprimatur and civil license are contained in the front matter of the first edition of *De Uno.* See Vico, *De universi iuris uno principio, et fine uno liber unus* (Naples: Felice Mosca, 1720). In this paragraph, I am drawing on the information provided by these reports and imprimaturs to reconstruct the publication history. Interestingly, Vico's ecclesiastical censor, Giulio Nicola Torno, proved to be one of Giannone's most ardent critics within the Neapolitan Church. See Ricuperati, *L'esperienza civile e religiosa,* 228.

67. *Sinopsi:* Cristofolini edit., 5; Pinton trans., lxi. Because further evidence regarding the drafting and completion of *De constantia* is wanting, it is difficult to assess the veracity of Vico's claim that he submitted both volumes to Mosca in March 1720, although it seems unlikely.

68. Again, this procedure conforms to that outlined by Belli in "I fondi archivistici napoletani e la storia di librai, stampatori e biblioteche," esp. 831. The experience of Giannone provides further evidence of how this concretely worked. See Giannone, *La vita di Pietro Giannone,* vol. 1, ed. Bertelli, 68–70.

69. My own work with the papers of the Secretary of the Viceroy, the Chancellery of the Consiglio Collaterale, and the Cappellano Maggiore from the year 1720 conserved in the ASN has not identified any indications regarding the civil censorship of *De uno.*

70. Letter from Apostolo Zeno to Pier Caterino Zeno dated Vienna, 24 August 1720, printed in Zeno, *Lettere di Apostolo Zeno,* vol. 3, no. 517. Therein, Apostolo wrote: "Che il Sig. di Vico ha incontrata difficoltà nel proseguimento della stampa del suo libro: perchè il P. de Miro, Presidente oggi de' Casinesi, ha ricusato di approvarla, dichiarandola affatto contraria alle sue idee: che l'uno, e l'altro abboccatosi insieme ultimamente si partirono scambievolmente amareggiati:... che ora il Vico fa istanza che gli sia assegnato un altro revisore." ([That] Mr. Vico has encountered difficulty in the process of publishing his book, because the Padre de Miro, currently President of the Benedictine Order, has refused to approve its publication, declaring the [publication of the] work entirely contrary to his ideas, so that when they last met they both departed embittered... and [that] now Vico has appealed for another reviewer.)

71. *Bibliografia vichiana,* vol. 1, 186–87.

72. Pinton, Introduction to Vico, *The One Principle and the One End of Universal Right,* in *Universal Right,* ed. and trans. Pinton and Diehl, xxvii.

73. For my biography of De Miro here and immediately below, I am drawing on: "Joannes Baptista de Miro," in Mariano Armellini, *Bibliotheca Benedictino[-]Casinensis...* (Assisi: Feliciani, & P. Campitelli, 1731), 27–31. I am indebted to Prof. Elena Bonora for this reference. From the documentation in the ASN it is clear that Vincenzo De Miro was a regent of the Collaterale in the second decade of the eighteenth century. However, his career would shortly take him to Austrian Lombardy. His activities there have been noted by Domenico Sella and Carlo Capra, *Il Ducato di Milano* (Turin: Utet, 1984), 217.

74. For the de Miro review of Gravina's monumental legal work, see, for example, the Neapolitan edition entitled the *Originum iuris civilis libri tres* published by Felice Mosca in 1713.

75. See "Joannes Baptista de Miro," in *Bibliotheca Benedictino[-]Casinensis...,* 28. I have found the nomination (dated 4 April 1696) of De Miro to the office of

qualificatore for the Congregation of the Roman Inquisition in ACDF, Priv. S.O., 1669–99, 838.

76. There is no entry for Vico in the ACDF catalogue of authors discussed by the Congregation of the Index, namely, ACDF, S.C. Indicis/ Schedulae/ Nominum Auctorum. More important, mention of Vico's *De uno* does not appear in the Protocol of the Congregation of the Index from the first few years immediately following its publication. ACDF, Indice, Protocolli, DDDD through FFFF.

77. Similarly, there is no entry for *De uno* in the ACDF catalogue of books reviewed by the Congregation of the Inquisition, namely, ACDF, Rubricella, C.L., 1570–1850. What is more, mention of Vico's *De uno* appears in neither the archive of the Roman Inquisition conserving requests for the licensing of books, the Tituli Librorum, nor in the one conserving the reports of its final decisions, the Censura Librorum. I have partially consulted ACDF, S.O., Tituli Librorum, 1710–21 and 1722–28, and ACDF, S.O., Censura Librorum, 1718–21.

78. According to the ACDF catalogue entitled S.C. Indicis/ Schedulae/ Nominum Auctorum, the collaboration of De Miro with the Congregation of the Inquisition as a *qualificatore* was limited to a single review from 1697 and conserved in ACDF, S.O., Censura Librorum, 1690–1714. What is more, Nicolini has claimed that this same De Miro kept the company of "anti-ecclesiastics" in Naples. "Gaetano Argento," in Fausto Nicolini, *Uomini di spada di chiesa di toga di studio ai tempi di Giambattista Vico* (1942; repr., Bologna: Il Mulino, 1992), 336. While the veracity of this assertion is hard to assess, from the correspondence of Giannone conserved in the SNSP it does seem that after his excommunication Giannone counted De Miro among his most sympathetic friends in Naples. See the copy of the letter by Pietro Giannone written from Vienna and dated 14 August 1723, conserved in the SNSP XXXI.B.4, vol. 1., 113r.

79. At the time, the Archbishop of Naples was Cardinal Francesco Pignatelli (from 1703), who was a high-ranking patrician, the nephew of Pope Innocent XII (reigned 1691–1700), and, not surprisingly, known for the stubborn independence with which he exercised the stewardship of his see.

80. While further research on this decade is necessary to clarify what was normative procedure for the various Italian states, it is clear from the works I have found in the Tituli Librorum that the Neapolitan Curia did not defer its authority to the Congregation of the Inquisition, unlike other Italian localities. ACDF, S.O., Tituli Librorum, 1710–21 and 1722–28. Nor does the catalogue of books reviewed by the Congregation of the Inquisition—the ACDF, Rubricella, C.L., 1570–1850—list books reportedly published in Naples around 1720. However, the list of the above-cited ACDF catalogue must be checked against the actual contents of the ACDF, S.O., Censura Librorum, 1718–21 to draw harder and faster conclusions about the demonstrable investigation of Neapolitan books circa 1720 by the Inquisition.

81. On the autonomy of the Neapolitan Inquisition, see the classic Luigi Amabile, *Il Santo Officio della Inquisizione in Napoli,* 2 vols. (Città di Castello: S. Lapi, 1892).

82. This is evidenced by the list of Neapolitan books censored by the Roman Index and the dates of their prohibition provided by Eugenio Di Rienzo and Maria Formica in their article "Tra Napoli e Roma: Censura e commercio librario," in *Editoria e cultura a Napoli,* ed. Rao. Interestingly, the prohibition of Neapolitan books usually occurred in clusters and at times of conflict; and among the titles prohibited

were often works that had been published several years earlier. In this context, it is perhaps interesting to note that the dear friend of Vico, Biagio Garofalo, had found his *Considerazioni intorno alle poesia degli Ebrei e dei Greci* (1707) discussed by the Index and then prohibited by its decree issued on 7 February 1718. ACDF, Indice, Protocolli, DDDD, 55r; 61r and ff; 212r and ff; 368. It bears mentioning that this same work originally had been published with the ecclesiastical imprimatur.

83. Torno's office is recorded in the "Registro de' Ministri del Tribunale del S. Officio della Curia Arcivescovile di Napoli dal tempo dell' Em.mo Cardinale Filomarino sin al tempo dell' Em.mo Cardinal Francesco Pignatelli" in ACDF, S.O., St. St., Inquisizione di Napoli, HH 2B, 72v. And it is confirmed by the list of ministers of the Tribunal of the Neapolitan Inquisition conserved in the ASDN, Fondo Sant'Ufficio, Processi, uninventoried. This second document has been published by Luciano Osbat in his "Il Sant'Ufficio nella Napoli di Giannone," in *Pietro Giannone e il suo tempo,* vol. 2, ed. Raffaele Ajello (Naples: Jovene, 1980), 635–58.

84. It is possible that Torno influenced Vico's revision of the second edition of the *Scienza nuova* (1730), as David Armando has noted in his "Vico, Giambattista" for the *Dizionario dell'Inquisizione,* ed. Adriano Prosperi (Pisa: Edizioni della Scuola Normale, 2010).

85. Based on my study of books published in Naples around 1720, it is clear that a large number of the books published with licenses were authored by members of the university professoriate.

86. This episode has been recounted in Girolamo De Miranda, "*Nihil decisum fuit.* Il Sant'Ufficio e la *Scienza nuova* di Vico: Un'irrealizzata edizione patavina tra l'imprimatur del 1725 e quello del 1730," *Bollettino del Centro di Studi Vichiani* 28–29 (1998–99): 5–69; and among works by Gustavo Costa, "Vico e l'Inquisizione," *Nouvelles de la République des Lettres* 2 (1999), 93–124; "Ancora su Vico," *Giornale critico della filosofia italiana* 79, no. 1 (2000); "Vico e la Sacra Scrittura alla luce di un fascicolo dell'Inquisizione," in *Pensar para el nuevo siglo: Giambattista Vico e la cultura europea,* ed. Emilio Hidalgo-Serna et al. (Naples: La Città del Sole, 2001).

87. Giannone would print precisely one thousand copies of his *Istoria civile* in 1723. See Giannone, *La vita di Pietro Giannone,* vol. 1, ed. Bertelli, 70. Vico would do the same for the first edition of the *Scienza nuova.* See "De Uno," in *Bibliografia vichiana,* vol. 1, 24–25.

88. Again, Giannone speaks of how he distributed copies of the *Istoria civile* among the regents of the Collaterale and heads of the tribunals, "to whom they were due," as he put it. Giannone, *La vita di Pietro Giannone,* vol. 1, ed. Bertelli, 70.

89. Letter from Vico to Bernardo Maria Giacco dated 12 October 1720, in *Epistole,* 88.

90. This dictum is inscribed on the inside of the cover of the copy of *De uno* conserved in the Department of Rari e Manoscritti in the BNN with the call number XX.E.18.

91. Letter from Vico to Bernardo Maria Giacco dated 12 October 1720, in *Epistole,* 88–90.

92. Ibid., 89.

93. As a point of comparison, it is interesting to note that the application process for the imprimatur and license of the first edition of the *Scienza nuova* took about four months.

94. Both the reports of the ecclesiastical and civil censors as well as the ecclesiastical imprimatur and civil license are contained in the front matter of the first edition of *De constantia.* See Giambattista Vico, *De constantia iurisprudentis* (Naples: Felice Mosca, 1721). In this paragraph, I am drawing on the information provided by these reports and imprimaturs to reconstruct the history of the publication.

95. According to the front matter of *De constantia,* the Curia had submitted that volume to its censor, Giulio Nicola Torno, on 18 February 1721, and then released the imprimatur for it on 22 August 1721, although the report by Torno himself would be dated 13 September 1721. This dating is extremely curious, as the approval of the Curia theoretically hinged on the report by Torno. Indeed, the imprimatur itself reads: "Attenta supradicta relatione D. Revisoris, quod potest imprimi, imprimatur." (According to the above cited report of the reviewer, this can be printed, may it be printed.) Similarly, the Consiglio Collaterale submitted *De constantia* to its censor, Nicola Galizia, on 18 August 1721, and released the license for it on 27 August 1721, although the report by Galizia would be dated 10 September 1721. At the very least, it is evident that there was reason for Vico and Mosca to present the granting of the imprimaturs for *De constantia* as decisions that effectively had been taken by the higher authorities themselves, rather than their individual censors.

96. Letter from Vico to Bernardo Maria Giacco dated 9 September 1721, in *Epistole,* 94.

97. Among the sample of books published in Naples around 1720 that I have studied to date, the only other work with an imprimatur predating the alleged date of its reviewer's report was a religious work that was also exceptional for having not only requested but also received its ecclesiastical imprimatur first. Interestingly, it was also published by Felice Mosca. See Sebastiano Paoli, *De ritu ecclesiae Neritanae exorcizandi aquam in Epiphania dissertatio* (Naples: Felice Mosca, 1719).

98. See "Clarissimorum virorum censurae extra ordinem," in Giambattista Vico, *De constantia iurisprudentis* (Naples: Felice Mosca, 1721), 242–60. This appendix has been reprinted in an abbreviated form in Vico, *Universal Right,* ed. Pinton, 533–35.

99. Letter from Vico to Bernardo Maria Giacco dated 27 October 1721, in *Epistole,* 99.

100. Letter from Anton Maria Salvini to Marchese Rinuccini dated 3 December 1720, in *Opere,* vol. 5, 2nd ed., 156. Also see Vico's most interesting comments on the reception of *De uno* by Salvini in *Autobiografia:* Croce and Nicolini edit., 41; Fisch and Bergin trans., 157.

101. Letter from Tommaso Maria Minorelli to Vico dated 27 September 1721, in *Epistole,* 96.

102. Letter from Biagio Garofalo to Vico dated 13 September 1721, in *Epistole,* 94–95, in which Garofalo acknowledges receipt of *De constantia.* More important, see: Letter from Vico to Eugene von Savoy dated 25 July 1722, in SAW, Grosse Korrespondenz, 148 a, 183r–v, no. 24, in which Vico acknowledges learning from Garofalo that Eugene happily has received and placed within his grand library Vico's legal treatise. This letter has been reprinted in *Epistole,* 101. Although Garofalo's letter to Vico is now lost, my research in the SAW has uncovered a reference to a letter from Eugene to Garofalo (dated 20 May 1722) commanding the latter to thank Vico for the gift of the *Diritto universale.* Thus, Vico must have involved Garofalo in the placement of his treatise in Vienna not long after he first had sent Biagio a copy of *De*

constantia. See: Letter from Biagio Garofalo to Eugene von Savoy dated Rome, 6 June 1722, in SAW, Grosse Korrespondenz, 86b, 173r. According to my own research in the ONB, it seems that both *De uno* and *De constantia* were sent to Eugene and included in his collection of books. Today they are conserved in the Prunksaal of the ONB, where they bear the call nos. BE.8.M.9 and MF 7158.

103. Letter from Vico to Jean Le Clerc dated 9 January 1722, in *Epistole*, 100–101.

104. Letter from Jean Le Clerc to Vico dated 8 September 1722, in *Epistole*, 102; 246–47 (modern translation).

105. *Autobiografia:* Croce and Nicolini edit., 47–48; Fisch and Bergin trans., 164–65.

106. Le Clerc did indeed review both *De uno* and *De constantia* in "Article VIII" of the *Bibliothèque ancienne et moderne* (Amsterdam: Frères Wetstein, 1722) vol. 18, part 2, 417–33.

107. *Autobiografia:* Croce and Nicolini edit., 47–48; Fisch and Bergin trans., 164–65.

108. Le Clerc, in "Article VIII" of the *Bibliothèque ancienne et moderne,* vol. 18, part 2, 430, 432.

109. Le Clerc, in "Article VIII" of the *Bibliothèque ancienne et moderne,* vol. 18, part 2, 424.

110. For a longer and more detailed treatment of the relationship between Vico and Le Clerc, see Mario Sini, *Vico e Le Clerc, tra filosofia e filologia* (Naples: Guida, 1978).

111. On Eugene's interest in radical religious ideas in The Hague, see Margaret C. Jacob, *The Radical Enlightenment* (London: Allen & Unwin, 1981), 224–32. On the radicalism of the Italian circle in Vienna and its relationship to Eugene, see Ricuperati, *L'esperienza civile e religiosa,* esp. chap. 6, 408–9. Indeed, in his autobiography Giannone speaks about his warm reception by Eugene in Vienna and the circle of intellectuals that he patronized. See Giannone, *La vita di Pietro Giannone,* vol. 1, ed. Bertelli, 102, 121, and 126–30.

112. Letter from Eugene to Vico dated 29 August 1724, in *Epistole,* 108.

113. Letter from Althann to Eugene von Savoy dated 18 December 1719, in SAW, Grosse Korrespondenz, 75a, 333r.

114. According to Ricuperati, Eugene advocated the removal of Althann from the office of viceroy of the Kingdom of Naples. Ricuperati, *L'esperienza civile e religiosa,* 277.

115. Letter from Aniello Spagnuolo to Vico dated 15 August 1721, in *Epistole,* 92–93.

116. Ibid., 92.

117. Ibid., 93.

118. Ibid.

119. See Grotius, Prolegomena to *De iure belli ac pacis,* 11, which again is known in the historiography as the *etiamsi daremus* passage, and Hobbes, *Leviathan,* esp. part 1, chap. 12, entitled "On Religion."

120. Letter from Giovanni Chiaiese to Nicola Geremia dated 13 August 1721, in *Opere,* vol. 5, 2nd ed., 162–69; also translated from the Latin into English by Elio Gianturco and printed in *Forum Italicum* 2, no. 4 (December 1968): 315–25.

121. Cicero, *De legibus,* Loeb Classical Library, I.v.17. (Keyes trans.)

122. Seneca quoted in: Letter from Giovanni Chiaiese to Nicola Geremia dated 13 August 1721, in *Opere,* vol. 5, 2nd ed.,163, and in English trans. by Gianturco in *Forum Italicum* 2, no. 4 (December 1968): 316–17. My translation of the Seneca is taken from the Loeb edition. See Seneca, "De otio," in his *Moral Essays,* vol. 2, Loeb Classical Library, IV.1. For further discussion of Seneca's cosmopolitanism and this quote in particular, see chapter 2.

123. See Keimpe Algra on "Stoic Theology," in Inwood, *Cambridge Companion to the Stoics,* 153–78, esp. 167.

124. I am paraphrasing and interpreting the quote presumably taken from the *Astronomica* by Manilius in: Letter from Giovanni Chiaiese to Nicola Geremia dated 13 August 1721, in *Opere,* vol. 5, 2nd ed., 163, and in English trans. by Gianturco in *Forum Italicum* vol. 2, no. 4 (December 1968): 317. In Latin, the quote reads: "Nec quicquam in tanta magis est admirabile mole,/ Quam ratio et certis quod legibus omnia parent." In early modern Europe, the *Astronomica* was most famously edited by Joseph Scaliger. See Anthony Grafton, *Joseph Scaliger: A Study in the History of Classical Scholarship* (Oxford: Clarendon Press, 1983), 180–226.

125. Ibid. Compare Cicero, *De republica,* Loeb Classical Library, VI.xxiv.26 through VI.xxvi.29.

126. See Keimpe Algra on "Stoic Theology," in Inwood, *Cambridge Companion to the Stoics,* 165–70, esp. 167.

127. In this paragraph, I am drawing on Dorothea Frede, "Stoic Determinism," in Inwood, *Cambridge Companion to the Stoics,* 179–205, esp. 192. For the documents of and commentary on the Stoic notions of causation, fate, and moral responsibility, see Long and Sedley, *Hellenistic Philosophers,* vol. 1, 333–43, and 386–94.

128. White, "Stoic Natural Philosophy," in Inwood, *Cambridge Companion to the Stoics,* 124–52, esp. 138. For evidence of this view, see "Zeno," in Diogenes Laertius, *Lives of Eminent Philosophers,* 7.134–36, cited in Long and Sedley, *Hellenistic Philosophers,* vol. 1, 268 and 275: "They [the Stoics] think that there are two principles of the universe, that which acts and that which is acted upon. That which is acted upon is unqualified substance, i.e., matter; that which acts is the reason [*logos*] in it, i.e., god.[268]...God, intelligence, fate and Zeus are all one.[275]" (Long and Sedley trans.) For further evidence of this view, also see the letter by Seneca, the great Roman popularizer of Hellenic Stoicism, in which he pithily explains: "Our Stoic philosophers, as you know, declare that there are two things in the universe which are the source of everything—namely, cause and matter. Matter lies sluggish, a substance ready for any use, but sure to remain unemployed if no one sets it in motion. Cause, however, by which we mean reason, moulds matter and turns it in whatever direction it will, producing thereby various concrete results.[65.2]...Do we ask what cause is? It is surely Creative Reason—in other words, God.[65.12]" Seneca, *Epistles,* trans. Richard M. Gummere, vol. 1, Loeb Classical Library (1917; repr., Cambridge, MA: Harvard University Press, 2006), letter 65.2 and 65.12. (Gummere trans.)

129. As Eusebius, bishop and historian of the Church in the late antique period, had reconstructed Stoic cosmogony in his *Evangelical Preparations:* "(1) At certain fated times the entire world is subject to conflagration, and then is reconstituted afresh. (2) But the primary fire is as it were a sperm which possesses the principles [*logoi*] of all things and the causes of past, present, and future events. The nexus and

succession of these is fate, knowledge, truth, and an inevitable and inescapable law of what exists. (3) In this way everything in the world is excellently organized as in a perfectly ordered society." This is the citation of Aristocles in Eusebius, *Evangelical Preparation* 15.14.2, which I am quoting from Long and Sedley, *Hellenistic Philosophers,* vol. 1, 276. For further evidence of necessitarianism, also see the citation of the Stoic Quintus Cicero in Cicero, *On Divination* 1.125–26, cited in Long and Sedley, *Hellenistic Philosophers,* vol. 1, 337: "Consequently, nothing has happened which was not going to be, and likewise nothing is going to be of which nature does not contain causes working to bring that very thing about." (Long and Sedley trans.)

130. See Frede, "Stoic Determinism," in Inwood, *Cambridge Companion to the Stoics,* 180. For the documents of and commentary on the Stoic notions of causation, fate, and moral responsibility, see: Sedley and Long, *The Hellenistic Philosophers,* vol. 1, 333–43 and 386–94.

131. Letter from Giovanni Chiaiese to Nicola Geremia dated 13 August 1721, in *Opere,* vol. 5, 2nd ed., 168, and in English trans. by Gianturco in *Forum Italicum* vol. 2, no. 4 (December 1968): 323.

132. See, for example, *De constantia,* part 1, chap. 6: Cristofolini edit., 367; Pinton edit., 311. In English translation, that short chapter reads: "The teaching of Fate (*Fatum*) by the Stoics is, therefore, false, if Fate is understood as the necessary series of events that drags away with its power all things, including the human free will. However, if considered as the word (*verbum*) with which God speaks (*fatur*) the eternal true to the human mind, it is, then, the *fas* that the philosophers called *ius naturale posterius,* that is a right absolutely immutable. This opinion is indeed most plainly true." (Pinton trans.)

133. See, for example, the discussion of Chyrsippus in Cicero, *On Fate,* 39–43, cited in Long and Sedley, *Hellenistic Philosophers,* vol. 1, 386–88, in which Cicero seeks to reconstruct the Stoic differentiation between primary and proximate causes as well as the Stoic doctrine of assent as it pertained to events dominated by proximate causes.

134. Frede, "Stoic Determinism," in Inwood, *Cambridge Companion to the Stoics,* esp. 191.

135. For Spinoza, God composed the one substance of the universe and all things had followed from his divine nature, including human conduct. Consequently, it was an anthropomorphic misconception to speak of human freedom, which Spinoza not only denied but also famously ridiculed as an illusion. For my account of Spinoza, I am drawing on a variety of secondary sources, including Jonathan Israel, *Radical Enlightenment* (Oxford: Oxford University Press, 2001), esp. 230–57; Steven Nadler *Spinoza's Ethics: An Introduction* (New York: Cambridge University Press, 2006); and Robert Sleigh Jr. et al., "Determinism and Human Freedom," in *The Cambridge History of Seventeenth-Century Philosophy,* ed. Daniel Garber and Michael Ayers (New York: Cambridge University Press, 1998), 1226–36.

136. The literature on this subject is vast. For an overview of the Italian examples, see Mario Rosa, *Cattolicesimo e lumi nel Settecento italiano* (Rome: Herder, 1981).

137. As we have seen, Chiaiese interpreted Vico's treatises as committed to a brand of Stoic monism. For my understanding of Stoic cosmology and theology, I am indebted to the fine contributions by Michael J. White on "Stoic Natural Philosophy" and Keimpe Algra on "Stoic Theology," in Inwood, *Cambridge Companion to the Stoics.*

138. In the ASDN the documentation of Inquisition trials from the first few decades of the eighteenth century makes plain that in Naples the reading of authors such as Spinoza was considered evidence of heresy. For example, in the trial from May 1731 of Michele Cannone(?), a thirty-year-old ecclesiastic from Puglia resident in Naples suspected of heresy, the defendant declared that he had been induced to doubt the divine authorship of the Bible, the divinity of Christ, and the morality of the Apostles, and, what was more, that he had been led to suspect the sacraments were nothing more than a "political invention" (*invenzione politica*) of the Church, the means by which Rome maintained its followers as "subjects" (*sudditi*) and defended its "interests in the monetary domain" (*interesse in materia di denari*). According to the defendant, the source of these ideas were the writings of Hobbes, Spinoza, Calvin, and Giannone, whom the defendant apparently had read and discussed in the company of other educated Puglians resident in Naples. Among their topics of conversation was the question whether or not it was right to consider Spinoza an atheist. The defendant abjured his beliefs on 26 September. The manuscript of this trial is in a section of the ASDN that is currently being reordered and inventoried anew, wherein it tentatively bears the call number Sant'Ufficio, Processi, 265–845/A. I am indebted to Giovanni Romeo for information about this trial and his notes on it.

139. De Miranda, "Nihil decisum fuit," 12–13.

140. For a brief overview of legal humanism, see Stein, *Roman Law in European History*, 75–82, esp. 75; and for a book-length overview, see Myron P. Gilmore, *Humanists and Jurists* (Cambridge: Harvard University Press, 1963). For erudite introductions to Italian and French legal humanism, see Donald R. Kelley's "Civil Science in the Renaissance: Jurisprudence Italian Style" and his "Civil Science in the Renaissance: Jurisprudence in the French Manner," both reprinted in Kelley's, *History, Law and the Human Sciences* (London: Variorum, 1984), article nos. 6 and 7. For excellent classics on French legal humanism, see Donald R. Kelley, *Foundations of Modern Historical Scholarship* (New York: Columbia University Press, 1970) and, in Italian, Domenico Maffei, *Gli inizi dell'umanesimo giuridico* (Milan: Giuffrè, 1956), as well as Vincenzo Piano Mortari, *Diritto, logica, metodo nel secolo xvi* (Naples: Jovene, 1978).

141. *De uno,* Prologue, para. 7: Cristofolini edit., 25; Pinton and Diehl edit., 5. Compare *De uno,* chap. 51, para. 9: Cristofolini edit., 67; Pinton and Diehl edit., 43, where Vico defines as the "vir bonus" the ancient Roman judges who exclusively worked on behalf of the utilities of others.

142. Indeed, the title of the second volume of the *Diritto universale, De constantia,* itself was borrowed from the political magnum opus of the Flemish Neo-Stoic, Justus Lipsius, who had identified in the bureaucracy of the emerging modern state a cohort of eminently reasonable administrators for the polity subject to the vicissitudes of historical change. Vico surely meant to cite and build on his authority. See Justus Lipsius, *De constantia* (Leiden: C. Platini, 1584) and in English *On Constancy,* trans. Sir John Stradling (Exeter, UK: Bristol Phoenix Press, 2006). Vico also speaks of the constancy of the Roman jurist in *De uno,* Prologue, para. 38: Cristofolini edit., 39; Pinton and Diehl edit., 13.

143. *Digest,* 1.1.10. Vico himself cites this Ulpian formula in *De uno,* chap. 58: Cristofolini edit., 71; Pinton and Diehl edit., 46.

144. *De uno,* chap. 43: Cristofolini edit., 57; Pinton and Diehl edit., 37.

145. Indeed, Vico expounded a notion of distributive justice in the *Diritto universale*—which he confusingly called the "ius aequatorium," or "commutative justice"—in refutation of Grotius's understanding of the same. See *De uno,* chap. 62: Cristofolini edit., 77; Pinton and Diehl edit., 48.

146. See Cicero, *De finibus,* Loeb Classical Library, III.xix.62 through III.xx.68, where Cicero employs the metaphor of one's seat in the theater to argue for natural possession predicated on usage; Grotius, *On the Free Sea,* chap. 5, 22–23; and, more famously, Locke, *Second Treatise on Government,* chap. 5, esp. paras. 27–28, 34, and 37–38.

147. *De uno,* chap. 44, para. 2: Cristofolini edit., 59; Pinton and Diehl edit., 38. In Latin, Vico wrote: "Haec autem fluxarum utilitatum aequalitas aeterna inter omnes constat."

148. *De uno,* chap. 44, para. 2: Cristofolini edit., 59; Pinton and Diehl edit., 38. As Vico continued: "Igitur ius est in natura utile aeterno commensu aequale. Quod iurisconsultis dicitur 'aequum bonum,' fons omnis naturalis iuris." It bears mentioning here that in this same chapter Vico had defined the art of justice as a means by which to adjudicate circumstances so that the human spirit (*animus*) would be free of perturbations, legitimating his material notion of justice in terms of the psychological impediments to freedom created by the inequality of things.

149. *Sinopsi:* Cristofolini edit., 6; Pinton and Diehl edit., lxii.

150. *De uno,* chap. 45, para. 2, "The Human Being Is Social by Nature": Cristofolini edit., 59; Pinton and Diehl edit., 39. In Latin, Vico wrote: "Igitur homo natura [est] factus ad communicandas cum aliis hominibus utilitates ex aequo bono. Societas est utilitatum communio..."

151. *De uno,* chap. 60, para. 6: Cristofolini edit., 75; Pinton and Diehl edit., 47.

152. For a summary of how this argument was developed in Enlightenment literature, see the classic Ronald L. Meek, *Social Science and the Ignoble Savage* (New York: Cambridge University Press, 1976). Also see Albert O. Hirschman, *The Passions and the Interests* (Princeton: Princeton University Press, 1977).

153. *De uno,* chap. 45: Cristofolini edit., 59; Pinton and Diehl edit., 39. (Pinton trans.)

154. *Sinopsi:* Cristofolini edit., 6; Pinton and Diehl edit., lxii.

155. Cicero, *De officiis,* Loeb Classical Library, I.vii.20.

156. Cicero, *De officiis,* Loeb Classical Library, I.vii.23.

157. *Digest,* 1.1.10.1.

158. *De uno,* chap. 51: Cristofolini edit., 65; Pinton and Diehl edit., 42.

159. *De uno,* chap. 52: Cristofolini edit., 69; Pinton and Diehl edit., 44.

160. For example, see Jean Domat, *Les lois civiles dans leur ordre naturel* (Paris: La Veuve de Jean Baptiste Coignard, 1695–1702), which was reprinted throughout the eighteenth century; Antoine-Yves Goguet, *De l'origine des arts, des loix, et des sciences* (Paris, Desaint & Saillant, 1758); and Adam Smith's lectures on jurisprudence, delivered at the University of Glasgow in 1763–64, and published as Adam Smith, *Lectures on Jurisprudence* (Oxford, 1978; repr., Indianapolis: Liberty Fund, 1982). On the concept of legal evolution and its advocates, see Peter Stein, *Legal Evolution* (New York: Cambridge University Press, 1980).

161. Over the course of the seventeenth and eighteenth centuries, there were efforts throughout Europe to produce national codes of laws, which both codified

statutes and borrowed from Roman and customary law. See Stein, *Roman Law in European History,* 104–14, esp. 110.

162. In the *Diritto universale* "authority" was a key concept that connoted the "certain." See *De uno,* chap. 83: Cristofolini edit., 101; Pinton and Diehl edit., 63.

163. *De uno,* chap. 47: Cristofolini edit., 63; Pinton and Diehl edit., 40.

164. *De uno,* chap. 48, esp. para. 2: Cristofolini edit., 63; Pinton and Diehl edit., 40.

165. On the variety of association with "natural law," see the excellent overview by Jan Schroder, "The Concept of (Natural) Law in the Doctrine of Law," in *Natural Law and Laws of Nature in Early Modern Europe,* ed. Daston and Stolleis.

166. For an excellent discussion of the meaning of the *ratio legis* in the Renaissance, which was indeed used interchangeably with the *mens legis,* see Ian Maclean, *Interpretation and Meaning in the Renaissance: The Case of Law* (New York: Cambridge University Press, 1992), esp. 153–55. For the roots of this idea in antiquity, see *Digest,* 1.1.9, where Gaius is cited as having defined the *naturalis ratio* as those precepts shared by all peoples.

167. *De uno,* chap. 75, para. 1: Cristofolini edit., 91; Pinton and Diehl edit., 57.

168. Compare Ulpian's first definition of the *ius naturale,* which he calls "that which nature had taught to all animals." *Digest,* 1.1.1.3.

169. See especially Hobbes, *Leviathan,* part 1, chap. 14, where he defines the "right of nature" (*ius naturale*) as the "liberty each man hath, to use his own power, as he will himselfe, for the preservation of his own Nature" and the "law of nature" (*lex naturalis*) as "a Precept...found out by reason, by which a man is forbidden to do, that, which is destructive of his life." Compare Locke, *Second Treatise on Government,* chap. 3, para. 21, 323, and Pufendorf, *On the Duty of Man and Citizen,* bk. 1, chap. 3, para. 7.

170. *De uno,* chap. 75, para. 6: Cristofolini edit., 95; Pinton and Diehl edit., 59. Compare Vico, *De uno,* chap. 35: Cristofolini edit., 53; Pinton and Diehl edit., 35, where Vico writes: "This reason is the power of truth (*vis veri*) in the corrupted human."

171. *De uno,* chap. 77: Cristofolini edit., 97; Pinton and Diehl edit., 61.

172. *Sinopsi:* Cristofolini edit., 6; Pinton and Diehl edit., lxii.

173. However, Vico's claims were closer to those of Leibniz's jurisprudential thought on this count. As Klaus Luig has explained, in the case of Leibniz's universal jurisprudence: "*ius* is the right of the individual that results from *lex* (of nature)." Klaus Luig, "Leibniz's Concept of jus naturale and lex naturalis—defined 'with geometric certainty,'" in *Natural Law and Laws of Nature,* ed. Daston and Stolleis, 233–48. From his many citations of predecessors and contemporaries, it seems that Vico had no knowledge of Leibniz's works, despite this resemblance.

174. That said, Vico did make some claims to the contrary. See his pronouncement about the indivisibility of natural rights in *De uno,* chap. 185, para. 11: Cristofolini edit., 281; Pinton and Diehl, edit., 174.

175. A number of studies have examined the peculiarities of Vico's Roman history in the *Scienza nuova* and many of their observations would hold for the *Diritto universale* as well. In particular, see the classic articles on the former by Arnaldo Momigliano, "La nuova storia romana di G. B. Vico," *RSI* 77 (1965), 773–90, and, in translation, his "Vico's *Scienza Nuova:* Roman 'Bestioni' and Roman 'Eroi,'" *History*

and Theory 5, no. 1 (1966): 3–23; Giuliano Crifò, "Vico e la storia romana: Alcune considerazioni," in *Giambattista Vico nel suo tempo e nel nostro,* ed. Mario Agrimi (Naples: Cuen, 1999) and, more recently, the observations in Anthony Grafton, "An Introduction to the *New Science,*" reprinted in his, *Bring Out Your Dead* (Cambridge: Harvard University Press, 2001).

176. Contrast Vico's universal history with that of his Roman contemporary Francesco Bianchini, who famously employed (Roman) artifacts as evidence for the claims of his historical scholarship, which sought to reconstruct a history of the world since biblical times inclusive of non-European peoples. On the genre of universal history around 1700, see Tamara Griggs, "Universal History from Counter-Reformation to Enlightenment," *Modern Intellectual History* 4, no. 2 (August 2007): 219–47, whose work beautifully evidences this transition from the baroque to the Enlightenment and whose argument I restate here.

177. On Vico's contribution to the debate on chronology, see Paolo Rossi, *Dark Abyss of Time: The History of the Earth and the History of Nations from Hooke to Vico,* trans. Lydia G. Cochrane (Chicago: University of Chicago Press. 1984), chap. 1.

178. I have demonstrated this argument in Barbara Naddeo, "Vico Anthropologist: From Civic to World History," *Bollettino del Centro di Studi Vichiani* 33 (2003): 103–18. Contrast Montesquieu, *The Spirit of the Laws* (1748), where the physical nature of the "law" results in a pluralism of customary and statutory laws worldwide.

179. Since antiquity, the cycle of constitutional change in Rome had been associated with the passage of the polity from kingship to tyranny and, then, to a republic, which authors from Polybius and Livy to Machiavelli all had noted as the source of Rome's greatness. For example, see Machiavelli, *Discourses on Livy,* esp. chap. 2.

180. See *De uno,* chap. 170: Cristofolini edit., 241 and 243; Pinton and Diehl edit., 152, where Vico writes about "heroic etymology" and projects an "etymologicon" that would ascertain the purportedly common origin of all languages.

181. See *De constantia,* part 2, chap. 19: Cristofolini edit., 513; Pinton and Diehl edit., 399–400, where Vico sketches the five epochs of early human history.

182. *De uno,* chap. 102, para. 2: Cristofolini edit., 117; Pinton and Diehl edit., esp. 76. Contrast *De constantia,* part 2, chap. 20 in its entirety, which nowhere restates this same notion of the family as a community of goods.

183. *De uno,* chap. 104, para. 13: Cristofolini edit., 123; Pinton and Diehl edit., 79. Also see *De constantia,* part 2, chap. 5, esp. para. 8: Cristofolini edit., 415 and 417; Pinton and Diehl edit., 347. Compare *De constantia,* part 2, chap. 20, section. 6: Cristofolini edit., 545 and 547; Pinton and Diehl edit., 417–18, where Vico talks at some length about how the occupation, use of, and what he calls "adherence" to the land by the so-called *viri* entitled them to its natural possession, which Vico further equates with the Roman legal term "bonitary possession."

184. Cicero, *De finibus,* Loeb Classical Library, III.xx.67.

185. *De uno,* chap. 104, esp. para 15: Cristofolini edit., 123; Pinton and Diehl edit., 79. Compare *De constantia,* part 2, chap. 21, section 1: Cristofolini edit., 573; Pinton and Diehl edit., 433–34.

186. It is important to note here that the form of slavery that property instituted was a literal one for Vico, and not merely that political form of slavery that Rousseau discusses in the *Social Contract,* bk. 1, chap. 4.

187. This scenario is especially well told in *Sinopsi:* Cristofolini edit., 11–12; Pinton and Diehl edit., lxix–lxx. Also see *De uno,* chap. 104, paras. 16–18: Cristofolini edit., 123 and 125; Pinton and Diehl edit., 80. Compare *De constantia,* part 2, chap. 21: Cristofolini edit., 571 and 573; Pinton and Diehl edit., 433–35.

188. Vico speaks about the advent of "coniugium" (conjugal union), the creation of the family unit, the exercise of paternal power, tutelage, and succession, as well as the first dominions of the earth and ownership of divided lands, which, Vico argued, derived from the literal "adherence" of the Optimates to those plots that they already possessed by natural right. See *De constantia,* part 2, chap. 20, esp. paras. 76–80: Cristofolini edit., 545 and 547; Pinton and Diehl edit., 417–19. Vico very briefly restates these themes at the beginning of chap. 21, where he further introduces his hallmark notion that the first cities were founded on agriculture and thus called *urbs* from *urbum,* the curvature of the plough. See *De constantia,* part 2, chap. 21, esp. paras. 1–2: Cristofolini edit., 563 and 565; Pinton and Diehl edit., 428–29. He further recapitulates the origin of agricultural holdings in *De constantia,* part 2, chap. 21, para. 15: Cristofolini edit., 571; Pinton and Diehl edit., 433.

189. Vico speaks of the right of asylum, "asylorum ius antiquissimum," and conjectures about the first instances of taking asylum in *De uno,* chap. 104, para. 19: Cristofolini edit., 125; Pinton and Diehl edit., 80. Compare *De constantia,* part 2, chap. 21, section 2 "Origin of the Asylums": Cristofolini edit., esp. 577 and 579; Pinton and Diehl edit., esp. 436–38. Importantly, here Vico contradicts what was a minor point in Livy concerning the motivations for the foundation of the asylums. Vico insisted that the asylums were not the product of the decision of a counsel but rather that of the compassion that the Optimates felt for the refugees of war, underscoring the relationship he sought to establish between feeling and the first unions of humans.

190. *De uno,* chap. 104, para. 18: Cristofolini edit., 123 and 125; Pinton and Diehl edit., 80. Compare *De constantia,* part 2, chap. 21, esp. para. 39: Cristofolini edit., 585; Pinton and Diehl edit., 441, where Vico most clearly states the obligations of the clients to their patrons.

191. *De uno,* chap. 106: Cristofolini edit., 127; Pinton and Diehl edit., 82, where Vico equates the foundation of the "respublica" with that of the "civitas," terms that he uses interchangeably throughout. Also see *De uno,* chap. 104, esp. paras. 19–20: Cristofolini edit., 125; Pinton and Diehl edit., 80, where he rather talks about the foundation of the *urbs,* which he uses interchangeably with *respublica,* and ibid., paras. 22–23: Cristofolini edit., 125; Pinton and Diehl edit., 81, where he speculates about how the *ius nexi,* or right of bonding, followed from the granting of asylum. Compare *De constantia,* part 2, chap. 21, esp. paras. 25–29: Cristofolini edit., 577 and 579; Pinton and Diehl edit., 436–38, although here again, Vico underscores the humanity of the founders of the first cities.

192. As Vico put it in *De uno:* "And, thus, while the patricians, that is, those who could name with certainty their own fathers, possessed fields, used auspices, were part of the Gentes, had solemn matrimony (*connubia*), sacred places (*lucri*), and altars (*arae*), the clients, on the contrary, could have none of all these." (Pinton and Diehl trans.) *De uno,* chap. 104, para. 18: Cristofolini edit., 125; Pinton and Diehl edit., 80. Similarly, Vico declared: "The term 'Optimates' meant those who held the right of tutelage for the preservation of their status, while the 'plebs' referred to those who wanted to introduce some changes (*res novae*)." (Pinton and Diehl trans.) *De uno,* chap. 104, para. 24: Cristofolini edit., 127; Pinton and Diehl edit., 81.

193. As Vico declared, in the city there were "within the same walls two body politics that had no commonality of (equal) rights," or what we might call juridical equality. *De constantia,* part 2, chap. 22, para. 14: Cristofolini edit., 607; Pinton and Diehl edit., 454.

194. On the *ius nexi,* see *De uno,* chap. 104, para. 23: Cristofolini edit., 125; Pinton and Diehl edit., 81. Compare *De constantia,* part 2, chap. 21, esp. para. 56: Cristofolini edit., 595; Pinton edit., 446, where Vico most clearly states the powers of the *ius nexi.*

195. *De uno,* chap. 127, para. 1: Cristofolini edit., 149; Pinton and Diehl edit., 94. Compare *De constantia,* part 2, chap. 22, esp. para. 2: Cristofolini edit., 603; Pinton and Diehl edit., 451.

196. Vico reiterates this point throughout *De uno* and *De constantia.* It is first stated with the utmost clarity in *De uno,* chap. 128, para. 1: Cristofolini edit., 151; Pinton and Diehl edit., 95, where Vico states: "Hence, you unmistakably see that the *ius optimum,* which hitherto has been thought to be the law proper to the Romans, is instead a law that originated from the ius gentium, which the Romans made their own by custody," and, Vico would add, by the law of victory (*ius victoriae*).

197. For an overview of alternative ways of recounting the origins of Rome in the early modern era, see Johannes Hendrik Erasmus, *The Origins of Rome in Historiography from Petrarch to Perizonius* (Assen, Netherlands: Van Gorcum, 1962). Also see Alexandre Grandazzi, *The Foundation of Rome: Myth and History,* trans. Jane Marie Todd (Ithaca: Cornell University Press, 1997).

198. Vico's chronology is outlined in *De constantia,* part 2, chap. 1: Cristofolini edit., 387–91; Pinton and Diehl edit., 329–32.

199. See Livy, *Ab urbe condita,* Loeb Classical Library, esp. bks. 1–2.

200. *De constantia,* part 2, chap. 7: Cristofolini edit., 425; Pinton and Diehl edit., 353. (Pinton and Diehl trans.) Compare Vico, *De uno,* chap. 118: Cristofolini edit., 149; Pinton and Diehl edit., 89, where Vico claims that all nations followed the same path of development from the law of the greater gentes to the civil law.

201. In particular, see *De constantia,* part 2, chap. 32: Cristofolini edit., 681–89; Pinton and Diehl edit., 502–7. These views challenged not only those of Livy but also Plutarch. See "Romulus," in Plutarch, *The Lives.*

202. Ibid., esp. paras. 3–4: Cristofolini edit., 683; Pinton and Diehl edit., 503. Compare *De uno,* chap. 123, para. 2: Cristofolini edit., 143 and 145; Pinton edit., 91.

203. For Livy, the patricians were the descendents of the "fathers" of the clans of archaic Rome, whose status Romulus reinforced with political appointment to the Senate. Livy, *Ab urbe condita,* Loeb Classical Library, I.viii.4–7. In other accounts, the differences between patricians and plebeians derived from original discrepancies in wealth. See Dionysius of Halicarnassus, *Roman Antiquities,* II.8, and Cicero, *De re publica,* Loeb Classical Library, II.ix.16. Also see "Romulus," in Plutarch, *The Lives,* where Plutarch offered a number of accounts for the origins of the patricians, which, in the end, he attributed to a designation by Romulus that was intended to smooth over the tensions between rich and poor. Therein, Plutarch wrote: "The city now being built, Romulus enlisted all that were of age to bear arms into military companies, each company consisting of three thousand footmen and three hundred horse. These companies were called legions, because they were the choicest and most select

of the people for fighting men. The rest of the multitude he called the people; an hundred of the most eminent he chose for counsellors; these he styled patricians, and their assembly the senate, which signifies a council of elders. The patricians, some say, were so called because they were the fathers of lawful children; others, because they could give a good account who their own fathers were, which not every one of the rabble that poured into the city at first could do; others, from patronage, their word for protection of inferiors, the origin of which they attribute to Patron, one of those that came over with Evander, who was a great protector and defender of the weak and needy. But perhaps the most probable judgment might be, that Romulus, esteeming it the duty of the chiefest and wealthiest men, with a fatherly care and concern to look after the meaner, and also encouraging the commonalty not to dread or be aggrieved at the honours of their superiors, but to love and respect them, and to think and call them their fathers, might from hence give them the name of patricians." (Dryden trans.)

204. *De uno,* chap. 123, para. 2: Cristofolini edit., 143 and 145; Pinton and Diehl, edit., 91. Compare *De constantia,* part 2, chap. 21, paras. 8–9: Cristofolini edit., 567; Pinton and Diehl edit., 431. Despite his claims, it seems that Vico was indebted to Varro for the etymology of *quir.* See Livy, *Ab urbe condita,* Loeb Classical Library, I.xiii.4–5n1.

205. *De constantia,* part 2, chap. 21, para. 36: Cristofolini edit., 585; Pinton and Diehl edit., 440.

206. *De constantia,* part 2, chap. 21, para. 38: Cristofolini edit., 585; Pinton and Diehl edit., 441.

207. *De constantia,* part 2, chap. 21, para. 28: Cristofolini edit., 579; Pinton and Diehl edit., 437. As Vico clarified, the sacred asylum Romulus had established was of such great importance to the life of the community that once defunct it would be designated to house the Roman Senate. And directly challenging Livy, Vico insisted that the Roman historian had been mistaken to speak about that asylum as a product of "counsel" rather than as a spontaneous establishment of the fathers that was rooted in their sympathy for the unfortunate and concern for their plight.

208. In the nineteenth century a number of notable modern scholars also argued that the origins of the Roman plebeians lay in warfare and that their initial status was that of clients. In particular, Theodor Mommsen argued that the ranks of the plebeians derived from emancipated slaves, bondsmen (*clientes*), foreign guests in need of protection, Latin settlers, and, no less, Latins conquered by the Romans. Together, these people constituted what Mommsen called the Roman *metoeci,* who were dependents of the burgesses and would band together as "plebeians" to struggle for their political equality. As he put it: "Out of the clients arose the plebs." Theodor Mommsen, "The Non-Burgesses and the Reformed Constitution," in his *History of Rome,* vol. 1, trans. William P. Dickson (London: Richard Bentley, 1864), 94. This position elaborated on the earlier one adopted by Niebuhr, who thought that the distinction between the patricians and plebeians had its basis in ethnic difference. As he put it at the start of his second volume: "The Republic existed at that time under a polity, to which nothing exactly parallel is discoverable in history. The state consisted of two nations, united together, living within the same walls, close to each other, yet not intermixed." G. B. Niebuhr, *The Roman History,* vol. 2, trans, F. A. Walter (London: C. and J. Rivington, 1827), 7. The resemblance this claim bears to that of the *Diritto universale* and the *Scienza*

nuova is stunning and worthy of further historical inquiry. Indeed, like Vico in the
Scienza nuova, Niebuhr claimed that the rights of the plebeians were "universal" and
derived from their status as a separate nation entitled to the rights of war and peace.
On Niebuhr's debt to the German Enlightenment, see Peter Hanns Reill, "Barthold
Georg Niebuhr and the Enlightenment Tradition," *German Studies Review* 3, no. 1
(Feb. 1980): 9–26. For evidence that Niebuhr's ballad theory was similar to Vico's
theory of poetry but derived from Perizonius, as Vico apparently had no knowledge
of ballad theory, see Arnaldo Momigliano, "Perizonius, Niebuhr and the Character
of the Early Roman Tradition," *Journal of Roman Studies* 47, no. 1–2 (1957): 104–14.
However true Momigliano's speculation about the source of Niebuhr's ideas might be,
it is important to note that his assertion about Vico's poetic theory was premised on
an oversight. For Vico evidently was familiar with the "ballad theory," which he cited
and adapted to his own ends in the *Diritto universale.* See *De constantia,* part 2, chap. 13,
para. 22: Cristofolini edit., 477; Pinton and Diehl edit., 380–81, where Vico states that
the formulae of the laws were called *carmina* by the Romans because they were, like
songs, composed of refrains. Also see *Notae,* Dissertation 13, paras. 11–12: Cristofolini
edit., 909; Pinton and Diehl edit., 695–96, where Vico talks about the origins of lyric
poetry, whose earliest content was that of customary law. As he therewith claimed:
"Apollo, the legislator, sang the *carmina.*" In contrast to Momigliano's position on
Niebuhr and Vico, see the position of Renate Bridenthal, who argues that Niebuhr's
use of poetry as a source for the writing of history had a "Vichian ring." Renate Bridenthal, "Was There a Roman Homer: Niebuhr's Thesis and his Critics," *History and
Theory* 11, no. 2 (1972): 193–213, esp., 197, from which I am quoting. If Vico set an
important precedent for successive interpretations of the "plebeians," his own theory
was not without its precedents. Notably, in the fifteenth century Leonardo Bruni
argued for an "ethnic" difference among the patricians and plebeians based on the
differences in their speech. Cited in H. J. Rose, "Patricians and Plebeians at Rome,"
Journal of Roman Studies 12 (1922): 106–33.

209. Most notably, in the nineteenth century the British ethnologist Henry
Maine would interpret the familial corporation as a unit of society and law, as well
as a set of practices that evolved from those associated with the *pater familias,* to those
associated with equity and natural law. In particular, Maine's typology of societal
forms, and his ideas about the nature of feudalism and the fictionality of law, bore a
striking resemblance to Vico's own. On Maine's *Ancient Law,* see Stein, *Legal Evolution,* 86–98. More generally on Maine, see Robert Redfield, "Maine's *Ancient Law* in
the Light of Primitive Societies," *Western Political Quarterly,* 3, no. 4 (1950): 574–89;
Henry Orenstein, "The Ethnological Theories of Henry Sumner Maine," *American
Anthropologist* 70, no. 2 (1968): 264–76; Kenneth E. Bock, "Comparison of Histories:
The Contribution of Henry Maine," *Comparative Studies in Society and History* 16,
no. 2 (1974): 232–62; and Roslyn Jolly, "Robert Louis Stevenson, Henry Maine and
the Anthropology of Comparative Law," *Journal of British Studies* 45, no. 3 (2006):
556–80. More generally on the Victorian context of these ideas, see J. W. Burrow,
Evolution and Society: A Study in Victorian Social Theory (Cambridge: Cambridge University Press, 1966); George W. Stocking Jr., *Victorian Anthropology* (New York: Free
Press, 1987); and Peter J. Bowler, *The Invention of Progress: The Victorians and their Past*
(Oxford: Basil Blackwell, 1989). For the impact of Vico's thought on the social theory
of post-Revolutionary France and in particular Michelet and Sorel, see Patrick H.

Hutton, "Vico's Theory of History and the French Revolutionary Tradition," *Journal of the History of Ideas* 37, no. 2 (1976): 241–56.

210. On this dualism of the Roman civic community and its importance for the trajectory of Roman history, see *De constantia,* part 2, chap. 22, para. 15: Cristofolini edit., 607; Pinton and Diehl edit., 454. There, Vico wrote: "The diversity of these two bodies within the walls of the same city will be for us the source of the entire Roman polity, history and jurisprudence." (Pinton and Diehl trans.)

211. On this count, Vico's history most starkly contrasted with the models provided by not only Livy but also Polybius and Machiavelli.

212. Indeed, immediately after treating the territories, or *arae,* of the *inclyti,* Vico treated the right of *postliminium,* presumably due to those who sought asylum in those same territories. As he put it, the postliminium was "introduced by the law of the lesser gentes, according to which the prisoners of war, after they returned within the boundaries of their own cities, recuperate their pristine liberty and rights. This allows us to conjecture that *postliminium* was a constant right of the *gentes,* and a valid one." (Pinton and Diehl trans.) *De constantia,* part 2, chap. 21, section 3, para. 59: Cristofolini edit., 595 and 597; Pinton and Diehl edit., 447. Compare Niebuhr's justification of the "universal" rights of the plebeians.

213. See Livy, *Ab urbe condita,* Loeb Classical Library, II.xxxiii. Contrast Dionysius of Halicarnassus, *Roman Antiquities,* VI.83.4 and VI.88.3.

214. See Livy, *Ab urbe condita,* Loeb Classical Library, III.liv.5 and III.lv.1–15.

215. For Livy's example of the first of the agrarian laws, see Livy, *Ab urbe condita,* II.xli.1–12; and for his well-known (and often cited) account of the Lex Licinia Sextia, which capped holdings of public lands to five hundred *iugera,* see Livy, *Ab urbe condita,* VI.xxxv.5. Contrast Vico's interpretation of the first secession of the plebs as yielding the first agrarian law or what was the right of bonitary possession: Vico, *De uno,* chap. 127, para. 2: Cristofolini edit., 149; Pinton and Diehl edit., 94. And in contrast to the specifics of Vico's own positions in *De uno,* also see *De constantia,* part 2, chap. 21, para. 32: Cristofolini edit., 581; Pinton and Diehl edit., 438, where the first agrarian law confers asylum and its concomitant duty to work the lands and the second agrarian law confers bonitary dominion, which, it seems, was formalized by the institution of the census by Servius Tullius. It bears noting here that in *De constantia* Vico predated the plebeians' acquisition of bonitary dominion to the late monarchy, and that the chronological discrepancies between these two interpretations of the agrarian laws by Vico also reflect two distinct timetables for the admission of the plebeians to citizenship within the Republic in the *Diritto universale.* For a brief history of how ancient Roman historians more generally treated the agrarian problem, see Arnaldo Momigliano, "Niebuhr and the Agrarian Problems of Rome," *History and Theory* 21, no. 4 (1982): 3–15. In his essay "Vico's *Scienza nuova*: Roman Bestioni and Roman Eroi," first published in *History and Theory* 5, no. 1 (1966): 3–23, Arnaldo Momilgiano noted that Vico's association of the Servian constitution and the Twelve Tables with agrarian laws was most unusual, to say the least, and speculated that this association was particular to Vico, as he had not found any predecessors to him on this count. To my knowledge, no one has overturned Momigliano's claim, although it has been shown that the agrarian laws were of some interest to early modern historians and that there were indeed a number of early modern interpretations of them that may have influenced Vico, such as Machiavelli's association of the

first agrarian law with Servius Tullius. See *Discourses on Livy,* bk. 1, chap. 37. On the history of the representation of the "agrarian laws" in early modern literature, see Ronald T. Ridley, "*Leges agrariae:* Myths Ancient and Modern," *Classical Philology* 95, no. 4 (2000): 259–67, where Ridley briefly treats the views of Machiavelli and, among others, Vico, whose position he does not fully represent. Be that as it may, the preexisting tradition of discourse about the agrarian laws by no means makes any less relevant Momigliano's ultimate question: What inspired Vico to think in such bold terms about agrarian problems?

216. *De uno,* chap. 127, para. 2: Cristofolini edit., 149; Pinton and Diehl edit., 94. Contrast *De constantia,* part 2, chap. 22, paras. 6–7: Cristofolini edit., 603 and 65; Pinton and Diehl edit., 451–52, where the second "agrarian law" first offers the plebeians bonitary dominion over the lands they cultivate and commutes the obligation of laboring for the Optimates into one of tribute.

217. *De uno,* chap. 127, para. 2: Cristofolini edit., 149; Pinton and Diehl edit., 94.

218. *De uno,* chap. 104, para. 24: Cristofolini edit., 127; Pinton and Diehl edit., 81, and *De constantia,* part 2, chap. 22, para. 1: Cristofolini edit., 601; Pinton and Diehl edit., 450. (Pinton and Diehl trans.)

219. On the permutation on the *ius nexi,* see *De uno,* chap. 127, para. 2: Cristofolini edit., 149; Pinton and Diehl edit., 94, and *De constantia,* part 2, chap. 29, para. 16: Cristofolini edit., 657; Pinton and Diehl edit., 486. On the patrician practice of usury, see *De uno,* chap. 173, para. 8: Cristofolini edit., 253; Pinton and Diehl edit., 159.

220. For Vico's interpretation of the Lex Poetelia Papiria, see *De uno,* chap. 173, para. 1: Cristofolini edit., 251; Pinton and Diehl edit., 157. Compare *De uno,* chap. 187, para. 3: Cristofolini edit., 285; Pinton and Diehl edit., 176, where Vico most emphatically repeats his claim that the Lex Poetelia outlawed debt bondage. Compare Livy, *Ab urbe condita,* Loeb Classical Library, VIII.xxiii, where Livy explains that this enactment designated as collateral for a loan the debtor's goods and not his person.

221. This claim resembles one that was central to the work of the great Italian Renaissance jurist Alciato. On this point, see Tuck, *Natural Right Theories,* 36.

222. On the association of the Roman *civitas* with its citizenry and the rule of law, see the Introduction to this book.

223. My reading of Vico confirms some of the claims made by Annabel Brett for Vasquez and, more generally, about the occasion for the modernization of natural law theory. In particular, see the stimulating and incisive article by Annabel Brett, "The Development of the Idea of Citizens' Rights," in *States and Citizens: History, Theory, Prospects,* ed. Quentin Skinner and Bo Straeth (New York: Cambridge University Press, 2003), 97–114.

224. I am drawing on some of the observations made by Pocock with reference to English history in *Virtue, Commerce, and History,* esp. 37–50.

225. On the forms of the Roman constitution, see *De uno,* chap. 138: Cristofolini edit., 169 and 171; Pinton and Diehl edit., 105–6, and, esp. *De uno,* chap. 144: Cristofolini edit., 177; Pinton and Diehl edit., 111–12, where Vico explicitly guts the "Republic" of its associations, inverts the traditional order of the forms of the Roman constitution, and asserts that the legal nature of the polity follows from the nature of its constituency.

226. This was the definition offered by Giovanni da Viterbo, who penned that "civitas" was an acronym for "citra vim habitas." Cited in Costa, *Civitas,* 32.

227. See Polybius, *Histories,* bk. 6, and Machiavelli, *Discourses on Livy,* bk. 1, chap. 2.

228. *De uno,* chap. 106: Cristofolini edit., 127; Pinton and Diehl edit., 82, where Vico literally defines the "republic" as a "commonality of all civil utilities" (*omnium civilium utilitatum communio*), and *De uno,* chap. 107, esp. para. 2: Cristofolini edit., 129; Pinton and Diehl edit., 82–83, where he specifies that the Republic contained within itself "all the goods of civil life."

229. *De constantia,* part 2, chap. 22, esp. paras. 11–13: Cristofolini edit., 605 and 607; Pinton and Diehl edit., 453, where Vico unusually defines the census as "a contract by which a parcel of land was given in usufruct to someone else by the full right of minor dominion, under the obligation of paying to the owner of the land a fixed tribute or a sum of money." (Pinton and Diehl trans.)

230. Livy, *Ab urbe condita,* Loeb Classical Library, I.xlii.4–5.

231. Contrast *De uno,* chap. 171, esp. paras. 2–3: Cristofolini edit., 243 and 245; Pinton and Diehl edit., 153, where Vico notes how the census destabilizes extant categories of patricians and plebeians and makes wealth the primary criterion for office.

232. As is well known, Marx admired Vico's thought and quoted him in *Das Kapital,* 2nd ed., vol. 1 (Hamburg: Otto Meissner, 1872), 385n.89. While much ink consequently has been spilled about Vico and Marx, among their many points of comparison little attention has been paid to the centrality of property to law. For example, see the fine article comparing Vico and Marx by Lawrence H. Simon, "Vico and Marx: Perspectives on Historical Development," *Journal of the History of Ideas* 42, no. 2 (1981): 317–31, which focuses on their respective explanations of historical change. Also see the (less satisfying) volume of essays edited by Giorgio Tagliacozzo, *Vico and Marx: Affinities and Contrasts* (Atlantic Highlands, NJ: Humanities Press, 1983).

233. For example, see Bacon, Preface to his "Wisdom of the Ancients," in *The Works of Francis Bacon,* ed. James Spedding, vol. 6: *Literary and Professional Works,* vol. 1, new ed. (London: Longmans and Co., 1878), esp. 695–96.

234. Much has been written about Vico's approach to mythology in the *Scienza nuova* and little about the origins of his own interest in it as illustrated by the *Diritto universale.* The historiographical literature on myth in the *Scienza nuova* is extensive and cannot be summarized here. To begin, in English, see Joseph Mali, *The Rehabilitation of Myth: Vico's* New Science (New York: Cambridge University Press, 1992) and, in Italian, see Gianfranco Cantelli, *Mente, corpo, linguaggio: Saggio sull'interpretazione vichiana del mito* (Florence: Sansoni, 1986).

235. *De constantia,* part 2, chap. 13, esp. para. 17: Cristofolini edit., 475; Pinton and Diehl edit., 380.

236. *De uno,* chap. 168, esp. para. 2: Cristofolini edit., 235 and 237; Pinton, edit., 149, where Vico poses the rhetorical question: "Is it possible to assume that the fables of the Heroic Time were nothing but the histories of the Dark Time?"

237. *De constantia,* part 2, chap. 23, paras. 14 and 17: Cristofolini edit., 621 and 623; Pinton and Diehl edit., 461–62.

238. *De constantia,* part 2, chap. 24: Cristofolini edit., 625–29; Pinton and Diehl edit., 465–66.

239. *Notae,* Dissertation 4.

240. *De constantia,* part 2, chap. 29: Cristofolini edit., 651–57; Pinton and Diehl edit., 483–86. Compare Plutarch, *The Lives,* chap. 25.

241. See *De constantia,* part 2, chap. 13: Cristofolini edit., 471–79; Pinton and Diehl edit., 378–82, and *De uno,* chap. 168, esp. para. 2: Cristofolini edit., 233–37; Pinton and Diehl edit., 148–49.

242. *De uno,* chap. 136, para. 2: Cristofolini edit., 163; Pinton and Diehl edit., 103.

243. *De uno,* chap. 124, esp. paras. 1–2: Cristofolini edit., 145; Pinton and Diehl edit., 92, where Vico identifies a number of the fictions employed in legal transactions that were literally symbols of the formerly coercive practices of the greater gentes, or what Vico called "imitations of violence." (Pinton and Diehl trans.)

244. *De uno,* chap. 129, para. 4: Cristofolini edit., 153 and 155; Pinton and Diehl edit., 97.

245. *De uno,* chap. 182: Cristofolini edit., 263 and 265; Pinton and Diehl edit., 164–65, which is entitled: "Ancient Law Abounds with Fictions."

246. *De constantia,* chap. 26, para. 4: Cristofolini edit., 632–33; Pinton and Diehl edit., 470.

247. It is worth noting that the word "constitution" was not used in ancient and early modern political theory to describe feudalism. However, as feudalism was one of the social forms that Vico described, I have extended its usage to feudalism as well, especially as the sorts of concerns and methods that Vico brought to the study of the ancient *civitas* and *respublica* applied in this case as well.

248. For Vico's account of the origins of the fief, see *De uno,* chap. 192: Cristofolini edit., 293; Pinton and Diehl edit., 181, entitled "The Origin of Fiefs," where Vico restates the "Germanist" thesis that the fief arose after the invasions of the barbarous *gentes* and was a form of compensation for "fidelity," which was regularly identified as the etymon for the "fief." For an important instance of Vico's analogy between feudal law and the law of the archaic Romans, also see *De uno,* chap. 129: Cristofolini edit., 153 and 155; Pinton and Diehl edit., 96–98, entitled "The Law of the Quirites Was a Feudal Roman Law." There, Vico explicitly interprets the customs of the *ius Quiritium* through the lens of medieval typologies, and he asserts that the law that the German barbarians brought to Europe marked the reappearance of the ancient ius gentium. Within the *Diritto universale,* Vico's position on the origins of the fief and feudal customs was not perfectly consistent, however. For Vico's reconstruction of the origins of feudal customs, in particular, see *De constantia,* chap. 21, paras. 41–62, esp. 46: Cristofolini edit., 587–97; Pinton and Diehl edit., 442–48, where Vico adopts the "Romanist" argument that the Roman culture of patronage bore the seeds of feudalism, and, by implication, that the Roman Empire bore the foundation of feudal institutions and their law. On the Renaissance debate about the origins of the fief and feudal law, see Donald R. Kelley, "*De origine feudorum:* The Beginnings of an Historical Problem," originally published in *Speculum* 39 (1964): 207–28.

249. In the historiography on the Enlightenment in the Kingdom of Naples, the idea that the Enlightenment was synonymous with reform and that reform entailed dismantling feudal prerogatives has long held sway. In particular, see the monumental work of Franco Venturi, *Settecento riformatori,* 5 vols. (Turin: Einaudi, 1969–90), esp. vol. 1. As more narrowly concerned the jurisdictional and fiscal privileges of the baronage, also see Raffaele Ajello, *Il problema della riforma giudiziaria e legislativa nel*

Regno di Napoli durante la prima metà del secolo XVIII, 2 vols. (Naples: Jovene, 1965–68). This historiographical emphasis derives from the rhetoric of the *illuministi* themselves, who spoke about the state of the countryside in the most abject terms and, in part, blamed that state on the tenacity of feudal privilege. In particular, see Galanti, "Del sistema feudale," in his, *Della descrizione geografica e politica delle Sicilie,* vol. 1, 126–28. Also see the writings of Galanti's protégé, Vincenzo Cuoco, who wrote about the feudalism of the Kingdom from afar in the most hyperbolic and censorious of terms, especially in the *Saggio storico della rivoluzione napoletana del 1799.* Among the classics on the empirical state of feudalism in the eighteenth-century Kingdom and its political reform, see Pasquale Villani, *Feudalità, riforme, capitalismo agrario* (Bari: Laterza, 1968); Rosario Villari, *Mezzogiorno e contadini nell'età moderna* (Bari: Laterza, 1977); the many studies of Aurelio Lepre on Campania; Angelo Massafra on Puglia; and Anna Maria Rao, *"L'amaro della feudalità": La devoluzione di Arnone e la questione feudale a Napoli alla fine del '700* (Naples: Guida, 1984). For more recent case studies of feudal communities, see Astarita, *Continuity of Feudal Power* and Benaiteau, *Vassalli e cittadini* (Bari: Edipuglia, 1997). For a synthesis of the historiographical debate on feudalism in the Kingdom, see Anna Maria Rao, "Morte e resurrezione della feudalità: Un problema storiografico," in *Dimenticare Croce?,* ed. Musi.

250. Indeed, critics of the *Scienza nuova* have noted the conspicuous resemblance that the Roman orders bore to those of the Middle Ages, and have posed the open question of why Vico would cast the Romans and their social history as if it were a template for the course (and, indeed, end) of the Middle Ages. As Momigliano has briefly noted, drawing on observations made by Giuseppe Giarrizzo, the Roman patricians and plebeians of the *Scienza nuova* bore such a striking resemblance to the barons and serfs of feudalism that one could almost say that Vico reconstructed the history of Rome through the lens of medieval typologies. See Momigliano, "La nuova storia romana di G. B. Vico," esp. 776 and 786, and, in translation, his "Vico's *Scienza Nuova:* Roman 'Bestioni' and Roman 'Eroi,'" esp. 18–23. However, Momigliano both reasoned that the explanation for Vico's analogy lay in the exigencies of his contemporary world and concluded that the evidence for an analogy between the conditions of the medieval-like Roman plebeians and the Kingdom's own peasants was wanting. Contrast the further astute assertions made by Giarrizzo concerning the contemporaneity of Vico's analogy, which, nonetheless, remained suggestive: Giarrizzo, "La politica di Vico," in *Vico, la politica e la storia,* esp. 107. Evidently, internal to the career of Vico's own thought, this resemblance between ancient and medieval times derived from his critical examination of the origins of the fief and feudal customs in the *Diritto universale.* On the contemporary reasons for Vico's preliminary reflections on the origins of the fief and feudal customs, see my discussion later in this chapter and, in particular, at the outset of chapter 4.

251. Momigliano, "La nuova storia romana," 783. In particular, on the Romanism of those Humanists, see Kelley, *"De Origine Feudorum,"* 216–19.

252. Strangely, Vico not only adopted both positions, as I have indicated, but he also marshaled the evidence associated with the Germanist position within his elaboration of the Romanist one. For example, in *De constantia,* chap. 21, para. 47: Cristofolini edit., 589; Pinton and Diehl edit., 443, Vico offers etymological evidence for the origins of the Romanist fief that was typical of Germanist arguments. Compare the etymology of Hotman and Le Caron, as discussed in Kelley, *"De Origine Feudorum,"* 225 and 226n89.

253. Kelley, *"De Origine Feudorum,"* esp. 218–19.

254. See *De constantia,* chap. 21, paras. 41–43: Cristofolini edit., 587; Pinton and Diehl edit., 442, where Vico specifically comments on the practices of clientelism in the "free republic" of Rome—such as, the retinue, or military escort provided by the plebeians of their patron; the *coena* (evening meal) offered by the Roman patron to the plebeians; and the gift baskets, *sportulae,* distributed among the plebeians.

255. *De uno,* chap. 129, para. 4: Cristofolini edit., 155; Pinton and Diehl edit., 97.

256. Vico discusses these institutions under the rubric of "Laws," "Senatusconsults," and "Judgments" *ex ordine* and *extra ordinem* in *De uno.* See *De uno,* chaps. 194–97: Cristofolini edit., 295–301; Pinton and Diehl edit., 183–86. It is interesting to note that Vico distinguished between the *leges* introduced by the tribunes to the plebeian assembly (the *concilium plebis*) and the plebiscites, which, in reality, were the same thing. For Vico, however, the most ancient plebiscites denoted royal decrees. See *De uno,* chap. 150: Cristofolini edit., 193–97; Pinton and Diehl edit., 121–22.

257. *De uno,* chap. 171, esp. paras. 1–3: Cristofolini edit., 243 and 245; Pinton and Diehl edit., 153–54.

258. *De uno,* chap. 171, esp. para. 6: Cristofolini edit., 245 and 247; Pinton and Diehl edit., 155, and Vico, *De uno,* chap. 173, esp. para. 8: Cristofolini edit., 251–53; Pinton and Diehl edit., 159.

259. *De uno,* chap. 171, esp. para. 5: Cristofolini edit., 245–47; Pinton and Diehl edit., 154, and *De uno,* chap. 173, esp. para. 1: Cristofolini edit., 249–51; Pinton and Diehl edit., 157.

260. *De uno,* chap. 170: Cristofolini edit., 241 and 243; Pinton and Diehl edit., 152. Also see *De uno,* chap. 149: Cristofolini edit., 185–93; Pinton and Diehl edit., 116–21, which speculates about the nature and language of the first laws.

261. On the "rigorous jurisprudence" of the patricians, see *De uno,* chap. 177: Cristofolini edit., 259; Pinton and Diehl edit., 162.

262. According to tradition, the Twelve Tables were the product of a tribunitial demand that a commission be drawn up to publish legal principles and to restrict consular power. See Livy, *Ab urbe condita,* Loeb Classical Library, III, esp. xxiii–liv, and Dionysius of Halicarnassus, *Roman Antiquities,* Loeb Classical Library, x.1–xi.50. What was more, those same laws reportedly had derived from the laws of Solon and had been brought by a commission to Rome from Greece, an origins legend that Vico would fully reject in the *Scienza nuova.* See *Scienza nuova* (1725), bk. 2, ch. 36. For an overview of Vico's treatment of the Twelve Tables, see Max Harold Fisch, "Vico on Roman Law," *New Vico Studies* 19 (2001): 5–9. However, the very transparency of the Twelve Tables neither abated the secrecy nor the rigor of patrician jurisprudence, which, according to Vico, the patriciate perpetuated in the form of arcane legal formulae for the strict application of the published law. *De uno,* chap. 184: Cristofolini edit., 275; Pinton and Diehl edit., 170. Here Vico rather freely interprets the *Digest* 1.2.2.4 (but 5!), where Pomponius is cited regarding the emergence of jurisprudence.

263. *De uno,* chaps. 194–95: Cristofolini edit., 295–97; Pinton and Diehl edit., 183–84. Compare *De uno,* chaps. 163–64: Cristofolini edit., 227–31; Pinton and Diehl edit., 140–42.

264. For example, it is curious that in the *Diritto universale* Vico did not discuss more centrally the Lex Canuleia (445 BCE), which permitted marriage between patricians and plebeians (Livy IV.1–6), or even mention either the Leges Valeriae Horatiae (449 BCE), which made plebiscites law and ruled that no Roman citizen could be executed without appeal (Livy III.55), or the landmark Leges Liciniae Sextiae (367 BCE), which instituted pathbreaking reforms concerning land, debt, and the allocation of offices among patricians and plebeians (Livy VI.39–42).

265. *De uno,* chap. 173: Cristofolini edit., 251–57; Pinton and Diehl edit., 158–60. In reality, the legislation of the *concilium plebis* primarily concerned political legislation.

266. *De uno,* chap. 174: Cristofolini edit., 257; Pinton and Diehl edit., 161.

267. Papinian in *Digest* 1.1.7.1.

268. *De uno,* chap. 187, paras. 1–3: Cristofolini edit., 283 and 285; Pinton and Diehl edit., 175–76. Compare Marcian citation in the *Digest* 1.1.8.

269. Ibid.

270. Ibid.

271. Ibid. In reality, according to Stein, the *regulae* were superseded by the development of natural jurisprudence. See Peter Stein, *Regulae iuris: From Juristic Rules to Legal Maxims* (Edinburgh: University Press, 1966).

272. Ibid.

273. On the *interpretatio,* see Jolowicz, *Historical Introduction to the Study of Roman Law,* 88–97, and Nicholas, *Introduction to Roman Law,* 28–31.

274. Jolowicz, *Historical Introduction to the Study of Roman Law,* 232.

275. On the praetorian interdict and bonitary ownership, see Jolowicz, *Historical Introduction to the Study of Roman Law,* 99 and 263–67.

276. *De uno,* chap. 187, para. 7: Cristofolini edit., 287; Pinton and Diehl edit., 177.

277. *De uno,* chap. 187, para. 8: Cristofolini edit., 287; Pinton and Diehl edit., 177. On "common sense" in Vico, see Schaeffer, *Sensus Communis: Vico, Rhetoric, and the Limits of Relativism* (Durham: Duke University Press, 1990); and on "common sense" in early modern thought more generally, see Sophia Rosenfeld, "Before Democracy: The Production and Uses of Common Sense in Early Eighteenth-Century England," *Journal of Modern History* 80, no. 1 (2008): 1–54.

278. For Vico's distinction between the legal *persona* and *homo,* see *De constantia,* chap. 20, para. 69: Cristofolini edit., 287; Pinton and Diehl edit., 543.

279. Strangely, the foremost work on Vico's Roman history and on his legal philosophy both have overlooked the specificity and meaning of Vico's reconstruction of praetorian law. In particular, I am thinking of the silence on this topic in Fisch, "Vico on Roman Law"; Momigliano, "La nuova storia romana di G. B. Vico"; Ajello, *Il problema della riforma,* vol. 1, *Il preilluminismo giuridico;* Ajello, *Arcana Juris;* Pasini, *Diritto, società e stato in Vico;* Mazzarino, *Vico, l'annalistica e il diritto;* Berlin, *Vico and Herder;* Kelley, "Vico's Road: From Philology to Jurisprudence and Back"; Lilla, *G. B. Vico;* Crifò, "Vico e la storia romana"; and Schaeffer, *Sensus Communis.* However, it should be noted that the following have stressed Vico's concern about equity: Franco Amerio, *Introduzione allo studio di G. B. Vico* (Turin: Società editrice internazionale, 1947); Carlo Cantone, *Il concetto filosofico di diritto in Giambattista Vico* (Mazara, Sicily: Società editrice siciliana, 1952); A. Robert Caponigri, "*Jus et aevom:*

The Historical Theory of Natural Law in Giambattista Vico," *American Journal of Jurisprudence* 24 (1979): 3–26; Francesco Lomonaco, "Diritto naturale e storia: Note su Gravina e Vico," in *Pensar para el nuevo siglo,* ed. Hidalgo-Serna et al.; and Giarrizzo, *Vico, la politica e la storia* (1981). The oversight of the former group is probably best explained by the change in Vico's own attitude toward praetorian law in the *Scienza nuova,* wherein it would figure far less centrally than it had in the *Diritto universale.*

280. *De uno,* chap. 187, paras. 8–10: Cristofolini edit., 287 and 289; Pinton and Diehl edit., 177–78.

281. This was the definition of justice coined by Celsus and reported in the very first lines of the *Digest.* See *Digest* 1.1.1.1.

282. See *De uno,* chap. 188: Cristofolini edit., 289; Pinton and Diehl edit., 179, where Vico defines "benevolent jurisprudence." (Pinton and Diehl trans.)

283. *De ratione,* section 7: Gentile and Nicolini edit., 91–92; Gianturco edit., 34. Also see Vico, *Institutiones oratoriae,* ed. Crifò, chap. 8, 34–37. Compare Vico's comments about forensic eloquence in contemporary Naples in *De uno,* chap. 199: Cristofolini edit., 303–5; Pinton and Diehl edit., 187.

284. In particular, Vico noted the innovation of the *fideicommissum. De uno,* chap. 209: Cristofolini edit., 297; Pinton and Diehl edit., 195. On that legal instrument, see Nicholas, *Introduction to Roman Law,* 267–69.

285. For example, Vico treated at some length the fiat of the *ius (publice) respondendi.* See: *De uno,* chap. 211, para. 1: Cristofolini edit., 321; Pinton and Diehl edit., 197. On that fiat, see Jolowicz, *Historical Introduction to Roman Law,* 359–63 and 374–75.

286. Vico was attuned to the diminution of the discretionary powers of the praetors by the Perpetual Edict. See: *De uno,* chap. 211, paras. 3–5: Cristofolini edit., 323; Pinton and Diehl edit., 198, and *De uno,* chap. 213, para. 2: Cristofolini edit., 329; Pinton and Diehl edit., 201. Compare Jolowicz, *Historical Introduction to Roman Law,* 357.

287. *De uno,* chap. 187, para. 10: Cristofolini edit., 287 and 289; Pinton and Diehl edit., 178.

288. *De uno,* chap. 206, para. 1: Cristofolini edit., 315; Pinton and Dihel edit., 193.

289. In reality, the Edict would indeed become the "chief text for the lawyer" and consequently the subject of innumerable commentaries. Jolowicz, *Historical Introduction to Roman Law,* 376.

290. *De uno,* chap. 212: Cristofolini edit., 323–27; Pinton and Diehl edit., 198–200. On the school, see Schulz, *History of Roman Legal Science* (Oxford: Clarendon, 1946), 119–23; Jolowicz, *Historical Introduction to Roman Law,* 378–84; and Nicholas, *Introduction to Roman Law,* 32–33.

291. See Tacitus, *Annals,* III.75. Cited in Jolowicz, *Historical Introduction to Roman Law,* 379. This contrast is also noted by Vico, but without citation. See *De uno,* chap. 212, para. 3: Cristofolini edit., 325; Pinton and Diehl edit., 199.

292. *De uno,* chap. 218, para. 1: Cristofolini edit., 337; Pinton and Diehl edit., 206.

293. *De uno,* chap. 218, para. 2: Cristofolini edit., 337; Pinton and Diehl edit., 206–7.

294. *De constantia,* bk. 2, chap. 4, para. 4: Cristofolini edit., 413; Pinton and Diehl edit., 345.

295. The most famous example of this is the Prammatica *De Vagabundis* (1724), which is discussed in Grimaldi, *Istoria delle leggi, e magistrati del Regno di Napoli,* vol. 11, 261.

Chapter 4

1. Stone, *Vico's Cultural History,* 257–58.

2. Emmanuele Duni, *Origine e progressi del cittadino e del governo civile di Roma,* 2 vols. (Rome: Francesco Bizzarrini Komarek, 1763).

3. I am quoting from paras. 81 and 162 of the modern editions of the *Principii di una scienza nuova intorno alla natura delle nazioni per la quale si ritruovano i principii di altro sistema del diritto naturale delle genti,* herewith abbreviated as *Scienza nuova* (1725), reprinted in Giambattista Vico, *Opere,* ed. Andrea Battistini (Milano: Mondadori, 1990), 1026 and 1062, and translated into English as Giambattista Vico, *The First New Science,* ed. Leon Pompa (New York: Cambridge University Press, 2002), 59 and 101. (Pompa trans.)

4. Among those entitlements and duties numbered the right to vote and hold public office and the duty to pay taxes and serve in the legions.

5. For the juridical definition of *libertas,* see *Digest* 1.5.4, where Florentinus is cited as writing: "Libertas is the natural liberty of doing whatever one pleases unless something is prohibited by force or law."

6. Momigliano, "Vico's *Scienza Nuova:* Roman Bestioni and Roman Eroi," 16–19.

7. Giarrizzo, *Vico, la politica e la storia,* esp., 106–7.

8. R. Villari, *Mezzogiorno e contadini,* esp. 135–47.

9. Lucio Villari, "Aspetti e problemi della dominazione austriaca sul Regno di Napoli (1707–34)," *Annali della Scuola speciale per archivisti e bibliotecari dell'Università di Roma* 4, nos. 1–2 (1964): 45–80, and Lucio Villari, "La Calabria nel viceregno austriaco," in *Atti del terzo Congresso storico calabrese* (Naples: F. Fiorentino, 1964). Also see Muto, "Istituzioni dell'*universitas* e ceti dirigenti locali," 57.

10. On the number of grievances brought before the courts under the Austrians, see chapter 2.

11. *Scienza nuova* (1725), para. 165: Battistini edit., 1063–64; Pompa edit., 103. (Pompa trans.)

12. For an early example, see Doria's political-economic tract in which he proposes the relocation of capital dwellers: "Del Commercio del Regno di Napoli," a manuscript now published in Giulia Belgioioso, ed., *Manoscritti napoletani di Paolo Mattia Doria,* vol. 1 (Galatina: Congedo, 1982), 141–208, esp. 165.

13. For Vico's use of the term "society" in his early works, see chapter 2.

14. See Barbara Naddeo, "Neapolitan Itineraries: Re-collecting the City in Topographical Studies of Naples, 1650–1800," (paper presented at a workshop held at CRASSH of Cambridge University), *Exoticizing Vesuvius,* Cambridge University, 18 September 2009. Of the many histories I treat therein, the following are particularly relevant to my argument here: Giovanni Antonio Summonte, *Historia della Città e Regno di Napoli* (Naples, 1601; repr., Naples: Domenico Vivenzio, 1748); Giulio

Cesare Capaccio, *Il forastiero* (Naples, 1634; repr., Naples: Lucca Torre, 1989); and Camillo Tutini, *Dell'origine e fundazion de' Seggi di Napoli* (Naples, 1644; repr., Naples: Raffaele Gessari, 1754).

15. For Neapolitan concessions and resistance to Habsburg directives to naturalize select subjects, see SAW XVII, 5, Neapel Collectanea, box 9, fascicle 8: "Naturalisation."

16. For evidence of this debate, see SAW XVII, 5, Neapel Correspondenz, box 93, fascicles 7 and 8, pages 56–61.

17. For an overview and assessment of the economic initiatives undertaken by the Austrians, see Antonio Di Vittorio, *Gli austriaci e il regno di Napoli, 1707–34: Ideologia e politica di sviluppo* (Naples: Giannini, 1973).

18. See the instructions to Viceroy Althann authored in the name of the emperor, "Instruccion de lo que Vos el Cardenal de Althann...haveis de hacer en el administracion...de Napoles," in SAW XVII, 5, Neapel Collectanea, box 19 [old], fascicle 12. That memorandum observed: "Tambien es digno de reflexion, que entre el gran numero de pueblo que hay en la Ciudad, se halla mucha Gente ociosa sin applicacion alguna, la qual siempre ama las nobedades...para cuyo [ri]medio es muy importante fomenteis las maniobras, y todas suertes de fabricas, y Comercio." (It is worthy of notice that among the large number of people in the City there are many who are idle, without any sort of application, and love the nobility...and for their remedy it is very important that one create handiwork and all sorts of workshops and commerce.)

19. For example, a Giunta del Commercio had been designed in 1714 to promote the commerce of the Kingdom and had had among its primary plans the expansion of the Kingdom's ports and commercial fleets, plans that should have targeted the city of Naples. Yet, as Giuseppe Ricuperati has noted, the results of this organ were stymied by its own cultural prejudices regarding the plebeians of Naples, namely, the concern to keep the Neapolitan populace away from the port area. Consequently, the port of nearby Pozzuoli would be designated for enlargement and promotion. Giuseppe Ricuperati, "Napoli e i vicerè austriaci (1707–1734)," in *Storia di Napoli,* vol. 6, esp. 393. What is more, one of the leitmotifs of the Italian memoranda conserved in the SAW was the inappropriateness of the sort of initiatives undertaken by the Austrians; they expressed doubts concerning the effectiveness of their initiatives and resistance to them. See the memoranda in SAW, Neapel Collectanea, box 9, fascicles 13 and 14 on "Schiffarth u. Handel, 1710–27." Be that as it may, Viceroy Althann did try to implement a more radical set of economic reforms, which threatened the interests of elites dependent on revenues, such as the nobility. Consequently, Althann was vigorously opposed by the *piazze* of Naples, as well as some of the Neapolitan ministers. Some of Althann's plans and frustrations dating from 1723 are expressed in his correspondence to Rialp from this year in SAW Neapel, Correspondenz, box 56.

20. From a brief consultation of the (mere) topics of the *consulte originali* by the Collaterale from this period catalogued in the ASN it is clear that the Collaterale was not in the position to fight a frontal war against the power and organization of the municipality and its governance of Naples. See the manuscript catalogue of the ASN, Coll., Consulte originali. However, both Fleischman and the magistracy of the Collaterale did seek to limit the most damaging abuses of the municipality in a piecemeal

way. For example, the famed magistrate Gaetano Argento challenged the municipality's administration of the *annona,* or bread supply, which notoriously favored the agricultural interests of the barons over the public welfare of the residents of Naples. See Luongo, *Vis jurisprudentiae,* esp. 270–75, which cites the discussion recorded in ASN, Coll., Notamenti, vol. 125, 4

21. Paolo Mattia Doria, *La vita civile,* 2nd ed. (Augusta [but Naples?]: Hoepper, 1710).

22. The instructions for Viceroy Althann authored in the name of the emperor, "Instruccion de lo que Vos el Cardenal de Althann...haveis de hacer en el administracion...de Napoles," in SAW XVII, 5, Neapel Collectanea, box 19 [old], fascicle 12, dedicated points 7–37 to the Neapolitan courts and their administration of justice. Interestingly, point 15 explicitly stated that the Consiglio [Collaterale] ought not to take on cases within the jurisdiction of the lower courts, seeking to limit the great breadth of its powers.

23. See SAW, XVII, 5, Neapel Collectanea, box 19 [old], especially fascicle 3, containing several reports on the "Regia Camera della Sommaria," and fascicle 4, containing a few reports on the "Consiglio Collaterale," including the meaty "De los Ministros, Y Abogados de Napoles,/ Embiada de su orden/ Al Excel.mo S. Arzobispo de Valencia,/ Presidente del Gran Consejo de Espana/ en Vienna," which includes a highly censorious description of the activities of Argento.

24. Ibid., fascicle 4, "De los Ministros..."

25. Indeed, in the past he had commanded Garofalo to communicate a number of his preferences to Cappellano Maggiore Vidania in Naples. Evidence for Eugene's recommendations are in SAW, Prinz Eugen von Savoyen, Grosse Correspondenz, box 152b. Similarly, in the future he would recommend Garofalo for appointment to the important position of Cappellano Maggiore of the Kingdom.

26. The intellectual companionship of the two is especially plain in the letter by Vico to Garofalo, in which the former praises the latter's recent work. See the letter by Vico dated 4 October 1721, edited and published by Silvia Caianiello and Manuela Sanna in "Una lettera inedita di G.B. Vico a B. Garofalo del 4 ottobre 1721," *Bollettino del Centro di Studi Vichiani* 26–27 (1996–97): 325–30.

27. Vico to Eugene of Savoy dated 12 December 1722, in SAW, Prinz Eugen von Savoyen, Grosse Correspondenz, box 148a, no. 24, 183r–v, published in *Epistole,* 103–4.

28. Ibid. As Vico put it in an Italian riddled with redundancy: "di tutti i Lettori ha particolarmente di me argomenti di particolare atto di osservanza." This letter clearly was written in the utmost haste. Furthermore, it is important to note that the syntax of this sentence is unusual, and that my interpretative translation essentially modernizes Vico's Italian. (By the same token, it is worthy of consideration whether by "argomenti di...atto di osservanza" Vico intended something else entirely, especially given the connotations of the verb "osservare.")

29. Indeed, it was on behalf of Giannone that Biagio Garofalo eventually wrote to Eugene. For example, see Garofalo to Eugene in SAW, Prinz Eugen von Savoyen, Grosse Correspondenz, box 86b, 173r. This letter is dated 4 January 1726, however, and I have not found correspondence by Garofalo to Eugene concerning Giannone's difficulty with the Church prior to this date.

30. See ASN, C.M., Affari Diversi, 718, III, 321r–v.

31. Fourteen days are noted in Coll., Con., Affari Diversi, first series (IV 37), no. 69, unpaginated letter signed by Vidania and dated 30 December 1722. But the actual window was longer.

32. Coll., Con., Affari Diversi, first series (IV 37), no. 68.

33. C.M., Affari Diversi, 718, III, 257r.

34. C.M., Affari Diversi, 718, III, 300r–301v.

35. C.M., Affari Diversi, 718, II, 50r–v.

36. C.M., Affari Diversi, 718, III, 158r.

37. C.M., Affari Diversi, 718, III, 185r–v.

38. Evident from: C.M., Affari Diversi, 718, III, 272bis through 273r.

39. For Vidania's bios of the candidates, see C.M., Affari Diversi, 718, III, 323r–325r.

40. Famously, Vico is not among the individuals listed as recipients of the doctorate of law in the papers of the Collegio dei Dottori of Naples conserved in the ASN and now available online at *http://patrimonio.archiviodistatonapoli.it*. However, it bears mentioning that Vico did sign his manuscript orations with the title of doctor of law.

41. *Autobiografia:* Croce and Nicolini edit., 8; Fisch and Bergin trans., 117. It is noteworthy that although Vico presented cases before the courts, this does not necessarily mean that he had received a degree, as it was not unusual in eighteenth-century Naples for individuals to practice law without the actual title of "Doctor of Law." See Anna Maria Rao, "Intellettuali e professioni a Napoli nel Settecento," in *Avvocati, medici, ingegneri: Alle origini delle professioni moderne (secoli XVI–XIX),* ed. Maria Luisa Betri and Alessandro Pastor (Bologna: Cooperativa Libraria Universitaria Editrice, 1997), 49–50.

42. Recorded in: C.M., Affari Diversi, 718, III, 273r. Law recorded in *Digest* 19.5.1.

43. *Autobiografia:* Croce and Nicolini edit., 44; Fisch and Bergin trans., 161.

44. *Autobiografia:* Croce and Nicolini edit., 45–46; Fisch and Bergin trans., 162.

45. Contrast the work of Vico's contemporary Pietro Giannone, which is more influenced by the Germanists, and, like them, takes an interest in medieval history.

46. *Autobiografia:* Croce and Nicolini edit., 46; Fisch and Bergin trans., 163.

47. In the archival documentation, there are annotations in the margins of the list of candidates and the topics of their addresses that suggest that the evaluation Vico received was poorer than that of his competitors. Vico has a clearly written "Med." next to his name, which distinguishes him from the "B." assigned to his higher-ranking and more successful colleagues in the Faculty of Law. C.M., Affari Diversi, 718, III, 273r. To date, I have yet to find any discussion of these annotations anywhere in the historiography, including the excellent discussion of this event in Ascione, *Seminarium doctrinarum.*

48. *Autobiografia:* Croce and Nicolini edit., 46; Fisch and Bergin trans., 163.

49. *Autobiografia:* Croce and Nicolini edit., 44; Fisch and Bergin trans., 161.

50. C.M., Affari Diversi, 718, III, 326r.

51. C.M., Affari Diversi, 718, III, 304r.

52. C.M., Affari Diversi, 718, III, 305r.

53. Vico, Letter to Bernardo Maria Giacco, 25 October 1725, in *Epistole,* 113–15. This letter is also reproduced in modern English translation in Fisch, Introduction to *Autobiography,* 14–15. (Fisch trans.)

54. Nicolini, Annotazioni to the *Autobiografia* in *Opere,* vol. 5, 2nd ed., 119–20.

55. Vico, Letter to Filippo Monti, 18 November 1724, in *Epistole,* 108–10.

56. Vico, Letters to Lorenzo Corsini, 25 and 26 December 1724, in *Epistole,* 110–11.

57. Lorenzo Corsini, Letter to Vico, 20 July 1725, in *Epistole,* 111–12.

58. *Autobiografia:* Croce and Nicolini edit., 48–49; Fisch and Bergin trans., 166. (Fisch trans.)

59. Ibid. (Fisch trans.)

60. On those imprimaturs, see De Miranda, "Nihil decisum fuit," 11–13. From the date of the ecclesiastical review, it seems most probable that Vico used the review that was written for his so-called *Scienza nuova in forma negativa.*

61. See the note that Vico transcribed on the back of the letter he received from Cardinal Corsini, wherein he notes his selling of his diamond ring for the printing and binding of the *Scienza nuova.* Reprinted in Sanna, Introduzione to the *Epistole,* 14–15.

62. Dedication in the *Scienza nuova* (1725): Battistini edit., 977–78; Pompa edit., 3. (Pompa trans.)

63. *Scienza nuova* (1725), para. 21: Battistini edit., 989; Pompa edit., 17. (Pompa trans.)

64. Galileo, *Discourses and Mathematical Demonstrations concerning Two New Sciences.*

65. *Scienza nuova* (1725), para. 399: Battistini edit., 1175; Pompa edit., 233. (Pompa trans.)

66. Compare *Scienza nuova* (1725), book 5: Battistini edit., 1175–1222; Pompa edit., 231–70, and *Scienza nuova* (1744), book 4: Nicolini edit., vol. 2, 49–127; Bergin and Fisch edit., 335–93.

67. *Scienza nuova* (1725), para. 20: Battistini edit., 988–89; Pompa edit., 16. (Pompa trans.)

68. *Scienza nuova* (1725), para. 400: Battistini edit., 1175; Pompa edit., 234. (Pompa trans.)

69. *Scienza nuova* (1725), para. 251: Battistini edit., 1104; Pompa edit., 150; *Scienza nuova* (1725), para. 305: Battistini edit., 1128–29; Pompa edit., 178.

70. *Scienza nuova* (1725), para. 249: Battistini edit., 1103; Pompa edit., 149. (Pompa trans.)

71. *Scienza nuova* (1725), para. 367: Battistini edit., 1153; Pompa edit., 207–8; *Scienza nuova* (1725), para. 374: Battistini edit., 1158; Pompa edit., 213. (Pompa trans.)

72. *Scienza nuova* (1725), paras. 255–60: Battistini edit., 1105–7; Pompa edit., 151–53; *Scienza nuova* (1725), para. 306: Battistini edit., 1129; Pompa edit., 179.

73. *Scienza nuova* (1725), para. 91: Battistini edit., 1033; Pompa edit., 67. (Pompa trans.)

74. *Scienza nuova* (1725), para. 148: Battistini edit., 1055; Pompa edit., 92. (Pompa trans.)

75. See *Scienza nuova* (1725), para. 162: Battistini edit., 1062; Pompa edit., 101. As Vico also put it: the ancient "law of the Roman citizens" was "identical with the law of the gentes of Lazio." *Scienza nuova* (1725), para. 156: Battistini edit., 1058–59; Pompa edit., 97. (Pompa trans.)

76. *Scienza nuova* (1725), paras. 184–90, esp. 188: Battistini edit., 1071–75, esp. 1074; Pompa edit., 112–16, esp. 115.

77. *Scienza nuova* (1725), paras. 188: Battistini edit., 1074; Pompa edit., 115. (Pompa trans.)

78. *Scienza nuova* (1725), paras. 152–54: Battistini edit., 1057; Pompa edit., 94–95, and *Scienza nuova* (1725), paras. 159–73: Battistini edit., 1060–66; Pompa edit., 98–105.

79. *Scienza nuova* (1725), para. 205: Battistini edit., 1081; Pompa edit., 124. (Pompa trans.)

80. *Scienza nuova* (1725), para. 390: Battistini edit., 1169; Pompa edit., 227. (Pompa trans.)

81. *Scienza nuova* (1725), paras. 226–32: Battistini edit., 1091–93; Pompa edit., 135–37; *Scienza nuova* (1725), paras. 350–59: Battistini edit., 1078–81; Pompa edit., 198–204.

82. Strangely, Vico did not note the Antonine constitution—which granted citizenship to the residents of the provinces of the Empire—as the event that equalized the status of the provinces with that of the metropole but rather noted Justinian's abolition of the distinction between things *mancipi* and *nec mancipi,* which concerned things whose ownership was transferable only by the solemn act of *mancipatio. Scienza nuova* (1725), para. 231: Battistini edit., 1092–93; Pompa edit., 137.

83. *Scienza nuova* (1725), para. 230: Battistini edit., 1092; Pompa edit., 136–37. (Pompa trans.)

84. *Scienza nuova* (1725), para. 41: Battistini edit., 1001; Pompa edit., 30. (Pompa trans.)

85. *Scienza nuova* (1725), paras. 354–56: Battistini edit., 1147–48; Pompa edit., 200–202.

86. Donald Kelley, "Vera Philosophia: The Philosophical Significance of Renaissance Jurisprudence," *Journal of the History of Philosophy* 14 (1976): 279.

❧ SOURCES CITED

Manuscripts

Anonymous. *Succinta Relattione del Tumulto successo/In Napoli il giorno del 23 7bre/ 1701....* SNSP MS XXVI.D.10(3.

Baconcopia, Garonne [pseudo.]. *Storia dell'ultima congiura di Napoli/ nel 1701/ Versione dal francese di/ Garonne Baconcopia.* SNSP MS XXI.A.15.

Bulifon, Antonio. *Quarant'hore del Principe di Macchia.* SNSP MS XXVIII.C.12.

Capasso, Nicola. "Se la Ragion di Stato possa derogare alla legge Naturale." In *Delle/ Lezioni Accade-/miche/ De' Diversi Valentuo-/mini de' Nostri Tempi/ Recitate Avanti/ L'Eccellentissimo Signore/ Duca di Medina-Coeli/ Vice-Re, che fù del Regno di Napoli. Parte III.* BNN MS XIII.B.73(5.

Caravita, Filippo. Untitled Memorandum on University Reforms by the Consultore of the Cappellano Maggiore dated 29 September 1714. BNN MS XI.B.17, pp. 282r–289v.

Confuorto, Domenico. *Notitiae/ D'Alcune famiglie Popolari/ Della Città, e Regno/ di Napoli./ Divenute riguardevoli per causa/ di Ricchezze, ò Dignitadi./ Opera del fù Domenico Conforto./ Con le note marginali/ Del Dottor Domenico Bertelli./ L'autore scrive circa il 1693; e/ poco appresso./ E le note son fatte dal 1706 in/ avanti.* BNN MS I.D.5.

———. *Notizie/ di Alcune famiglie Popolari/ Della Città e Regno di Napoli/ Che per ricchezze, e dignità sono divenute/ nobili, e riguardevoli* (1693). BNN MS X.A.15.

———. *Il/ Torto, Òvero Il/ Dritto della Nobilità Napo-/litana/ Esposta al/ Vetro della Verità./ Del Dr. Domenico/ Confuorto.* BNN MS X.A.25.

Contegna, Pietro. *Alcune riflessioni intorno al presente governo del Regno di Napoli sotto l'Augustissimo Imperatore Carlo VI.* SNSP MS XXI.A.7.

Gizio, Andrea Giuseppe. *Prerogative, Genealogie e discorsi di/ diverse famiglie/ con varie cose notabili e singolari.* BNN MS Biblioteca Brancacciana. IV.D.1.

Inventario/ De' Libri/ Prohibiti/ Della/ Libraria/ Brancaccio. BNN MS II.G.14.

Maiello, Carlo. *Conjuratio/ Inita et extincta Neapoli anno MDCCI....* SNSP MS XXII.B.17(2; SNSP MS XXVIII.C.17 and SNSP MS Cuomo I.6.21(2.

———. *Congiura formata e distrutta in Napoli l'anno 1701.* SNSP MS XXVI.A.18.

Marchese, Elio et al. *Esame/ Della Nobiltà Napolitana/ distribuita/ Nei cinque Seggi, cioè/ Capuano, Montagna, Nido, Porto, e Portanova/ Trattenimento dispassionato/ d'Incerto Autore del 1695./ In fine il trattato dell'Origine delle/ Nobili Famiglie della Città di Napoli di Elio Marchese.* BNN MS X.B.72.

Vico, Giambattista. "Delle Cene sontuose de'Romani." In *Delle/ Lezioni Accade-/miche/ De'Diversi Valentuo-/mini de'Nostri Tempi/ Recitate Avanti/ L'Eccellentissimo Signore/ Duca di Medina-Coeli/ Vice-Re, che fù del Regno di Napoli. Parte III.* BNN MS XIII.B.73(1.

———. *Institutionum/ Oratoriarum/ Liber Unus/ exposuit/ Utriusque Juris Doctor Iohannes Baptista a Vico/ In almo Neapolitano Gymnasio/ Die 24 mensis Aprilis Anno/ 1711.* BNN MS XIX.42.IV(1.

Printed Sources

Primary Sources

Ageta, Nicola Gaetano. *Annotationes pro regio aerario ad Supremi Regiae Camerae Summariae senatus Regni Neapolis decisiones.* Naples: Raillard, 1692; repr., Naples: Voccola, 1736.

Aldimari, Biagio, ed. *Pragmaticae, edicta, decreta, regiaeque sanctiones Regni Neapolitani.* First edition. Naples: Raillard, 1682.

Aristotle. *Politics.* Translated by Jonathan Barnes. New York: Cambridge University Press: 1996.

Armellini, Mariano. *Bibliotheca Benedictino[-]Casinensis....* Assisi: Feliciani, & P. Campitelli, 1731.

Bacon, Francis. *Of the Dignity and Advancement of Learning. Books II–VI.* In *The Works of Francis Bacon.* Edited by James Spedding. Vol. 4: *Translations of the Philosophical Works,* Vol. [i.e., part] 1. New edition. London: Longmans and Co., 1875.

———. "Wisdom of the Ancients." In *The Works of Francis Bacon.* Edited by James Spedding. Vol. 6: *Literary and Professional Works,* Vol. [i.e., part] 1. New edition. London: Longmans and Co., 1878.

Biscardi, Serafino. *Epistola pro augusto Hispaniarum monarcha Philippo quinto qua & ius ei assertum successionis universae monarchiae, et omnia confutantur, quae pro investitura Regni Neapolitani, & pro caeteris regnis a Germanis scripta sunt.* Naples: Giuseppe Roselli, 1703.

Bodin, Jean. *The Republic.* Edited and Translated by Julian H. Franklin. New York: Cambridge University Press, 1992.

Calogerà, Angelo, ed. *Raccolta d'opusculi scientifici, e filologici.* Vol. 1. Venice: C. Zane, 1728.

Capaccio, Giulio Cesore. *Il forastiero.* Naples, 1634. Reprint, Naples: Lucca Torre, 1989.

Caravita, Nicola, ed. *Componimenti recitati nell'accademia a' dì 4 di novembre anno 1696 ragunata nel real palagio in Napoli per la ricuperata salute di Carlo II re di Spagna, di Napoli, ec.* Naples: Domenico Antonio Parrino, 1697.

——— *Nullum ius Pontificis maximi in Regno Neapolitano.* Alethopoli [but Naples]: n.p., n.d. [but 1707]. Reprint, Naples, 1788. Italian ed., Naples, 1790.

———, ed. *Varii componimenti in lode dell'eccellentissimo signore don Francesco Benavides conte di S. Stefano ...raccolti da don Nicolò Caravita.* Naples: Giuseppe Roselli, 1696.

———, ed.[?] *Pompe funerali celebrate in Napoli per l'eccellentissima signora donna Caterina d'Aragona....* Naples: Giuseppe Roselli, 1697 [but 1699].

Chiaiese, Giovanni. Letter to Nicola Geremia dated 13 August 1721. In Vico, *Opere,* vol. 5, second edition. And in English translation in *Forum Italicum* 2, no. 4 (December 1968): 315–25.

Cicero. *De finibus bonorum et malorum.* Translated by H. Rackham. Loeb Classical Library. 1914. Reprint, Cambridge: Harvard University Press, 1961.

———. *De legibus.* Translated by C. W. Keyes. Loeb Classical Library. 1928. Reprint, Cambridge: Harvard University Press, 2000.

———. *De officiis*. Translated by Walter Miller. Loeb Classical Library. 1913. Reprint, Cambridge: Harvard University Press, 2005.

———. *De re publica*. Translated by C. W. Keyes. Loeb Classical Library. 1928. Reprint, Cambridge: Harvard University Press, 2000.

———. *Tusculan Disputations*. Edited by J. E. King. Loeb Classical Library. 1927. Reprint, Cambridge: Harvard University Press, 2001.

Columna, Antonio Romano. *De praestantia Sacri Regii Consilii*. Naples: Carlo Porsile, 1704.

Coustel, Pierre. *Les règles de l'éducation des enfants*. 2 vols. Paris: E. Michallet, 1687.

Cuoco, Vincenzo. *Saggio storico della rivoluzione napoletana del 1799*. Edited by Antonino De Francesco. Manduria: P. Lacaita, 1998.

D'Andrea, Francesco. *Avvertimenti ai nipoti*. Edited by Imma Ascione. Naples: Jovene, 1990.

De Luca, Giovanni Battista. *Il Dottor volgare, overo il compendio di tutta la legge civile, canonica, feudale, e municipale, nelle cose piu ricevute in pratica*. Rome: Giuseppe Corvo, 1673.

Diogenes Laertius. *Lives of the Eminent Philosophers*. 2 vols. Translated by R. D. Hicks. Loeb Classical Library. 1925. Reprint, Cambridge: Harvard University Press, 1972.

Dionysius of Halicarnassus. *Roman Antiquities*. With an English translation by Earnest Cary, on the basis of the version of Edward Spelman. 7 vols. Loeb Classical Library. Cambridge: Harvard University Press, 1937–50.

Domat, Jean. *Les lois civiles dans leur ordre naturel*. Paris: La Veuve de Jean Baptiste Coignard, 1707.

Du Perier, Jérôme. *Histoire de la dernière conjuration de Naples en 1701*. Paris: Chez Pierre Giffart, 1706.

Galanti, Giuseppe Maria. *Breve descrizione della Città di Napoli e del suo contorno*. Naples: Gabinetto Letterario, 1792.

———. *Della descrizione geografica e politica delle Sicilie*. Edited by F. Assante and D. Demarco. 2 vols. Naples: Edizioni Scientifiche Italiane, 1969.

Galileo. *Discourses and Mathematical Demonstrations concerning Two New Sciences*. Chicago: University of Chicago Press, 1950.

Genovesi, Antonio. *Lezioni di commercio, o sia di economia civile*. 2 vols. Second edition. Naples: Simoniana, 1768–70.

Giannone, Pietro. *La vita di Pietro Giannone*. Edited by Sergio Bertelli. 2 vols. Turin: Einaudi, 1977.

———. *Istoria civile del Regno di Napoli*. Edited by Antonio Marongiu. 7 vols. Naples, 1723. Reprint, Milano: Marzorati, 1972.

Giornale de' letterati d'Italia. 43 vols. Venice, 1710–40.

Giustiniani, Lorenzo. *Memorie istoriche degli scrittori legali del Regno di Napoli*. 3 vols. Naples: Stamperia Simoniana, 1787.

Goguet, Antoine-Yves. *De l'origine des lois, des arts, et des sciences, et de leurs progrès chez les anciens peuples*. 3 vols. Paris: Desaint & Saillant, 1758.

Gravina, Gian Vincenzo. *Originum iuris civilis libri tres*. Naples: Felice Mosca, 1713.

Grotius, Hugo. *De iure belli ac pacis libri tres*. (1646). In English translation: *The Rights of War and Peace*. Edited by Jean Barbeyrac. Translated by John Morrice. London: D. Brown, 1738. Reprint, Indianapolis: Liberty Fund, 2005.

———. *Mare liberum*. (1609). In English translation: *The Free Sea*. Edited by David Armitage. Indianapolis: Liberty Fund, 2004.

Hobbes, Thomas. *De cive*. Edited by Richard Tuck and Michael Silverthorne. New York: Cambridge University Press, 1998.

——. *Leviathan*. Edited by Richard Tuck. New York: Cambridge University Press, 1991.

Le Clerc, Jean. "Article VIII." In *Bibliothèque ancienne et moderne*. Amsterdam: Frères Wetstein, 1722.

Lipsius, Justus. *De constantia*. (1584). In English: *On Constancy*. Translated by Sir John Stradling. Exeter, UK: Bristol Phoenix Press, 2006.

——. *Politicorum sive civilis doctrinae libri sex*. (1589). In English: *Politica: Six Books of Politics or Political Instruction*. Edited, with translation and introduction by Jan Waszink. Assen, Netherlands: Royal Van Gorcum, 2004.

Livy. *History of Rome*. Translated by B. O. Foster. 11 vols. Loeb Classical Library., 1919. Reprint, Cambridge: Harvard University Press, 2002.

Locke, John. *The Second Treatise on Government*. A critical edition with an introduction and apparatus criticus by Peter Laslett. New York: Cambridge University Press, 1960. Reprint, New York: New American Library, 1965.

Machiavelli. *Discourses on Livy*. Translated by Julia Conaway and Peter Bondanella. New York: Oxford University Press, 2003.

Marcus Aurelius. *Meditations*. Edited and translated by C. R. Haines. Loeb Classical Library. 1913. Reprint, Cambridge: Harvard University Press, 2003.

Montesquieu, Charles de. *The Spirit of the Laws*. (1748) Edited by Anne Cohler, Basia Miller, and Harold Stone. New York: Cambridge University Press, 1989.

Origlia, Gian Giuseppe. *Istoria dello Studio di Napoli*. 2 vols. Naples: Giovanni di Simone, 1754.

Parrino, Domenico Antonio. *Napoli, città nobilissima, antica e fedelissima*. Naples: Parrino, 1700.

——. *Teatro eroico, e politico de'governi de'viceré del Regno di Napoli dal tempo del re Ferdinando il Cattolico fino al presente*. 3 vols. Naples: Nella nuova stampa del Parrino, e del Mutii, 1692–94.

Plutarch. *The Lives of the Noble Grecians and Romans*. Translated by John Dryden and Arthur Hugh Clough. New York: Modern Library, 1979.

Polybius. *Histories*. Translated by W. R. Paton. 6 vols. Loeb Classical Library. Cambridge: Harvard University Press, 1922–27.

Porzio, Camillo. *La congiura de' baroni del Regno di Napoli, contra il Re Ferdinando Primo*. Naples: Stamperia di G. Gravier, 1769.

Pufendorf, Samuel. *On the Duty of Citizen and Man*. Edited by James Tully. Translated by Michael Silverthorne. New York: Cambridge University Press, 1991.

Riaco, Carlo Francesco. *Il giudicio di Napoli: Discorso del passato contaggio, rassomigliato al Giudicio Universale., in cui si specificano le qualità, e numeri de'morti, con tutti gl'accidenti intervenuti*. Perugia: Pietro di Tomasio, 1658.

Riccardi, Alessandro. *Considerazioni sopra al nuovo libro intitolato* Regni neapolitani.... Cologne [but Naples]: Pier Martello [pseud.], 1709.

——. *Ragioni del Regno di Napoli nella causa de' suoi beneficii ecclesiastici*. n.p., n.d. [but Naples, circa 1708].

Rousseau, Jean-Jacques. *The Social Contract*. Edited by Victor Gourevitch. New York: Cambridge University Press, 1997.

Sallust. *The War with Catiline*. Translated by J. C. Rolfe. Loeb Classical Library. 1921. Reprint, Cambridge: Harvard University Press, 2005.

Seneca. *Moral Essays*. Translated by John W. Basore. 3 vols. Loeb Classical Library. 1932. Reprint, Cambridge: Harvard University Press, 1970.

Seneca. *Epistles*. Translated by Richard M. Gummere. 3 vols. Loeb Classical Library. 1917. Reprint, Cambridge: Harvard University Press, 2006.

Soria, Francesco Antonio. *Memorie storico-critiche degli storici napoletani*. 2 vols. Naples: Stamperia Simoniana, 1781–82.

Summonte, Giovanni Antonio. *Historia della Città e Regno di Napoli*. Naples, 1601. Reprint, Naples: Domenico Vivenzio, 1748.

Toppi, Niccolò. *De origine omnium tribunalium nunc in castro Capuano fidelissimae Civitatis Neapolis existentium*. 2 vols. Naples: Onofrio Savio, 1655.

Tutini, Camillo. *Dell'origine e fundazion de' Seggi di Napoli*. Naples, 1644. Reprint, Naples: Raffaele Gessari, 1754.

Ussia, Salvatore. *L'epistolario di Matteo Egizio e la cultura napoletana del primo settecento*. Naples: Liguori, 1977.

Vergerio, Pier Paolo. "De ingenuis moribus et liberalis studiis adulescentiae" (1403). In *Il pensiero pedagogico dell'umanesimo*. Edited by Eugenio Garin.

Vico, Giambattista. *Acta funeris* in *Publicum Caroli Sangrii et Josephi Capycii nobilium Neapolitanorum funus a Carolo Austrio III Hispaniarum Indiarumque et Neapolis rege indictum*. Naples: Felice Mosca, 1708.

——. *The Art of Rhetoric (Institutiones Oratoriae, 1711–41)*. Edited and translated by Giorgio A. Pinton and Arthur W. Shippee (from the Crifò edition). Amsterdam: Rodopi, 1996.

——. *Autobiography*. Translated by Max Harold Fisch and Thomas Goddard Bergin. First edition. Ithaca: Cornell University Press, 1944.

——. *La congiura dei principi napoletani, 1701 (Prima e seconda stesura)*. Edited by Claudia Pandolfi. Naples: Morano, 1992.

——. *Epistole*. Edited by Manuela Sanna. Naples: Morano, 1992.

——. *The First New Science*. Edited and translated by Leon Pompa. New York: Cambridge University Press, 2002.

——. *Le gesta di Antonio Carafa*. Edited by Manuela Sanna. Naples: Guida, 1997.

——. "In funere excellentissimae Catharinae Aragoniae Segorbiensis ducis, etc." In *Pompe funerali celebrate in Napoli per l'eccellentissima signora donna Caterina d'Aragona....* Naples: Giuseppe Rosselli, 1697 [but 1699].

——. *Institutiones oratoriae*. Edited by Giuliano Crifò. Naples: Istituto Suor Orsola Benincasa, 1989.

——. *Liber alter qui est de constantia iurisprudentis*. Naples: Felice Mosca, 1721.

——. *Minora: Scritti latini, storici e d'occasione*. Edited by Gian Galeazzo Visconti. Naples: Guida, 2000.

——. *De nostri temporis studiorum ratione*. In *Opere*. Vol. 1: *Le orazioni inaugurali, Il De Italorum sapientia e le polemiche*. Edited by Giovanni Gentile and Fausto Nicolini. Bari: Laterza, 1914.

——. *The New Science: Unabridged Translation of the Third Edition, 1744*. Translated by Thomas Goddard Bergin and Max Harold Fisch. First edition. Ithaca: Cornell University Press, 1948.

——. *Notae in duos libros alterum de uno universi iuris principio, etc. alterum de constantia jurisprudentis*. Naples: Felice Mosca, 1722.

——. *On Humanistic Education (Six Inaugural Orations, 1699–1707)*. Translated by Giorgio A. Pinton and Arthur W. Shippee. Ithaca: Cornell University Press, 1993.

——. *On the Most Ancient Wisdom of the Italians.* Translated by L. M. Palmer. Ithaca: Cornell University Press, 1988.

——. *On the Study Methods of Our Time.* Translated by Elio Gianturco. Ithaca: Cornell University Press, 1990.

——. *Opere.* Edited by Andrea Battistini. 2 vols. Milan: Mondadori, 1990.

——. *Opere.* Edited by Fausto Nicolini with Benedetto Croce and Giovanni Gentile. 8 vols. Bari: Laterza, 1911–41.

——. *Opere giuridiche: Il diritto universale.* Edited by Paolo Cristofolini. Florence: Sansoni, 1974.

——. *Le orazioni inaugurali, I–VI.* Edited by Gian Galeazzo Visconti. Bologna: Il Mulino, 1982.

——. *Panegyricus Philippo V Hispaniarum, Indiarumque, utriusque Siciliae potentissimo regi.* Naples: Felice Mosca, 1702.

——. *Princìpi di una scienza nuova.* In *Opere.* Edited by Andrea Battistini. Vol. 2. Milan: Mondadori, 1990.

——. *Risposta del signore Giambattista di Vico nella quale si sciogliono tre gravi opposizioni fatte da dotto signore contro il primo libro* De antiquissima Italorum sapientia, *ovvero della metafisica degli antichissimi filosofi Italiani tratta da'latini parlari.* Naples: Felice Mosca, 1711.

——. *Risposta di Giambattista di Vico all'articolo X del tomo VII del* Giornale de' letterati d'Italia. Naples: Felice Mosca, 1712.

——. *Universal Right.* Translated from the Latin and edited by Giorgio Pinton and Margaret Diehl. Amsterdam: Rodopi, 2000.

——. *De universi iuris uno principio et fine uno liber unus.* Naples: Felice Mosca, 1720.

——. *Varia.* Edited by Giangaleazzo Visconti. Naples: Guida, 1996.

——, ed. *Varii componimenti per le nozze degli eccellentissimi signori don Giambattista Filomarino prencipe della Rocca &c., e donna Maria Vittoria Caracciolo de'marchesi di Sant'Eramo.* Naples: Felice Mosca, 1721.

——, ed. *Varii componimenti per le nozze degl'illustrissimi & eccellentissimi signori don Adriano Carafa duca di Traetto, conte del S.R.I., grande di Spagna &c., e donna Teresa Borghesi de' prencipi di Sulmona, di Rossano, &c.* Naples: Felice Mosca, 1719.

——. *Vita di Giambattista Vico scritta da se medesimo.* In *Opere.* Vol. 5: *L'autobiografia, il carteggio e le poesie varie.* Edited by Benedetto Croce and Fausto Nicolini. Second edition, revised and enlarged. Bari: Laterza, 1929.

Vitoria, Francisco de. *Political Writings.* Edited by Anthony Pagden. New York: Cambridge University Press, 1991.

Zeno, Apostolo. *Lettere di Apostolo Zeno.* 6 vols. Second edition. Venice: Francesco Sansoni, 1785.

Secondary Sources

Ajello, Raffaele. *Arcana Juris: Diritto e politica nel Settecento italiano.* Naples: Jovene, 1976.

——. "Il Banco di San Carlo: Organi di governo e opinione pubblica nel Regno di Napoli di fronte al problema della ricompra dei diritti fiscali." *Rivista Storica Italiana* 81 (1969): 812–81.

——. "Dal facere al factum." *Bollettino del Centro di Studi Vichiani* 12–13 (1982–83): 343–59.

———. *Il problema della riforma giudiziaria e legislativa nel Regno di Napoli durante la prima metà del secolo XVIII.* 2 vols. Naples: Jovene, 1965–68.

Amerio, Franco. *Introduzione allo studio di G. B. Vico.* Turin: Società editrice internazionale, 1947.

Ascione, Imma. *Il governo della prassi: L'esperienza ministeriale di Francesco D'Andrea.* Naples: Jovene, 1994.

———. *Seminarium doctrinarum.* Naples: Edizioni Scientifiche Italiane, 1997.

Astarita, Tommaso. *The Continuity of Feudal Power: The Caracciolo of Brienza in Spanish Naples.* New York: Cambridge University Press, 1992.

Badaloni, Nicola. *Introduzione a G. B. Vico.* Milan: Feltrinelli, 1961.

Baron, Hans. *The Crisis of the Early Italian Renaissance.* Revised edition. Princeton: Princeton University Press, 1966.

Belgioioso, Giulia, ed. *Manoscritti napoletani di Paolo Mattia Doria.* 5 vols. Galatina (Lecce): Congedo, 1982.

Belli, Carolina. "I fondi archivistici napoletani e la storia di librai, stampatori e biblioteche." In *Editoria e cultura a Napoli nel XVIII secolo.* Edited by Anna Maria Rao. Naples: Liguori, 1998.

Benaiteau, Michèle. *Vassalli e cittadini: La signoria rurale nel Regno di Napoli attraverso lo studio dei feudi dei Tocco di Montemiletto (XI–XVIII secolo).* Bari: Edipuglia, 1997.

Benedikt, Heinrich. *Das Koenigreich Neapel unter Kaiser Karl VI.* Vienna: Manz Verlag, 1927.

Bentley, Jerry H. *Politics and Culture in Renaissance Naples.* Princeton: Princeton University Press, 1987.

Berlin, Isaiah. *Vico and Herder: Two Studies in the History of Ideas.* New York: Viking Press, 1976.

Bianchi, Lorenzo, ed. *Cosmopolitismo.* Naples: Liguori, 2004.

Bizzocchi, Roberto. *Genealogie incredibili: Scritti di storia nell'Europa moderna.* Bologna: Il Mulino, 1995.

Bock, Kenneth E. "Comparison of Histories: The Contribution of Henry Maine." *Comparative Studies in Society and History* 16, no. 2 (1974): 232–62.

Bot, Hans, and Françoise Wacquet. *La République des lettres.* Paris: Belin, 1997.

Bowler, Peter J. *The Invention of Progress: The Victorians and Their Past.* Oxford: Basil Blackwell, 1989.

Bowsky, William. "Medieval Citizenship: The Individual and the State in the Commune of Siena, 1287–1355." In *Studies in Medieval and Renaissance History.* Vol. 4. Edited by William M. Bowsky. Lincoln: University of Nebraska Press, 1967.

Brett, Annabel. "The Development of the Idea of Citizens' Rights." In *States and Citizens: History, Theory, Prospects.* Edited by Quentin Skinner and Bo Straeth. New York: Cambridge University Press, 2003.

———. *Liberty, Right, and Nature: Individual Rights in Later Scholastic Thought.* New York: Cambridge University Press, 1997.

Bridenthal, Renate. "Was There a Roman Homer: Niebuhr's Thesis and his Critics." *History and Theory* 11, no. 2 (1972): 193–213.

Burke, Peter. Review of *Neostoicism and the Early Modern State* by Gerhard Oestreich. *English Historical Review* 100, no. 395 (1985): 403–4.

———. "A Survey of the Popularity of Ancient Historians, 1450–1700." *History and Theory* 52, no. 2 (1966): 135–52.

———. "Tacitism." In *Tacitus.* Edited by T. A. Dorey. London: Routledge and Paul, 1969.

———. "Tacitism, Scepticism, and Reason of State" In *The Cambridge History of Political Thought, 1450–1700.* Edited by J. H. Burns. New York: Cambridge University Press, 1991.

———. "The Virgin of the Carmine and the Revolt by Masaniello." *Past and Present,* no. 99 (1983): 3–21.

Burrow, J. W. *Evolution and Society: A Study in Victorian Social Theory.* Cambridge: Cambridge University Press, 1966.

Cantone, Carlo. *Il concetto filosofico di diritto in Giambattista Vico.* Mazara (Trapani): Società Editrice Siciliana, 1952.

Capasso, Bartolommeo. *Sulla circoscrizione civile ed ecclesiastica sulla popolazione della città di Napoli dalla fine del secolo XIII fino al 1809.* Naples: Tipografia della Regia Università, 1882.

Caponigri, Robert. *Time and Idea: The Theory of History in Giambattista Vico.* Chicago: Henry Regnery, 1953.

Caporali, Riccardo. *Heroes Gentium: Sapienza e politica in Vico.* Bologna: Il Mulino, 1992.

Clark, Peter, and Bernard Lepetit, eds. *Capital Cities and Their Hinterlands in Early Modern Europe.* Brookfield, VT: Ashgate, 1996.

Cochrane, Eric. *Historians and Historiography in the Italian Renaissance.* Chicago: University of Chicago Press, 1981.

Colapietra, Raffaele. *Vita pubblica e classi politiche del viceregno napoletano.* Rome: Edizioni di storia e letteratura, 1961.

Colussi, Roberta. "Diritto, istituzioni, amministrazione della giustizia nel Mezzogiorno vicereale. I: La struttura regalistica." In *Storia del Mezzogiorno.* Edited by Giuseppe Galasso and Rosario Romeo. Vol. 9: *Aspetti e problemi del medioevo e dell'età moderna,* part 2. Naples: Edizioni del Sole, 1991.

Comparato, Vittor Ivo. "From the Crisis of Civil Culture to the Neapolitan Republic of 1647: Republicanism in Italy between the Sixteenth and Seventeenth Centuries." In *Republicanism: A Shared European Heritage.* Edited by Martin van Gelderen and Quentin Skinner. New York: Cambridge University Press, 2005.

———. *Uffici e società a Napoli (1600–47): Aspetti dell'ideologia del magistrato nell'età moderna.* Florence: Olschki, 1974.

Coniglio, Giuseppe. *I vicerè spagnoli di Napoli.* 1957. Reprint, Naples: Fausto Fiorentino, 1967.

Conti, Vittorio. *Le leggi di una rivoluzione: I bandi della repubblica napoletana dall'ottobre 1647 all'aprile 1648.* Naples: Jovene, 1983.

Cosgrove, Denis. "Globalism and Tolerance in Early Modern Geography." *Annals of the Association of American Geographers* 93, no. 4 (2003): 852–70.

Costa, Gustavo. "Ancora su Vico." *Giornale critico della filosofia italiana* 79, no. 1 (2000).

———. "Vico e l'Inquisizione." *Nouvelles de la République des Lettres* 2 (1999), 93–124.

———. "Vico e la Sacra Scrittura alla luce di un fascicolo dell'Inquisizione." In *Pensar para el nuevo siglo: Giambattista Vico e la cultura europea.* Edited by Emilio Hidalgo-Serna et al. Naples: La Città del Sole, 2001.

Costa, Pietro. *Civitas: Storia della cittadinanza in Europa.* Vol. I: *Dalla civiltà communale al Settecento.* Rome: Laterza, 1999.

Crifò, Giuliano. "Vico e la storia romana. Alcune considerazioni." In *Giambattista Vico nel suo tempo e nel nostro.* Edited by Mario Agrimi. Naples: CUEN, 1999.

Croce, Benedetto. *Bibliografia vichiana.* First edition. Naples: Alfonso Tessitore & Figlio, 1904.

———. *Bibiliografia vichiana.* Revised and enlarged by Fausto Nicolini. 2 vols. Naples: Ricciardi, 1947.

———. "I due concorsi universitari di G. B. Vico." *La critica* 6 (1908), 306–8.

———. *The Philosophy of Giambattista Vico.* Translated by R. G. Collingwood. 1913. Reprint, Brunswick, NJ: Transaction Press, 2002.

———. *Uomini e cose della vecchia Italia.* 1927. Second revised edition, Bari: Laterza, 1943.

D'Alessio, Silvana. *Contagi: La rivolta napoletana del 1647–48.* Florence: Centro editoriale toscano, 2003.

De Frede, Carlo. *Studenti e uomini di legge a Napoli nel Rinascimento.* Naples: L'arte tipografica, 1957.

De Giovanni, Biagio. "Il *De nostri temporis studiorum ratione* nella cultura napoletana del primo Settecento." In *Omaggio a Vico.* Edited by A. Corsano et al. Naples: Morano, 1968.

Del Bagno, Ileana. *Il Collegio napoletano dei dottori: Privilegi, decreti, decisioni.* Naples: Jovene, 2000.

———. *Legum doctores: La formazione del ceto giuridico a Napoli tra Cinque e Seicento.* Naples: Jovene, 1993.

Delille, Gerard. "Demografia." In *Storia del Mezzogiorno.* Edited by Giuseppe Galasso and Rosario Romeo. Vol. 8: *Aspetti e problemi del Medioevo e dell'età Moderna,* part one. Naples: Edizioni del Sole, 1991.

De Miranda, Girolamo. "Nihil decisum fuit." *Bollettino del Centro di Studi Vichiani* 28 (1998–99): 5–70.

De Seta, Cesare. *Storia della città di Napoli.* Rome: Laterza, 1973.

Donzelli, Maria. *Natura e humanitas nel giovane Vico.* Naples: Istituto per gli Studi Storici, 1970.

Erasmus, Johannes Hendrik. *The Origins of Rome in Historiography from Petrarch to Perizonius.* Assen, Netherlands: Van Gorcum, 1962.

Farraú, Giacomo. *Il tessitore di Antequera: Storiografia umanistica meridionale.* Rome: Istituto storico italiano per il Medio Evo, 2001.

Fassò, Guido. *Vico e Grozio.* Naples: Guida, 1971.

Findlen, Paula. "Translating the New Science: Women and the Circulation of Knowledge in Enlightenment Italy." *Configurations* 3, no. 2 (1995): 174–84.

Fisch, Max Harold. "Vico on Roman Law." *New Vico Studies* 19 (2001): 3–25.

Fragnito, Gigliola. "The Central and Peripheral Organization of Censorship." In *Church, Censorship, and Culture in Early Modern Italy.* Edited by Gigliola Fragnito. New York: Cambridge University Press, 2001.

Galasso, Giuseppe. "Ai tempi del Vico: Fra il tramonto del viceregno e l'avvento di Carlo di Borbone." In *Napoli capitale.* Edited by Giuseppe Galasso. Naples: Electa, 1998.

———. *Aspetti e problemi del medioevo e dell'età moderna.* Rome: Editalia, 1991.

———. *Napoli dopo Masaniello: Politica, cultura, società.* 2 vols. Florence: Sansoni, 1982.

———. "Napoli nel viceregno spagnolo (1696–1707)." In *Storia di Napoli.* Vol. 6: *Fra Spagna e Austria.* Naples: Edizioni Scientifiche Italiane, 1970.

———. "Il Vico di Giarrizzo e un itinerario alternativo." *Bollettino del Centro di Studi Vichiani* 12–13 (1982–83): 359–75.

Garin, Eugenio. "Da Campanella a Vico." In *Dal Rinascimento all'Illuminismo.* Pisa: Nistri-Lischi, 1970.

———. *Educazione umanistica in Italia.* Bari: Laterza, 1949.

———, ed. *Il pensiero pedagogico dello umanesimo.* Florence: Editrice Universitaria, 1958.

Gelderen, Martin van. "The Machiavellian Moment and the Dutch Revolt: The Rise of Neostoicism and Dutch Republicanism." In *Machiavelli and Republicanism.* Edited by Gisela Bock, Quentin Skinner, and Maurizio Viroli. New York: Cambridge University Press, 1990.

———. *The Political Thought of the Dutch Revolt, 1555–1590.* New York: Cambridge University Press, 1992.

Ghisalberti, Carlo. *Gian Vincenzo Gravina: Giurista e storico.* Milan: Giuffrè, 1962.

Giarrizzo, Giuseppe. "Giannone, Vico e i loro interpreti recenti." *Bollettino del Centro di Studi Vichiani* 11 (1981): 173–84.

———. *Vico, la politica e la storia.* Naples: Guida, 1981.

Gilbert, Felix. "Bernardo Rucellai and the Orti Oricellari: A Study on the Origin of Modern Political Thought." *Journal of the Warburg and Courtauld Institutes* 12 (1949): 101–31.

Gilmore, Myron P. *Humanists and Jurists: Six Studies in the Renaissance.* Cambridge: Harvard University Press, 1963.

Goldgar, Anne. *Impolite Learning: Conduct and Community in the Republic of Letters, 1680–1750.* New Haven: Yale University Press, 1995.

Goodman, Dena. *The Republic of Letters: A Cultural History of the French Enlightenment.* Ithaca: Cornell University Press, 1994.

Gordon, Daniel. *Citizens without Sovereignty: Equality and Sociability in French Thought, 1670–1789.* Princeton: Princeton University Press, 1994.

———. "Citizenship." In *The Encyclopedia of the Enlightenment.* Edited by Alan Kors. Oxford: Oxford University Press, 2005.

Gouwens, Kenneth. *Remembering the Renaissance: Humanist Narratives of the Sack of Rome.* London: Brill, 1998.

Grafton, Anthony. *Bring Out Your Dead: The Past as Revelation.* Cambridge: Harvard University Press, 2001.

———. *Joseph Scaliger: A Study in the History of Classical Scholarship.* Oxford: Clarendon Press, 1983.

Grandazzi, Alexandre. *The Foundation of Rome: Myth and History.* Translated by Jane Marie Todd. Ithaca: Cornell University Press, 1997.

Granito, Angelo, Principe di Belmonte. *Storia della congiura del Principe di Macchia.* 2 vols. Naples: Iride, 1861.

Griggs, Tamara. "Universal History from Counter-Reformation to Enlightenment." *Modern Intellectual History* 4, no. 2 (2007): 219–47.

Gualdo Rosa, Lucia. "L'elogio delle lettere e delle armi nell'opera di Leonardo Bruni." In *Sapere e\è potere.* Vol. 1: *Forme e oggetti della disputa delle arti.* Edited by Luisa Avellini.

———. "Leonardo Bruni." In *Centuriae Latinae: Cent une figures humanistes de la Renaissance aux Lumières offertes à Jacques Chomart*. Collected by Colette Nativel. Genève: Librairie Droz, 1997.

Guenter, Abel. *Stoizismus und fruehe Neuzeit: Zur Entstehungsgeschichte modernen Denkens im Felde von Ethik und Politik*. Berlin: De Gruyter, 1978.

Gueye, Cheikh Mbacké. *Late Stoic Cosmopolitanism*. Heidelberg: Universitaetsverlag, 2006.

Haakonssen, Knud. *Natural Law and Moral Philosophy: From Grotius to the Scottish Enlightenment*. New York: Cambridge University Press, 1996.

Haddock, B. A. *Vico's Political Thought*. Swansea, Wales: Mortlake Press, 1986.

Hankins, James. "The Baron Thesis after Forty Years and Some Recent Studies of Leonardo Bruni." *Journal of the History of Ideas* 56, no. 2 (1995): 309–38.

———. Introduction to *History of the Florentine People. Books I–IV*, by Leonardo Bruni. Cambridge: Harvard University Press, 2001.

Heilbron, Johan. *The Rise of Social Theory: Contradictions of Modernity*. Translated by Sheila Gogol. Minneapolis: University of Minnesota Press, 1995.

Herzog, Tamar. *Defining Nations: Immigrants and Citizens in Early Modern Spain and Spanish America*. New Haven: Yale University Press, 2003.

Hills, Helen. *Invisible City: The Architecture of Devotion in Seventeenth-Century Neapolitan Convents*. New York: Oxford University Press, 2005.

Hirschman, Albert O. *The Passions and the Interests: Political Arguments of Capitalism before Its Triumph*. Princeton: Princeton University Press, 1977.

Hochstrasser, T. J. *Natural Law Theories in the Early Enlightenment*. New York: Cambridge University Press, 2000.

Hohenberg, Paul M., and Lynn Hollen Lees. "Urban Systems and Economic Growth: Town Populations in Metropolitan Hinterlands, 1600–1800." In *Capital Cities and Their Hinterlands*. Edited by Peter Clark and Bernard Lepetit.

Hont, Istvan. *Jealousy of Trade: International Competition and the Nation-State in Historical Perspective*. Cambridge: Harvard University Press, 2005.

Hutton, Patrick H. "Vico's Theory of History and the French Revolutionary Tradition." *Journal of the History of Ideas* 37, no. 2 (1976): 241–56.

Ianziti, Gary. "A Humanist Historian and His Documents: Giovanni Simonetta, Secretary to the Sforzas." *Renaissance Quarterly* 34, no. 4 (1981): 491–516.

Intorcia, Gaetana. *Magistrature del Regno di Napoli*. Naples: Jovene, 1987.

Inwood, Brad, ed. *The Cambridge Companion to the Stoics*. New York: Cambridge University Press, 2003.

Israel, Jonathan. *Radical Enlightenment: Philosophy and the Making of Modernity, 1650–1750*. Oxford: Oxford University Press, 2001.

Jacob, Margaret C. *The Radical Enlightenment: Pantheists, Freemasons, and Republicans*. Boston: Allen & Unwin, 1981.

———. *Strangers Nowhere in the World: The Rise of Cosmopolitanism in Early Modern Europe*. Philadelphia: University of Pennsylvania Press, 2006.

Jedin, Hubert. *A History of the Council of Trent*. 2 vols. St. Louis: B. Herder, 1957–61.

Jolly, Rosyln. "Robert Louis Stevenson, Henry Maine and the Anthropology of Comparative Law." *Journal of British Studies* 45, no. 3 (2006): 556–80.

Jolowicz, H. F. *Roman Foundations of Modern Law*. Oxford: Clarendon Press, 1957.

Jolowicz, H. F., and Barry Nicholas. *Historical Introduction to the Study of Roman Law.* Cambridge: Cambridge University Press, 1972.

Kelley, Donald R. "*De origine feudorum:* The Beginnings of an Historical Problem." *Speculum* 39 (1964): 207–28.

———. *Foundations of Modern Historical Scholarship: Language, Law, and History in the French Renaissance.* New York: Columbia University Press, 1970.

———. *History, Law, and the Human Sciences.* London: Variorum, 1984.

———. *The Human Measure: Social Thought in the Western Legal Tradition.* Cambridge: Harvard University Press, 1990.

———. "The Pre-history of Sociology: Montesquieu, Vico, and the Legal Tradition." *History of the Behavioral Sciences* 16, no. 2 (1980): 133–44.

———. "Vera Philosophia: The Philosophical Significance of Renaissance Jurisprudence." *Journal of the History of Philosophy* 14 (1976): 279.

Kirshner, Julius. "*Ars Imitatur Naturam:* A Consilium of Baldus on Naturalization in Florence." *Viator* 5 (1974): 289–331.

———. "Between Nature and Culture: An Opinion of Baldus of Perugia on Venetian Citizenship as Second Nature." *Journal of Medieval and Renaissance Studies* 9, no. 2 (1979): 179–208.

———. "*Civitas Sibi Faciat Civem:* Bartolus of Sassoferrato's Doctrine on the Making of a Citizen." *Speculum* 48, no. 4 (1973): 694–713.

Kleingeld, Pauline. "Six Varieties of Cosmopolitanism in Late Eighteenth-Century Germany," *Journal of the History of Ideas* 60, no. 3 (1999): 505–24.

Kohl, Benjamin G. "Humanism and Education." In *Renaissance Humanism.* Vol. 3: *Humanism and the Disciplines.* Edited by Albert Rabil. Philadelphia: University of Pennsylvania Press, 1988.

Koselleck, Reinhart. "Historia Magistra Vitae: The Dissolution of the Topos into the Perspective of a Modernized Historical Process." In Idem. *Futures Past: On the Semantics of Historical Time.* Cambridge: MIT Press, 1985.

Labrot, Gerard. *Baroni in città: Residenze e comportamenti dell'aristocrazia napoletana, 1530–1734.* Naples: Società Editrice Napoletana, 1979.

Lilla, Mark. *Vico: The Making of an Anti-Modern.* Cambridge: Harvard University Press, 1993.

Lomonaco, Fabrizio. *Le Orationes di G. Gravina: Scienza, sapienza e diritto.* Naples: La Città del Sole, 1997.

Long, D. N., and A. A. Sedley. *The Hellenistic Philosophers.* 2 vols. New York: Cambridge University Press, 1987.

López García, José Miguel, and Santos Madrazo Madrazo. "A Capital City in the Feudal Order: Madrid from the Sixteenth to the Eighteenth Century." In *Capital Cities and Their Hinterlands.* Edited by Peter Clark and Bernard Lepetit.

Luce, James T., and A. J. Woodman, eds. *Tacitus and the Tacitean Tradition.* Princeton: Princeton University Press, 1993.

Luongo, Dario, ed. *All'alba dell'illuminismo: Cultura e pubblico studio nella Napoli austriaca.* Naples: Guida, 1997.

———. *Serafino Biscardi: Mediazione ministeriale e ideologia economica.* Naples: Jovene, 1993.

———. *Vis jurisprudentiae: Teoria e prassi della moderazione giuridica in Gaetano Argento.* Naples: Jovene 2001.

Maclean, Ian. *Interpretation and Meaning in the Renaissance: The Case of Law.* New York: Cambridge University Press, 1992.

Maffei, Domenico. *Gli inizi dell'umanesimo giuridico.* Milan: Giuffrè, 1956.

Maffei, Scipione, ed. *De origine iuris civilis.* Naples: Gennaro Matarazzo, 1822.

Mali, Joseph. *The Rehabilitation of Myth: Vico's New Science.* New York: Cambridge University Press, 1992.

Marin, Brigitte. "Mythes ou Mystification." In *Naples: Démythier la ville,* by Collette Vallat, Brigitte Marin, and Gennaro Biondi. Paris: L'Harmattan, 1998.

———. "Naples: Capital of the Enlightenment." In *Capital Cities and Their Hinterlands in Early Modern Europe.* Edited by Peter Clark and Bernard Lepetit.

———. "Town and Country in the Kingdom of Naples, 1500–1800." In *Town and Country in Europe, 1300–1800.* Edited by S. R. Epstein. New York: Cambridge University Press, 2001.

Masi, Giorgio. *Dal Collenuccio a Tommaso Costo: Vicende della storiografia napoletana fra Cinque e Seicento.* Naples: Editoriale scientifica, 1999.

Massafra, Angelo. "Nota sulla geografia feudale del Regno di Napoli alla fine del XVIII secolo." In *Le mappe della storia.* Edited by Giuseppe Giarrizzo and Enrico Iachello. Milan: FrancoAngeli, 2002.

Mastellone, Salvo. *Francesco D'Andrea politico e giurista (1648–1698): L'ascesa del ceto civile.* Florence: Olschki, 1969.

———. *Pensiero politico e vita culturale a Napoli nella seconda metà del Seicento.* Messina/Florence: Casa Editrice D'Anna, 1965.

Mayer, Ronald. "Personata Stoa: Neostoicism and Senecan Tragedy." *Journal of the Warburg and Courtauld Institutes* 57 (1994): 151–74.

Mazzarino, Santo. *Vico, l'annalistica e il diritto.* Naples: Guida, 1971.

Mazzotta, Giuseppe. *The New Map of the World: The Poetic Philosophy of Giambattista Vico.* Princeton: Princeton University Press, 1999.

McCrea, Adriana. *Constant Minds: Political Virtue and the Lipsian Paradigm in England, 1584–1650.* Toronto: University of Toronto Press, 1997.

McCuaig, William. "Bernardo Rucellai and Sallust." *Rinascimento* 32 (1982): 75–98.

Meek, Ronald L. *Social Science and the Ignoble Savage.* New York: Cambridge University Press, 1976.

Miles, Geoffrey. *Shakespeare and the Constant Romans.* New York: Oxford University Press, 1996.

Miletti, Marco Nicola. *Tra equità e dottrina: Il Sacro Regio Consiglio e le "decisiones" di V. De Franchis.* Naples: Jovene, 1995.

———. *Stylus judicandi: Le raccolte di "decisiones" del Regno di Napoli in età moderna.* Naples: Jovene, 1998.

Miller, Peter N. "Nazis and Neo-Stoics." *Past and Present* no. 176 (2002): 144–86.

———. *Peiresc's Europe: Learning and Virtue in the Seventeenth Century.* New Haven: Yale University Press, 2000.

———. "Stoics Who Sing: Lessons on Citizenship from Early Modern Lucca." *Historical Journal* 44, no. 2 (2001): 313–39.

Momigliano, Arnaldo. *The Classical Foundations of Modern Historiography.* Berkeley: University of California Press, 1990.

———. "Niebuhr and the Agrarian Problems of Rome." *History and Theory* 21, no. 4 (1982): 3–15.

——. "La nuova storia romana di G. B. Vico." *Rivista Storica Italiana* 77 (1965): 773–90.

——. "Perizonius, Niebuhr, and the Character of the Early Roman Tradition." *Journal of Roman Studies* 47, no.1–2 (1957): 104–14.

——. "Vico's *Scienza Nuova:* Roman 'Bestioni' and Roman 'Eroi.'" *History and Theory* 5, no. 1 (1966): 3–23.

Mommsen, Theodor. *History of Rome.* Translated by William P. Dickinson. London: Richard Bentley, 1864.

Monserrat, Gilles D. *Light from the Porch: Stoicism and English Renaissance Literature.* Paris: Didier-Edition, 1984.

Monti, G. M. "Legislazione statale ed ecclesiastica sulla stampa nel Viceregno austriaco di Napoli." In *Scritti giuridici in onore di Santi Romano.* Padua: Cedam, 1940.

Monti, Salvatore. *Sulla tradizione e sul testo delle orazioni inaugurali di Vico.* Naples: Guida, 1977.

Mooney, Michael. *Vico in the Tradition of Rhetoric.* Princeton: Princeton University Press, 1985.

Morford, Mark. *Stoics and Neostoics: Rubens and the Circle of Lipsius.* Princeton: Princeton University Press, 1991.

Mortari, Vincenzo Piano. *Diritto, logica, metodo nel secolo XVI.* Naples: Jovene, 1978.

Musi, Aurelio, ed. *Dimenticare Croce? Studi e orientamenti di storia del Mezzogiorno.* Naples: Edizioni Scientifiche Italiane, 1991.

——. *La rivolta di Masaniello nella scena politica barocca.* Naples: Guida, 1989.

Muto, Giovanni. "Gestione politica e controllo sociale nella Napoli spagnola." In *Le città capitali.* Edited by Cesare De Seta. Rome: Laterza, 1985.

——. "Istituzioni dell'universitas e ceti dirigenti locali." In *Storia del Mezzogiorno.* Edited by Giuseppe Galasso and Rosario Romeo. Vol. 9: *Aspetti e problemi del medioevo e dell'età moderna,* part 2. (Naples: Edizioni del Sole, 1991).

——. " Problemi di stratificazione nobiliare nell'Italia spagnola." In *Dimenticare Croce?* Edited by Aurelio Musi.

——. "I segni d'honore. Rappresentazioni delle dinamiche nobiliari a Napoli in età moderna." In *Signori, patrizi, cavalieri in Italia centro-meridionale nell'Età moderna.* Edited by Maria Antonietta Visceglia.

——. "I trattati napoletani cinquecenteschi in tema di nobiltà." In *Sapere e/è potere.* Vol. 3: *Dalle discipline ai ruoli sociali.* Edited by Angela De Benedictis.

Naddeo, Barbara. "Neapolitan Itineraries: Re-collecting the City in Topographical Studies of Naples, 1650–1800." Paper presented at the conference "Exoticizing Vesuvius" at The Centre for Research in the Arts, Social Sciences and Humanities (CRASSH), Cambridge University, Cambridge, England, 18 September 2009.

——. "Topographies of Difference: Cartography of the City of Naples, 1629–1798." *Imago Mundi* 56, no. 1 (2004): 23–47.

——. "Vico Anthropologist: From Civic to World History." *Bollettino del Centro di Studi Vichiani* 33 (2003): 103–18.

Nadler, Steven. *Spinoza's Ethics: An Introduction.* New York: Cambridge University Press, 2006.

Nicholas, Barry. *An Introduction to Roman Law.* Oxford: Oxford University Press, 1979.

Nicolet, Claude. *The World of the Citizen in Republican Rome.* Translated by P. S. Falla. Berkeley: University of California Press, 1980.

Nicolini, Fausto. *Giambattista Vico nella vita domestica.* 1927. Reprint, Venosa (Potenza): Edizioni Osanna, 1991.

—— *La giovinezza di Giambattista Vico (1668–1700).* Second revised edition. Bari: Laterza, 1932.

——. *Uomini di spada di chiesa di toga di studio ai tempi di Giambattista Vico.* 1942. Reprint, Bologna: Il Mulino, 1992.

——. "Vicende e codici della *Principum neapolitanorum coniuratio* di Giambattista Vico." In *Atti della Reale Accademia Pontaniana di Scienze Morali e Politiche* 59 (1938): 122–63.

Niebuhr, G. B. *The Roman History.* Translated by F. A. Walter. London: C. and J. Rivington, 1827.

Nussbaum, Marta. "Kant and Stoic Cosmopolitanism." *Journal of Political Philosophy* 5, no. 1 (1997): 1–25.

Oestreich, Gerhard. *Neostoicism and the Early Modern State.* Edited by Brigitta Oestreich and H. G. Koenigsberger. Translated by David McLintock. New York: Cambridge University Press, 1982.

Olin, John C. *Catholic Reform: From Cardinal Ximenes to the Council of Trent.* New York: Fordham University Press, 1990.

Orenstein, Henry. "The Ethnological Theories of Henry Sumner Maine." *American Anthropologist,* New Series 70, no. 2 (1968): 264–76.

Osmond, Patricia. "*Princeps Historiae Romanae:* Sallust in Renaissance Political Thought." *Memoirs of the American Academy in Rome* 40 (1995): 101–43.

Palonen, Kari. *Quentin Skinner: History, Politics, Rhetoric.* Cambridge: Polity Press, 2003.

Pandolfi, Claudia. *Per l'edizione critica della* Principum neapolitanorum coniurationis anni mdcci historia *di G. Vico.* Naples: Guida, 1988.

Pasini, Dino. *Diritto, società e stato in Vico.* Naples: Jovene, 1970.

Petraccone, Claudia. *Napoli dal Cinquecento all'Ottocento: Problemi di storia demografica e sociale.* Naples: Guida, 1974.

——. *Napoli moderna e contemporanea.* Naples: Guida, 1981.

Peytavin, Mireille. "Espanoles y italianos en Sicilia, Nápoles y Mílan durante los siglos XVI y XVII: Sobre la oportunidad de ser 'nacional' o 'natural.'" *Relaciones* 19, no. 73 (Winter 1998): 87–114.

Pii, Eluggero. "L'utile e le forme di governo nel Vico politico." *Il pensiero politico* 23 (1997): 105–34.

Pocock, J. G. A. *Barbarism and Religion.* Vol. 3: *The First Decline and Fall.* New York: Cambridge University Press, 2003.

——. "The Ideal of Citizenship since Classical Times." In *Theorizing Citizenship.* Edited by Ronald Beiner. Albany: State University of New York, 1995.

——. *Virtue, Commerce, and History: Essays on Political Thought and History, Chiefly in the Eighteenth Century.* New York: Cambridge University Press, 1985.

Pontieri, Ernesto. *Camillo Porzio storico.* Naples: Società Napoletana per la Storia Patria, 1953.

Quondam, Amodeo. *Cultura e ideologia di Gianvincezo Gravina.* Milan: Murisa, 1968.

Rak, Michele, ed. *Lezioni dell'Accademia di Palazzo del duca di Medinaceli.* 5 vols. Naples: Istituto Italiano per gli Studi Filosofici, 2000–2005.

Rao, Anna Maria. *L'amaro della feudalità: La devoluzione di Arnone e la questione feudale a Napoli alla fine del '700*. Naples: Guida, 1984.

——. "The Feudal Question, Judicial Systems, and the Enlightenment." In *Naples in the Eighteenth Century: The Birth and Death of a Nation State*. Edited by Girolamo Imbruglia. New York: Cambridge University Press, 2000.

——. "Intellettuali e professioni a Napoli nel Settecento." In *Avvocati, medici, ingegneri: Alle origini delle professioni moderne (secoli XVI–XIX)*. Bologna: Cooperativa Libraria Universitaria Editrice, 1997.

——. "Morte e resurrezione della feudalità: Un problema storiografico." In *Dimenticare Croce?* Edited by Aurelio Musi.

——. "Nel Settecento napoletano: La questione feudale." In *Cultura, intellettuali e circolazione delle idee nel '700*. Edited by Renato Pasta. Milan: Franco Angeli, 1990.

——. *Il Regno di Napoli nel Settecento*. Naples: Guida, 1983.

Redfield, Robert. "Maine's Ancient Law in the Light of Primitive Societies." *Western Political Quarterly* 3, no. 4 (1950): 574–89.

Reill, Peter Hanns. "Barthold Georg Niebuhr and the Enlightenment Tradition." *German Studies Review* 3, no. 1 (1980): 9–26.

Reumont, Alfred van. *The Carafas of Maddaloni: Naples under Spanish Dominion*. London: H. G. Bohn, 1854.

Riccio, C. Minieri. *Cenno storico delle accademie fiorite nella città di Napoli*. Napoli: Francesco Giannini, 1879.

Ricuperati, Giuseppe. "A proposito dell'Accademia Medina Coeli." *Rivista Storica Italiana* 84 (1972): 57–79.

——. "Alessandro Riccardi e le richieste del 'ceto civile' all'Austria nel 1707." *Rivista Storica Italiana* 81 (1969): 745–77.

——. *L'esperienza civile e religiosa di Pietro Giannone*. Naples: Ricciardi, 1970.

——. "La prima formazione di Pietro Giannone: L'Accademia Medina-Coeli e Domenico Aulisio." In *Saggi e ricerche sul Settecento*. Naples: L'Istituto Italiano per gli Studi Storici, 1968.

Ridley, Ronald T. "*Leges agrariae*: Myths Ancient and Modern." *Classical Philology* 95, no. 4 (2000): 259–67.

Riesenberg, Peter. "Civism and Roman Law in Fourteenth-Century Italian Society." *Explorations in Economic History* 7, nos. 1–2 (1969): 237–54.

Rispoli, Guido. *L'Accademia Palatina del Medinaceli*. Naples: Nuovo Cultura, 1924.

Robertson, John. *The Case for the Enlightenment: Scotland and Naples, 1680–1760*. New York: Cambridge University Press, 2005.

Rose, H. J. "Patricians and Plebeians at Rome." *Journal of Roman Studies* 12 (1922): 106–33.

Rosenblatt, Helena. *Rousseau and Geneva: From the First Discourse to the Social Contract, 1749–62*. New York: Cambridge University Press, 1997.

Rosenfeld, Sophia. "Before Democracy: The Production and Uses of Common Sense in Early Eighteenth-Century England." *Journal of Modern History* 80, no. 1 (2008): 1–54.

Rossi, Paolo. *The Dark Abyss of Time: The History of the Earth and the History of Nations from Hooke to Vico*. Translated by Lydia G. Cochrane. Chicago: University of Chicago Press, 1984.

———. *I segni del tempo: Storia della terra e storia delle nazioni da Hooke a Vico.* Milan: Feltrinelli, 1979.

Rovito, Pier, Luigi. "La rivoluzione costituzionale di Napoli (1647–48)." *Rivista Storica Italiana* 118, no. 2 (1986): 367–462.

Rowe, Christopher, and Malcolm Schofield, eds. *The Cambridge History of Greek and Roman Political Thought.* New York: Cambridge University Press, 2000.

Sahlins, Peter. *Unnaturally French: Foreign Citizens in the Old Regime and After.* Ithaca: Cornell University Press, 2004.

Salmon, J. H. M. "Cicero and Tacitus in Sixteenth-Century France." *American Historical Review* 85, no. 2 (1980): 307–31.

———. "Stoicism and the Roman Example: Seneca and Tacitus in Jacobean England." *Journal of the History of Ideas* 50, no. 2 (1989): 199–225.

Sapere e/è potere. Vol. 1: *Forme e oggetti della disputa delle arti.* Edited by Luisa Avellini. Bologna: Istituto per la Storia di Bologna, 1990.

Sapere e/è potere. Vol. 3: *Dalle discipline ai ruoli sociali.* Edited by Angela De Benedictis. Bologna: Istituto per la Storia di Bologna, 1991.

Schaeffer, John D. *Sensus Communis: Vico, Rhetoric, and the Limits of Relativism.* Durham: Duke University Press, 1990.

Schellhase, Kenneth. *Tacitus in Renaissance Political Thought.* Chicago: University of Chicago Press, 1976.

Schlereth, Thomas, J. *The Cosmopolitan Ideal in Enlightenment Thought.* Notre Dame, IN: University of Notre Dame Press, 1977.

Schofield, Malcolm. *The Stoic Idea of the City.* New York: Cambridge University Press, 1991.

Schroder, Jan. "The Concept of Natural Law in the Doctrine of Law and Natural Law of the Early Modern Era." In *Natural Laws and Laws of Nature in Early Modern Europe.* Edited by Lorraine Daston and Michael Stolleis. Burlington, VT: Ashgate, 2008.

Schulz, Fritz. *Classical Roman Law.* Oxford: Clarendon Press, 1954.

Sellars, John. *Stoicism.* Berkeley: University of California Press, 2006.

Sherwin-White, A. N. *The Roman Citizenship.* Oxford: Clarendon Press, 1939.

Shifflet, Andrew. *Stoicism, Politics, and Literature in the Age of Milton: War and Peace Reconciled.* New York: Cambridge University Press, 1998.

Simon, Lawrence H. "Vico and Marx: Perspectives on Historical Development." *Journal of the History of Ideas* 42, no. 2 (1981): 317–31.

Skinner, Quentin. *The Foundations of Modern Political Thought.* 2 vols. New York: Cambridge University Press, 1980.

———. *Hobbes and Republican Liberty.* New York: Cambridge University Press, 2008.

———. *Liberty before Liberalism.* New York: Cambridge University Press, 1998.

———. *Machiavelli.* New York: Oxford University Press, 1981.

———. "Meaning and Understanding in the History of Ideas." *History and Theory* 8, no. 1 (1969): 3–53.

———. *Reason and Rhetoric in the Philosophy of Hobbes.* New York: Cambridge University Press, 1996

———. *Visions of Politics.* 3 vols. New York: Cambridge University Press, 2002.

Siegel, Jerrold. "Civic Humanism or Ciceronian Rhetoric? The Culture of Petrarch and Bruni." *Past and Present* 34 (1966): 3–48.

Sleigh Jr., Robert, et al. "Determinism and Human Freedom." In *The Cambridge History of Seventeenth-Century Philosophy*. Edited by Daniel Garber and Michael Ayers. New York: Cambridge University Press, 1998.

Smith, Adam. *Lectures on Jurisprudence*. Edited by R. L. Meek, D. D. Raphael, and P. G. Stein. Oxford: Oxford University Press, 1978. Reprint, Indianapolis: Liberty Fund, 1982.

Soll, Jacob. "Amelot de la Houssaye: Annotates Tacitus." *Journal of the History of Ideas* 61, no. 2 (2000): 167–87.

——."Empirical History and the Transformation of Political Criticism in France from Bodin to Bayle." *Journal of the History of Ideas* 64, no. 3 (2003): 297–316.

Soria, Francesco Antonio. *Memorie storico-critiche degli storici napoletani*. Naples: Stamperia Simoniana, 1781–82.

Stein, Peter. "Equitable Principles in Roman Law." In *Character and Influence of Roman Civil Law*. Edited by Adolf Berger. London: Hambledon Press, 1988.

——. *Legal Evolution: The Story of an Idea*. New York: Cambridge University Press, 1980.

——. *Regulae iuris: From Juristic Rules to Legal Maxims*. Edinburgh: The University Press, 1966.

——. *Roman Law in European History*. New York: Cambridge University Press, 1999.

Stone, Harold Samuel. *Vico's Cultural History: The Production and Transmission of Ideas in Naples, 1685–1750*. New York: Brill, 1997.

Storia del Mezzogiorno. Edited by Giuseppe Galasso and Rosario Romeo. 15 vols. Rome: Edizioni del Sole, 1986–94.

Storia di Napoli. 11 vols. Naples: Edizioni Scientifiche Italiane, 1967–78.

Swain, Simon, and Mark Edwards, eds. *Approaching Late Antiquity: The Transformation from Early to Late Empire*. New York: Oxford University Press, 2004.

Tagliacozzo, Giorgio. *Vico and Marx: Affinities and Contrasts*. Atlantic Highlands, NJ: Humanities Press, 1983.

——. *Vico, Past and Present*. Atlantic Highlands, NJ: Humanities Press, 1981.

Tagliacozzo, Giorgio, and Donald Philip Verene, eds. *Giambattista Vico's Science of Humanity*. Baltimore: Johns Hopkins University Press, 1976.

Tagliacozzo, Giorgio, and Hayden V. White, eds. *Giambattista Vico: An International Symposium*. Baltimore: Johns Hopkins University Press, 1969.

Tierney, Brian. "Dominion of Self and Natural Rights before Locke and After." In *Transformations in Medieval and Early-Modern Rights Discourse*. Edited by V. Maekinen and P. Korkman. Dordrecht, Netherlands: Springer Verlag, 2006.

——. *The Idea of Natural Rights*. Atlanta: Scholars Press, 1997.

Toffanin, Giuseppe. *Machiavelli e il Tacitismo*. Padua: Draghi, 1921.

Torraca, Francesco et al. *Storia della Università di Napoli*. Naples: Riccardo Ricciardi, 1924.

Tuck, Richard. *Natural Right Theories: Their Origin and Development*. New York: Cambridge University Press, 1979.

——. *Philosophy and Government, 1572–1651*. New York: Cambridge University Press, 1993.

——. *The Rights of War and Peace*. New York: Oxford University Press, 1999.

Tully, James. *An Approach to Political Philosophy: Locke in Contexts.* New York: Cambridge University Press, 1993.

———. Introduction to *On the Duty of Man and Citizen,* by Samuel Pufendorf. Translated by Michael Silverthorne. New York: Cambridge University Press, 1991.

Vaughan, Frederick. *The Political Philosophy of Giambattista Vico.* The Hague: Martinus Nijhoff, 1972.

Ventura, Piero. "Le ambiguità di un privilegio: La cittadinanza napoletana tra Cinque e Seicento." *Quaderni storici* 89, no. 2 (1995): 385–416.

———. "Privilegio di cittadinanza, mobilità sociale e istituzioni statali a Napoli tra Cinque e Seicento." In *Disuguaglianze: Stratificazione e mobilità sociale nelle popolazioni italiane (dal secolo XIV agli inizi del secolo XX).* Edited by Società Italiana di Demografia Storica. Vol. 2. Bologna: Clueb, 1997, pp. 515–30.

Venturi, Franco. *Settecento riformatori.* 5 vols. Turin: Einaudi, 1969–90.

Verene, Donald Philip. Introduction to *On Humanistic Education,* by Giambattista Vico. Translated by Giorgio A. Pinton and Arthur W. Shippee.

———. *Knowledge of Things Human and Divine: Vico's New Science and Finnegan's Wake.* New Haven: Yale University Press, 2003.

Villani, Pasquale. *Documenti e orientamenti per la storia demografica del Regno di Napoli nel Settecento.* Rome: Istituto Storico Italiano per l'età moderna e contemporanea, 1968.

———. *Feudalità, riforme, capitalismo agrario.* Bari: Laterza, 1968.

———. "Territorio e popolazione: Orientamenti per la storia demografica." In his *Mezzogiorno tra riforme e rivoluzione.* Second revised edition. Rome: Laterza, 1973.

Villari, Lucio. "Aspetti e problemi della dominazione austriaca sul Regno di Napoli (1707–34)." *Annali della Scuola speciale per archivisti e bibliotecari dell'Università di Roma,* nos. 1–2 (1964): 45–80.

Villari, Rosario. "Masaniello: Contemporary and Recent Interpretations." *Past and Present,* no. 108 (Aug. 1985): 117–32.

———. *Mezzogiorno e contadini nell'età moderna.* Rome: Laterza, 1977.

———. *The Revolt of Naples.* Cambridge: Polity Press, 1993.

Viroli, Maurizio. *From Politics to Reason of State: The Acquisition and Transformation of the Language of Politics, 1520–1600.* New York: Cambrdige University Press, 1992.

Visceglia, Maria Antonietta. *Identità sociali: La nobiltà napoletana nella prima età moderna.* Milan: Edizioni Unicopli, 1998.

———, ed. *Signori, patrizi, cavalieri in Italia centro-meridionale nell'Età moderna.* Rome: Laterza, 1992.

Zangari, Domenico. *Gaetano Argento: Reggente e presidente del Sacro Regio Consiglio.* Naples: La cultura calabrese, 1922.

✖ INDEX

Accademia Medinaceli
  natural law theory, and, 74–75
  Nicola Capasso, and, 74–75
  Vico's admission to, 21
agrarian laws, interpretation of, 147
  Diritto universale, in, 143–44, 164
  historiography, in the, 164
  Scienza nuova, in, 164–65, 184
Albani, Cardinal Giovanni Francesco, and
    Pope Clement XI, 95
Alciato, Andrea, 150, 174
Althann, Cardinal Friedrich Michael von,
    114–15, 167–69, 171–72, 176–77
anthropology, 55, 186
  anti-rationalism, and, 74
  moral realism, and, 67–68
  oikeiosis, 55, 68
  original sin, and, 80
  social, 142
De antiquissima Italorum sapientia ex linguae
    Latinae originibus eruenda, 89–90
  Etruscan civilization in, 137
  Ionian civilization in, 137
Antonine constitution, 12
apatheia, 57–58, 65, 124
  qualification for office, as, 65
  second oration, in, 57–58
archives, 39, 40, 91, 107, 109, 166, 168
  Archive of the Congregation for the
    Doctrine of the Faith, 109, 237n29,
    243n76–43n80, 244n83
  Archivio di Stato di Napoli, 39, 40, 107,
    212n59–12n64, 213n73–13n75,
    232n143, 233n145–33n146,
    239n47, 242n69, 267n30,
    268n31–68n42, 268n50–68n52
  State Archive of Vienna, 166, 168,
    245n102, 266n15–66n19,
    267n22–67n29
Argento, Gaetano, 86
  Oratio of 1719, and, 103–5
  president of the Sacro Consiglio, as, 105

secret report on, 168–69
  vice decano of the Collaterale, as, 104
Aristotle
  polis, idea of, 11
  psychology, and, 81
Ascione, Imma, 239n47
Astarita, Tommaso, 18
Astronomica, (Manilius' poem), 118
asylum, right to
  debt for, 139
  foundation of Rome, and, 137, 139, 141
  foundation of the *civitas,* and, 139, 145
  inequality of the orders, and, 137
  Livy, in, 141
  Naples, in, 159
  Scienza nuova, in, 183–84
atheism
  Diritto universale, in, 116
  Spinoza, and, 121
  trial of atheists, Vico and, 111, 121
Athens, 51, 148
Augustine, Saint, 102
Aurelius, Marcus, (Roman) Emperor, 51, 54
Austria, 25, 49, 79, 86, 91, 159, 160, 166–67
Autobiografia, 6, 20, 89, 94–96, 101, 107,
    173–75
  Coniuratio, on the, 23
  Diritto universale, on the, 101
  isolation of Vico, on the, 89, 107
  patronage of the *Scienza nuova* ('25),
    on the, 178
  De rebus gestis, on the, 91, 94
  university competition of 1723, on the, 174
  Vico's faith, on, 95
  Vico's legal career, on, 173
Avvertimenti ai nipoti, 16, 62

Bacon, Francis, 78, 82, 147
Baker, Keith Michael, 70
Bari, 11
barons. *See* nobility
Bayle, Pierre, 128, 178